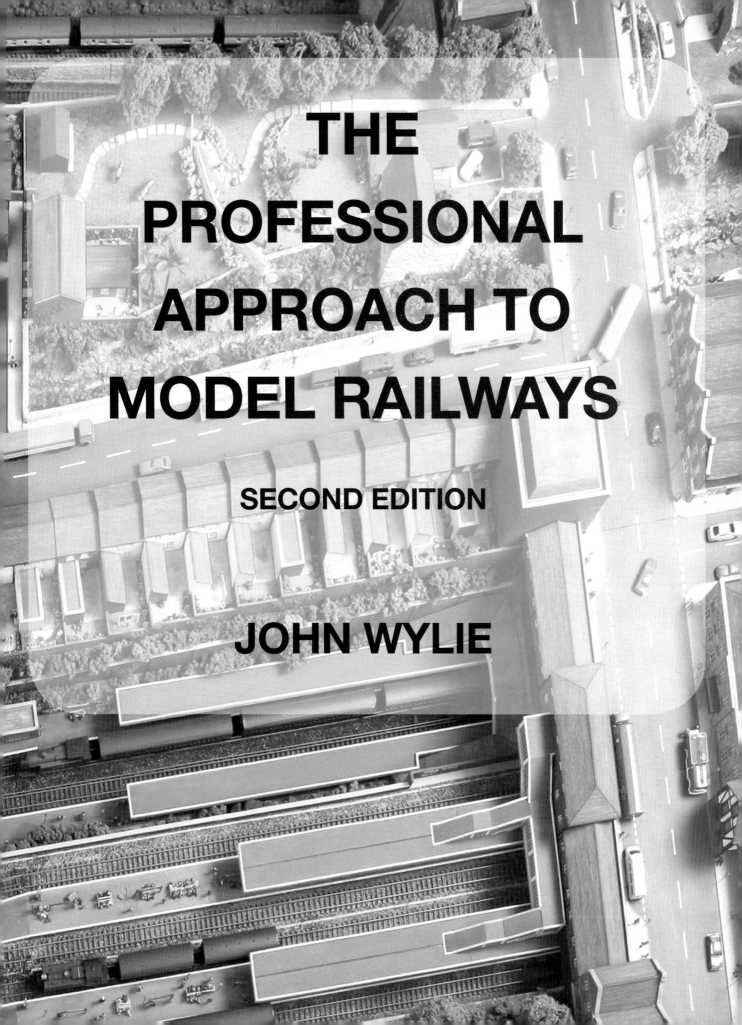

THE PROFESSIONAL APPROACH TO MODEL RAILWAYS

SECOND EDITION

JOHN WYLIE

First Edition 1987 (Patrick Stephens Limited)
Reprinted 1992 & 1993
Second Edition published March 2009
Reprinted July 2009 and March 2010
A catalogue record for this book is available.

ISBN 978 184425 679 2

Library of Congress catalog card no. 2008939604

Published by Haynes Publishing,
Sparkford, Yeovil, Somerset BA22 7JJ, UK
Tel: +44 (0)1963 442030 Fax: +44 (0)1963 440001
Email: sales@haynes.co.uk
Website: www.haynes.co.uk

Printed and bound in the USA

Haynes North America Inc., 861 Lawrence Drive,
Newbury Park, California 91320, USA

Front and Endpapers:
Bases 01, 02 and 03 joined together to form a large oval layout. The scenic setting of the layout also contains scale size roads and buildings etc, therefore the layout looks more realistic. The layout also has more track, therefore more rolling stock movements can be carried out. Compare this with the basic small oval layout, whereby the single track restricts running.

Title page: The changing levels of the multilevel oval base makes the landscape look more realistic. The points and coloured signals can be automatically operated. The track is split into electrical sections, so that a series of operations can be carried out. The layout can accommodate ten trains, i.e. two trains continually running on the up and down lines, two trains wait in the station, three trains in the sidings and three trains can be stored underneath.

CONTENTS

Left: 00 Scale Modelling. This typical country station scene is easily modelled using the ready to fit Scenecraft® 'Market Hampton' building produced by Bachmann® which has been customised by adding hanging baskets, (map pins covered with coloured foam texture) gas lamps (cut down street lamps pinned to the wall) etc, and painted as detailed on page 132. The engine has been painted to look dirty and details of how to weather the building and rolling stock are shown on pages 133 to 141. To make the situation interesting people are placed as if watching the photographer. The location could well be a busy branch line, providing a service to the local community. The rails in the foreground depict the engine 'run around the train track' used to change the engine's position from the front of the train to the back, for return running. For the photographer you will find in Chapter 12 a brief outline of how to take model and information gathering photographs.

PREFACE

Below: The oval layout's basic construction using plywood battens and 'Contiboard' edging. Expanded polystyrene foam forms the foundation for the embankments. The step-by-step construction methods, shown for this layout and others are shown within the book. The concept of the book is to show the reader how to design a baseboard, make the base and how to make the landscape look realistic. The methods shown in the book reveal many of the interesting techniques I have used as a professional model maker for almost a half of a century.

In welcoming you as a reader to this book perhaps I ought to tell you a little about myself, for more than 45 years I have worked as a professional model maker. The first rough draft of this book was prepared in 1983, printed in 1987, reprinted in 1992 and 1993 and little did I know that in the year 2000 I would start to completely revise the book which would take me until the year 2008 to finish.

The book has been completely revised, much has been rewritten and updated. Not all the time has been spent on the book because I was commissioned to build two large castle models. The first model was to show Rochester Castle, as it was in the 13th century, and the second was to portray Upnor Castle (both in Kent) at the time of the castle's only battle in 1677. Each model took more than year to research and to build. For the reader the interesting part is that I used the methods shown in this book, to make the baseboards. The buildings were constructed by casting replica stone walls, modelled at 1:200 scale using rubber moulds. (The solid rubber moulds were 300 mm square and used the method shown on page 116.) The painting and weathering of the castles used exactly the same methods as per Chapter 7, and

the same applied to the landscape. Both models are on public display at the appropriate castles.

My work during this time has also involved photography and lecturing to various students in numerous colleges, on how to make models. This background has allowed me to produce a book that is based upon years of experience and is designed to help you to progress from beginner through to expert status in easy-to-follow stages.

Each chapter contains progressive step-by-step procedures, starting with the easier models to allow the beginner to the hobby to learn the very basic techniques of model making, using the book as a reference for gathering information.

While the basic knowledge will be learnt very quickly, the development of craft skills takes longer, so as the modeller improves his/her skills they will be able to undertake far more difficult and complex types of model making. To illustrate this, compare two photographs. The first on page 63, is constructed on a flat baseboard with track, and is ready for some houses and trees; this simple layout is ideal for the beginner to make. The layouts shown below are more advanced and have contoured baseboards portraying rolling landscape.

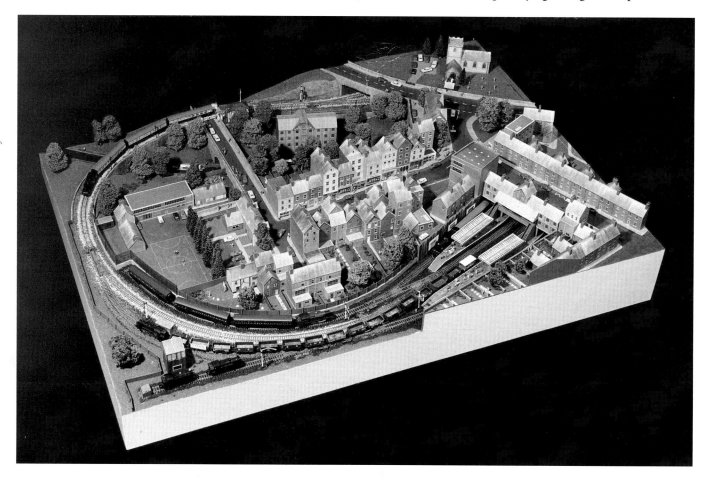

Such a layout could be easily constructed by the average modeller, but would be far too complex a project for the inexperienced modeller to start with.

My advice to the newcomer to the hobby is always to start with a simple layout and find out the problems involved. Remember the layout can always be rebuilt at a later date, when skills, experience and knowledge have been learnt.

With this in mind, the book shows how to construct an interesting small layout for use with one or two controllers, which is initially built on a flat base, but can be landscaped afterwards. The design of the layout is based on a simple oval with passing loops and a siding. This will allow up to three locomotives to be run, one at a time using a single controller, two with the double controller system, etc.

Alternatively, the very simple shelf layout shown on page 70 & 71 could be built or the '00' scale 'Wishton Halt' layout shown on pages 40, 41, 151, 152, 153 & 154 could be made.

The Wishton Halt layout has been designed for use with Digital Command Control, so that the track wiring is kept to a minimum. The number of points used also fits the readymade point controller produced by Gaugemaster® to make life easier. Instructions can also be found in the book for wiring the layout, including signals that change automatically as the turnouts (points) are set, and for sectioning the layout so that several operators can use the layout simultaneously.

The progressive method of construction shown in the book is favoured by many modellers, because it allows improvements to be carried out whilst still being able to operate the layout.

The experienced modeller, having developed their basic skills, will never cease to learn. In fact it is quite often that the newcomer, having fresh ideas, can cause the expert to rethink their own methods of model making. The newcomer should remember that the experts have also made their disasters as they learnt the hard way, Therefore do not be disappointed if your first model is not as good as you would have hoped.

John Wylie, FSAI, ABIPP, ARPS
June 1986, December 2000 and April 2008

Below: The finished multi-level oval layout as constructed from the photographs shown in this book. The layout looks realistic because all the roads and buildings are made to the same scale and the ground levels change above and below the track's level. This layout mimics reality with the choice of colour. The size of this layout built at N scale is 3ft wide by 5ft 9in long (0.9 x 1.75 m).

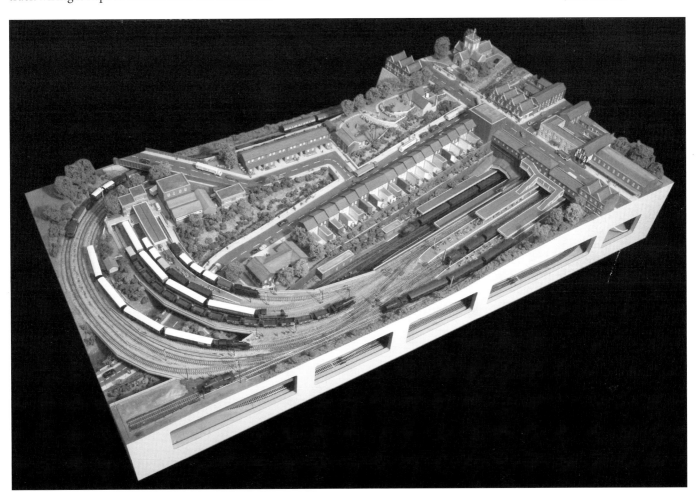

INTRODUCTION

Above: The hand over the 00 scale *Flying Scotsman* locomotive clearly shows its size. 00 and HO scale rolling stock use the same track gauge but are of different scales.

Modelling railways is a hobby that is followed by millions of people throughout the world. For many it is the fascination of modelling replicas of magnificent engineering feats which in full size are enormously powerful, and capable of pulling many times their own weight, and in model form producing their very own engineering problems.

It is a challenging and relaxing pastime to model the peaceful scenic settings and the modeller will gain considerable knowledge and probably gain a number of useful household skills, i.e. learn to fix shelving in place. As a hobby it is only as expensive as the amount of money a person invests, but note that I say invest, for a model railway is always a re-saleable item.

A railway layout will provide hours of enjoyment irrespective of age. How many new dads I wonder have, at the excuse of a first baby, rushed off and started a model railway? Or perhaps when the youngster grows up, having reached the age of six or seven, they might say: 'Dad can you make me a model railway?' These are typical beginnings to a hobby that for many remains into old age.

In the early stages the beginner, or indeed the old hand returning to the hobby, is often overwhelmed by the choice of rolling stock available and the wide variety of scales. Coming across a term such as HO/00 can be very confusing, for although the track gauge remains the same size the modelling scale is very different. The smallest commercially produced scale is Z gauge from Marklin. This ultra-tiny scale has a track gauge of 6 mm (0.24in) and uses mainly German rolling stock. Its size is so small that a complete layout can be built on a coffee table and a locomotive fits comfortably into a matchbox.

At the other end of the scale are 5.5-inch gauge live steam locomotives that will allow passengers to be carried. These live steam models are in many respects not so much 'models' as simply small locomotives, especially those which are a freelance design rather than based on a full-size prototype.

Right: Minitrix 'N' scale locomotive shown on a box of matches to display its size. The same track gauge is also used for other scales.

Miniature steam locomotives are subject to the same boiler pressure checks, maintenance problems and so on that one would find on the largest counterpart. For practical reasons, this book does not attempt to cover this type of modelling.

Scales Available

Gauge 1: (10mm to 1ft, previously 3/8 inch to 1ft) This gauge is normally accepted as the start of model as opposed to miniature railways, but because of size they are usually found laid out in a garden. This is also a popular scale for model town layouts that visitors flock to see, as due to its size it is very impressive. It is a specialist scale usually involving the use of steam, heated by coal, oil, methylated spirit or gas firing, although model village layouts are generally electrically driven.

0 Gauge: (7mm to 1ft) This is the largest scale suitable for an indoor model railway layout, but is also found as a garden layout, perhaps starting from inside the garden shed. The 0 gauge live steam locomotive is often these days controlled by radio, as the advent of small transmitters, reliable receivers and servos has made this possible. This method of control is also useful for electric outdoor layouts, overcoming the problems of the weather short-circuiting the track and the restrictions of being only able to run a very limited amount of rolling stock on a single track.

Electrically-powered rolling stock carries their own rechargeable battery and its movements are controlled through radio. This allows not only forward and reverse operation in a completely scale-like manner, but most important of all multi-use of a single line track, because the transmitters and receivers have up to 24 frequencies, allowing up to 24 locomotives to be operated at the same time along a single length of track, all independently controlled.

S Gauge: (3/16 of one inch to 1ft) This is half the size of gauge 1 and being so close to 00 scale has not really caught on, there being little or no trade support for it apart from in North America.

00 Gauge: (4mm to 1ft) The most popular gauge in Britain, although not a true scale track gauge-wise,

is 00. It is extremely well catered for commercially. The history of the gauge is derived from HO (3.5mm to 1ft) which is popular with European and American manufacturers. The large electric motors, which were all that were available at the time, could be fitted into model American and European locomotives but unfortunately not into British locomotives which are considerably smaller in average size. So the British manufacturers decided to change the scale from 3.5mm to 1ft to 4mm to 1ft and rename it 00 for British outline rolling stock, but to retain the same track gauge to allow a running compatibility. Therefore the choice of modelling scale is important, not the track gauge. It is the smallest practical size for live steam running, although in recent years smaller scales have been built and successfully run by an expert.

Below: A live steam gauge locomotive, capable of pulling driver and passenger. When such a locomotive is constructed to the builder's own design it ceases to be a model and becomes a small real locomotive.

Right: The classic beginner's mistake is joining a layout together without using insulators, sections or switches. The layout does not work due to the built-in electrical short circuit. See Chapter 8 on wiring for a complete explanation (page 145).

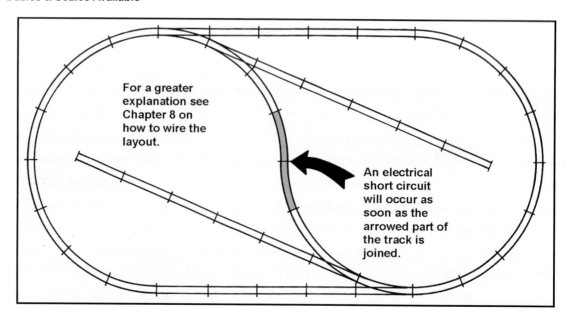

For a greater explanation see Chapter 8 on how to wire the layout.

An electrical short circuit will occur as soon as the arrowed part of the track is joined.

UNDERSTANDING SCALE SIZE

The scale chosen for the construction of the layout is often governed by the space available. For example the layout shown on page 70 is designed to fit on a shelf and to auto run two separate trains, one at a time. The scale is 'HOe' which is 3.5mm to the foot (same as HO Scale) but runs on 'N' scale track because it represents a narrow gauge railway. This provides the benefit of the larger scale and the smaller bends associated with narrow gauge trains. The oval track design is generally the first step towards building a fixed track layout. Unfortunately it can have its wiring problems as shown above. The track configuration can be made to work, but will need the understanding of how to use insulated sections of track and wiring switches. Note: this includes Digital Command Control (DCC) wiring of the layout.

Unfortunately mixing HO and 00 does not work because an HO scale locomotive run alongside a 00 scale model looks very wrong, as the HO locomotive is smaller than the 00 locomotive at model size whilst in real life it is the reverse. Buildings also become extremely noticeable as HO scale buildings are dwarf-like compared with 00 scale buildings, so again they should not be mixed.

EM Gauge: Modellers who were disillusioned with 00 gauge, as the track gauge is really much too narrow for its correct scale, began to remake the axles and wheels, moving the wheels outwards to give the maximum track width possible (18mm gauge). Then came the introduction of specialised components in 18.25 mm track gauge. This dimension remains to the present, but as always the true scale modeller was not really satisfied with this which led to the development of the next gauge listed.

Scale four or Protofour: This is the final development to date of the 4 mm to 1ft scale. It is a virtually accurate 18.83mm track gauge and is building up a following in Britain, although as yet it is still very much a specialist's and expert's scale as the vast majority of components have to be hand-built.

HO Scale: (3.5mm to 1ft) The most popular scale of all in Europe and America is HO, standing for half 0 gauge, which dates from about 1920. It was established by manufacturers producing models in the early years of railway modelling and is very accurate. This scale provides the modeller with the widest choice of additional components of any scale; buildings, cars, people and other accessories, all with appropriate national characteristics to the countries of origin.

TT Gauge: (3mm to 1 foot) TT stood for the table top. This gauge has now ceased to be commercially produced in quantity in Britain although it flourishes in America. It was the first of the smaller scales to be developed, but like HO/00 two variations arise. (A) The scale ratio 120:1 was adopted by American and European manufacturers. (B) British manufacturers worked to a scale of 100:1. As with HO/00, this means that the British models are not strictly to scale and true scale and specialist modellers change the wheels and track gauge in order to create the correct gauge for the British rolling stock modelled at 3mm to 1ft.

N Gauge or nine gauge refers to the track gauge of 9mm. This is unquestionably the smallest of the standard gauges but as with HO/00 and TT the scales vary: (A) 160:1 for North American and European prototypes; (B) 148:1 (2mm to 1ft) for British outline rolling stock; 000 Gauge (152:1) is half 00 Gauge etc. Once again it was the problem of fitting of the electric motors into the smaller 'British Outline' models that caused the change – it is quite surprising just how small our locomotives are compared with those of other countries. British specialist scale modellers therefore started hand-building to the wider 9.5mm track gauge so as to keep to the true track gauge for 2mm to 1ft scale. This is the N gauge equivalent of EM gauge and Protofour/ scale four. Poor old Britain always seems to be left struggling with a non-standard international scale size.

Z Gauge: The smallest of all the model sizes and is the micro-miniature modelling scale (1.4mm to 1ft). The track gauge is 6.5mm (0.25in) established by Marklin, and depicts mainly German rolling stock.

LAYOUTS

Obviously the larger the modelling scales chosen, the larger the layout will be. 0 gauge layouts require an enormous amount of room which is why they are

generally built in gardens, whilst a Z gauge layout requires the area of a coffee table. The middle of the range, and the most popular scale, is HO or 00. To build a reasonable oval layout at this scale will require a 2m x 1.2m (6ft 6in x 4ft) baseboard area. An equivalent N gauge layout will require a baseboard 2 m x 0.75 m (6ft 6in x 2ft 5in), the size of a standard door panel.

An oval layout is a good compromise in that it allows continuous running and has provision for sidings, landscaping and buildings, all built on a single baseboard which allows access from all sides. It is ideal for the younger modeller.

The alternative is to build an end-to-end layout, fixed to a wall. By utilising further walls the layout can then be extended until it runs around all the walls of the room, leaving a clear space in the middle for the operator. This type of layout arrangement allows for greater scale-like curves of the track and considerable room for landscaping, buildings and backdrop. This all looks far more realistic. but unfortunately it also requires a large permanent room. If you have the opportunity, the loft is ideal for this purpose and has the added advantage that you can retract the ladder behind you when solitude is required!

Garden Layouts: The gauge 1 locomotive that was run at 'Tucktonia' is a classic example of a large scale open air layout, the down side is that real grass and shrubs have to be used for the landscape, which need looking after.

PHOTOGRAPHY
When photographing model railway layouts, you will find that eye level photographs look more realistic than the bird's eye view.

Right: The gauge 1 locomotive that was run at 'Tucktonia' open air seaside attraction at Christchurch. (1975) Unfortunately the layout was troubled with a short circuit problem, whereby morning dampness across hundreds of sleepers short circuited the track. (A shower of rain also stopped the layout from working.) The ideal solution for outdoor layouts is to run radio controlled electrically powered models that carry their own batteries. This means that the track no longer needs an electrical supply.

Diagrams right and below: The overall size of different countries' rolling stock varies. This caused manufacturing problems in the early days, resulting in HO scale and 00 scales running on the same track gauge.

Pictures below: The design of the engines and rolling stock vary. In many cases the country of origin will have a distinctive style. Compare the British engine to the lower American wood-burning locomotive.

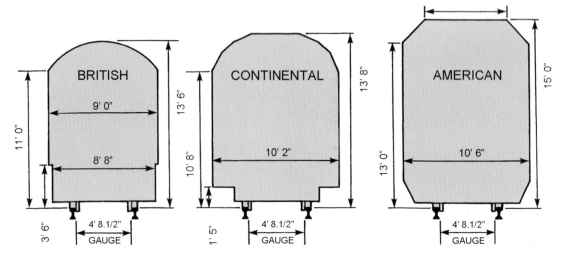

SCALE SIZES

With all the different types of scales and ratios, it is very difficult at first to understand the relationship between scale and ratio, so let us see precisely what is meant, for example 32:1 – we take a full-size object 32 inches long and divide this by 32 and the answer would be 1 inch. Thus, if we were to make a model of our object totalling 1 inch long this would represent a full size to model ratio of 32 to 1 (32:1) as our real object is 32 times bigger. This forms a straight division scale by dividing up one inch by 32 equalling 1/32 of an inch, each 1/32 of an inch on the model equalling 1 inch full size. If the object was bigger, say 32 foot long, and the finished model is 1 foot long, the ratio remains the same (the 32 foot divided by 32 equals 1 foot). Imperial measurements consist of 12 inches that make 1 foot (ft). Each inch (in) can be divided by 1/2, 1/4, 1/8, 1/16, 1/32 etc. Therefore divide 12 inches by 96, the answer is 96:1 scale (1/8 inch multiplied by 96 equals 12 inches). If we divide the 12 inches by 32 we get 3/8. This 3/8 of 1 inch now represents 1 foot full size. Instead of our ratio of 32 to 1, we could have used inches, by saying each inch represents a foot, so our 32-foot full size object would become 32 inches long; this is a one-twelfth scale model. (1:12 full size.)

It is the same with metric dimensions. One metre divided by 100 equals 1:100, but note the way the figures have changed over and are now reversed, one being 32:1 and the other 1:100. The main difficulty arises when scales of 4mm to 1 foot occur and how the conversion to metric is accomplished (1m equals 39.37 inches). The nearest we can get conveniently is 39 inches, as 1mm now equals 3 inches full size, therefore 13mm equals 39 inches full size (this is arrived at by dividing 39 by 3 equalling 13 so that at 4mm to 1ft scale 1mm equals 3 inches full size). Next we have 13mm to 1m giving a full-size ratio of 76:1 (00 scale). This 13mm is a close approximation

which is convenient, but when it is multiplied over a considerable length the error becomes exaggerated due to the 0.37 inch ignored. Fortunately in Britain one rarely mixes these dimensions, modelling either in Imperial or metric measurements, but Continental modellers have a worse problem as the HO scale is 3.5mm to 1ft. Hence the ratio of 87:1 is used, the metric measurement of 1m being divided up by 87 providing a close approximate equivalent dimension of 11.5mm (model size) to 1 metre full size. These dimensions for convenience are rounded up or down; for example, N gauge at 160:1 and 000 gauge 152:1, yet both are modelled at 2mm to the foot.

GAUGES

When George Stephenson first invented the *Rocket* railway engine and decided a distance between the tracks of 4ft 8½in, it was only the start of the great track gauge debate. This gauge was not, of course, adopted throughout the world or even by other British companies, and different gauges were introduced, both narrower and wider. The narrow gauge name has remained, its gauge (or distance between the tracks) being anything less than the 'Stephenson standard 1 width'. A wider gauge introduced by Brunel became known as broad gauge. The terms narrow, standard and broad gauge are still used throughout the world today but, since different countries use various gauges, the modeller should ideally use the correct gauge and rolling stock of that country, all modelled to a common scale. In practice, and for commercial reasons, a series of standard model track gauges have appeared. HO and 00 share the same track gauge as explained earlier, the scale of the model changing, to allow for the interchangeability of rolling stock upon the layout.

Below: A comparison of sizes showing the popular scales used and their relationship to each other.

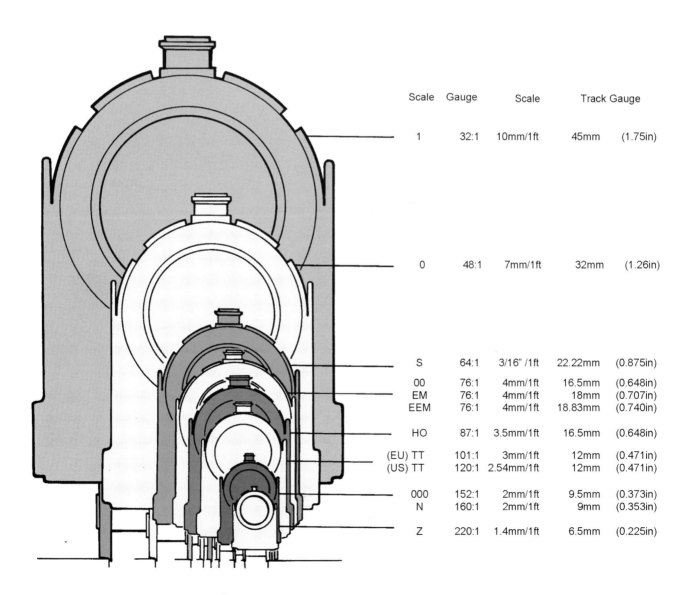

Scale	Gauge	Scale	Track Gauge	
1	32:1	10mm/1ft	45mm	(1.75in)
0	48:1	7mm/1ft	32mm	(1.26in)
S	64:1	3/16" /1ft	22.22mm	(0.875in)
00	76:1	4mm/1ft	16.5mm	(0.648in)
EM	76:1	4mm/1ft	18mm	(0.707in)
EEM	76:1	4mm/1ft	18.83mm	(0.740in)
HO	87:1	3.5mm/1ft	16.5mm	(0.648in)
(EU) TT	101:1	3mm/1ft	12mm	(0.471in)
(US) TT	120:1	2.54mm/1ft	12mm	(0.471in)
000	152:1	2mm/1ft	9.5mm	(0.373in)
N	160:1	2mm/1ft	9mm	(0.353in)
Z	220:1	1.4mm/1ft	6.5mm	(0.225in)

Right: The British loading gauge: this is a device used to size the load within its limitations. The maximum height is 13 feet 6 inches and the maximum width is 9 feet. The Continental and American loading sizes are larger.

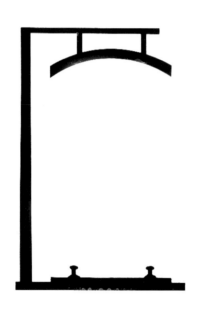

CLEARWAY
This is the gap between the pair of tracks (i.e. up and down line). The scale distance between the tracks is much too small for model use, so increase the gap to suit, with extra clearance on the curves.

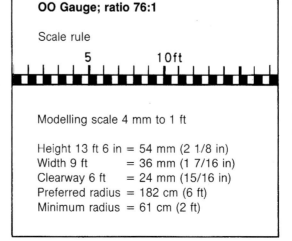

Above: The Standard Class 5MT 73068 BR Green Late Crest and BR 1C tender 00 scale 'Bachmann' locomotive. This is reproduced scale size (Model Size) the top rule shows HO 3.5mm/ 1 foot scale and the lower ruler shows 00 4mm/ 1 foot scale, for the same locomotive.

This actual size difference of rolling stock and buildings is the reason why 'HO & 00' should not be used on the same layout. Cars and people are so close in scale size that they can be used.

The locomotive shown has been slightly weathered to dull the pristine livery. The model can be purchased as pristine or as weathered, with normally only a running number change.

Gauge 1; ratio 32:1

Scale rule

Modelling scale 10 mm to 1 ft

Height 13 ft 6 in = 135 mm (5 5/16 in)
Width 9 ft   = 90 mm (3½ in)
Clearway 6 ft   = 60 mm (2 3/8 in)
Preferred radius = 1,220 cm (40 ft)
Minimum radius   = 610 cm (20 ft)

O Gauge; ratio 48:1

Scale rule

Modelling scale 7 mm to 1 ft

Height 13 ft 6 in = 94½ mm (3 11/16 in)
Width 9 ft   = 63 mm (2½ in)
Clearway 6 ft   = 42 mm (1 21/32 in)
Preferred radius = 366 cm (12 ft)
Minimum radius   = 183 cm (6 ft)

S Gauge; ratio 64:1

Scale rule

Modelling scale 3/16 in to 1 ft

Height 13 ft 6 in = 66 mm (2 19/32 in)
Width 9 ft   = 43 mm (1 11/16 in)
Clearway 6 ft   = 29 mm (1 1/8 in)
Preferred radius = 274 cm (9 ft)
Minimum radius   = 137 cm (4 ft 6 in)

OO Gauge; ratio 76:1

Scale rule

Modelling scale 4 mm to 1 ft

Height 13 ft 6 in = 54 mm (2 1/8 in)
Width 9 ft   = 36 mm (1 7/16 in)
Clearway 6 ft   = 24 mm (15/16 in)
Preferred radius = 182 cm (6 ft)
Minimum radius   = 61 cm (2 ft)

HO Gauge; ratio 87:1

Scale rule

Modelling scale 3.5 mm to 1 ft

Height 13 ft 6 in = 47¼ mm (1 7/8 in)
Width 9 ft = 31½ mm (1¼ in)
Clearway 6 ft = 21 mm (53/64 in)
Preferred radius = 182 cm (6 ft)
Minimum radius = 61 cm (2 ft)

TT Gauge (EU); ratio 101:1

Scale rule

Modelling scale 3 mm to 1 ft

Height 13 ft 6 in = 40½ mm (1 19/32 in)
Width 9 ft = 27 mm (1 1/16 in)
Clearway 6 ft = 18 mm (47/64 in)
Preferred radius = 152 cm (5 ft)
Minimum radius = 45 cm (1 ft 6 in)

N Gauge; ratio 160:1

Scale rule

Modelling scale 2 mm to 1 ft

Height 13 ft 6 in = 27 mm (1 1/16 in)
Width 9 ft = 18 mm (47/64 in)
Clearway 6 ft = 12 mm (15/32 in)
Preferred radius = 91 cm (3 ft)
Minimum radius = 23 cm (9 in)

Z Gauge; ratio 220:1

Scale rule

Modelling scale 1.4 mm to 1 ft

Height 13 ft 6 in = 18.9 mm (¾ in)
Width 9 ft = 12.6 mm (½ in)
Clearway 6 ft = 8.4 mm (21/64 in)
Preferred radius = 69 cm (2 ft 3 in)
Minimum radius = 14.5 cm (5 3/16 in)

Peco Ltd produce an excellent number of booklets on track information which include layout plans and the company also produce rolling stock for both narrow and standard gauge modelling. In addition to this the company also produces a wide range of modelling accessories and a monthly magazine.

Note: The minimum radius should always be checked against the rolling stock that is used, because with some rolling stock the buffers become locked on tight bends and on points, whilst being reverse shunted. (Pushed by the engine around a bend or over points.)

1. UNDERSTANDING MAPS AND CONTOURS

To successfully model a landscape with its hills, trees and rivers requires a basic knowledge of how the landscape is formed. This can easily be accomplished through studying books, magazines, visiting and studying the countryside etc. It provides one with a natural instinct for knowing just what could happen at a particular point. For example, where the edge of a field adjoins a stream, one forms a mental picture of how the ground may have been eroded away, the possible colour of the soil and the plant life that grows upon its banks.

Basic information on how the ground heights are shaped (known as contours) can be obtained from maps. The 6in to 1 mile maps produced in Britain by Ordnance Survey will show the rivers, the roads and the railways. For modelling purposes these larger scale maps show information far more clearly than the smaller scales.

A 1:1.250 scale map will contain detailed information on the house shapes and boundaries, shown in plan form, and since these maps have been reduced from larger scale maps they are extremely accurate. Unfortunately some of the larger-scale maps do not show the contour lines and are marked out in spot heights only. Spot heights are normally shown in the centre of the road but on occasions they will be located on a wall. These are called 'Bench marks' and since they are located on the wall, the heights indicated can be a few feet above the actual ground level. Reading the map only, this 'Bench mark' level cannot be assessed so a site visit will be needed. Spot heights at ground level are

Above: A typical hilly landscape, with a road, railway and stream following the ground levels around the lowest part of the valley. The railway will follow a reasonably constant level, whilst the stream will become lower, from one end of the valley to the other end. The level of the roads could vary, but not lower than the stream's level, or the road would flood. To indicate the changing levels on a map, contour lines and spot heights are used (see illustration right).

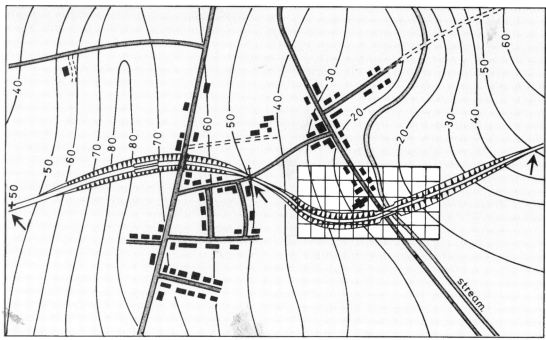

shown as plus signs, followed by a number representing height above sea level. A benchmark above ground level is shown as the plus sign, number, and then an arrow underneath to denote that it is above ground level.

Since the scale of any map obtainable is too small to make the model directly from it, the map will have to be enlarged in size. One of the easiest ways of doing this is to grid the map with squares then redraw it. Do not redraw to the actual size of the layout, but to a convenient sketch size, and just show the main features, i.e. the roads, railways, rivers and buildings; so as to form an outline map. This will provide an idea of how the landscape, the contours and other heights of the ground work in relationship with each other; ultimately these will probably need to be changed to fit the base board of the layout.

PROBLEMS OF OLDER MAPS

Modern maps are marked out in metric dimensions but older ones are in Imperial, so it is important first to establish the way that the map has been measured out. Older maps quite often contain imperial and metric measurements, the heights of the contours being shown in metric, the longitude distances in miles, with the grid of the map in kilometres. This was due to the British changeover from Imperial to metric. Because modern maps now use international symbols, it has affected the way in which the information is shown; i.e. The symbols that represent trees, woodland, etc, are different to that shown on the older style maps.

GRIDDING

I have found through practice that the best way of gridding up is to use the existing grid on the

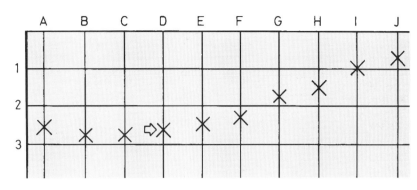

Above: By estimating the position of the intersecting lines, the small map can be enlarged. Mark a cross where lines intersect on the large grid.

small-scale map and sub-divide this by ten. Then you re-grid to a convenient sketch scale, by plotting the intersecting points on both the small and the larger grid by eye, estimating the intersecting point on each line. Start with the railway. Having plotted the intersections, the points can be joined up by freehand sketching the radii of the track's curves (see illustration). Then plot in the roads, followed by the rivers or streams, thus slowly building up the enlarged portion of the map. Having completed this, next mark in the spot heights shown on the roads and join up corresponding heights of the same level, or using the grid follow the contour lines marked out so as to establish how the ground levels change.

The railway line itself tends to run at an almost continuous level, very slowly changing height; the track either running through a cutting or built up upon an embankment, whilst roads change height very quickly in comparison. In reality there is a restriction upon the gradient of a hill, a 1 in 5 hill being extremely steep. (One in five means one-metre rise in five metres distance expressed as a percentage of 20 percent.) This should be the maximum gradient we use on our roads that travel up or down hill, so the roads on the layout look more natural.

Opposite page: A typical small-scale map showing a hilly countryside. Reading the map from left to right, the track is at ground level + 50, then it runs through a cutting and has a road bridge over the track, confirmed by the raised contours: the ground then falls to meet the track level at the next road crossing on the 50 contour level. The ground continues to fall away and the track now becomes raised on an embankment with a road and stream passing underneath it. The ground then rises to meet the track level. At + 50, this provides us with three track spot heights.

Left: Then join the crosses up, starting with the railway track, followed by the road, the stream, then the contours. Below the +20ft contour level no contours are shown, but the stream could well be at +11ft, thus effectively obscuring the next lower contour line.

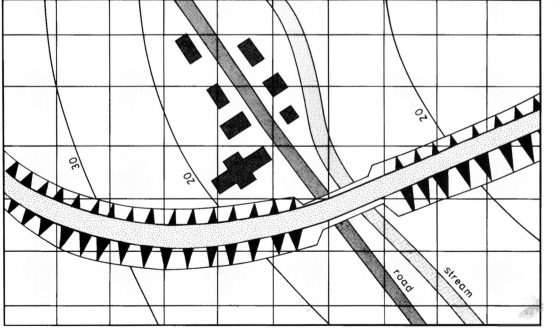

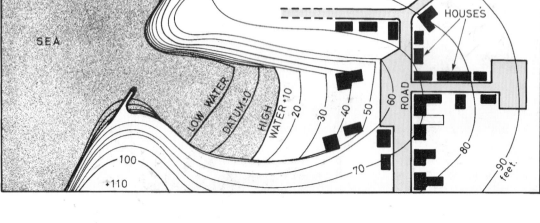

Right: A typical Cornish cove found within a hilly landscape. The gap between the cliff faces forms a natural harbour. The beach is formed by sand and small stones being washed into the cove, and from the landscape deposited by the weather over thousands of years; the ground level rising from the water datum of zero (mean tide) to 90ft, is shown in 10ft contour intervals. The maximum height of the ground is 110ft on top of the cliff. The road shown drops in its levels from both sides to its lowest at +60ft, dwellings being built alongside it. Since these houses are built into the hillside they will have the ground changing all around their foundation levels.

UNDERSTANDING CONTOURS

It is a matter of common observation that hillsides and valleys vary greatly in size and to indicate this on a map contour lines are used to show the changes of level. So that all maps have a zero level or datum, a common level is necessary, and this generally is the sea's mean tide level, i.e., the tide is neither in nor out. Low and high water marks are also shown on maps to indicate the lowest and the highest levels at spring and neap tides, so there are three points that can be used as the datum zero level.

As one travels inland the ground level generally rises above the sea level, therefore to make it clear on the map, the heights that form the contour lines are marked with a plus sign, showing that they are indeed above sea level. The ground itself varies in height due to the formation of the Earth's crust, the ice age, wind and weather. Then with the passing of time the elements have eroded away the softer layers of soil, leaving the harder rock as high ground, the earth being washed down by the rain into the valleys producing good soil areas with plenty of growth, whilst the rock faces remain barren.

The rain that has fallen forms streams which join up to form rivers which eventually reach the sea. Since the ground varies in its levels the streams and rivers always follow the lowest ground level available. The steeper the slope the faster the water flows, causing considerable erosion of the streams' or rivers' banks. The flatter the ground the more likely the water is to form lakes, wide shallow streams or meandering rivers. The direction of the flow of water could well have changed over the years, and formed ponds etc. Man has also contributed by building sea walls and reclaiming land that is below sea level. This is shown as a minus sign on the contour levels of the maps. Drainage ditches now become above ground level with a series of banks on each side, the water from the lower ditches being pumped up into each higher level of ditch.

To interpret the contour lines shown one simply looks at their height above or below the datum level. The slope of the ground determines how the contour lines will be spaced out. If the ground is very steep, i.e., on a hillside, the contour lines will be close together. If the ground is very flat the contour lines will hardly exist and will be spaced extremely far apart. When a very sharp fall occurs in the contour level, e.g., a man-made embankment, the contour lines are replaced with a series of signs like an arrow head, wide and heavily marked at the top becoming a point at the bottom of the slope, so as to denote which is the top and bottom of the embankment or fall in the ground's level.

To translate the heights from the map on to the model, first establish the scale it is going to be enlarged to and then draw the zero datum line; from this measure vertically either to the scale you are using on the model, 00/HO, etc, or to the scale being used on the working drawing. Mark the height of the first contour, and then scale out the spacing of the next. Repeat this for each contour level required then finally join up these points in a series of radii so that the ground level looks natural. This forms a section through the landscape.

By carefully studying the photograph, and the two illustrations, the road spot heights can be seen along with the contour lines marked across the road. The highest contour on the road is at the top of the hill (+100ft) and the lowest is just under the railway bridge (+30ft). The track level remains at +50ft. The water level is shown at +35ft and +25 ft, suggesting that the stream flows from right to left (Map Base 6). Compare the photograph with the photograph on page 54.

Below: Part of a map showing the levels of a drainage ditch above ground level. The water is raised from the −10 level to the datum zero level (shown as WL − + 0) – compare the map and the drawing of the same area.

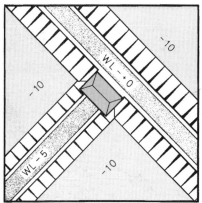

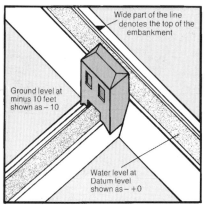

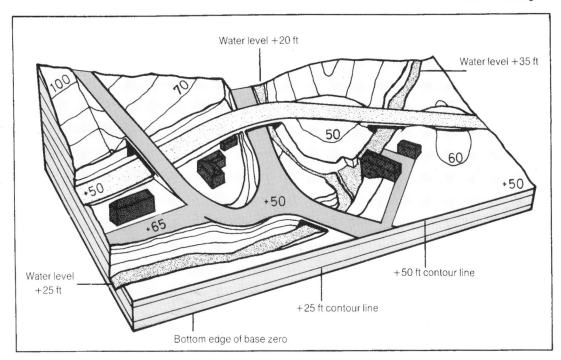

Water level +20 ft

Water level +35 ft

Water level +25 ft

+50 ft contour line

+25 ft contour line

Bottom edge of base zero

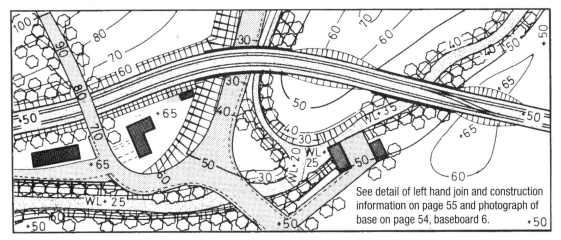

See detail of left hand join and construction information on page 55 and photograph of base on page 54, baseboard 6.

Left: The landscape of this baseboard is identical to the way the contours are described for the cove. By studying the map **(centre)** direct comparisons can be made. The water level starts at +25ft and drops to +20ft, whilst the water level on the top right-hand side is at +35ft and drops down to +25ft, then +20ft. This drop gives an indication as to the direction of flow of the water as it travels downhill. The ground contours start at the lowest water level of +20ft and rise to 100ft in the top left-hand corner. The road changes in its levels from +30ft, passing under the track level, rising to form a road bridge over the stream at +50ft and continuing to climb, passing over the track level at 75ft to reach its maximum of 100ft, whilst the track's level remains constant at +50ft. The contours' spacing on the left hand side indicates rapid change in ground levels, whilst on the bottom right is a comparatively flat area, the contours being spaced wide apart.

Below: The view shown in the photograph is from the railway bridge side.

Right: This portrays a totally unrealistic situation whereby the boats could not go under the bridges, the river has no embankments, the car could not go over the bridge and the car looks very small compared with the person in the boat.

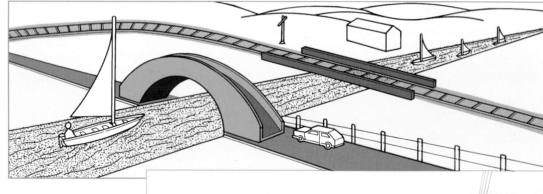

Right: This shows a railway over a road and stream, situated in Athlone (Ireland). The rail bridge over the road shows a 12ft 11in clearance. The traditional style Athlone West junction cabin (c.1981) is built on the side of the embankment and there are a lot of telephone and power lines. The banks of the stream are overgrown and the water level is much lower than that of the road. See hatch 4 & 5 page 73, 198 & 199, these have a stream running alongside the road.

Left: A small lifting bridge over the canal. The bridge when raised is closed to road traffic by gates on one side and on the other side by the bridge itself which now being vertical blocks the road. This is a good place to position people and cars queuing to go over the bridge, because it can portray a real life situation.

Right: This image portrays a typical railway scene and was taken from a road bridge over the track. Because this is a public location no permission was needed. But if the photograph had been taken on the platform (Private property) permission to take the photograph would have been needed if it was for commercial gain, but not for private use. The easiest way is to see the station master, and avoid any misunderstanding! Consult www.nationalrail.co.uk for further information.

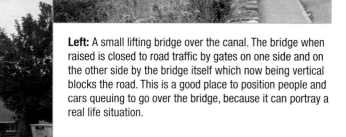

ROADS AND BRIDGES

Roads and bridges form a very important part of the layout, in the way they provide a scale to the model. The eye seeing this automatically sizes things to the reality it knows. If a model is made of an area of landscape in an unnatural way the eye simply will not accept what it sees as being realistic; for example, a model hump-back road bridge over a canal might have the angle of the road almost approaching 45 degrees to go up each side of the bridge and have a small radius at the top. In practical terms the approach road either side would be too steep to allow the safe transportation of a vehicle up the slope of the bridge and due to the small radius at the top of the bridge, the passing vehicle would hit its underside on the crest of the bridge (see illustration) leaving its wheels airborne.

Alongside this hump-back bridge might be a railway bridge, level with the river banks and having just a few inches clearance over the water. If the railway bridge is fixed in position and not a 'swing out of the way type,' this is an impractical situation that is not true to life so the mind does not accept what it is seeing as being realistic especially if the modeller puts canal barges travelling up and down the canal either side of the railway bridge. (Because the onlooker will know that the barges simply could not have passed underneath the bridge.)

To avoid this type of situation careful planning of the layout is required and an understanding of the rules and regulations that have been laid down. These rules cover public road usage; they lay down maximum recommended gradients for the approaches to bridges and the radius of the bridge so as to provide clearance for traffic passing over the bridge or under it. Many hump-back bridges are still in existence today but their use has been restricted, in many cases to pedestrians only, or they have been considerably modified to meet the demands of today's traffic, but with restrictions on vehicle length, axle weight, etc. Roads are also built to regulations that govern the radii of bends, so that two-way traffic can negotiate them without using the other side of the road. Similarly there will be recommendations as to the maximum gradient of a hill, for the provision for emergency escape bays on the long downhill stretches of roads should the brakes fail, etc.

Finally the width of the road will be regulated for the type and volume of traffic using it. In many countries the minimum width of a public road is the single width of a private motor car, and in country lanes, passing places must be provided at regular intervals, to allow two-way traffic to pass. When traffic constantly travels in both directions, the road will be wider and as the road width increases so does the radius of a bend in it. Thus small country lanes are notorious for their steep hills and sharp bends whilst motorways are noted for their billiard table flatness and gentle curves.

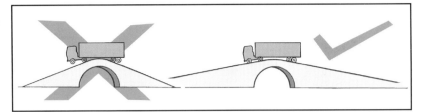

What actually happens in practice? The gradient of a hill can be reduced in many ways. Steep roads travelling up or down hills can be reduced in gradient by forming cuttings or embankments, the same as found on the railways. Roads (and railways) which travel diagonally up a hill are generally half excavated into the hillside; the earth removed being used to form an embankment on the other side of the road (or track). This also applies to

Above The lorry going over the humpback bridge that hits its chassis leaving its wheels airborne; by extending the approaches to the bridge this should be prevented.

Below: A rock-strewn stream going under bridge.

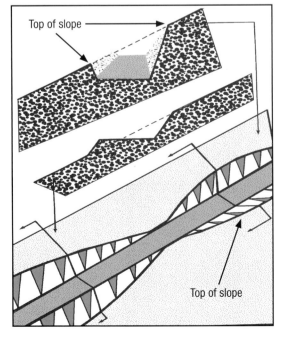

Left: The sections through the ground show the cutting made for the road across a hillside. This keeps the road flat across its width and the gradient at a reasonable angle up the hillside. Note the way the embankment is cut away and shown with tapering arrows to indicate man-made earthworks on the plan. The wide part of the arrow indicates the top edge of the ground. This is how the stream in the photo could be shown on a map.

Top of slope

Top of slope

Right: The photographs used in the making of this plan have their real locations miles apart from each other and by combining this real information and then using selective compression the baseboard's plan can be designed to look real yet meet the restricted size of the available space and the track shape. The unknown areas outside the photograph's view are invented to suit the joining of each situation together.

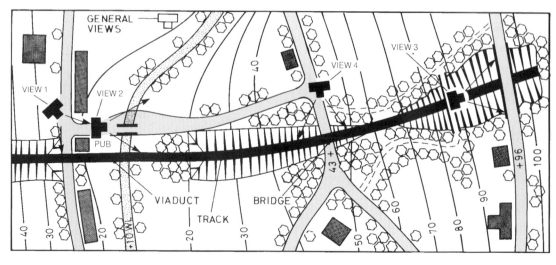

Opposite from top: The public house and viaduct joined together from a series of photographs. (South Darenth, Kent); The ford and humpback bridge (Eynsford, Kent); Road bridges over a track, located in a cutting (Rochester, Kent); Rail bridge over a road. (Sutton at Hone, Kent).

Below: The level Crossing, could replace the bridge (view 4) by changing the ground levels.

Right: A single photo of the pub, while several are used to make up the top right photograph.

roads (or track) travelling along a hillside which will be built this way for economy reasons, since it is far cheaper to half excavate and fill with the excavated material (see illustration) on the other side of the road (track).

The same form of economy measures are also applied to bridges and viaducts by redirecting the road to travel under the railway alongside a stream or river, thus building one bridge instead of two. The height of the embankment quite often equals the volume of the excavated material from the cutting. (This is because it is less expensive to transport large volumes of earth short distances.) Therefore it is worth keeping in mind this type of practice whilst designing the layout to suit the baseboard size, because it adds interest and realism to the model railway.

RESEARCH AND COMPROMISE

If it was decided to try to make a true to scale layout which included every item modelled in great detail, it would require an enormous amount of research, time and effort, plus a very large space in which to assemble the finished layout. The involvement of making just one fully detailed model that is in

fact a small part of the overall layout, will require a considerable amount of research. (The internet is ideal, especially the sites that have maps and aerial views.) Try to include in your research plans, photographs, notes, etc, cross-checked for accuracy, especially if a layout is being modelled of a subject from the past, when authenticity of the information could be doubtful. If the subject still exists, it can be far easier to make a visit to the place to gather one's own information.

Say a particular situation is required, of a railway bridge over a road and stream. Start by studying a series of updated maps, following the railway lines, until a suitable bridge is found, then study the map's ground contours, as this will provide an indication as to the setting. Finally, make an internet

search for an aerial photo. If all is still suitable make a site visit.

Unfortunately at times the map will fail to show the number of trees surrounding the subject, which of course one finds on arrival obscuring the majority of the bridge from view. In this situation all one can do is to make a series of sketches, take photographs of the bits visible and prepare notes, and then at home piece all the information together.

The important information to obtain is: the clearance between the road's surface and the underside of the bridge; the construction style of the bridge, e.g., stone, brick or metal, and its colour; and an estimate of the difference in the ground levels around the site. Finally take a series of photographs looking away, from and around the bridge, so as to gather all the reference material required for the bridge and its setting.

Whilst it is also possible to work from photographs of other people's models shown in books and magazines, one has to be very careful not to model a model. Use the modelling techniques described but study and work from reality, using notes and photographs, as the model shown could easily be the author's interpretation of what he has seen, adapted to suit his layout.

A decision will be required at some time as to whether the layout is going to be true to scale in every way, or will it be a series of different well-researched and convincingly made buildings, rolling stock, etc, all made to the same scale and set in a realistic condensed situation to suit the layout's size restrictions. The latter type of modelling is generally referred to as 'being based upon', for example 'Little Bovington'. It allows considerable wider scope in design, content, and interpretation of the layout. It uses real situations which may in reality, be miles apart. These are adapted to suit the layout with its limitations of baseboard size and above all the model must be practical to operate.

The plan illustrated shows how a selection of different area photographs can be combined and formed into a layout plan, whilst each subject in real life is miles away from the others. The way I have set about this is to keep the track at a constant height, estimated from the viaduct as being 58ft above ground level. Since the ground level at the stream is given as the height of +10ft above sea level, this is added to the viaduct's height, to total 68ft above sea level. The rail bridge over the road is estimated at 25ft above the road's surface. The track height is 68ft less 25ft, making the road height at +43ft, to form a spot height. The ground then has to rise to track level at 68 feet, then continue to around 100 feet, so as to allow for the tunnel, through which the track level passes. This provides a series of heights along the track's length. Starting at the water level of 10ft to the highest level of 100ft, it is divided up using the heights established, into a series of levels to suit.

2. DESIGNING THE LAYOUT

Right: The construction of a simple baseboard can be made using 9mm MDF for the top and 75 x 30mm timber for the frame and legs. A good starting size is 2m long x 0.75m wide x 0.70m high (door size).

Opposite top: The oval layout measures 7ft x 4ft, but dismantles into convenient sections for storage.

Opposite bottom: The one piece oval layout measures 3ft x 4ft, and fits into the back of an estate car's boot.

Note: There is an extremely wide choice of pre-packed layouts produced by numerous manufacturers. The very basic introductory set contains sufficient track to make a simple oval, with some rolling stock to use. Any additional items required have to be purchased separately and generally from manufacturers specialising in accessories.

Below: Graham Farish produced these simple to make buildings using self adhesive elevations.

LAYOUTS BOXED

In some ways the small oval layout is ideal for the beginner and manufacturers produce basic boxed sets suitable for assembly on a tabletop. It is the same with buildings, whereby many specialist companies have designed simple to assemble buildings. Graham Farish for example produced a range of buildings, using plastic blocks, (similar to Lego) over which self-adhesive pre-printed building elevations are fixed. These stick elevations hold the blocks in place so that no additional glues are used.

Since the blocks are not glued together, at a later date the buildings can be stripped of their elevations and rebuilt using home-made elevations as described in a later chapter. It is this advantage that makes them ideal for the beginner to purchase, and they are very different from the hollow cardboard buildings, which are far more difficult and time-consuming to construct.

SIZE OF LAYOUT

The storage of a layout after use is a common problem, but a solidly constructed one-piece baseboard can simply be picked up and stored away, e.g. under the bed as in many cases the bedroom is used for the hobby room, or another good storage space is behind the wardrobe. Storage of the layout is one of the major problems of a model railway, since the layouts require room both in use and afterwards and can force the decision of which scale to model in.

If you live in a small flat and space is at the premium then you have little choice but to build a small layout. If you live alone then you can put up with some inconvenience, but if you are married one's other half may not share these thoughts, thus requiring the layout to be put away after use, especially if there are little fingers in the house! The layout therefore has to be designed to get around these problems.

If you are a member of a club, then the layout problem could be of less concern at home because

Pre-cut length of square metal tubing fixed into push fit corner pieces.

Driven home with a mallet, to secure. Once assembled do not dismantle.

Alternatively construct a table using wood and screws, cross brace as required.

Finally fix a top in place, Paint layout design, assemble track, add buildings, trees etc.

you can help build and run the club's layout, and at home have a short length of test track to keep the rolling stock in good working order, using display cases or even boxes for storage. Alternatively the layout could well be designed to fit into a piece of furniture, for example a long sofa which really is a disguised storage chest with cushions on, allowing two or three baseboards to be stored inside. Such a layout through necessity would have to be of a back and forth design due to its long narrow storage.

If one has a larger house then the problems of storage are reduced considerably as many houses have a loft, cellar or garage, and these are points to consider when purchasing a house.

USABLE SPACE

The location of the layout normally influences the design, the loft could well be converted by boarding it for use as a hobby room. The hatch size into the loft will then pre-decide the maximum size of baseboard, (Build the layout in sections, so that each base goes through the hatch; just in case you move.) The cellar makes an ideal layout area especially if you expect a lot of visitors. Failing this it's the garage, the layout being built around three walls leaving the door clear as an entrance.

The car can be garaged in the middle overnight. But remember the height of the layout will need to be sufficient to allow the bonnet of the car to go underneath the baseboard, and don't forget to leave sufficient room on one side for the driver to get out. Alternatively, you could leave the car outside, carpet the floor and make the garage feel very homely!

Having a hobby room in a loft, cellar or garage gives you almost unlimited freedom in designing a layout. However, there are other considerations than just those of space. Few people have unlimited money or time, so a small layout is often dictated by circumstances rather than by choice.

The self-contained layout under average circumstances can have many advantages, and a concealed fiddle yard greatly expands the layout's running programmes for it allows one to undertake all the non-realistic situations; it is a behind the scenes operation and 'fiddled' so as to make the layout work conveniently in the minimum of space.

LAYOUT PLANS

The simplest form of layout for the younger modeller to build is the basic oval and siding, laid out on a solid board. The manufacturers encourage this by producing various types of train layouts to suit all budgets and pre-packed ready for use. These 'train sets' generally consist of a number of standard track lengths, a modern Digital Command Control (DCC) controller, two engines, plus some carriages or wagons. The first stage in expanding the layout is to purchase additional track and some points.

Note: If larger engines (mainline) are planned to be used on the new layout, larger radius curves will be required (see page 156).

The next stage is to carefully plan a layout and fix the track down permanently into position. The next stage is to paint the baseboard with emulsion paints to represent roads, paving, grass, etc, and by adding buildings and other structures; the expanded layout can be made to look more attractive. (All items that can be undertaken by the younger modeller under parental supervision.) These stages can be further expanded until eventually a large-scale layout is constructed.

Unfortunately, by building on a flat board the layout will not look as visually attractive as it might, being just a series of loops on a flat landscape, but the landscape can be made far more attractive by varying the levels, raising the ground level above and below the track level, so that a stream, for example, can be modelled at the lowest level, providing an excuse to build railway and road bridges over it. By similarly raising other levels to a sufficient height above the track, the landscape's shape suggests the reason for the building of tunnels, road bridges or viaducts. By now adding buildings, gardens, paving with kerbs, grass with texture and trees with various colours, the layout becomes even more visually interesting.

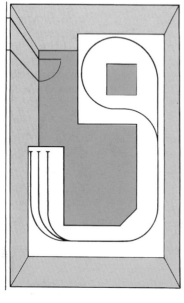

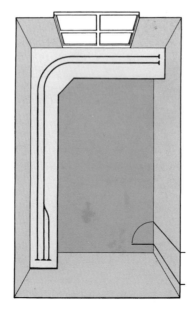

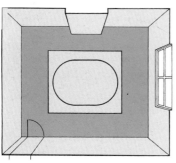

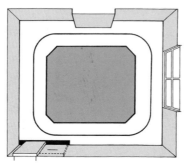

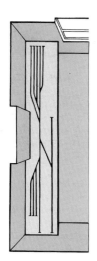

Top left: The G shaped design is a layout that permits a departing train to travel around the layout and back to its starting place, engine first. This will allow for the engine to be turned around on a turntable, as part of the departure procedure.

Top Right: the back and forth 'L' layout.

Above: The oval in the middle of the room is cramped for space compared with the around the room layout.

Left: The back and forth layout is ideal as a shelf display, whereby the landscape is the prime subject.

Bottom: The shelf brackets need to be firmly fixed to the wall, using cavity wall fixings for most internal plasterboard walls. These should not be less than 18 inches (45cm) apart and the shelf extending from the wall no more than 15 inches (40cm). Shelf displays make ideal portable layouts.

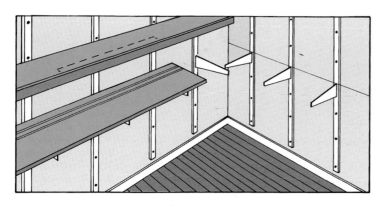

THE 'L' AND 'U' SHAPE LAYOUTS

These types of layout are ideal for building along the walls of a room and are generally modelled to represent a small terminus. The object of building this type of layout is to try to follow full size practice, by keeping the tracks, curves, distances, etc, as realistic as possible. This is impossible with the small oval layout, as a railway is in reality a route from A to B with stations along the way. All one can do with the oval layout is to try and disguise this fact as much as possible. The back and forth layout loses the continuous running facility, but the gain is the advantage of displaying a sky and landscape backdrop which considerably enhances the layout. This again is almost impossible with the oval layout, due to the fact that it requires access from all sides.

THE 'G' SHAPE LAYOUT

The 'G' shape layout is an extension of the 'L' and 'U' layout but has the advantage of a return loop which allows rolling stock to depart and return (coupled with a fiddle yard), the return loop generally being disguised under a hill.

THE AROUND-THE-ROOM LAYOUT

The around-the-room layout really is the ultimate, the operator standing in the middle of the room surrounded by a panoramic view of railway. It has all the advantages of the oval layout's continuous running facilities, large radius curves for fast mainline running programmes, provision for sidings, stations, fiddle yards, etc, and section control, enabling several operators to work the layout together, passing on each scheduled train to the next operator, just as happens in real life. The only disadvantage is that it requires a complete room to itself. The style and shapes of the layouts are endless, generally only limited by the cost and space available. One way of reducing cost is to join a club and share in the facilities. Some clubs work on the principle that each member builds a baseboard to a specification. This standardises all the key dimensions so that the baseboards become interchangeable, and on club nights the owners arrive with their baseboards and rolling stock and join them all together for running.

RESEARCH

If one wishes to undertake one's own research there is a vast number of books, magazines and posters to call upon to aid this. For example, if one wishes to model a railway set in the south of England, a book on the subject can be borrowed from the local library, showing the type of countryside, housing, streets, and industrial areas etc. The book need not be about railways, but a general guide to the area, providing an idea of the locality, preferably with maps and colour photos showing a selection of very different types of

locations, rather than for example a book on south of England churches, which is too specialised.

What one is looking for is a selection of modelling possibilities showing how the towns and villages look, the materials in which they are built, the type of roofs, an idea of the landscape's contours and its ground cover, i.e., what type of growth is shown in the way of trees and crops, etc, and how are the fields enclosed. The characteristic style of the roads and bridges can also be seen, so that one forms an overall picture. Once this is obtained and one is satisfied, then deeper research into the railway locations can be undertaken and having established an area of interest further specialised research can be carried out.

Since for practical reasons the layout will not be of true scale proportions, one can use artistic licence by moving situations around. An attractive village that is miles away in real life can be sited on the layout to suit, the same applies to the hillsides, landscape, bridges, roads, streams, all placed in appropriate positions to enhance the visual appearance of the layout and being designed to match the overall effect of the area as found in the general locations book showing the vicinity.

The amount of planning now depends entirely upon the modeller. Some modellers prefer to try to keep the layout as realistic in terms of scale distance as possible; others just try to capture a feeling of the area, as the object in most cases is to landscape the baseboard so that it looks attractive, with a selection of carefully chosen subjects.

Having now researched into the locality and an idea formed of the buildings, one needs now to find out what kits are available of suitable buildings, stations, etc, so that an indication can be assessed of what is easily obtained and what needs to be scratch-built.

This information is required so as to decide the physical area that the buildings will occupy on the baseboard for design purposes, especially if one is planning a series of buildings going down a hill or along a main road with no front gardens. Careful planning will be required at this point so as to disguise the variations of levels, as kit cardboard and plastic buildings tend to have flat base levels which will require careful remodelling to fit the street's change in level. A point worth remembering!

From top left: The old Abbey Wood Station Building (c.1980) being demolished to make way for the modern station. Settle Station and footbridge kept in immaculate condition. Typical stone built building, Settle, North Yorkshire. Typical wooden roof structure of a privately owned French dwelling.

Note: The location that the layout is to represent will mean that the architecture typical of the location will need to be studied.

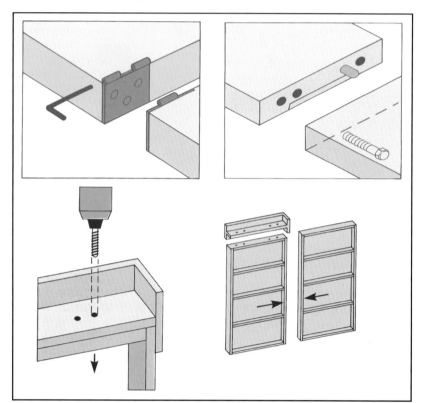

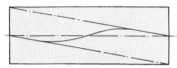

Top Left: By removing the pin from the hinge, and making a new pin that fits, the baseboards can be quickly assembled and dismantled.

Top Right: Alternatively the baseboards can be doweled and bolted, which provides a very secure join, and track alignment that does not move once the bolts are tightened.

Middle: Use a jig to standardise fixing holes, drill 4 holes, 2 for the pegs, 2 for the bolts each end, etc.

Above: Agree a standard track alignment for the bases so that other bases can be fitted together. The illustration shows a standard 2ft x 6ft (610 x 1830mm) baseboard, with a centre line. From the centre line a line is drawn at an angle to the top left hand. This is repeated, from the right hand bottom corner, which sets the track angle. When two tracks are being used this forms the centre line between the tracks.

Right: This illustration shows how a number of bases could be joined together to form various layouts which could be for example, set up in the loft and dismantled for exhibition, or stored and assembled on a club night, or members building individual bases etc.

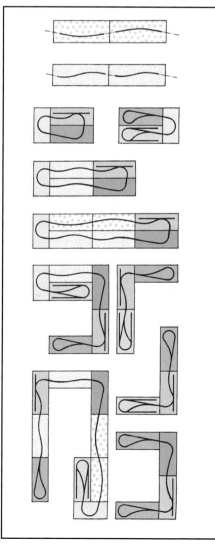

DESIGN CONSIDERATIONS

Since the design of the layout in many situations is completely influenced by the restrictions on the available space, and since for practical reasons the building of the layout uses stock timber size sheets, why not design the layout from the very beginning as a series of separate interlocking baseboards? The finished size of each board can then be planned so that they are portable and will fit into the available storage space, can be manoeuvred through doors and are not too heavy to carry. There is also the possibility of moving home to be taken into consideration. This factor can well be turned into an advantage rather than an inconvenient nuisance by making the baseboard sections in such a way that the layout is interchangeable. This gives more flexibility in the way the layout is arranged than does building a fixed one-piece layout which will be extremely difficult to alter at a later date without major rebuilding, during which time the layout could well be unworkable.

Most modellers find that their modelling skills increase as they work, so that as they progress around the layout, the first area to have been modelled does not look as good as later ones. Dissatisfaction with the early work may mean complete re-planning and rebuilding, at the cost of considerable delay in getting the layout completed. This situation can be avoided by designing the layout in interchangeable sections in the first place, as then one area can be built and left and the second worked upon and built. Then at a later date a completely new first area can be built if required as a separate baseboard which completely replaces the old first one. During the construction time required to make the new baseboard the layout remains in operation, which is a great advantage. By using this method the layout can grow in stages and if a standard size can be agreed between groups of people, who belong to a club, baseboards can be loaned or exchanged between the members or their friends from other clubs. This then allows an even greater flexibility than normal. Also, at exhibition time the combined series of baseboards could well be assembled to create a vast layout and producing even more enjoyment in their use.

By designing and building in this way, using a standard size of base, the baseboard could well be sold to a friend thereby making room and raising funds for the next new baseboard should the need arise. This is a very valid point to consider, as the N gauge society in Britain and the USA has already agreed on a standard specification, so it is worth considering. Although this specification does not need to be followed in a home layout, for club use it becomes very important so that a standard specification can be maintained throughout the country, which allows easy interchange and assembly of the layouts.

If it is wished, adapter baseboards can be made that allow the link-up of the standard size board

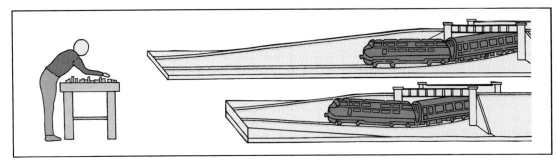

Left: By splitting the levels of the track, so that one track descends whilst the other climbs, it reduces the length of track required before both tracks reach the same level.

to a board of one's own design. This linking base must remain the same width as standard, only the rail alignment being moved to suit one's own layout at one end, and to meet the standard alignment at the other. So as to retain the grid that the standard baseboards make when assembled, the linking base will probably be an unusual length and then further problems accumulate. So at this point a decision should be taken as to the size of the baseboard, standard or non-standard.

Whatever the choice the same design considerations apply to the detail of planning the baseboard. Due to the restrictions of the board, the track layout shape is the first to consider (the minimum radius guide will be found at the front of the book). Plan the layout starting from the outside and working inwards across the baseboard so that maximum radii curve can be used. Make sure if laying two or three parallel tracks close to each other to allow sufficient clearance room between them, especially on the curves. The clearance necessary is best established by running the longest piece of rolling stock that you plan to use around the smallest bend and drawing a line from the front outside overhang so as to establish its arc of travel; then draw a line

from the mid-point, so as to establish its overhang inside the track's radius. These two lines inside and outside the radius of the track establish its clearance requirements (see illustration below).

An additional point to be taken into consideration is the distance of the track from the edge of the baseboard, so that in case of a derailment you can easily reach to put things right; similarly, track should not be laid too close to the edges of the baseboard in case valuable stock falls on the floor after an accident.

Finally, if one is using a multi-level layout the angle of rise or fall in the track's gradient must be very shallow, approximately two metres length being required to clear a 00/HO gauge locomotive (10 cm high rise). Allow for a thin 10 mm track support under the bridging track for a single rise above a baseboard level. Halve this distance if using the split rise and fall method each side of the bridge, so that one track rises whilst the other drops in its level. This second method, whilst considerably reducing the overall length required, can sometimes cause other problems by weakening the support batten underneath the layout if it is not properly planned for.

Note: The length of the gradient will vary because gradients on curves need to be less steep than those in a straight line. This is because wheel friction increases on the curves, and the outcome is that the same engine can pull less coaches or trucks up hill on a curve than in a straight line.

Below: It is vitally important that the tracks align between baseboards. Because it is impossible to align every baseboard with each other, it is advisable to build in some form of adjustment, so that the tracks can be aligned. This is particularly important at club meetings, when a selection of members bring their baseboards.

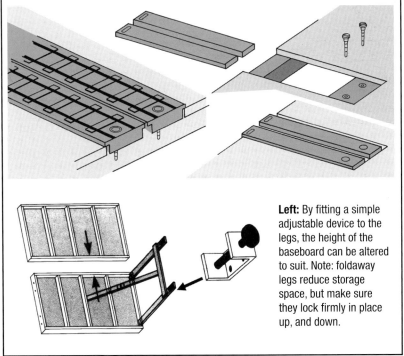

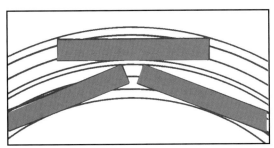

Left: By fitting a simple adjustable device to the legs, the height of the baseboard can be altered to suit. Note: foldaway legs reduce storage space, but make sure they lock firmly in place up, and down.

Above: Blundiz Main Station in Austria, which has international trains passing through its platforms. Continental rolling stock is very different to British stock, as are the platforms etc., which are far lower than the British counterpart.

Opposite: A series of photographs taken at Settle Station, North Yorkshire, which is an extremely well preserved and maintained traditional older style station building. The points of interest are: Just how clean everything is, including the roof! The flower arrangements and the oil stain down the centre of the track and rust deposit on the rails & ballast etc.

CHOICE OF SUBJECT

Railways run throughout the world, which provides enormous scope for the modeller. Much will depend upon the modeller's skill as to whether he/she chooses to scratch-build or use commercially available rolling stock. Availability of stock will vary from country to country, as will the scales in which the models are produced. Each country tends to support its own type of outline, so that difficulties could well be encountered with an overseas modelling choice. The choice of country is very important, for not only is rolling stock of that country required, but information on buildings and scenery, which can be considerably different to one's own surroundings.

As previously mentioned the scales vary from country to country and you will find that other factors also have to be taken into consideration. Fortunately many specialist dealers run a mail order or internet service, so that items unavailable locally can be purchased through the post. This is a mixed blessing, because one cannot inspect the purchase beforehand.

One answer to finding supplies is to obtain a catalogue or hobby magazine from the country that has been chosen to be modelled. From this the required information about modelling supplies can be gathered, plus an indication of trade support as well as some idea of the local scenery and stations.

Since most magazine contributors tend to model subjects of their own country rather than from abroad, they provide all sorts of valuable information obtained locally or easily accessible to them. Thus, if an overseas modeller writes to the author of an article via the magazine, a contact could be made in another country and useful information exchanged.

Alternatively the name of a particular club or layout can be found that is of interest, and since most modellers enjoy the exchange of ideas a reply could be possible. (Enclose an international reply coupon with the letter.) One problem really does exist, and that of course is language, so that the country you are writing to really needs to be English-speaking.

English is also spoken in America, as well as most European and Scandinavian countries. If you cannot read, write or speak a foreign language needless to say overseas correspondence will be difficult. If you are asking for information also offer a service in lieu of the inconvenience possibly caused to the person who has taken the trouble to reply. The internet is a good source of obtaining and exchanging information!

Above: Craig Semplis captured this night time image at Bury Station. Craig has been photographing railways for years and was able to supply another image he captured of a semaphore signal shown at halt, way ahead blocked.

Right: This is a typical photograph that is easily captured from the end of the station. Notice how untidy the track bed is and the discolouring of the ballast.

Opposite top: The station at Ford with its rust stained weathered paintwork in need of refurbishment. (Buildings and rolling stock need to be weathered.)

Opposite bottom: The trees in the background look like a poor attempt at making model trees.

Above: The lock gates being closed by helpers whilst a barge exits Gauxholme's lock 22.
Left: This shows a substantial heavy duty railway bridge over a canal.
Below: Eynsford ford, photographed in the evening sunlight of an autumn day.

All of these photographs have modelling potential on a water theme. The camera used to produce reference photos need not be expensive, just capable of producing sharp images.

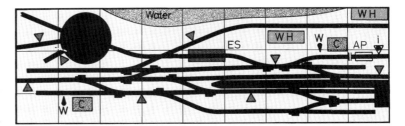

THE COMPROMISE LAYOUT DESIGN

The first baseboards made by the beginner should be kept as simple as possible, with a shelf layout being ideal to start with. The above illustration shows a true life situation, known as a branch line. This is because it is a spur off the main line, located some miles away, and the line performs a local service, for the arrival and departure of both goods and passengers. The plan shows it to be 240m (787ft) long.

This scales at the 2mm/ft 'N' gauge model size 1.57m long (5ft 2in) and twice this length at '00' scale. By using 6 inch squares we can use selective compression, the overall length of the branch line can be reduced and our model base now becomes 1.37m (4ft 6in) long.

The around the room layout uses 12in squares and is designed as a '00' gauge 4mm/1ft scale layout. The layout needs a room size of 6ft x 9ft with a maximum reach depth of 2ft 6in to the back of the layout; important when rolling stock comes off the track.

Using the information found in Chapter One and establishing the available room space for the layout, you could well by now have decided to work with a group of friends, all of whom have limited storage space and money. This really forces you to build a series of baseboards that plug into each other, and since each baseboard will be subject to a lot of carrying around, they will have to be light yet very sturdy and easily secured together.

A ready-made basic structure will be required unless all the members of the group are capable of woodwork, and the answer to this problem could well be to purchase a series of lightweight doors, of the type that are hardboard-surfaced, filled with a criss-cross of cardboard and edged with thin batten, designed for domestic internal use. This now fixes the baseboards' sizes in a very convenient way that is easily added to. The track now needs to be designed; the most convenient practical way is to run the tracks in straight lines parallel to one edge, allowing for the scenery at the back. This unfortunately looks very uninteresting and considerably worse after several baseboards have been joined together. It also restricts assembly configurations as each board has a front and back.

This problem can be overcome by running the track down the middle of the baseboard so that the baseboard may be turned around and viewed from both sides. Now if the track is also built in a series of curves greater visual interest can be created, whilst maintaining the interchangeability of the baseboards (see page 28). The next problem to arise is

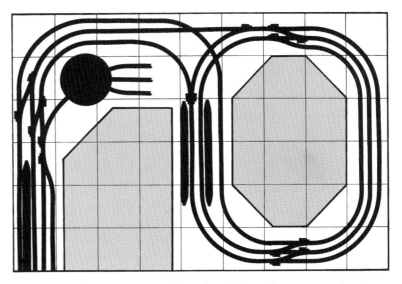

the joining of the contours, as these obviously need to be at a common level at each end of the baseboard, so the track joins at a standard level and angle.

The baseboard size could be too big for N gauge or too small for 00/HO gauge, or laying the track in a series of curves could present problems in joining the baseboards together. So a compromise has to be reached, especially since carpentry is nearly always a stumbling block, due either to lack of facilities or skill.

So even if you decide to retain the large door size as the basic baseboard size, you may decide to lay the track off centre, sacrificing the facility of turning the baseboards around but allowing a greater modelling area on the back edge, providing depth to the layout.

The track can be laid as a 'home and away' configuration with a hidden return loop and a fiddle yard at the other end. If the scale of the layout is to be N gauge, so as to allow maximum scenic modelling, the buildings, trees, hills, etc, will be proportionately smaller than 00/HO gauge, so you will require more of them to cover the baseboard. This is a real swings and roundabout situation, gain in one direction, lose on the next. However, an N gauge layout could be smaller and the baseboard thinner and lighter, so you can see there are many different valid points to consider when selecting the scale of the layout.

Top: This map of a branch line is based on 'Bude' a branch line terminus that no longer exists. The information has been extracted from an old aerial photograph, plus maps so it contains a lot of reasonably accurate guess work.

Middle: The selective compression version of the 'Bude' terminus using a 6in square grid. (75ft squares at 2mm/1ft scale) which will allow good running potential coupled with a fiddle yard.

Bottom: The around the room layout has both out and back plus continuous running potential. From the running of the trains point of view, this configuration is ideal.

The 00/HO scale layout (below) using the 'N' scale design, (right) condensed so that it is not twice as large but one and a half times. The N scale base is 4ft by 3ft, the 00/HO scale base is 6ft by 4ft 6in. Notice the way the roads have been increased in their width and the way buildings have been removed on the 00/HO version.

Multi level plan
Compare these plans with the plans shown in chapter 11. The right hand side of the track now drops in its level to form an underground storage. This considerably increases the working potential of the layout.

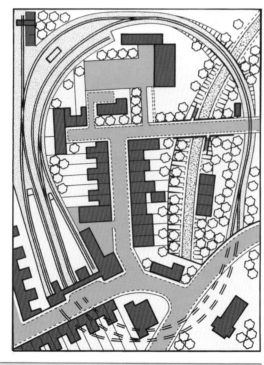

Note: A criticism of this layout design is that you cannot run two trains at the same time, therefore I recommend that the single track loop is replaced with two tracks, via points so that rolling stock can be moved from track to track.

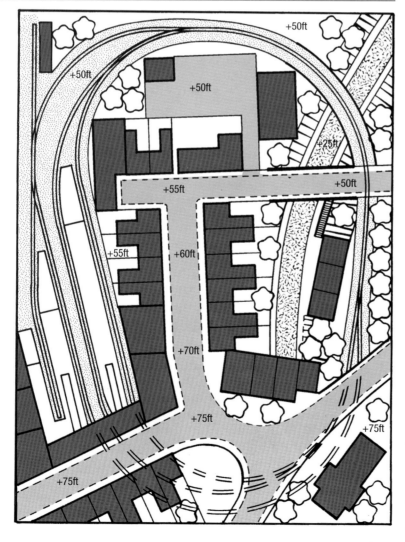

00/HO SCALE BASEBOARDS

By using the 2mm to the foot N gauge layout plans shown (base size 5ft x 2ft) and doubling up the size to 4mm to one foot (00 scale) a new base size is formed of 10ft by 4ft (3m x 1.22m), or slightly smaller at HO scale. This is far too large to construct in one piece and remain practical. It is also unnecessary because a complete 00/HO oval layout can be constructed on a 6ft x 4ft 6in (2m x 1.5m) baseboard including passing loops and sidings.

An easy way of reducing the area of the plans shown is to model the centre strip only on a 2ft 6in wide by 10ft long base, which will remove a lot of the unwanted surrounding ground detail. Alternatively selective condensing could well be used so that the base becomes 6ft 6in by 2ft 6in, about the size of a standard door. This second method allows a similar type of layout to be built, but this time in greater detail, especially if you opt for narrow gauge modelling.

This is much the same as running N gauge track width wise but the locomotives are at 00/HO scale because it is just the track width (gauge) that is narrower. This opens up a completely new zone of modelling not discussed as yet and really provides the best of both worlds. Quarries, chalk pits, coal mines, etc. can now be modelled with their own working rolling stock, which can link up with the standard gauge at terminals and therefore allowing two types of layout to be run in conjunction with each other on the same baseboard.

Although N gauge can be run on 00/HO layouts as a backdrop to create the effect of distance, this of course only really works when viewing the layout from ground level and not from the bird's eye view at which it is seen most of the time.

The method used for condensing length is to widen the roads and increase the buildings' size to suit, working on top of the existing plans, in this particular case by half size (e.g. a building or road width of 2in (50mm) becomes 3in (75mm). Where the buildings are too close together, to increase size remove some of the buildings: compare the two oval layouts shown on this page.

This method effectively reduces the surrounding area to the buildings, making them closer together. The base drawing is then re-scaled so that the base becomes 6ft 6in instead of the 5ft length and contour distances also become closer together so that the landscape becomes hillier. The spacing of the contours 6in (150mm) apart means that scale distance 38ft for a 10ft road rise is the critical distance for the maximum 25 per cent gradient of road.

Ideally embankments should not be steeper than 45 degrees, so use a retaining wall at the bottom when the angle of the embankment exceeds this for sandy soils, but rock or chalk faces can be vertical. Cover embankments with plenty of plant life, including lots of ground cover, but keep the trees back from the track's edge. (Because in reality you get leaves on the line.)

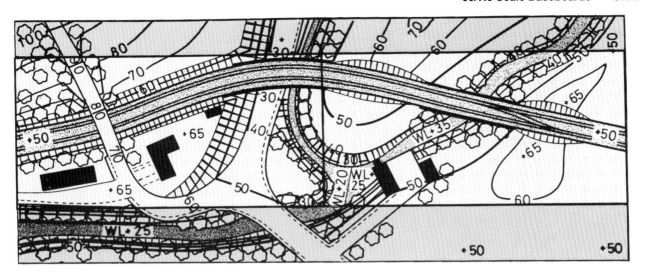

1. Modelling the centre strip of this plan and doubling its size makes it 10ft by 2ft; it also puts the join of the track between the bases in an awkward position, being right at the back.

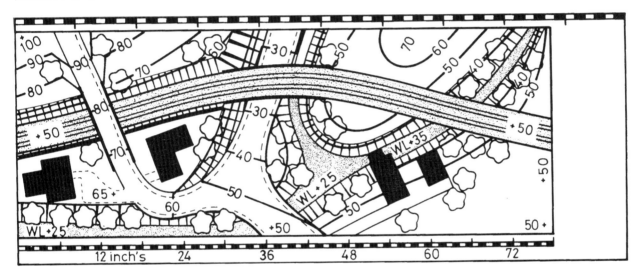

2. By rescaling the base and thickening up both the track and the road width, the design and content of the base can be much the same. In terms of scale and distance, items have moved closer together, which will make the slope of the ground that much steeper. This is a very important factor, because roads do not go up hill at 45 degrees (height by length = 100% slope). The maximum is around 25%, a 1 in 4 gradient, but this is a very steep slope.

Therefore it is probably better to move the existing road bridge from the middle of the base and move it to the right, and move the stream over to suit. The buildings can be turned sideways to allow for the road, and remove the

stream that runs under the bridge in the middle of the base. This would considerably reduce the ground's slope.

3. By reducing the track's radius, room can be created in the foreground. The lower area ceases to be water, but now becomes a self-contained narrow gauge layout, built into one of the bases. Incorporating narrow gauge within a design considerably increases the visual impact of the layout. To reduce the slope of the road, the bridge could well become a level crossing; this would avoid a steep 30 foot rise over a short distance.

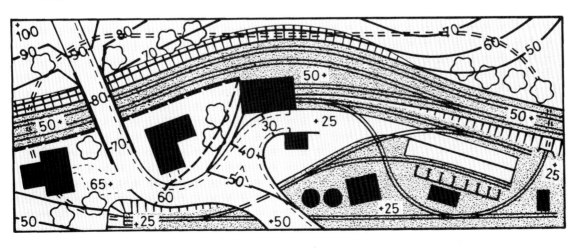

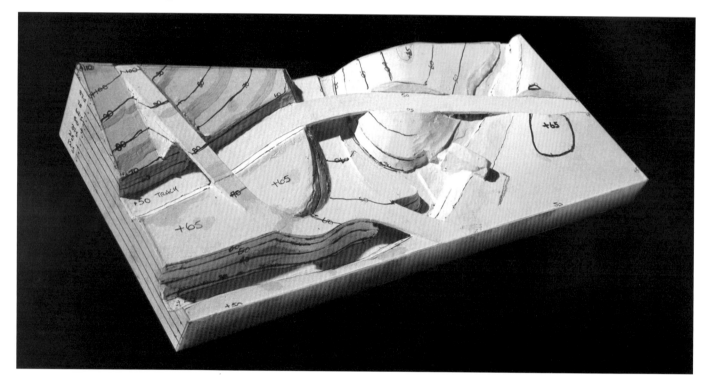

Above: The design model of base 6, showing the contour lines. The design model is made from card and balsa wood, with Plasticine® being used to shape the awkward bits. Both design models were then painted white using oil paint, and the contour lines applied using the height gauge or bridge method. Scaling: With the event of digital photography it becomes a simple task of photographing the design model directly from above and downloading it onto the computer. The next stage is to print out an image, grid the picture up, and using the gridlines enlarge the photo to model size. (See page 16, 17 & 19 for further details).

THE DESIGN MODEL

Among the biggest problems facing the modeller are the changes required from reality to make the layout work, not just in a practical sense, in that the tracks line up and function well, but also in the overall visual effect of the layout, since the majority of its design is a compromise rather than reality scaled down. This is due to the restrictions of the baseboard's size which means the landscape, buildings, roads, etc. all have to be moved around and re-sited to suit the baseboard, yet at the same time need to look as natural and realistic as possible – just as if, in fact, it is modelled on reality and nothing has been changed.

This is a very difficult task to undertake in plan form alone, especially when the ground levels are constantly changing. This is when the design model assists the understanding of the plans, because drawings are very difficult at times to mentally interpret into three dimensions. i.e., how the contours and levels relate to each other. At times problems also arise within the design of the layout, when several ramps or levels coincide with each other, and each 'bit' requires a certain clearance. This problem is generally due to the gradient required by the track or road, being long in length, which affects an area a long way away from the source. Therefore by solving one problem, a new problem can be created elsewhere. Unless it is very clear in one's mind precisely what is occurring, mistakes happen, resulting in a lot of hard work and effort needed to alter, and all because a design point was overlooked and to much annoyance only discovered during the construction stage.

Fortunately a lot of these design problems can easily be resolved in the design stage by making a mock model of the layout first. This mock-up design model needs only to be simple, but can assist the design and visual effect immensely, since it gives you a solid visual impression of the proposed layout for study and from which working dimensions can be obtained. By simply producing the 'model' of the layout using card, balsa wood, Plasticine® or modelling clay, alterations can be quickly made as problems are discovered during the design process stage.

The mock-up modelling technique used is to cut out a piece of cardboard, scaled to a convenient size. This is used to represent the plywood baseboard level; then, using card and balsa wood, add the basic rail and road levels, the card being used to represent the plywood and the hardboard, the balsa to represent wood battens. The construction methods are the same as if it was the full size base, including the building of the below ground slab levels that the buildings are going to sit on (so as to establish the additional below ground level requirements of the buildings).

Finally fill in the gaps left with Plasticine® or modelling clay to represent the contours, all of which can easily be changed around whilst undertaking the design process of the layout. Therefore each step or alteration can be studied in solid form, rather than trying to form a mental picture allowing a much clearer interpretation to be made of the progress of the design. The outline of buildings and trees can be added in 'block and blob' form so that a complete three-dimensional representation of the layout can be made for study.

On completing the design and being satisfied with the overall effect, the model is painted using household oil-based white undercoat, and when dry dimensions and heights are taken from the

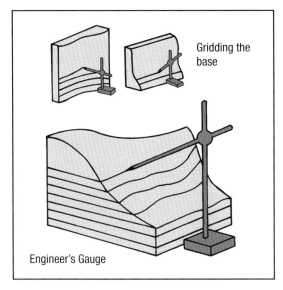

Gridding the base

Engineer's Gauge

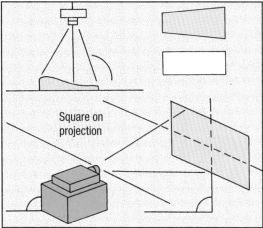

Bridge Height Gauge

Work on a flat surface

Square on projection

Far left: An engineer's height gauge is used to mark out the contours.

Left: A home made 'Bridge' that uses pieces of wood of the same height, spanned by a strip of wood. The pencil height is adjusted to suit each contour.

Left: The photograph of the model on transparency (slide) film and projected onto a wall covered with paper. Keep the projector parallel to the wall to prevent the projected image from distorting, and move the projector back and forth to size the image.

Note: Lining paper used on walls is an ideal source of cheap drawing paper.

model using the scriber or the bridge method, so as to translate the information back into two dimensions or to work from. The outside of the model can also be drawn around so as to obtain the baseboard's edge contour levels, and by using the grid method these can then be enlarged to layout size. The use of proportional dividers and scale rules helps keep estimating to the minimum.

Alternatively, the design model can be photographed on slide film in plan form and then projected on to the full-size baseboard; the image is then 'traced' onto the baseboard to suit. This method is a very quick, simple and accurate way of enlarging the drawings or mock-up models to working size.

In practice, I have found that working with the aid of a small scale model has saved hours of wasted time. The second advantage is that quite often the design changes, as other ideas occur and are implemented, which leads to other ideas so that in the end a new and better design evolves.

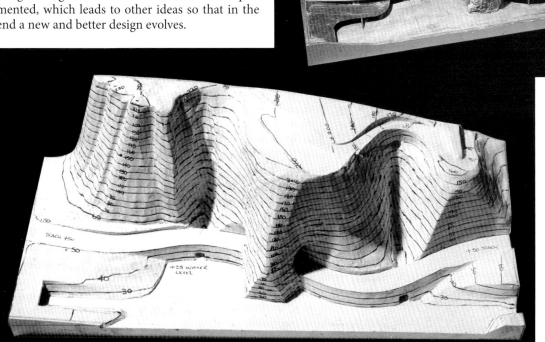

Above: The 'N' gauge layout baseboard closely resembles the design model shown on the left.

Further details of how to construct this baseboard at model size are shown in Chapter 3.

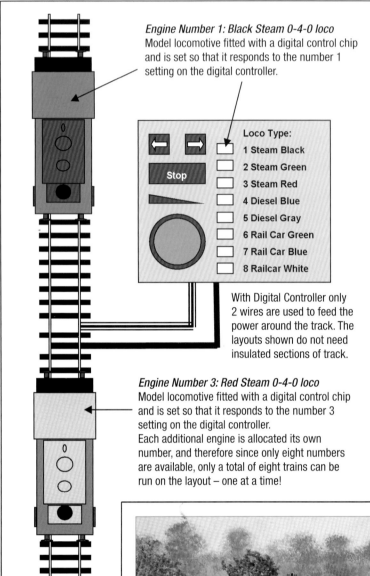

Engine Number 1: Black Steam 0-4-0 loco
Model locomotive fitted with a digital control chip and is set so that it responds to the number 1 setting on the digital controller.

	Loco Type:
← →	1 Steam Black
Stop	2 Steam Green
	3 Steam Red
	4 Diesel Blue
	5 Diesel Gray
	6 Rail Car Green
	7 Rail Car Blue
	8 Railcar White

With Digital Controller only 2 wires are used to feed the power around the track. The layouts shown do not need insulated sections of track.

Engine Number 3: Red Steam 0-4-0 loco
Model locomotive fitted with a digital control chip and is set so that it responds to the number 3 setting on the digital controller.
Each additional engine is allocated its own number, and therefore since only eight numbers are available, only a total of eight trains can be run on the layout – one at a time!

Right & Below: The Wishton Halt layout is wired solely for DCC running. This means that the track is not broken up into electrical sections, but power supplied throughout the track at all times. (This permits lights & sound etc. to remain functioning at all times.) It would require complex wiring and the track split into numerous electrical sections to run several trains without digital control.

DIGITAL CONTROL

With the development of digital control, the railway modeller's dream of running two or more trains on the same length of track was realised. Whilst the concept of digital control is not new, it is only after 20 years' development and the drop in the prices of electronic components that it has become affordable.

In the past, running two trains on the same track without digital control was only possible by breaking the track into electrical sections, and passing the trains from one section of track to another section. Whilst it is possible to operate two trains using a single conventional controller, both trains moved or stopped simultaneously, because there was no independent control on each train. For example if both the trains were running on an oval track, in due course one train would catch the other one up! Now with the advent of DCC control the trains can be independently controlled, so the train that is catching the other one up can be slowed down or the slower train can be speeded up; despite being on the same oval track!

Note: The number of trains that can be run simultaneously is restricted by the output of the controller.

Size affects installation of the microchip, therefore 00 and HO gauge rolling stock fitted with DCC controlling chips are commercially available, but it is not the case with N gauge; whilst it has been achieved it is at a price!

The way that individual control is achieved is to fit a microchip into each power unit, so that it recognises all the commands assigned to it, and will ignore all other commands issued to any other power unit (engine) on the same length of track.

This does not apply to just a single length of track, but to the entire network of track on the layout. In practical terms the wiring is made simpler, but at times it will still need isolated sections and isolated points to prevent cross-feed electrical short-circuits on tracks that loop back on themselves.

This is because certain track configurations, despite using track insulators, short circuit when the train's power unit bridges the insulated track join. Note: Return loops that link back onto the same length of track should be avoided, and the same applies to the oval (shown on page 10) because both short circuit unless isolated and wired correctly (see Chapter 8 on wiring). Therefore I recommend that neither method of track configuration should be used by the inexperienced modeller until the art of wiring is mastered.

WISHTON HALT

The plan of the layout shown on this page is based on Lynton Station, but the model was influenced by Swanage, Sidmouth and a number of other stations that had turntables. The change involved making the layout wider, from 12in (30cm) to 17in (43cm) and from 8ft (230 cm) to 9ft 2in (280cm). The new sizes were influenced by the available space in my estate car, which is taller, wider and longer than my old car – a point worth considering if you are going to transport layouts around!

CONCEPT

The station 'in theory' was once a small halt at the turn of the century (1900) near the seaside. *(The crane is used to lift the boats etc. off or onto the train.)* Because of its location it has grown in size due to the number of summer visitors who prefer to disembark here because it is nearer the sea, than to get off the train at the main Wishton Station (N gauge oval layout). Since the main station already exists, the halt could not be renamed as a station, and since the local railway authority failed to change the name to Wishton Sands, the old name remains to the present time.

The location is in the south of England, because Southern Rail runs through the main Wishton Station, therefore this sets the colours used on the station fittings and on the buildings etc. It also sets the style of architecture and the running of both steam and diesel set the time zone.

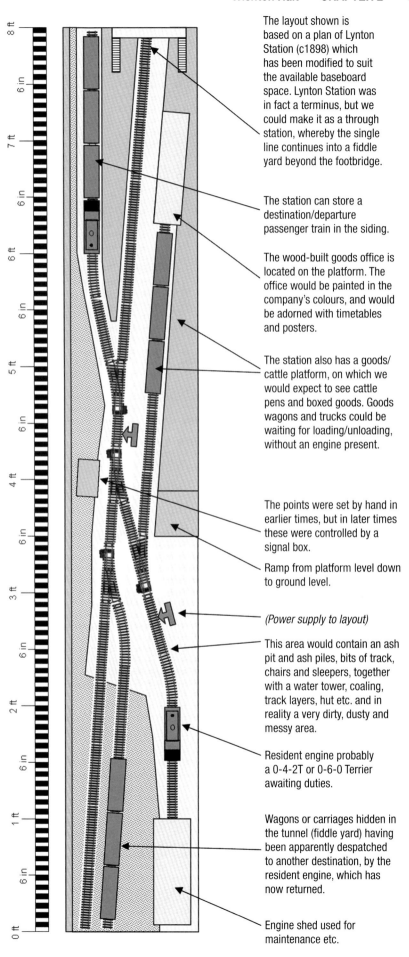

The layout shown is based on a plan of Lynton Station (c1898) which has been modified to suit the available baseboard space. Lynton Station was in fact a terminus, but we could make it as a through station, whereby the single line continues into a fiddle yard beyond the footbridge.

The station can store a destination/departure passenger train in the siding.

The wood-built goods office is located on the platform. The office would be painted in the company's colours, and would be adorned with timetables and posters.

The station also has a goods/cattle platform, on which we would expect to see cattle pens and boxed goods. Goods wagons and trucks could be waiting for loading/unloading, without an engine present.

The points were set by hand in earlier times, but in later times these were controlled by a signal box.

Ramp from platform level down to ground level.

(Power supply to layout)

This area would contain an ash pit and ash piles, bits of track, chairs and sleepers, together with a water tower, coaling, track layers, hut etc. and in reality a very dirty, dusty and messy area.

Resident engine probably a 0-4-2T or 0-6-0 Terrier awaiting duties.

Wagons or carriages hidden in the tunnel (fiddle yard) having been apparently despatched to another destination, by the resident engine, which has now returned.

Engine shed used for maintenance etc.

3. LAYOUT CONSTRUCTION

Right: The oval base shown during construction has changing levels making for a more realistic setting. The points and signals are planned to be operated electrically and the track is split into electrical sections. A single controller was used to control all the sections, but by using more than one controller, several different rolling-stock movements could be carried out simultaneously. i.e. the loop could be used for continuous running whilst the siding and platforms are used to prepare the next train.

Research: There are a number of internet map sites that also contain aerial photographs and this has made research so much simpler. Nowadays you can follow a railway line's progress through town and country, by using a few clicks of the computer's mouse. Having studied a suitable place that has modelling potential a visit should be arranged, to obtain ground level views. The best time for site surveys is during the winter months, when there is no foliage on the trees to block the view. The current trend is to use a digital camera, so fill the memory card with pictures, and include lots of detail pictures as well as location views.

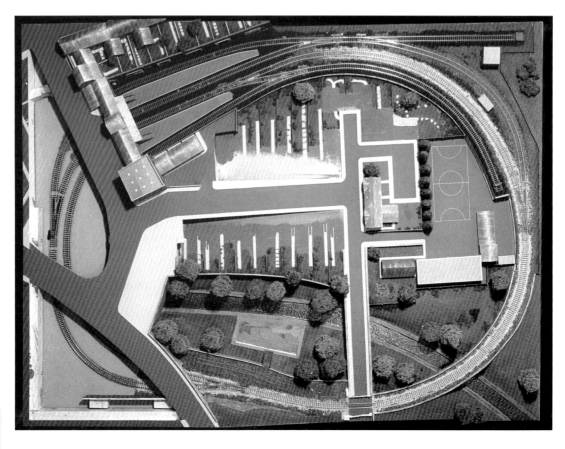

ADVICE FOR THE BEGINNER

For the beginner building his or her first baseboard, I recommend that a very simple layout is made first. This will allow you to experiment within the basic learning stage. Small separate samples can be made and if they do not work satisfactorily, these can be thrown away. By doing this, one is encouraged to try out different techniques, knowing that the outcome cannot damage the main layout. This is the procedure I still use today when trying out new methods.

The illustration on page 26 shows simple layouts built on a flat board. These can use a single controller and the points (turnouts) can be operated by hand. This type of layout is typical of a permanent layout that started with one of the many boxed commercial 'railway sets', which simply have its track pushed together and dismantled after use.

THE BASEBOARD

The content of each of the bases covers a particular construction problem in a progressive way. For example, base 01 is flat and simple to make whilst base 7 contains a cliff face rising some 200 scale feet above track level and is far more complex in its construction.

For the beginner, the construction sequence is designed to allow the easiest bases to be made first. These are bases 01, 02 and 03, and cover the basic construction methods; they are kept simple by building from the track datum level upwards, a well tried and tested standard method of construction. The history of the ideas behind the baseboards uses a method that will suit any design of layout. My research consisted of studying hundreds of miles of track, using a series of maps. Points of interest were noted and the most interesting places were visited, photographs taken and notes made. Local guidebooks were obtained which contained aerial photographs to provide and build up an overall idea of the locality.

The next stage was to plan out the track's position to suit the baseboards, the ground then being contoured to suit each locality being modelled. In the end, despite the places being miles apart, the situations were joined together by inventing surrounding areas and adjusting the real places to suit the restrictions imposed by the bases. Bases 01 and 02 are typical town areas, while bases 03, 4, 5, 6 and 7 are countryside. The various construction methods used to make the baseboards will vary so much that the beginner will find it very difficult to understand.

What will not help is that whenever help or advice is sought on a particular problem, each individual asked resolves the problem using a different method. Well, the truth of the matter is that there is no 'fixed way' to model anything.

The reasons for this are: material preferences, available space and equipment. Most modellers own a collection of hand tools only, whilst others own a selection of power tools etc. The vast majority of modellers work on the kitchen table, whilst others have garages or a room in which to work. Finally, skills and experience progressively develop over a number of years of making models.

These variable factors are the reason for producing a selection of answers, simply because each person they ask has a different level of knowledge and skill. You will also find that many methods shown in this book are different to methods shown in other books, this is normal.

KITCHEN TABLE MODELLING

This situation has gained enormous respect over the years. As previously mentioned, many modellers only have this facility at their disposal but, working at home with the minimum of tools, have devised methods and developed incredibly high skills. The newcomer to the hobby, I feel, should always keep this in mind.

CONSTRUCTION METHODS

To cover the wide range of construction methods used for the baseboards I advise the reader to read this entire chapter as a series of methods, all of which can be intermixed and applied to suit. My reason for choosing N scale as the prime example is the physical size of the baseboards, all of which have had to be constructed and photographed within my own limited available space. Also, N scale can be easily scaled up to HO/00 but the conversion does not work so conveniently the other way around, the reason being that the minimum radius of the track's curves become impractical when scaling down.

As an example of this, take the standard Peco 00/HO set track's minimum radius of 371mm (14.5in). If you halve this it becomes 185.5mm (7.25in). The minimum recommended standard radius curve of N gauge track is 228mm (9in), which is well over half the size of the 00/HO dimension for scaling-down purposes. Working in reverse, i.e., scaling up from N gauge to 00/HO gauge, a 228mm (9in) radius becomes 58mm (18in), an almost standard radius size. Finally, and very importantly, more problems could be encountered within each of the N scale bases and the reader should study these.

The construction methods for N, 00/HO and 0 scales, although progressively larger in physical size, hardly change, so that the methods shown can be used throughout these various scales. Larger scales such as gauge 1 are too large in practical terms to have a baseboard of this nature.

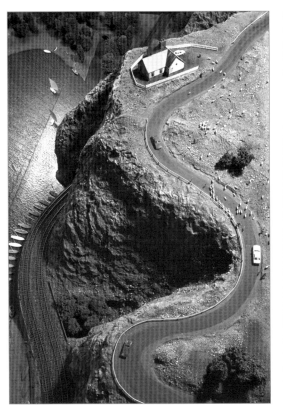

Left: The cliff baseboard, which forms part of a series, is a complex base to construct because of its changes of level.

BASEBOARD DETAILS

The design is known as a double loop, allowing two-train operation from a single controller. The oval layout (left) shows an extension of the double loop, an elaborate contoured single baseboard oval layout, complete with sidings, station, roads and other buildings. The points (turnouts) are operated electrically; the working signals correspond to the turnouts' settings. A single controller was used to operate the selection of rolling stock and the entire layout was visually attractive, due to its lifelike environment, complete with trees, cars and people.

The photograph at the top of the page shows a single baseboard that forms part of a series of bases that make up a large layout when joined together. Alternatively the layout could be built on a shelf and portray a small country terminus that deals with small amounts of rail traffic. The construction of this and other bases are explained elsewhere.

The concept of the book is to show the reader model making methods that are used by the professional, who will have a considerable amount of experience in using power tools. This knowledge is generally learnt in the first instance by attending college, and studying on one of the specialist 3D courses. Prior to this many hobbyists start by working on the kitchen table, possibly with the encouragement of dad, but in the way of mum when she wants to get dinner ready! Ideally the railway modeller needs a bit of space that he can walk away from at the end of the evening without the need to pack everything away after use. The loft is the main location for many a layout, but build it in sections, so that it can be removed through the loft hatch should you move! The alternative place is the garage, and the car is left outside. In America, they take their railroad modelling very seriously, and some construct enormous buildings to house the layout. In the United Kingdom space is at a premium so the small self contained layout is the norm, with the club layout allowing greater running space.

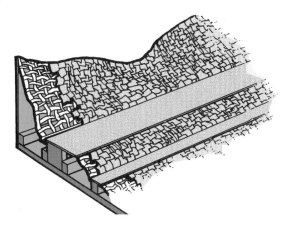

Left: On a layout that uses woven card or wire to support the scenery over the track, it is necessary to provide access into the covered area via cut outs in the side of the base.

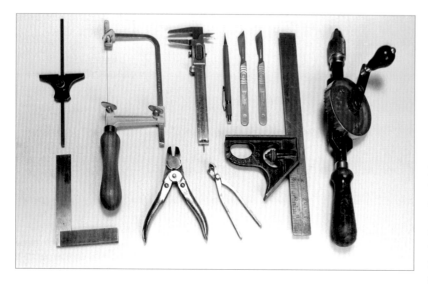

Above: A well used collection of hand tools, and despite the drill not being battery operated still gets used.

Far right: The band saw is extremely useful for cutting curves and random shapes, but not really satisfactory for cutting straight lengths of plastic or timber.

Right: the jig saw is similar, cuts curves and random shapes with ease, but very difficult tool to cut a straight line with. When using a jig saw it is better to clamp the material down to stop it moving, rather then using the other hand to hold it in place. Note how the material spans the gap, so that the material being cut is supported on both sides. Keep moving the material to avoid cutting through the workmate top.

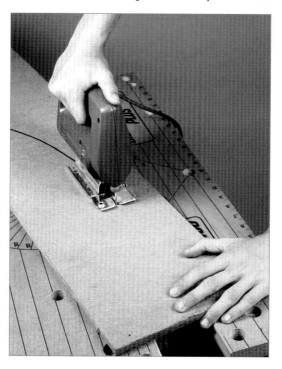

HAND AND POWER TOOLS

Since the majority of the material used for the construction of the average baseboard is wood, this simply becomes a carpentry procedure, requiring the use of some woodworking tools, etc. These are easily purchased in any good DIY shop. Surprisingly, the selection of tools required need not be elaborate for a simple baseboard. If the wood is purchased pre-cut to size, then it just becomes an assembly job requiring the use of a hammer, some nails and woodworking glue. On the other hand, if the baseboard is of a complex design, additional tools will be required.

The choice of tools is quite important as cheaply priced tools, generally, are of a poor-quality steel which means they do not retain their cutting edges for very long. Chisels are particularly prone to this. Alternatively, over-purchase or the acquisition of more tools than are required is easily done. The newcomer to the hobby is recommended to purchase equipment and tools as required and as skills develop.

Fortunately the majority of the hand tools initially required will already be found in the home, so seldom does one actually start from scratch. But if this is not the case then I recommend the purchase of the following: a 9in carpenter's square, a 3m steel Imperial/metric tape, an HB pencil, Stanley knife and a 300mm (12in) steel rule; followed by a tenon saw, a hand drill and a small set of twist drills including a counter sink, a set of screwdrivers, a hammer and a 15mm (6inch) plane.

This is a minimum selection of tools that will enable a start to be made. The carpenter's square is used to square things up, a very important point to remember as assemblies out of alignment create all sorts of problems, especially when a series of bases are to be assembled together. It is also useful to have a Stanley knife, not only used for cutting things out but for marking out, as this provides a finer line to work to, again very important when a number of items have to fit together. For sharpening knives

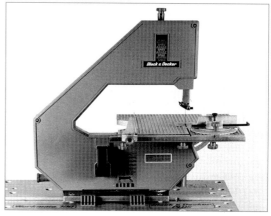

and chisels an oilstone will be required. For cutting large sheets of timber a ripsaw can be purchased, preferably Teflon-coated so that it cuts more easily, but if an old saw is available then it can be waxed with a candle to help it cut. Whether it is old or new this type of saw is only suitable for cutting straight lines. Therefore if one is going to the expense of purchasing a saw, then buy a more useful type which will also cut radii, e.g. a power jigsaw (and knowing today's prices it will not be very much more expensive).

I think the reader can quickly gather that it does not take long to acquire a basic selection of tools. My own choice of tools, remembering that I am a trained machinist, would further include a bandsaw and circular saw. The bandsaw is used to cut out curved shapes conveniently, the circular saw for machining material to size. In the professional world of model making the circular saw is one of the most important machines to be able to use, as the majority of all the materials used are cut on this machine. But for the home user of power equipment a bandsaw is a reasonably safe machine provided it is used sensibly, not only within the machine's working limits *but also within the individual's working limits.*

To use a bandsaw safely – and this applies to all power equipment – the machine needs to be set up properly on a firm foundation. A good method for this is to mount the equipment on to a thick board and clamp it down on to a solid workbench. Black and Decker make an ideal portable workbench known as a Workmate. This bench is ideal for mounting a bandsaw, plus many other items when awkward jobs need to be secured.

Burgess machine tools produce a small sanding disk which is also very useful for sizing pieces. Again a jig can be made which is taped into position with double-sided sticky tape. This fits on the down side of the disk (don't use the up side or the work will fly in the air), and fixed on to this can be wedges of wood at set angles – a 45 degree wedge being ideal for mitring corners.

So as to be able to produce continuous identical lengths of components make a another jig that controls the length of the item being sanded, and which fits the front edge of the sanding disk's table, or use a depth gauge.

Being a qualified machinist I also use other machines i.e. the circular saw, which by its very nature of having a fast rotating blade makes it dangerous, and it has to be used within current legislation. The prime task of the circular saw is to cut timber, but it is also used to cut plastics, which needs the saw to be set up in a different way to that of wood when cutting thin brittle plastic sheet. The blades are also different, and a wood cutting ripsaw blade is not suitable for cutting plastic, but more often than not it is the blade supplied with the machine. The pillar drill is also another machine that is extremely useful for drilling accurate vertical holes in various materials. Note: Always purchase metal cutting drills.

Left: The router fitted to a home made table that replicates the movements of a metal cutting milling machine. Whilst this looks crude it can produce extremely accurate work.
Below: The disk sander is a machine that I would be lost without, because it enables the trimming of materials, especially the squaring up of ends when the material has been cut out of square. Unfortunately this machine creates dust so that an extractor needs to be fitted, a domestic cylinder vacuum cleaner is ideal for this but the bag needs to be changed regularly.
Bottom: The use of power tools made the multilevel oval base easier to make.

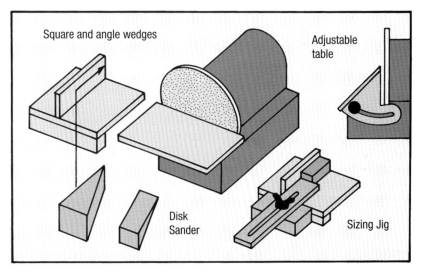

Square and angle wedges

Adjustable table

Disk Sander

Sizing Jig

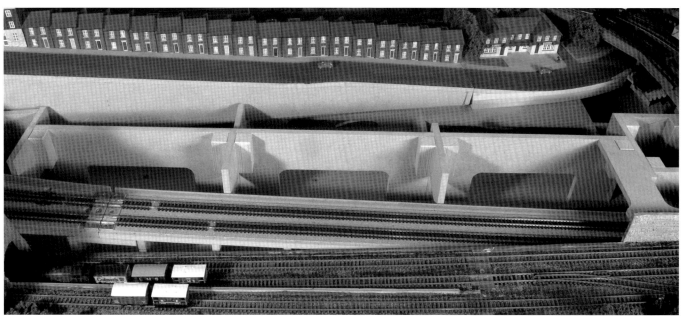

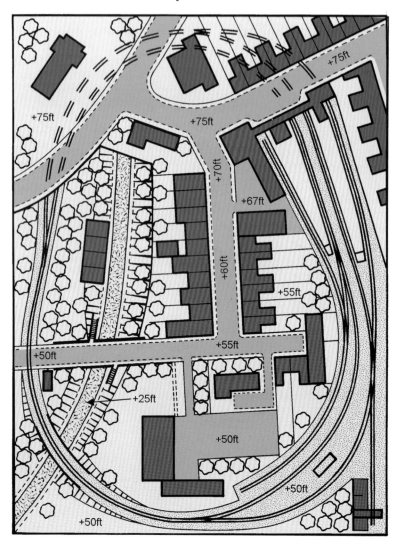

Above: The plan of the Oval base uses variable levels. The spot heights on the base show the ground levels (i.e. +50ft). This is the 50 scale feet measured from the bottom edge of the baseboard, which is counted as zero.

Note: The levels on the baseboards are shown in feet, because at 0, S, 00, EM, EEM, H0, TT, 000, N & Z scale, the bases can be made at correct scale heights.

THE OVAL LAYOUT

The self-contained layout is in many ways the easiest to build, because it does not join onto other baseboards. It can be built in stages; it can be constructed very simply on a flat board or built as a multi-level complex layout with its ground levels at various heights. For the beginner building their first base I recommend making a flat base and then to contour the landscape above the track level. I also recommend replacing the single length of track, with double track, so that two trains can be run simultaneously,

By building the track on a flat surface the layout will still look interesting, but it avoids all the problems associated with a curved track with gradients. (See the advanced oval layout with its curved gradients.) The illustration of bases 01, 02 and 03 (overleaf) shows a simple track layout with passing loops and sidings, constructed using the flat baseboard (+50ft) method, with additional ground levels (+75ft) added.

The illustration (top left) shows how the series of levels work. Starting with the track level, this remains flat throughout at a constant height of +50ft, the lowest area being the canal water level

at +25ft, the highest of the areas being the road bridges and surrounding ground over the track at +75ft. To make things easier the bottom edge of the baseboard is counted as zero.

The high areas over the track are constructed on top of the track level and have removable panels, which allow access to the track within the tunnel should a derailment occur. (Good access into tunnels is very important!) The levels of 25ft, 50ft and 75ft are derived from converting (N scale) 2mm to 1ft into standard wood size, i.e. 50mm wood batten divided by 2mm to the foot scale equals 25 foot model scale.

Unfortunately finished wood sizes quoted as being 50mm are generally 45mm in actual thickness. But when you add the 5mm plywood covering, the total thickness becomes 50mm (25ft model scale). Therefore the change in contour levels is worked around the available thickness of the materials used, i.e. 150mm (6in), a standard Contiboard® width equals 75 scale feet, the height of the edge the base.

The Contiboard® material is easily obtainable from DIY shops and is used for shelving, for the home construction of furniture and is available in various widths, etc. The material itself is chipboard covered with a thin layer of compressed resin impregnated paper, so it has a smooth white finish. It is this smooth finish that makes it ideal for edging the bases, because it can be easily cut using a wood saw. The material can also be glued and screwed in the usual way.

Therefore planning the layout, so that you use standard thickness of materials, as much as possible makes the building of the baseboard far easier.

AVAILABLE MATERIALS

Now it can be seen just how much available material sizes can influence baseboard construction, scrap material in many cases influencing a particular part of a base's construction. The baseboard's width, for practical reasons ceases to be exactly 2ft wide, because the available standard plywood unit is 2 feet wide, and the 12mm (1/2in) edges are added to the outside. Therefore this increases the size of the base to a true finished width of 63.5mm (2ft 1in) by 1,155mm (5ft 1in) long.

By looking at the top right illustration showing the basic levels the cutting programme of the base can be worked out, any part of the base less than +50ft being removed and lowered, levels above +50ft being added as separate overlays of wood. You can use either 5mm plywood or 6mm MDF. (Do not use 3mm hardboard, or any of the softboards used for floor underlay as they break easily.)

Difficult areas of the layout such as embankments are filled with expanded foam then carved to shape. The surface of the foam is then covered with rag or paper squares soaked in a white woodworker's glue (PVA) diluted 50:50 with water so as to form when dry a hard surface on top of the expanded foam that makes it more durable.

The reason for using a split level base instead of building up directly from the lowest level (i.e. +25ft – the canal level) is to allow access directly to the track support structure (+50 level) so that point motors, signals, etc can be easily installed. If the base was built up from the canal level, access holes would need to be cut into the low level of +25 to allow access to the +50 track support level.

The supporting and stiffening batten should be positioned so as to clear point motors or other miscellaneous items, therefore they are spaced at approximately 300mm (12in) centres. Due to the cutting out of the track level, the canal's water level will be cut into sections so it will need to be completely re-cut out, using a new single piece of material. A strip of hardboard is best suited as it has a smooth surface; whilst this raises the water level by the thickness of material being used, it does not matter.

The top right illustration shows the cut out lines of the overlays (black lines), the term overlay referring to anything that is applied on top of a surface, which in this case is on top of the battening used as a support. The most efficient way of cutting overlays out is to use a power hand-held jigsaw, because this involves a lot of curved cuts. The cutting of the supporting batten is best done by using a tenon saw and a jig to produce a square cut.

The final illustration shows how the levels work, and although it looks very complicated it is in fact a straightforward procedure, and the following pages show construction of seven other baseboards in greater detail and you will note that each baseboard becomes more complex to construct.

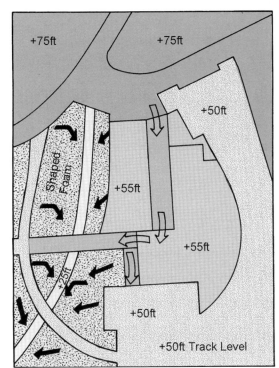

+75ft   +75ft

+50ft

Shaped Foam

+55ft

+55ft

+25ft

+50ft

+50ft Track Level

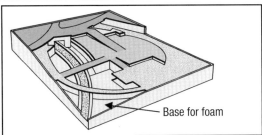

Base for foam

Left: This illustration shows the cutting plan for the Oval Layout. Start by drilling holes in the corners of the internal voids. The 50ft track level runs totally underneath the +75ft level, so that only the area marked as shaped foam (+25ft canal) should be cut out from the track level. The removed material is then fixed at the canal level to form a base for the foam. Cut a single piece of material for the canal, so that the water's surface does not have a join. The battening support is standard 50mm x 25mm finished planed softwood timber, with the thickness being used to form +25, +50 and +75ft baseboard heights.

Below: A low level view of the Oval Layout showing how the road goes over the canal, and the track enters into a tunnel.

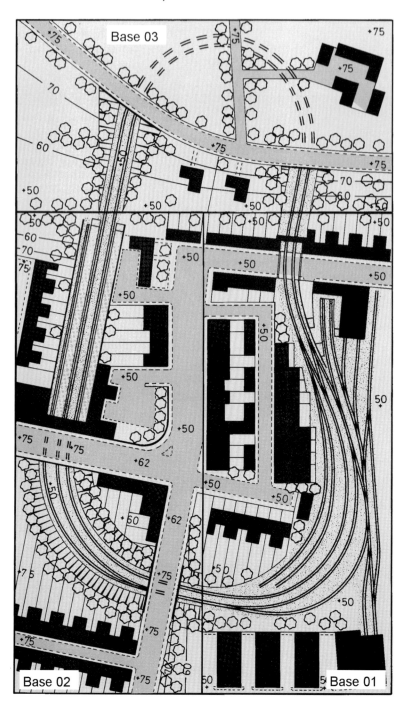

Above: I have numbered the interchangeable bases as follows; 01, 02 and 03 followed by 4, 5, 6, 7, 8 and 9. The first three make up the basic oval and are the core units. Bases 4, 5, 6 and 7 are interchangeable. Base 8 is a return loop and base 9 is a fiddle yard. Use the concept of the bases to produce baseboards of your own design.

CONSTRUCTION

The construction materials used should be of good quality, the plywood that forms the top should be 9mm (3/8in) thick and supported with cross battens. Plywood has the advantages over chipboard that it is stronger and it does not warp by absorbing moisture. The batten timber should be carefully selected so that it is as straight and knot-free as possible. The edging material, Contiboard®, which is of a wood chip base, does not warp either provided the edges are sealed, as its surface is covered with an impervious layer. The assembly method of the base 01 shows the basic construction of all the baseboards.

BASEBOARDS 01, 02 & 03

The plans for the layouts shown can easily be changed, because the modelling scale and baseboard size can be chosen upon their own merits. But do remember it does require a reasonable amount of room to portray acceptable realism. It is also worth doing your best to disguise the basic track shape, especially on an oval layout by using a long tunnel, because it will allow the train to momentarily vanish from sight and stop. Therefore when it re-emerges it appears to be another train.

The tunnel can be made to fool the eye with even greater effect if a storage loop is concealed within the tunnel and after a short delay a second train emerges.

The seven baseboards when joined together form a oval layout 17ft long by 4ft wide, providing a running track length of approximately 34ft. The arrangement of bases 01, 02 and 03 (layout size 7ft by 4ft) provides a running length of track of approximately 13ft. By placing baseboards 4 and 5 between bases 01 and 02 at one end and using base 03 (the U-shaped return), the layout's running length becomes approximately 23ft (layout size 12ft by 4ft.)

Baseboard 01: This uses a completely flat base at the +50ft level; the height being measured from the bottom of the base (see illustration), the road crossing the track via a level crossing.

Baseboards 02 and 03: Both of these bases retain the track level at +50 ft, the additional baseboard levels being built from this basic level.

Baseboard 4: This uses a two-part split-level base, the first part of one level being at +25ft, used for the water level, the second level at +50ft being used for the track and scenery. This base and base 5 can be interlocked sideways to form an extension of bases 01, 02 and 03.

Baseboard 5: This base uses a series of levels, the basic level at +50 ft, the track gaining height from +50 to +55 ft in the middle and then returning to the +50 ft level. The road starts at +50 then reduces in its levels so that it passes underneath the railway track and then increases in its levels until it rejoins the +50 level.

Baseboard 6: This is the most complex of baseboards, as the contour levels around the track's level of +50 ft constantly change above and below the track's level. The height of the water is also at three different levels and the road constantly changes in height, being at one point below track level, the next above it. This base and base 7 are designed as a pair of handed bases that interlock in the middle with each other. *Therefore they are always assembled as a pair of bases.*

Baseboard 7: This base, despite its change in levels, is in many ways an easier base to construct. It starts with a split-level of +25 ft for the water and +50 ft for the track, the cliffs above the track allowing considerable scope for artistic licence in their shape, or they can be built to follow the contour lines precisely.

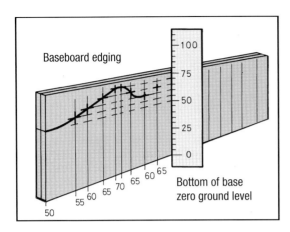

Baseboard edging

Bottom of base zero ground level

Baseboard 01:

1 Cut plywood to the size of the base including provisions for track aligners, and cut batten and fix into position by gluing and screwing.
2 Trim the baseboard to the finished dimensions using a hand plane and keeping edges square and straight.
3 Edge with Contiboard® fixed by screws from the inside and sand and fill as required to make good.

Baseboards 02 and 03:

1 Make as baseboard 01 excluding the instructions for part 3.
2 Draw out the layout on to the top of the plywood board and mark out the positions of the raised area of roads and high ground.
3 Mark out the heights of the raised levels on to the batten and join the heights together, blending the change in levels if required to look natural; do the same to the edging.
4 Cut the batten out to shape using a jigsaw or bandsaw and fix the batten into position on the base. Repeat with all other height-battened levels.
5 Mark out the hardboard for the roads and paving, etc., and cut out the hardboard along the change in level lines or in places not required.
6 Overlay hardboard on to base and check that it fits. When satisfied that the cutouts and changes in levels work correctly glue into position by using PVA glue and hardboard nails.
7 Fill in difficult areas of embankment with polyurethane or expanded polystyrene foam or use cardboard cut to shape.
8 Trim foam to shape allowing for the thickness of surfacing, and cover foam with newspaper or rag dipped in PVA glue to form a hard surface over the foam.
9 Trim off surplus material used for surfacing whilst still wet with a sharp knife and allow to dry.
10 Plane the base to size keeping the edges square and straight.
11 Drill holes in Contiboard® edging as required for location pins and securing bolts etc. (Cut, drill, etc. as pairs for adjoining base edges.)
12 Fix Contiboard® with screws from the inside and edge ends as required with iron-on strip. Sand and fill the landscape as necessary to make good and paint with oil-based undercoat.

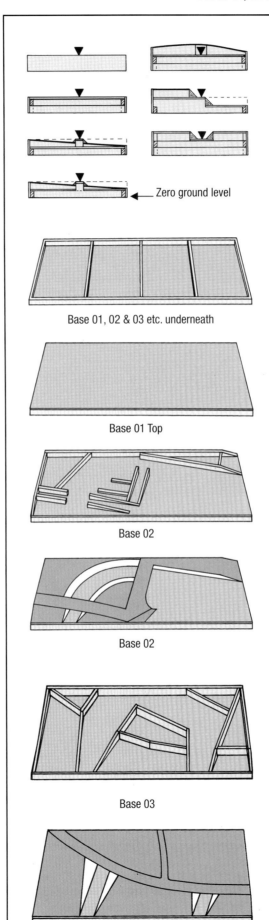

Zero ground level

Base 01, 02 & 03 etc. underneath

Base 01 Top

Base 02

Base 02

Base 03

Far Left: The edge of the bases marked out onto Contiboard® available from DIY shops. The bottom edge is our zero datum line.

Left: The base levels are made up using the 50 x 25mm batten (N Scale) or 100 x 25 mm (00 Scale) laid on edge to provide 25 scale feet heights. Carefully lay the track out on the flat board, so as to locate the cross battens, so that they miss the point motors that will fit under the baseboard's surface.

Baseboards 01, 02 and 03: These are designed to join on to the baseboards 4, 5, 6 and 7 (extension bases) so as to form a very large oval layout.

Construction: Bases 01, 02 and 03, since they form a complete layout within themselves, are recommended to be constructed first, followed by baseboards 4 and 5 to extend the basic oval layout. Bases 6 and 7 are built last as these two link together to form a long non-interchangeable section. Baseboards 8 and 9 are designed to assemble on to any of the bases so as to form an end return loop and fiddle yard, which provides a condensed yet self-contained layout. In other words, baseboards 8, 01 and 9 form an 'L' shape (see the page on layout variations) to provide the builder with multiple choice on the configuration of the layout. In some ways it is best to secure the bases together and assemble the track across the joins, and cut them apart using a razor saw.

The 'Cliff' base 7 and the 'Lake' base 4, shown on this page will need a good deal of practical DIY skills to make, because they are complex in their construction.

The methods used for these baseboards and the following baseboards should be used as a design study, whereby the methods of construction shown can be applied to any other baseboard design.

The object of showing each of these bases is so the reader can learn how to make complex baseboards that use spot heights and contour lines, as found on Ordnance Survey Maps.

The Lake and the Cliff bases start with the bottom edge of the base, (see page 49) being our zero datum level. Our first level is +25ft ('N' @ 2mm per foot and '00' @ 4mm per foot) which is made as base 01, but with the track cut out (access to underside of track for wiring). This is raised to +50 ft using spacers to suit. Further batten (strips of wood) are then cut to size and fixed in place. Finally mark out the formers and outside edges, cut and fix in place using screws from the inside to preserve the exterior appearance of the boarding.
(Continued top of page 51)

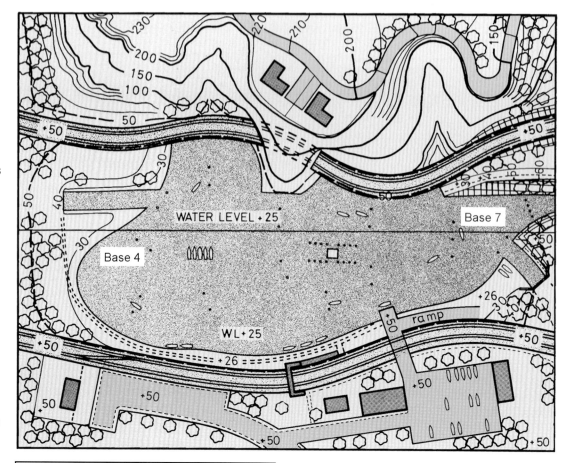

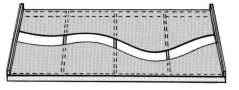

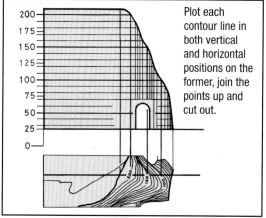

Plot each contour line in both vertical and horizontal positions on the former, join the points up and cut out.

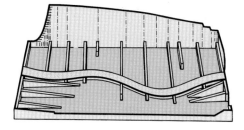

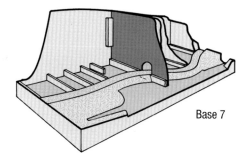

Base 7

Each former (shown in dark tone) will need to be plotted from the map or plan, if an accurate profile of the cliff face is to be made.

Fix the track in place at +50 ft and then secure the chicken wire to the formers. Fill the area between the track and the lake with expanded foam, carved to shape.

Finally two methods can be used to model the rock-face, The first is plaster, (which produces a very heavy baseboard) or the second method is to use old rags and woodworker's glue, (PVA) which is then sprinkled with broken texturing material and bits of plaster glued in place and dry new plaster powder.

Use a pressurised plant spray bottle filled with 75% water and 25% PVA, to soak the new and old plaster mixture.

The names to the bases are:
01: The Sidings
02: The Station
03: The Tunnel
 4: The Lake
 5: The Country Station
 6: The Countryside
 7: The Cliff
 8: The Junction
 9: Fiddle-yards

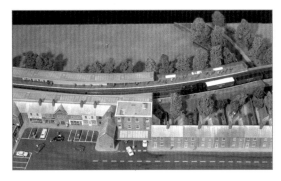

Top: This shows the 'Cliff' base 7, and the 'Lake' base 4 joined together.
Middle Photos:
Above left: This is a close-up view of the cliff base 7.
Above: Base 5, showing the station approach road.
Left: The 'Country Station' base 5 and the 'Lake' base 4, showing how they look when they are joined together.

Note: The angle of the track at each end of the base dictates the limitations of the track plan. Therefore the track shape is identical, but the landscape is different. The same applies to the road, it could only be in one place.

Pages 51, 52 and 54 contain a group of colour photographs that show bases 01, 02 and 03. These are designed to join on to the baseboards 4, 5, 6 and 7 (extension bases) so as to form a very large oval layout.

Construction

Bases 01, 02 and 03, because they form a complete layout within themselves, are recommended to be constructed first, followed by bases 4 and 5 to extend the basic oval layout.

Bases 6 and 7 are built last as these two link together to form a double length non-interchangeable section.

Baseboards 8 and 9 are designed to assemble on to any of the bases so as to form an end return loop and fiddle yard.

This will produce a narrow self-contained layout. Example: baseboards 8, 01 and 9 can be used to form an 'L' shape layout (see the page on layout variations).

Choice of colour:
The colouring of the bases is extremely important; my own colours are chosen to represent late summer, when the trees are fully matured with all their foliage and are just beginning to turn in colour. The same applies to the colour selected for the grass; instead of a rich green which would dominate the landscape, a browny-yellow is used which complements the trees and allows them to stand out in their own colours.

The overall colour of both trees and grass has been taken into consideration in the colouring of the buildings, roads and paving. (Note: Old style 'Graham Farish' buildings shown on page 52.)

Therefore the colour of the buildings' predetermined the colour of the landscape, so that they work in a harmony; a point to remember.

Finally cars and people are added to bring the model to life.

Top Left opposite page: Bases 01,02 and 03 joined together to form an oval layout.

Middle: This is a view over bases 01, 02 and 03.

Lower Left: The stables are portrayed on one of the removable hatches.

The photographs on this page are of the multilevel layout, a far more recent model but the colours used are similar.

The roads, paving and grass are my stock colours, and the same applies to the trees. The colours look different in the early photos, due to age related technical difficulties (taken 20 years ago) and modern day digital photography.

Baseboards 6 and 7

These are designed to be a matched pair of bases that have a contoured join in the middle.

The reason for this is to demonstrate within the construction of baseboards, how to make this type of join, and the other bases fit onto the overall landscape.

The contours and track alignment of bases 6 & 7 interlock therefore the 'middle joins' are not interchangeable.

Finally, bases 4, 5, 6 and 7 when joined together must have the visual appearance of being part of the same landscape, yet to look convincing must not be repetitive in their track shape.

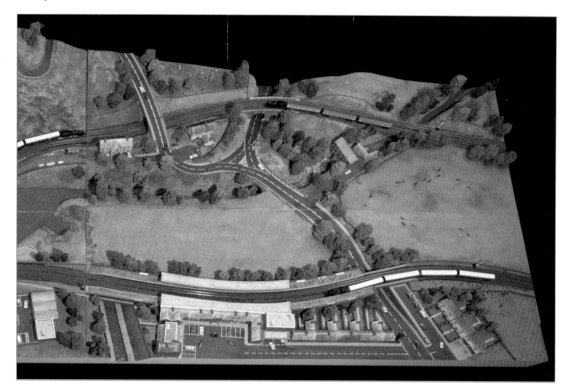

Far left: Base 6, showing the road passing under the track and the traffic problems caused by the farmer moving his cows.

Left: The busy high street creating the feeling that the area is bustling with life. Group cars and people adjacent to shops.

The Oval Layout:

This is ideal for showing at an exhibition because it is made in one piece and fits into an estate car. With hindsight I would replace the single length of track that the train occupies with double track, which would avoid the wiring problem associated with continually changing the electrical polarity of the track so that the trains can travel in alternate directions.

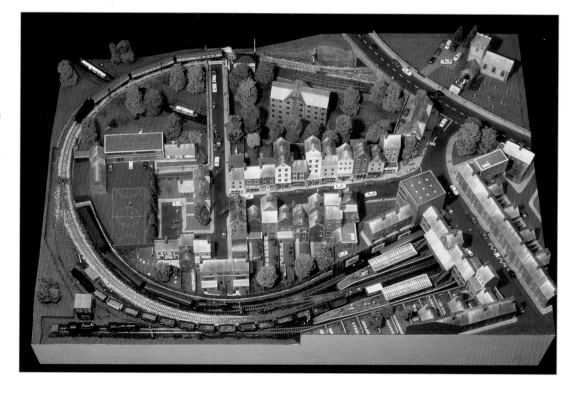

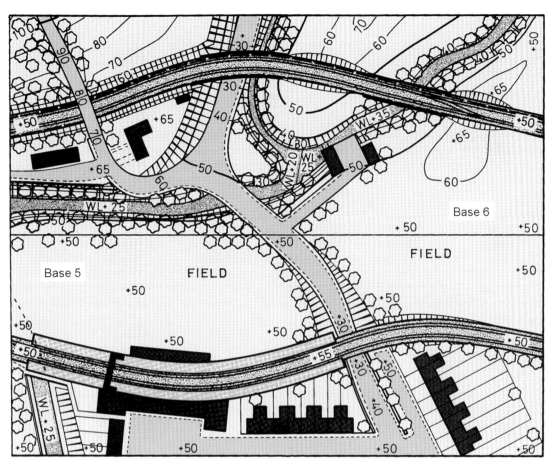

Base 6

Base 5

FIELD

FIELD

Left: Each base portrays a particular type of landscape and base 6 represents 'The Countryside' with rolling landscape that has streams, roads and track at different levels.

The same applies to the 'Country Station' base 5, which whilst it lies in flat countryside, the track level has risen to +55ft to provide extra clearance over the road that has been excavated under the track.

This is a typical example of how a road has become far busier over the years, and the level crossing has had to be replaced with a bridge. Normally a bridge over the tracks is built because they are cheaper, but the local people could have put pressure on the railway owners to run the road under the railway.

The baseboard's construction is similar to bases 6 and 7, in the way that the track is cut out and raised.

Only this time the road and the embankment are cut out and replaced with a new piece of road, fixed under the track.

Below: An untidy section of track, with signs of modernisation work in progress. Notice how cable covers are stacked along the embankment and kept away from the track.

Base 6

Fill difficult bits with foam, trimmed to shape.

Cut and fix the profiled ground level supports as required.

Cover with 3mm hardboard and fix with glue and nails as required.

Mark out and cut at the same time adjoining Contiboard® edging and drill location holes for bolts & pegs etc. Allow for thickness of edging i.e. two true length, two plus thickness on overall length.

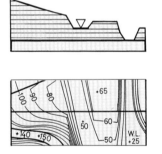

The methods shown for the construction of baseboards in this book are not the definitive methods of producing baseboards, but they are time tested and have been in common practice for more than 100 years.

Models using these methods of baseboard construction have been used by architectural illustrators, to show lay people what a design would look like because many people cannot understand technical drawings.

Rochester & Upnor Castles

I have two models on permanent public exhibition, one is at Rochester Castle the second is in Upnor Castle (Kent) and both use the methods of construction as shown in this book, not only for the bases but for the buildings and landscape etc.

The Rochester model is on view all year, but the Upnor model is on display during the summer months only.

Base 4: 'The Lake' shows how a baseboard with a series of levels can be modelled. The water level is at +25ft and the surrounding countryside is at +50ft. In reality it is unusual to have such a vast difference accruing naturally, but not with man made excavations.

Base 5: 'The Country Station' depicts a typical example of a small town station, that is adjacent to a bridge over the main road. To provide sufficient clearance for the traffic, the road's ground level has been lowered to go under the track, and the base shows how this can be modelled.

Baseboards 6 and 7

These are designed to be a matched pair of bases that have a contoured (profiled) join in the middle. The reason for this is to demonstrate within the book the construction of adjoining baseboards, how to make this type of join, and the landscape formations.

The track and the contours of these two bases pre-decide the join, therefore the middle 'joins' are not interchangeable. Secondly, bases 4, 5, 6 and 7 when joined together must have the visual appearance of being part of the same landscape, yet not be repetitive in their track shape.

Baseboard 6

All the methods used for the construction of this baseboard are a natural progression from techniques required on the earlier bases, but taken a stage further. (Note: The plywood level of this base is at +25ft and all other levels are constructed from this, above or below.)

1 Cut out the plywood and battens as per baseboard instructions 01. (6mm ply is ideal)
2 Draw the layout plan on to plywood including contour lines.
3 Cut out plywood for the lowest water level of +20. (Just fix under cut out in 6mm plywood top and forget true height in this case)
4 Fix batten in place (as base 01)
5 Insert +20 water level using scrap ply to underside of +25 level.
6 Cut one full length and one width batten and fix on top of the water level.
7 Trim the base to size using hand plane, keeping square and edges straight.
8 Mark and cut out the Contiboard® edging copying the edge of baseboard 5 along the join, and allow for the track adjusters.
9 Fix edging in place, keeping square and true.
10 Mark out and then cut out the roads using hardboard or thin ply (3 mm).

11 Mark out and then cut out the track level from 6 mm ply.
12 Cut out the track supports and fix so as to bring the track support level up to the +50 level from the plywood level of +25.
13 Cut out the stream at +35 level from 3 mm ply or hardboard.
14 Cut out and fix stream water level support blocks to bring the stream up to +35 level allowing for the thickness of material (i.e., material thickness 3 mm, stream level +35, plywood level +25, gives a scale difference of 10 ft. Multiplied by 2 mm to 1 ft (N gauge) this equals a 20mm rise, and 20mm less 3mm thickness of material equals 17mm block height). (Note The difference in the material thickness used on top of the blocks is subtracted from the total height required which is variable depending upon thickness used.)
15 Cut out and fix the various height supporting blocks for the roads allowing for road thickness material by using the spot heights on the roads.
16 Fix roads into place.
17 Fix track level in place; allow for the track adjusters.
18 Cut out and fix supporting structure for landscape using the contour lines drawn on the plywood, to provide the heights and allowing for the thickness of covering.
19 Cut out and fix hardboard covering material for landscape.
20 Fill difficult areas of hillside and embankments using expanded foam and surface (as base 02 parts).
21 Fill and make good as required in preparation for painting.
22 Prime expanded polystyrene with emulsion paint and wood with oil based undercoat.

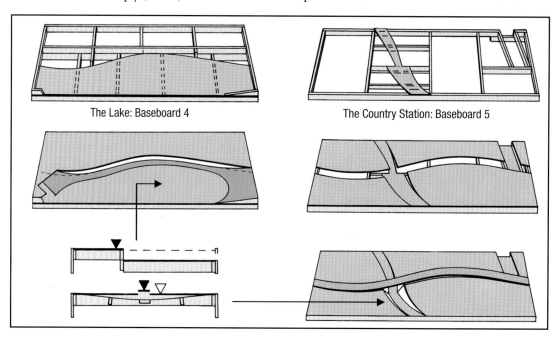

The Lake: Baseboard 4

The Country Station: Baseboard 5

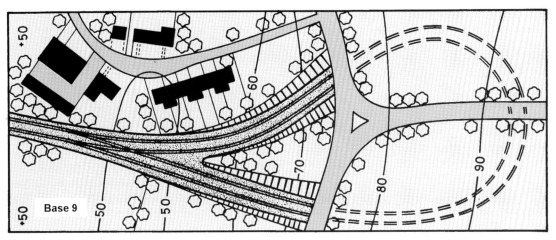

Left: This shows the return loop, with the tracks disappearing into a hillside. **Note:** When the covered part of the track is greater than the train's length, the train can be stored inside the tunnel, but don't forget that it is there, just in case you isolate that section of track and when you make the track live, the train appears, causing trouble at the crossing!

Baseboard 7

The construction of this base allows a great deal of artistic licence and could be constructed in several ways depending on the final effect required.

1   Cut out plywood and battens, as per baseboard instructions 01.
2   Draw the layout plan on to plywood and include contour lines below the +50 level only.
3   Cut out the track level of +50.
4   Assemble the base as per base 4.
5   Mark out the edges and assemble, taking care to align the end of the base which joins on to baseboard 6.
6   Cut assorted battens that fit on top of the +25 plywood level.
7   Cut out the formers as required and fix on to the batten (see illustration).
8   Fix formers in position and then fix track support level into position on top of the extending batten.
9   Cut and fix supporting material for the hardboard.
10 Mark and cut out the hardboard for the levels below the +50 level to the shape of the water line.
11 Cover the formers with chicken wire.
12 Fix road in position on top of chicken wire using hardboard cut to shape.
13 Fill difficult areas with expanded polystyrene, and landscape as described in the section on rock faces and cliffs.

Baseboard 8

The construction of the base for the marshalling yard uses the first two steps shown in the illustration on the right.

Baseboard 9

Follow the instructions as shown in the illustration on the right.

Fiddle yards: The construction of these bases will depend upon the type chosen. Sliding fiddle yards are a bit more complex than the swivel type, but the track on the sliding base is straight, therefore easier to lay. The swivel type needs the tracks to align with the pivot point at the tracks' join, and then change course to become parallel on the pivoting part of the board, but in practice rolling stock falls off the track through sudden sideways movement with the pivoting fiddle yard.

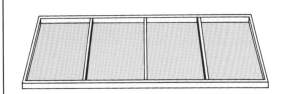

50 x 25 mm finished planed softwood timber frame (the same method as other bases).

6mm plywood top fixed in place with woodworker's glue & screws. (The same method as other bases.)

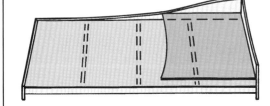

Contiboard® edging fixed in place with woodworker's glue & screws. Cut removable ply hatch cover, support on 50 x 25 mm timber. (N gauge.)

Cut alternative contour levels using easily shaped material. (Expanded polystyrene or soft board wood floor underlay)

Fix the contours in place using woodworker's glue, and allow to dry. (Make sure hatch is removable.)

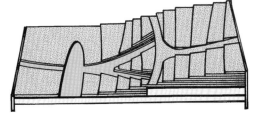

Sand contours as required to produce the landscape effect desired. Cut and fix cardboard road in place, cutting into landscape as required.

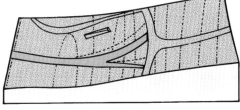

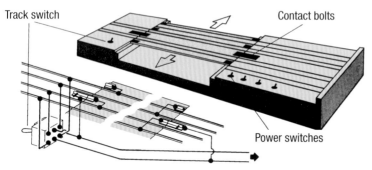

The sliding plate fiddle yard is the part of the layout where the unrealistic actions take place and is ideal for rearranging large scale heavy rolling stock, with which aligning the wheels with the track has its difficulties!

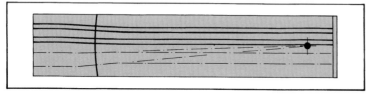

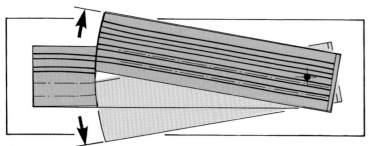

RETURN LOOPS, TUNNELS AND THE FIDDLE YARDS

The baseboard 03, both the self-contained oval layouts as well as this baseboard number 8 use tunnels to disguise the tracks' return. The length of the tunnel is important if its effect is to work satisfactorily, the ideal length being slightly longer than the longest length of rolling stock configuration to be used, so that the complete length of train disappears from view within the tunnel. As previously stated, when it re-emerges after a long pause, it appears to be a second train. The tunnel can be used to fool the eye with even greater effect if a storage loop or sidings are concealed within the tunnel and a different (second) train emerges.

This 'fooling the eye' can be taken further by using short lengths of rolling stock, three carriages instead of six, for example, and reducing the platform length accordingly. It is even better still if the platform and tunnel join each other; this way, six carriages can still be used although the platform is only three carriage lengths' long as the rest of the train's length can be hidden in the tunnel whilst it is in the station. The same effect can be created with buildings; instead of using one large structure, use a number of small buildings to create the illusion of distance. In this way you give an impression of greater variety within the same space.

Baseboard 9
The construction of the return loop and storage sidings base uses the instructions for base 01 because its track level is at +50. The turntable is fitted as per manufacturer's instructions or as a home build design. The advent of chip controlled power units has totally re-invented the wiring of a layout. With simplified wiring far more ambitious track configurations become practical.

Turntables
Turntables enable the rolling stock to be turned around either in single items, or as complete train lengths, and are very much up to the individual as far as choice and size are concerned. The manufacturers produce a number of different types, all of which have different fitting instructions.

Sliding fiddle yards
This method of fiddling the rolling stock to work convincingly uses parallel tracks which are pushed back and forth by hand so as to align with the incoming and outgoing tracks. The rolling stock is assembled on this in running order and is released as required on to the main layout. The main use of this method is for large scale rolling stock or when space is at a premium, as it saves a lot of valuable room on the layout. The disadvantage is that the rolling stock cannot be turned around, but it is ideal for the branch line layout when this is not required.

The construction of a sliding fiddle yard is very simple, as it can all be made from plywood

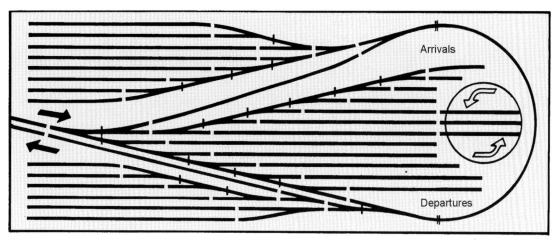

Left: The marshalling yard, in which the assembly of various train configurations is carried out in a more realistic way.

stiffened as necessary with battening then glued and screwed together. The tracks' alignments are secured into position at each end by brass bolts. These are wired up as shown, as they are also used for an electrical contact. The other side of the bridge, used for storing the rolling stock which is assembled in ready-to-run lengths, is switched on or off as required.

Alternatively a simple flat base can be used with a small number of sidings, depending on the space available. Careful design can permit hidden return tracks, tucked away behind the scenery, or under a raised embankment.

'L' GIRDER CONSTRUCTION

This method of construction relies on a basic open framework, similar to a table, and is constructed using two inverted 'L' girders. These are the weight carriers of the layout to which the legs are attached (see illustration). The cross members are fitted on top of these inverted 'L' girders. These are spaced at a suitable distance that will allow a screwdriver to be inserted in between for the fixing of the uprights and the uprights support the various track levels. The track supports are cut out of 1/2in ply shaped to suit the track plan and are wider than the track (see illustration). The exact width required would be determined by what is necessary for the fixing of the scenery supports, which can be chicken wire or canvas. The chicken wire is used as a base to support the actual scenery, additional timber supports being placed as required to help support the scenery, or to create an effect.

The advantage with this type of construction is that it allows limitless adjustment to the track levels, so that the track layout can be in full working order before landscaping. In addition, most of the timber used will be short off-cuts, which helps reduce cost. Finally, because the parts are all screwed together, they can be dismantled and reassembled in a different way, remaking the scenery to suit. The only real disadvantage is that once built, the layout is extremely difficult to move due to the lack of cross bracing.

LARGE SCALE LAYOUTS

The Helmshore '0' gauge layout shown in the photographs was built by Pemberton Engineering and is based on part of the East Lancashire railway line running from Accrington to Bury. Sadly the real line closed in 1966, but some stock is now on display in the Bury Transport Museum.

Below: The open framework makes for a lighter construction of a baseboard and is less rigid. But it is easier to wire because of the open framework.

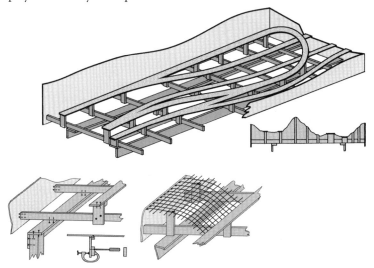

Right: The 125 at speed, emerging from a tunnel cut into a chalk embankment. Notice how a portal has been used to support the chalk from crumbling away at the mouth of the tunnel.

Below: This embankment is a mixture of stone and hard sand strata, which will wash away over time, but sufficiently solid so that it does not need additional support.

TUNNELS, EMBANKMENTS AND THE WATER CULVERTS

The construction of the scenic setting would not be complete without roads, embankments and tunnels. The last-named are very easy to construct as a number of manufacturers produce tunnel portals made in card, plastic or resin. A short length of cardboard is necessary to form the start of the tunnel. On a short stretch of tunnel it is recommended that you take the cardboard right the way through. The track is laid first then the tunnel is built over it, but do save the track from damage whilst doing so by covering it with a suitable protective material. One of the easiest materials to work with is foam polystyrene; (insulation foam) which is available in various thicknesses from builder's merchants.

CONSTRUCTION

The method of construction is reasonably straight forward, the foam is cut to size using a hacksaw blade, wrapped at one end to form a handle with masking tape. Using this basic tool, the foam is cut to the shape of the hillside, embankment etc. The foam is fixed together using white woodworker's glue (PVA) which is extremely slow drying when bonding foam polystyrene; Fill in gaps with newspaper, soaked in PVA glue, and let dry. When everything is firmly fixed together further work on the embankment can continue.

Left: The plastic tunnel portal fitted with a short piece of cardboard, that has been wrapped around a broom handle so that it forms part of a tube.

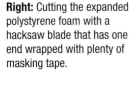

Right: Cutting the expanded polystyrene foam with a hacksaw blade that has one end wrapped with plenty of masking tape.

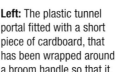

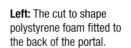

Left: The cut to shape polystyrene foam fitted to the back of the portal.

Right: The landscape being built up around the tunnel entrance, using a mixture of foam and newspaper fixed together using PVA woodworker's glue.

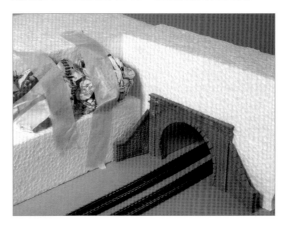

When a tunnel has been drilled out of solid rock (e.g. a cutting situation through a rock outcrop as modelled on baseboard 7) a portal would not be used, as the rock would be sufficiently strong to support itself. In a soft soil or chalk situation, however, portals would be used to secure the surface at the entrances of the tunnel and a brick or steel tube would support the tunnel inside. On the model a short length of cardboard is used behind the tunnel entrance to represent this.

On a longer tunnel access to the track will be required in the form of a lift-off hatch. In this situation it is easier to build the basic hillside first, leaving room to position the tunnel entrance, the track and a short length of card. Then fill around the tunnel entrance with foam polystyrene shaped to match the back of the tunnel entrance. Gaps can be filled at a later date with plaster and painted to suit. This method allows a small amount of track adjustment should the building of the tunnel be slightly out of alignment.

The embankment around the tunnel can be constructed from foam polystyrene cut to suit and glued in position with PVA or ceiling tile cement (don't use solvent glues or it will melt) then covered with a thin layer of plaster, so as to form a hard durable surface. This will finally be painted and textured. (See Chapter 4 on landscaping).

Roads can be modelled by using good quality thick card or hardboard cut to shape with a sharp knife or jigsaw. Don't try to slice through the card in one cut but use several lighter strokes; this gives more control over the cutting and is also safer as it reduces blade breakage. Keep the knife blade sharp by using a slip stone to re-sharpen. Do this regularly and cut on to an old piece of card or hardboard (not chipboard as it quickly blunts the blade).

Cut hardboard with a coping saw, fretsaw, a powered jigsaw or bandsaw. Use a metal cutting blade when using powered tools, so as to produce a clean cut, and also take care when cutting with the jigsaw not to cut through the power cable.

It is very important to support the hardboard firmly whilst cutting to prevent accidents so support the hardboard on both sides of the cut. The Workmate® portable bench makes this extremely simple because its top can be opened so there is a large gap between the vice jaws, forming a support either side of the cutting blade. The hardboard is placed on this surface and all cutting is carried out over the gap. *Safety Tip: it is safer to support the hardboard on each side of the cut and good workshop practice.*

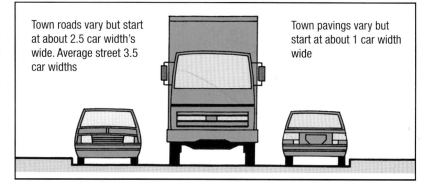

Town roads vary but start at about 2.5 car width's wide. Average street 3.5 car widths

Town pavings vary but start at about 1 car width wide

Above: When making tunnels or bridges for vehicles the height needs to provide sufficient clearance for large lorries.

Right: This is a deep cut rail tunnel that has its walls lined with stone. The material used to line the walls of cuttings will depend upon locality, London for example has an abundance of clay, and therefore there was an abundance of bricks. In the North of England stone is abundant; therefore stone was used for lining the walls, as well as building stations etc.

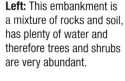

Left: This embankment is a mixture of rocks and soil, has plenty of water and therefore trees and shrubs are very abundant.

Far left: Walls and culverts come in all sorts of shapes and sizes, but they will need a reason for being there. In most cases it is to allow water drainage underneath a road or track etc. The best way to produce realistic modelling is to study reality, and with digital cameras fitted to mobile phones, when you see it, then photograph it for later!

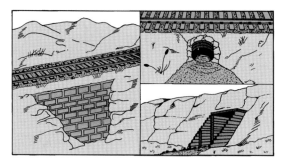

The '00' scale layout shown right because of its size has very little space in which to run the rolling stock.

A pair of standard coaches is around 132ft (530mm/21in long) whilst a two-car rail bus is 100ft (400mm/16in long).

Therefore if the train length is 21 inches, and we have a track length of 96 inches, (610 scale feet) it will leave only 75 inches (477.5 scale feet) for the train to move.

The summary is that the '00' track plan shown on the left is far too ambitious for the available space, yet at 'N' scale (opposite) the 8ft long base can contain a workable layout.

Compare this plan to the plan shown on page 41. (The space is the same.) This works because the engines and 4-wheel passenger coaches/wagons that make up a train length are shorter.

This has reduced the train's overall length to around 17 inches and also allows for a light engine (no carriages or wagons) to run on a good length of track, i.e. engine length 10 cm, (4 inches) track length 244cm (96 inches) equals 234cm (92 inches) for the engine to travel. Note: Read the schedule of moves on opposite page.

The number of tracks and points are also reduced and the passengers' platforms reduced to just one. What has been introduced is a goods platform and offices, signal box, engine shed, ash pit, coaling, etc. The ground could also be landscaped to provide ground level at platform height, so that the track looks like it is in a shallow cutting, and disappears into the hillside.

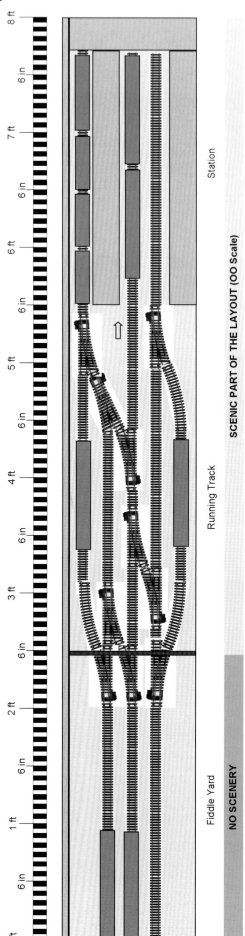

Station

SCENIC PART OF THE LAYOUT (OO Scale)

Running Track

Fiddle Yard

NO SCENERY

PASSENGER TERMINUS

The concept of the layouts shown is that of a busy local passenger line terminus, which handles a small amount of freight. The terminus also has a goods siding, which links to the fiddle yard. The trains depart from the station and after a short length of surface track disappear into a tunnel (the fiddle yard). Trains arrive at the station on all 3 tracks and divert at points just before the station into their designated 'up line' arrival platform.

Departing trains leave from any of the 3 platforms and change tracks as necessary to gain access to the 'down-line' which goes via the tunnel to the next station! (fiddle yard) Other trains instead of departing can go into the goods shed siding and parked etc.

00 Layout Size: The basic back and forth shelf layout shown left is designed for 3 units of 2 car passenger trains and 1 goods unit comprising of the engine and 3 trucks. The length of the train has been determined by available space; since the board is 244cm (8ft) long divided by 4 is 61cm (2ft) it provides us with two carriage lengths of 30cm (1ft) each. In practical terms the layout shown on the left is a poor design, because the base is overcrowded with long carriages and has very little usable track. Finally, The space between each of the points means that just a single coach can be stored in the gap. (see Plan on page 40).

N Layout Size: If the layout was built at N scale on the same length of board it would provide for the same number of trains, only this time the model trains are smaller, in fact half the size of the '00' version. The outcome is that we could reduce the width of the base to 30cm (12in) and still have room for some scenery. Finally instead of running 8 wheeled coaches, run four-wheel coaches and 0-6-0 Terrier engines or small diesel units.

Middle Level Oval Layout: The multilevel oval layout has a small back and forth totally independent set of track-work, that portrays the 3rd rail electric pickup still used in South London and Kent. The concept is that this part of the layout will be

Construct the base using the method shown on page 49 for the base 01 and fix 4 mm ply at the back, to support the background. Locate the cross battens to align with the shelf supports.

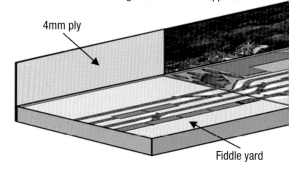

4mm ply

Fiddle yard

automatic, and that it will operate whilst the main layout is in use. Therefore this will create the movement of trains in the middle of the layout and will add interest, whilst the operator concentrates on running the main part of the layout. (See page 196).

Automatic Operation: Both the layouts shown can be operated automatically, and this is why 3 tracks leading into the station and into the fiddle yard are included on the layout. The principle is that a magnet is fitted under the train, and as it passes over a reed switch, it triggers a stopping circuit, followed by a predetermined short delay and the automatic application of reverse power, and the train moves back to the start. By setting all 3 tracks on automatic running, and because the stopping and starting will not be synchronised, the layout will look reasonably realistic, while you just sit and watch!

Construction: Materials required for the '00' scale layout, 1 off 244 x 38cm (8ft x 1ft 3in) Contiboard®, and 1 off 244 x 15cm (8ft x 6in) 4mm ply.

Materials required for the 'N' scale layout, 1 off 244 x 30cm (8ft x 1ft) Contiboard® and 1 off 244 x 15cm (8ft x 6in) 4mm ply.

You will also need three lengths of 50mm x 25mm x 3m long (2in x 1in x 9ft) softwood batten. The batten is cut into two lengths of 244cm (8ft) long and five lengths to act as cross spacers, cut to size to fit the gap.

You will also need some tools, some screws etc. The first task is to fix the batten and Contiboard® together so that it becomes ridged. Next, key the Contiboard's surface by rubbing with sand paper. Finally, paint the board's surface and the background with grey oil-bound paint.

Lay the track in place, working away from the points, using either flexi track or standard kit pre-cut lengths. Don't fix anything permanently to the baseboard until everything fits, including fitting the track insulators and wired the track. (Secure wiring in place with masking tape). When everything works then fix the track in place using double sided sticky tape (not under the points). Finally when totally satisfied that all is well then the layout can be landscaped.

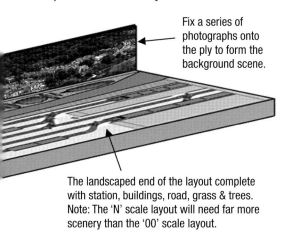

Fix a series of photographs onto the ply to form the background scene.

The landscaped end of the layout complete with station, buildings, road, grass & trees. Note: The 'N' scale layout will need far more scenery than the '00' scale layout.

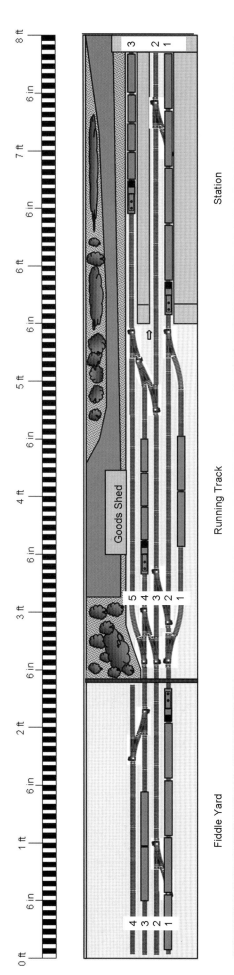

Station

SCENIC PART OF THE LAYOUT *('N' Scale)*

Running Track

Goods Shed

Fiddle Yard

NO SCENERY

Schedule: Move 1: Engine 3, the train in the fiddle yard track 1 moves to the vacant platform 2 section of track in the station and stops.

Move 2: Engine 1, the short goods train at platform 3 departs to the goods shed track 5, and uncouples its wagons.

Move 3: Engine 4, the train in platform 1 departs to fiddle yard track 1 and stops.

Move 4: Engine 1, the light engine (no wagons) track 5, at the goods shed departs to the fiddle yard track 3 and collects the coaches.

Move 5: Engine 2, The train at goods shed track 4 departs to platform 3.

Move 6: Engine 2 platform 3 departs to fiddle yard track 2.

Move 7: Engine 1 departs from fiddle yard track 3, to platform 3 and stops.

Move 8: Engine 4 departs fiddle yard track 1 to platform 1 and stops. *(Back to its start)*

Move 9: Engine 1, platform 3 departs to goods track 4 and stops.

Move 10: Engine 2 fiddle yard track 2 departs to platform 3 and stops. *(Back to start)*

Move 11: Engine 1 departs goods track 4 to fiddle yard 3 and uncouples the coaches.

Move 12: Engine 3, departs platform 2 to fiddle yard track 1 and stops. *(Back to start)*

Move 13: Engine 1, the light engine (no coaches) departs fiddle yard track 3 to goods track 5 and collects the wagons.

Move 14: Engine 2 departs to goods track 3 and stops.

Move 15: Engine 1 departs to platform 3. *(Both back to start)* Repeat as required.

4. MAKING THE SCENERY

THE LANDSCAPE

The scenery will probably cover more than 80% of the layout's surface, the rest being made up with buildings, track and the road. Landscaping the model is a love or a hate relationship, some modellers are only interested in modelling rolling stock, and the landscape is irrelevant. Other modellers totally enjoy modelling the buildings, the trees and the landscape. This is because any excuse to model a particular feature is used to enhance the layout.

The modelling of buildings is relatively easy, because kits can be purchased, but unfortunately the landscape has to be made. This is quite often the downfall of a layout, and the owner finds themselves making apologies!

For the reader to judge the quality of landscape modelling, they will need to visit one or two railway modelling exhibitions, which generally portray the full range of standards. You will find the junior, who with limited funds had made a very good attempt; the colours are not quite right, and the road textures are out of scale. Next comes the average modeller, who is more often only interested in running the layout, therefore the scenery is a bit of a nuisance, because it gets damaged every time the layout is moved.

Finally you get the serious modeller, who is invited to show their layout at an exhibition; their layout will be immaculate, and will keep you busy for hours just looking at the modelling. It is by close examination and asking questions that you will learn, but you will still need to go out and look and photograph the real thing!

Look at the landscape and say, expanded polystyrene cut to shape, covered with paper and rag soaked in glue with a bit of plaster. Painted a mixture of brown, yellows and shades of green; sprinkled with mixed textures of various colours. The embankment is bare earth, dark in colour adjacent to the water where it is wet but lighter where the ground is drier. The reeds could be modelled using dried grasses, coloured to suit. The water is a bit murky; I could use painted and varnished plaster to represent that.

The old wooden building is probably best modelled using thin real wood, rather than plastic, because some bits will need to be broken. If I move that building nearer to that building, and ignore that modern building, incorporate the pub at Dartford, and the bridge and stream at Edenbridge. That brochure my wife had, for our holidays, contained some good photographs of a village; you are beginning to take your landscape modelling seriously!

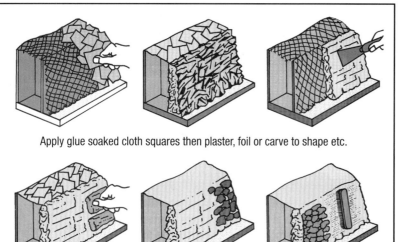

Apply glue soaked cloth squares then plaster, foil or carve to shape etc.

Apply plaster, cork bits, crumpled plaster, cat litter or small pieces of coal.

MODELLING

We have at our disposal several different types of modelling materials, all of various weights. E.g. plaster is heavy, expanded polystyrene is extremely light. Therefore much will depend upon the use of the layout, whilst expanded polystyrene is extremely light it is somewhat fragile and easily damaged compared to plaster.

On a layout which will not need to be moved I prefer the chicken wire and plaster method of modelling rock faces. The chicken wire is stapled to the framework of the baseboard and is cut and shaped to suit. This is then covered with a series of small cloth squares soaked in a mixture of builder's plaster (not Plaster of Paris, because it sets too quickly) and PVA white woodworker's glue, mixed at 75% water to 25% glue. Apply these squares in thin layers to prevent the plaster cracking. After covering the chicken wire framework with the cloth squares and they have hardened, apply a thicker mixture of plaster using crumpled-up tin foil. Work with about 30 cm (12 inches) square areas at a time.

The method is to spread the plaster onto the tin foil and whilst still soft, wet and runny, press this onto the hardened plaster-impregnated cloth, foil uppermost. Press and squeeze until a good shape is achieved. The edges of the tin foil will need to be pressed to shape to meet the contours of the adjoining surfaces. The plaster is then allowed to harden in place, still covered with the tin foil. When the plaster has almost completely set the tin foil is carefully removed, exposing a random rock face-like texture. This procedure is repeated along the length of the surface being modelled, slightly overlapping each join.

The joins are carefully knifed away to match the previously modelled surface, so that the join line becomes lost. This produces a very hard and realistic surface ready for painting, the texture of which can be varied by the amount that the tin foil is crumpled.

The above method can also be used with car body filler; this time polystyrene is used as a support, and is cut to shape as required. The surface is then covered with a thin layer of paper squares, followed by cloth squares, soaked in woodworker's (PVA) glue diluted 50/50 with water. When dry the car body filler is applied directly on top of this, using the tin foil method, only this time 15 cm (6 inch) squares are used. (Car body filler sets very quickly.) The tinfoil is removed as the material sets and do not worry if you fail to remove all the foil, the car body filler is designed to stick to metal!

ROCK FACES

Rock, whether naturally eroded to shape or cut by man, produces various types of surface. Therefore the type of surface will need to be modelled in a slightly different way to look realistic. Well-washed boulders, for example, found in a stream, tend to be rounded whilst loose boulders exposed to the elements through a landslide or excavation tend to have hard edges. Also, no two areas are alike, some contain rocky outcrops with no vegetation, whilst others contain boulders mixed with grass. Vertical cliff faces tend to be reasonably smooth, but do have a random pattern texture. Cliff ledges will generally contain some plant growth, thus adding colour to their otherwise barren surfaces.

The angle of the rock face will also vary depending upon its hardness. Granite and other hard rocks tend to form almost a vertical sheer drop, whilst loose sandy soils that dry, stack at about 45 degrees. This is easily demonstrated by pouring out some household salt into cones of approximately 3 cm high and noting the angles of the cones. Very dry salt will form a shallower angle than damp salt. It is the same with cliffs since hard rock faces tend to be sheer whilst softer surfaces become shallower in their angle. This is the reason for the various embankment angles found on railway cuttings, and also explains why plant life is encouraged to grow on the embankments; as it helps to hold together the topsoil and helps to prevent the ground being washed away by the elements. Plants somehow manage to grow in all sorts of niches!

The photographs show various types of near vertical surfaces, the one left is a cliff some 100 ft high, (N scale) made using plaster, and below rock face (HOe scale) modelled using fibre board; as used under laminated household flooring.

The materials chosen to represent the different scales should be carefully chosen, because the smaller scales need finer materials than the larger scales.

Track ballast is one of the main problems; 2mm/ 1 foot modelling scale needs almost coarse sand to represent ballast.

COAL or CORK

Both these materials can produce a very good landscape effect that is ideal for modelling large areas at a time. Shaped polystyrene is used as the foundation and primed with PVA white glue. (Thin the glue to suit.) The larger lumps are scattered over the surface of the wet PVA followed by sprinkling of the fine coal dust, cork or plaster powder.

When completely dry, (allow 24 hours) the smaller baseboard can be turned upside down, to remove any material that has not adhered to the surface of the polystyrene. If the layout is large, the material can be removed with a vacuum cleaner fitted with a new bag so as to recover the coal, cork etc, mixture. The coal, cork and plaster glued to the baseboard is now ready for painting.

CHALK FACES AND EMBANKMENTS

There are several ways of making chalk faces, and one method is the use of cardboard strips. This method is very useful when making a lightweight structure, the cardboard strips are stapled top and bottom, (see page 43) of the cliff or embankment and then further strips are threaded through to form a woven texture. These woven cardboard strips form a base on which screwed/rolled/crumpled newspaper is laid (sticky taping it in place). This crumpled newspaper in turn is covered with small flat strips of newspaper, pre-soaked in a mixture of white glue and water at the ratio of half glue to half water. Take care when overlaying the strips not to flatten the crumpled newspaper underneath, so crumple the strips so that they also produce an uneven surface.

When they have dried and hardened, the newspaper is painted white using emulsion paint. When the first layer of paint is completely dry, apply a second coat of paint and whilst this is still wet thinly sprinkle the surface with white Plaster of Paris powder through a sieve to form a texture. When dry and set add a third coat of white emulsion paint and this time sprinkle with stones, soil and grass texture to form the finished surface. The wet paint holds the texture permanently in place when dry. (See Chapter Seven for further information on painting, etc.)

SMALL HILLSIDE EMBANKMENTS

Many materials can be mixed together whilst constructing baseboards. The important thing to remember is which glue or solvent dissolves certain materials. For example, UHU® or Evostick® dissolve expanded polystyrene but do not dissolve expanded rigid polyurethane. (The type of material used in the building industry for heat insulation.) Similarly, some paints contain certain solvents that will dissolve some types of plastic, but will not stick or adhere to other types of plastic. Therefore care must be taken in the choice of materials, glues and paints. Fortunately emulsion paint (being water-based) does not cause many difficulties. If in doubt, test the paint or glue on the material to be used, for undesired effects.

The rigid expanded polyurethane material, although expensive, is an ideal material for filling in awkward areas, because it is easily cut with a bread knife, using a sawing action. It also carves and sands extremely well and accepts most types of paints and glues without dissolving.

The mixed method of constructing baseboards allows for large areas to be covered in solid sheet form to obtain a finished smooth surface whilst the tricky contoured areas are filled in with an easily workable material. Both surfaces can be painted and textured to suit, as described elsewhere.

Always consider the weight of the baseboard

Left: The layered base is a traditional way of modelling contours accurately. The method also allows very complex landscape to be simply made.

The retirement home hatch for the new oval layout is complex in its levels, (see page 200 for more details) because it is built on a slope.

The side nearest to us contains a small stream, approximately 4 metres (12ft) below street level, and indicated by the sloping kerb nearest to the front of the picture.

Because the hatches will need to withstand a lot of use, the material used for the contour thickness is 12mm MDF, which at 'N' scale is 6 feet, This did not cause many problems because the heights and the thickness of the layers totalled the desired overall height. i.e. 10 layers equalled 60 ft at N scale, the total fall on the hatch.

N.B. I refer to scale feet rather than 12mm thickness to avoid confusion. 6 scale feet is 12mm at N scale and 24mm at 00 scale!

because at some time in the future the base will be moved. Therefore a lightweight base is easier to move than a base that takes 6 people to lift. Also consider its size, will it go through the door, or the hatch in the loft; this is where size also plays a crucial role!

LAYERED BASES

The product known as Sundealer Board® or soft board etc. is very much like a fibrous soft pulp board that is not very strong, it does not bend and easily breaks. It is a very good sound insulating board and it compresses, making it an ideal material for laying under wood effect flooring. This is because being soft it moulds to the irregularities of the surface on which it is laid, therefore from the modeller's point of view because it also cuts, shapes and sticks easily, it is an ideal material for model-making.

The method of cutting is to use a sharp heavy duty craft knife and to cut on top of an old piece of board; taking care not to cut through both. The method that I used is to mark out onto a pair of boards the contour lines as found on your drawing or plan. (3 or 4 boards may be required) It will depend upon the gradient of the ground as to the number of boards used, i.e. steep cliff or ground requires more boards because the contours are much closer together compared to that of a shallow gradient of a slight hill. In most cases 2 boards will be sufficient, so that alternative contours are cut and alternatively stacked on top of each other.

So that the ground does not collapse, 1-inch wide supporting strips are fitted underneath each contour and everything is fixed in place with white woodworker's glue (PVA). Having fixed all the contours in place and the glue has hardened the contours can now be carved to shape. A mixture of methods can be used, i.e. carved to shape using a power chisel, or sanded to shape using a powered rotary disc or belt sander. Whilst both are exceptionally fast, they are also extremely messy; with dust everywhere. Therefore a dust mask and protective clothing is essential! The power chisel is relatively clean to use, producing wood chips, rather than dust.

Because I find it can be very difficult to obtain a satisfactorily smooth surface for the roads by just carving, I cut out a card overlay (Art board) and fix this in place on the roads with woodworker's glue.

Alternatively I use car body filler or Polyfilla® to fill the dips and gouges that appear whilst carving, and when the roads are smooth they are edged with a card paving strip, fixed in place with wood workers glue. The base is them primed with oil bound undercoat paint thinned 25 percent so that it soaks into the fibrous board and seals it, followed by a painting with matt household emulsion paint; the road, the paving and the grass basic colours. Then using a series of washes the final road and paving colours are achieved. Finally for the country scenes having finished the painting the grass texture is added, the holes drilled for the trees, the bushes and hedges added etc. For town scenes cars, people and buildings are added.

The soft board can also be laid under the track, instead of cork. I prefer to glue this to a backing 6mm thick plywood board, to provide some strength, because to fix it directly onto the battening can provide a weak baseboard. (You can break a hole through the baseboard's surface by leaning on the base.) The oval base uses MDF as the material for the contours, which is much harder and cannot be cut with a knife; therefore a jig or band saw has to be used, but the material carves and sands the same. It is also far more durable than polystyrene, foam or soft board.

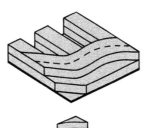

Expanded polystyrene, insulation sheet, or pulp board can be worked very easily with a sharp knife or with a hacksaw blade. Cut the contours and overlap as shown and support with strips. Fix together with white woodworker's glue (PVA).

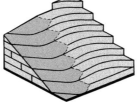

When set sand with very coarse sandpaper using a power tool or carve to shape.

Expanded polystyrene is very fragile therefore the surface will need to be covered with a layer of paper soaked in PVA. Cover small areas at a time and allow to dry to prevent the surface from warping.

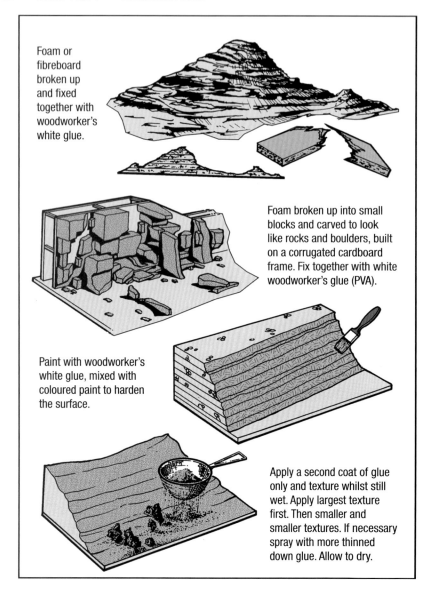

Foam or fibreboard broken up and fixed together with woodworker's white glue.

Foam broken up into small blocks and carved to look like rocks and boulders, built on a corrugated cardboard frame. Fix together with white woodworker's glue (PVA).

Paint with woodworker's white glue, mixed with coloured paint to harden the surface.

Apply a second coat of glue only and texture whilst still wet. Apply largest texture first. Then smaller and smaller textures. If necessary spray with more thinned down glue. Allow to dry.

The foam method of constructing baseboards goes back to flight simulators, when the contours of the ground were machine cut on a large milling machine. Then by hand the contours were sanded smooth, painted with white glue, to provide a durable surface and then painted. Finally its surface was covered with roads, fields and houses, all painted on by hand. For the best effect mix the colours with similar colours and stipple the colours so that the finish looks patchy, then texture with mixed colours and sizes and avoid bald spots.

SEDIMENT FACES

These type of faces are the result of the different layers of soil being formed over thousands of years, and through time changes have accrued, either made by man or by nature, and becoming exposed as a cross section. Each layer will have its own weathering characteristic. The harder the material the longer it takes to break down. Soft sand, for example, is very easily eroded away by the wind and rain, and thus exposes the harder material.

Each sediment layer will also vary in texture, because quite often these layers are a series of hard or soft materials. Therefore, each layer has its own characteristic of erosion and colour. Alum Bay on the Isle of Wight, as an example, has 21 different clearly definable colours within a very short length of cliff face. The colours range from black, white, red, yellow, grey and a mixture of softer tones in between. This, of course, is an exceptional case and far from normal, most areas having a predominant colour.

Devon, for example, is noted for its reddish soil, whilst in other areas it is darker or lighter in colour depending on the chalk or clay content of the soil. If one is modelling a particular area, then research will be required into soil and sediment layers.

From the modelling point of view this allows one to experiment with different layers and colours to enhance the layout so that the scenery becomes more interesting. By carefully making a selection of real rocks, stone and sand, these can be studied, modeled and painted to represent the material being portrayed.

Nowadays available on the market are various types of pre-packed textures replacing the old out-dated dyed wood sawdust. These new textures are produced from dyed cork granules, ground up foams and natural selected materials.

But of course one is not restricted to pre-packed materials as stones and different soils abound around us, all of which can be very easily gathered up and prepared for use. The method that I use is to collect a couple of jam or coffee jars full of each of the different types of very fine soil or stone. I then spread out in a thin layer each of the collected materials on sheets of newspaper; so that they dry out. The material is then sieved using different grades of sieves, so that in the end I obtain the various grades of texture; working from the largest to the smallest size of particle.

These sorted grades are now placed into self-seal plastic bags with the location, the type of material and a number written on, for identification at a later date. This is important so one can rematch the various bags and grades together, as after modeling for a number of years you can very easily gather several hundred sample bags, all of which are slightly different. Therefore it is useful to know the exact location it came from, when you require some more material at a later date.

The basic structure of a sediment face can be wood, chicken wire/plaster or polystyrene depending upon the baseboard. Broken up fibreboard and polystyrene ceiling tiles work well but both are difficult to vary in their thickness. In reality the sediment layers rarely maintain a consistent thickness or run in a straight line, so to help overcome this particular problem I use pieces of wood between the layers, spaced at different intervals so as to jack up and vary the sediments' contour levels.

Alternatively I use a block of expanded polystyrene and etch the contours in as required using a paintbrush dipped in cellulose thinners to melt the expanded polystyrene to shape. To guide the brush strokes I use a piece of cardboard cut in an irregular line, and this also helps plan out the contours. When the etching is finished paint with emulsion paint. With fibre board use oil paint similar in colour to the natural texture I am going to use.

The first coat should be allowed to completely dry out and will form the base sealant coat. The second coat can now be applied on the dried sealant coat using coloured matt emulsion paint mixed with woodworker's glue, because it remains wet longer and is more 'sticky'.

On to the wet paint surface sprinkle the textures, starting with the coarsest granules which form the rocks, then adding the medium textures followed lastly by the finest dust-like texture. The dust helps to fill in all the gaps between the larger stones. After a day or so, when the paint is completely dried out, the excess materials are removed either by turning the baseboard over or by the vacuum cleaner method.

In each case all the excess materials are re-gathered, re-sieved and then stored away for the next project. The outcome should be a realistic, naturally-textured sediment surface requiring no further work and which is also quite hard-wearing and easily repaired.

The problem with baseboards is the weight, the plaster and chicken wire type are extremely heavy, but very hard wearing, whilst the foam bases are more fragile, but extremely light. The ply bases 01, 02, 03, 4 & 5 are quite light, base 6 is heaver and base 7 requires two people to lift it. Base 7 could have been made lighter using expanded foam, but would have used a lot of foam, and would have been very expensive compared to the cost of the plaster and wire method used.

I use a mixture of methods, based on what is available for free. My preferred method is Sundealer® board, similar to the soft board that goes under wooden floors, because it is easily cut with a knife and is more durable than foam. It can also be broken and crumbled with rough edges with the use of pliers, and fixed in place with white woodworker's glue (PVA). I also use oil bound paint as the primer, because water based paints can affect soft boards, chipboard and MDF, because on the 'end grain' at times the water causes the material to swell and buckle.

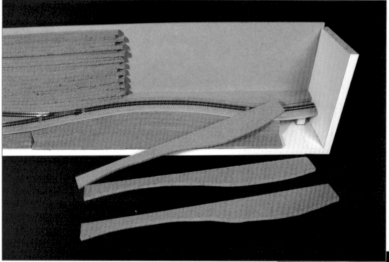

LAYERED BASES

The construction of this base uses Contiboard® MDF and a fibrous soft pulp board (used for laying under laminated household flooring) all of which are easily obtainable. The construction starts by having cut the 15cm wide Contiboard® shelving to length (in this case 2 required 830cm long) and the ends (2 required) 20cm high. Since the 20cm ends fit onto the 830cm long shelf, the 5mm thick backing board is cut at 830 long x 22.4cm wide (high). The track bed is cut from 9mm MDF and shaped at the front as required. The track bed is supported on scrap timber and MDF as required. The MDF track bed has the track fixed in place and wiring completed.

Right: The pulp board is laid in brick wall fashion, so that you do not get a straight join on the joins and the board is cut using a sharp knife to follow the shape of the rock face. Glue the layers together so that the glue does not dribble out and down the front surface. Keep the upper and lower pulp board components separate at this stage so that they can be carved to shape separately and then assemble making sure the rolling stock clears the rock face edges (adjust to suit). When satisfied the train runs well on the track, assemble everything and permanently fix in place.

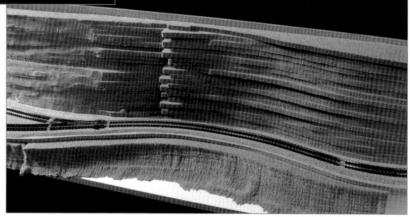

Left: The pulp board is shaped using an electric drill fitted with a rotary wire brush to remove the bulk of the surface. This is then followed by using smaller and smaller rotary brushes, powered by a hobby drill to produce the finer detail.

Warning 1: When using any form of powered hand tool always use face and eye protection because rotary wire brushes are notorious for losing strands of wire.

Warning 2: Always wear suitable dust masks when cutting and shaping wood based fibrous manmade materials because the dust produced is harmful to your health.

Right: The pulp board surface having been shaped using various rotary cutting tools should to begin to look like a rock or sediment surface. To get the best effect it is best to work from a photograph that shows the surface being modelled. The example shown was found in Italy; was grey in colour, with grasses and shrubs growing from the ledges. What was noticed was the lack of birds that normally live on rock faces, so the rocks remained very clean but very dusty. Colour changes with moisture, and these rocks looked very different when wet, because the colours became darker with a wider range of hues.

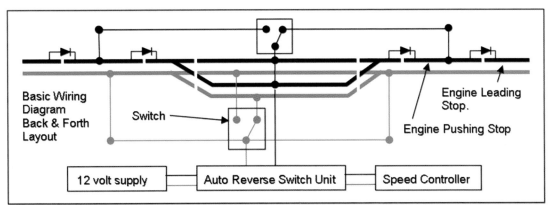

Top: The rock face was primed with grey household emulsion paint, whilst wet ballast was sprinkled on to the surface along the strata lines.

When dry lighter and darker colours were added following the strata lines.

The stone embankment wall beneath the track was added using Woodland Scenics® large stones, fixed in place with wood workers glue and Polyfilla® and when dry sanded to show a flat surface. Further stones were then added using glue and filler to shape the lower embankment. When dry everything was painted a series of grey and earth colours, given a dirty wash, followed by ballasting, grassing, trees and people as required.

Left: The wiring diagram is very basic for an auto run back & forth type layout.

Above: The view across bases 4, 5, 6 & 7.

Left: The 'Retirement Home' hatch has a mixture of landscape features. Pages 67, 198 & 200.

Below: This shows one of the many traditional methods of making a simple lightweight contoured base. This starts with the basic wood baseboard containing the track and edging. 2: Expanded foam or crumpled newspaper is then used to fill the void. 3: Newspaper is fixed in place with woodworker's white glue. 4: The newspaper is painted and textured. 5, 6, & 7: More colour and texture is added until the desired landscaping effect is achieved, followed by adding trees and bushes.

Left: The 'Retirement Home' hatch 4 (more details on page 198) is only one of the removable hatches on the 'Multi Level Oval layout'. The reason for having the hatches removable is to allow access to the track below; for cleaning, maintenance and for retrieving derailed rolling stock.

This base was constructed using layers of MDF, similar to that used for the rock face. But in this case layers were added above and below the chosen datum level. (See page 200)

The changing contour levels provided a good reason to add a shallow fast flowing stream.

Because the stream has been there for hundreds of years, the soil has been washed away, so it is around 10 feet below ground level, and on the banks of the stream a lot of vegetation will flourish.

For safety reasons local dwellings will have walls to the edge of their property. People and cars will add scale to the scene, and richness of colour will set the time of year.

Right Hatch 2: The stream flows under the bridge and onto hatch 4. Because the stream flows through a park, it is more accessible and therefore we have the excuse to show young people enjoying themselves, watched by the disapproving church warden!

The model shown was produced by John Piper, who in the early 1960s was the first person in Britain to produce acid etched trees. John together with Norman Finch, Rod Kitchen, I and other professional model makers at that time, all helped to develop a wide range of tree making methods and textures that is now taken for granted. The methods were developed for architects models. The earlier methods (pre 1960) were crude, with saw-dust for grass and twigs covered in lichen used for trees. Unfortunately this method has stayed with the hobbyist and it has only been in the last 10 years or so that some manufacturers ceased to produce coloured sawdust. Woodland Scenics® are now the brand leaders in this field.

PLOUGHED FIELDS, GRASS AND HEDGES

The furrows and planting of ploughed fields are very simple to reproduce in model form. The technique is first to cut a piece of plastic into a comb-like shape, by using a knife or file, at the scale that is being modelled. Secondly mix up some builder's plaster to a butter-like mixture using water and woodworker's white glue. (About 50:50 water/glue ratio) This is then spread over the baseboard's surface and, using the comb, is moulded to shape, the comb forming the small ridges and valleys and, at the end of each straight line, being pivoted around to represent the turning of the tractor and plough. This is repeated alongside the previous ploughed line, until the field is finished.

Finally, when the plaster has set and dried, the 'field' is painted with emulsion paint of a colour to suit the location being modelled. This first coat is allowed to dry out, then a very thin mixture of paint of the colour used plus some white is applied in a wash-like form so that it runs down into the 'valleys' and is allowed to dry. White glue is now mixed up with some of the ground colour paint to colour it. This mixture is then applied with a stiff brush or sponge to the tops of the plough marks. The glue is then sprinkled with foliage material, and when dry you remove unwanted foliage. The net result is the appearance that the tops of the ploughed furrows have plants growing!

Hedges and other clumps of grass, small bushes etc., all help to make the field look as if it is lived in, and will need to be modelled. The materials used will be dependant upon scale, because what looks right at one scale looks disastrously wrong when used at another scale. 'N' scale needs finer texture material than '00' scale, so whilst instructions can be found on how to make something the instructions may not apply to another scale.

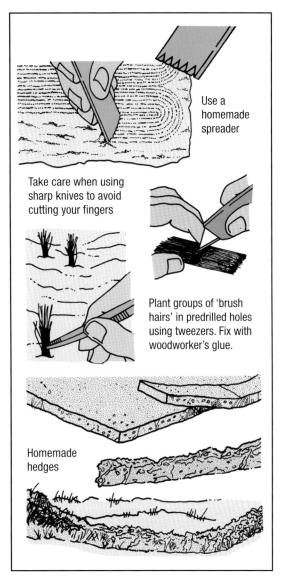

Use a homemade spreader

Take care when using sharp knives to avoid cutting your fingers

Plant groups of 'brush hairs' in predrilled holes using tweezers. Fix with woodworker's glue.

Homemade hedges

Left: The ploughed field effect is obtained by mixing up a soft butterlike plaster mixture and then spread using a homemade spreader that has 'V' shaped notches cut in the end. The spreader is dragged across the plaster so that it forms a series of mounds and troughs. When dry paint and texture to suit.

Old wallpaper paste brushes are an ideal source of long grass! Remove the metal binding and cut into small bundles that conveniently fit the drill size that you are using. Paint to suit when they are fixed in place.

Rubberised horse hair or non-scratch pot scourers make an ideal foundation on which to fix hedging texture. This is because it can be bent around curves and sufficiently flexible to go up and down hills. Fix in place on the baseboard (pin in place until the glue dries) using woodworker's water based white glue and apply grass texture on top of excess glue.

Left: The farmer in the ploughed field adds interest to an otherwise barren space.

The field could be growing several crops, each planted a week apart, so that later in the year they can be harvested a week apart. This will add interest, because the field can be split into several sizes of texture and colour. People can be in the field harvesting the crop and packing the goods in boxes, and the plants that have been harvested can look yet another colour.

Right: A typical etched leaf tree, measuring some 8 inches high. The trunk is made from twisted copper wire stripped from household 15-amp electrical cable.

To stop the strands untwisting most of the wires were soldered together. The trunk and main branches were then covered with acrylic filler, thinned down with water, so that it produced a smooth finish. When dry attached to the ends was fixed a leaf and branch brass etching, soldered in place. To make a tree like this is very expensive and time consuming.

Right: Polyfilla® or plaster mixed with a small amount of white woodworker's glue and water, mixed to a runny butter consistency, applied with a paint brush, and then painted with both colour and clear varnish creates realistic looking murky water.

Clear water is more difficult to model, and one of the better ways is a sheet of clear plastic fixed over the bottom of the stream or pond at water level. Alternatively clear casting resin can be poured on in thin layers, but this material tends to soak up the plants and also the embankment and the paint can become affected. But if done carefully and in very thin layers it can look very realistic.

The art is to add detail with each layer, so that weeds and plants appear to be floating under the water, and don't forget the fish, and a fisherman!

RIVERS, STREAMS AND PONDS

There are three basic ways of producing 'water'. The first is to simply paint the area being modelled with a mixture of muddy tones to represent the water, and apply several coats of clear varnish. To make the surface more lifelike stipple with a sponge or brush to represent the ripples on the water. Each coat of varnish must be allowed to dry before applying the next until the desired effect is obtained.

The second method is to use a sheet of clear plastic material, this being laid over the model river/stream bed and the banks, the clear plastic being varnished to represent the ripples on the water's surface, and streaks being added to represent weeds, etc.

The third method is the use of clear casting resin. This method requires the building up of the depth of water in thin layers; otherwise it will crack or shrink badly. This method is a very long process but carefully done allows weeds, etc, to be placed at various levels throughout the water, and this looks very realistic. Care must be taken when measuring the resin to obtain the exact mixing ratios, otherwise the resin will not set or alternatively ends up with a sticky surface. If this happens, with luck one can varnish the surface and save the situation. Around the water's edge reeds and grasses can be planted either by gluing or drilling holes and inserting long plants glued in place.

TREES

The trees form a major part of a scenic setting by helping to provide a scale to the layout. A fully-grown tree is very large, quite often exceeding 75ft (25m) in height, or at 00/HO scale 12in (30cm). Although trees vary in types and age, which affects their size, on average the majority of trees we see

are mature and at their full height. One of the reasons so many modellers make under-size trees is the difficulty of making large trees and the time they consume to produce, especially when you consider a small layout can require fifty trees.

The easiest of all the trees to make is at the smaller scales. The Z or N scale type, can be simply made from lichen or rubberised horse hair (used as a branch shaping material) cut into small pieces and glued on to a cocktail stick, or a long small-headed nail or length of wire, which forms the trunk. The branch material is then trimmed to shape with a pair of scissors, forming the basic winter tree shape. Then, by holding the trunk and dipping the 'branches' into clear nail varnish (allow the excess varnish to drain off) the summer foliage can be applied on to the 'branches'. Once this has dried, the unwanted foliage can be trimmed off. This method is ideal for making trees up to 3 inches (80mm) in height.

For the construction of very large trees requiring thick trunks I use brazing rod, as this material is available in various thicknesses and in straight lengths. Depending upon the size of the tree, between three and six lengths of rod can be bent to suit so that they form a series of prongs. The prongs are bound together at the base to form the trunk of the tree. Ideally, copper wire should be used for the binding (removed from old household power cable), then soldered to prevent movement.

The same with the finer branches, made from copper wire stripped from household cable and twisted as if a small tree and soldered in place. On top of the binding car body filler is applied that is mixed with some glass fibre resin to thin it down.

Painted Polyfilla® or plaster mixed with woodworker's glue stippled with gloss varnish.

Clear plastic sheet fixed into the embankment as the model is built. Note: the stream has to be finished first.

Layers of clear casting resin poured onto the finished stream bed.

Alternatively, acrylic paste could be used or pre-coloured plaster mixed with white glue can also be applied. The idea is to thicken up the trunk and cover the binding, so that the trunk looks natural. When this procedure has been completed the basic trunk is painted, and the finer branches added, using Woodland Scenic® foliage material.

For small trees rubberised hair (purchased as off cuts from good furniture or bedding repair specialists) is cut up into small random pieces and glued on to the prongs of the trunk. From experience I have found that UHU® (universal yellow and black tube) is the best glue to use as it is easy to apply and holds the rubberised horsehair firmly in position.

When the prongs of the trees' trunks are completely covered with the horsehair and the glue has hardened, continue by trimming the trees to shape using scissors. Cut the horsehair in a typical winter shape as found on the real tree being modelled. When this is finished the trunk and branches of the tree are sprayed a suitable colour with a matt oil-bound paint. Since trees vary in their basic colour this method works extremely well as the foliage for each tree is applied separately, allowing choice of colour for each individual tree.

COMMERCIAL TREE KITS

A wide selection of various types of tree kits are available today, ranging from the 'Britain's' all-plastic kits to the more realistic cast metal and etched ones. John Piper of 'Scale Link' first explored the possibility of etched trees; 4D now along with other companies continue to produce these very realistic trees. In the United States the American 'Woodland Scenes' produce kits which are imported into Britain. All of these companies produce an excellent range of texturing materials suitable for both ground cover and foliage, nowadays used by both the amateur and professional model maker.

All the tree kits contain the basic materials, but exclude glue and paint. Their construction varies only slightly since the techniques have not really changed for a considerable number of years, so the methods shown in this book are time-tested and found to be extremely reliable.

The actual construction of an etched brass tree kit is dependent upon the type and size, because some need soldering during the kit's construction. Small trees are etched in one piece, and are ideal for Z and N scale layouts. For 00/HO scale, the trees obviously have to be considerably larger and to overcome production problems, some trunks and branches are produced in sections and joined together by soldering, because glue joins break. The soldering is carried out with a hot iron, just using the tip to melt the pre-tinned solder. Once this has been completed the trunk and branches of the tree can be bent into the required shape to form the type of tree being modelled. Finally at this stage the tree is thoroughly washed to remove

all traces of grease, etc, and when dry the trunk is thickened. The tree is then painted with cellulose or oil paint to the desired colour. This forms the basis of the tree ready for the application of the foliage material.

The very large etched brass kits are constructed in a similar way. The etching is removed from the fret and a wire stalk is soldered on to the trunk so as to extend the base. Brazing rod is ideal material to use for this as the rod is of a constant thickness, and avoids the problem of constantly changing the drill's size when planting the trees, When the stalk has been soldered in place the tree is bent to shape and then car body filler of the resin type or an acrylic paste is applied to thicken up the trunk. The tree's finer branches are modelled from wire wool or pre-prepared commercially available foliage material. (Woodland Scenics® make a good range of materials.)

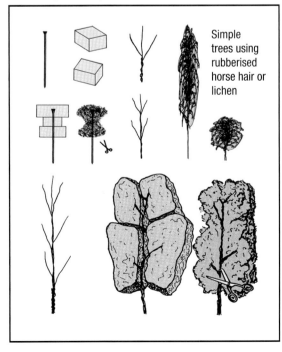

Simple trees using rubberised horse hair or lichen

Above: Because we now live in a multicultural society, and in a country that is now renowned for its innovative and exciting architecture, it gives the modeller the chance to break with traditional 'British style of architecture' and explore a wide range of building designs.Brighton, on the south coast boasts of a classic 'overseas' piece of architecture, built years ago!

Left: A very basic tree can be made using a nail and lichen (available from craft shops etc.). The alternative material is rubberised horse hair, used in upholstery. Both are used to form the basic tree shape, fixed in place on a nail or twisted wire. I prefer to use UHU® universal glue, which bonds most materials, for fixing the lichen/horse hair in place.

Allow to dry and trim to shape with sharp scissors, then fix in place the coloured foliage texture. Vary the colours to make a group of trees look more interesting.

Above: By taking photographs of trees in winter, a better study can be made of their basic shape. Ideally you also need to photograph the same tree in spring, summer and autumn, to understand the range of colours displayed by the tree throughout the year. Each type of tree has its own set of colours, which in spring can be extremely vibrant when the tree flowers.

Autumn is also another time of the year when the various trees display a wide range of colours.

WIRE WOUND TRUNKS

Wire wound tree trunks are very simple to produce; the 'trees' can be made at any scale and any variety of tree can be modelled. The basic construction material consists of a bundle of wire, twisted and bent to shape. For the construction of smaller trees brass picture wire is used. Do not use steel cable because it is difficult to cut and shape. The larger trees are constructed using 'Rose Wire' that is used in flower arranging. This soft iron wire is available in various thicknesses, lengths and by the roll.

The technique is to bind a series of wires together at what will be the base of the tree's main trunk. The top wires are then wound together. When using picture wire, the wire will require soldering in sections of about 1 inch (25 mm) of soldered wire to about 3 inches (75 mm) of unsoldered wire, before unwinding. One of the easiest methods of unwinding is to place the wire into a vice and fit the other end in a hand drill, and simply unwind the wire. The solder will hold sections together, whilst

other bits are unwound, cut and trim the wire to length. Place the short lengths back in the chuck of the drill and clamp the drill in a vice. Next you hold on to the other end of the wires with pliers and rotate the drill to rewind the wire to shape. For larger trees the number of wires used will depend upon the type and size of tree being modelled.

A silver birch, for example, will require fewer wires because it is tall and slender. The oak tree has a fat trunk and branches are considerably thicker, requiring far more wire, probably four times as much for the same tree height and old or young use different amounts of wire. Therefore the number of wires used is important in order to capture the overall feeling of the tree's shape.

WINDING THE WIRE

The wires are wound using a hand drill, secured in a vice. The pliers are used to hold the wire, whilst twisting the wire. Note: always twist the wire in the same direction, whilst forming the branches, otherwise it will all come undone. The technique is to separate a small bundle of wires out, folded through the middle as if plaiting, and to trap the selected bundle, as the main wires are twisted together. These separate lengths are also twisted to form the smaller branches until one ends up with two or three prongs of wire at the end of each length of twisted wire. Repeat this procedure until every wire is twisted together. Finally spread the wires out into a typical tree shape. (For a particular type of tree that you wish to model, work from photographs.)

Finally trim off unwanted lengths of wire with cutters. Remove the tree from the drill's chuck and embed the base of its trunk into a block of Plasticine® or modelling clay. The wire armature forming the tree is now ready for its application of filler. This can be pre-coloured plaster mixed up with white glue or acrylic paste or car body filler. Note: The car body filler is of the paste type used for repairing dents in automobiles and thinned down to make it runny with glass fibre resin. The selected mixture is applied to the trunk of the tree and allowed to run down the trunk so that it smoothes itself out, rather than being applied in blobs, that will require cleaning up or sanding to shape when the material has hardened.

WIRE AND STRING TREES

Trees can also be made of wire and string, a method probably dating from the bottle cleaners used to make conifer trees and developed further. By using this technique a mixture of materials can be used to form the branches, ranging from the stiff bristles found in a yard broom to sisal string, the type used for tying up parcels, white in colour and very much like thin strands of wood. The sisal string needs to be unwound so as to separate the strands. These are then cut in approximately 3in (8cm) lengths and are laid in between two wires.

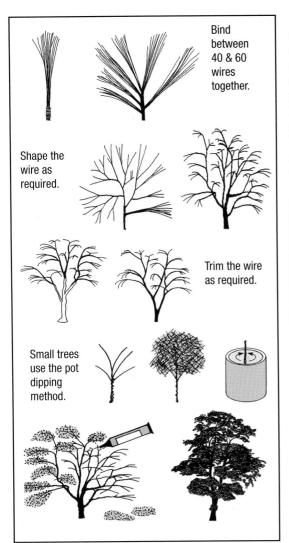

Bind between 40 & 60 wires together.

Shape the wire as required.

Trim the wire as required.

Small trees use the pot dipping method.

This technique of applying wire wool can be used with other trees as it enables the production of cedars or Scots pines, the foliage on these types of tree being very different from the types found on the oak and plane tree. The foliage of the Scots pine and cedar is very flat on the branches, forming layers, whilst the foliage and branches of the oak and other trees are bushier. The wire wool can also be teased out very thinly, making it an ideal material to use on silver birches noted for their fineness of foliage, whilst other trees are noted for their autumn colours.

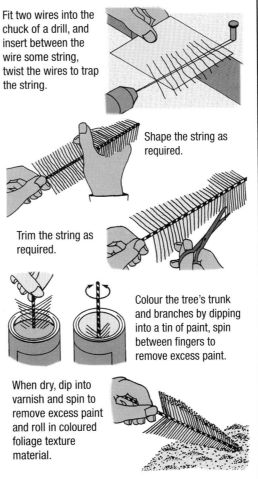

Fit two wires into the chuck of a drill, and insert between the wire some string, twist the wires to trap the string.

Shape the string as required.

Trim the string as required.

Colour the tree's trunk and branches by dipping into a tin of paint, spin between fingers to remove excess paint.

When dry, dip into varnish and spin to remove excess paint and roll in coloured foliage texture material.

Far left: Bind around 50 22 swg x 4 inches long wires together. Note: 15-amp stripped mains cable makes ideal tree armatures (trunk) for medium size trees and 30-amp cable for larger trees. Ideally strip 2m lengths at a time, and having removed the plastic with a sharp knife, laid across the wire, and pushed along. (Take care not to cut yourself.) The alternative method is wire strippers, a short length at a time. The method is to twist the wires together, and as you do so, split the wire up into smaller and smaller bundles until you get two or three wires. Repeat this as often as required, and then shape to the type of tree being modelled. Foliage as required.

Left: The wire and string method produces a tree armature similar to that of a bottle cleaner. This is trimmed to shape, and depending as to which direction the bristles are pointed, as to the type of tree it portrays.

Below: The conifer trees are made using the wire and string method, and the bristles are pointing slightly down, and trimmed cone shape, coated with a dark green texture.

The wires are then pulled tightly together by clamping one end in a vice, the other end being secured in a twist drill pulled taunt to keep the wires straight. A second person is needed to pass the separate strands through the two wires, which are then twisted together using the drill. This traps the strands in place. A good length to produce is 3 feet (1 m) in one wire twisting session. The length of wound wire complete with its bristles is cut into smaller lengths to suit the height of the tree, allowing an additional length of approximately 1 in (3 cm) which is used to fix the tree into the baseboard.

The tree's trunk is thickened by covering the lower wires with a drinking straw, glued in place. (Some of the bristles may need to be removed to make it fit.) The main part of the tree is now trimmed to shape using scissors. This is an ideal technique for producing poplar trees, as the branches can be bent upwards. Alternatively the tree can be trimmed to form a conifer shape and textured. The tree can also be trimmed to a different shape and wire wool applied to form the outer branches, the wool being secured in place by spraying with oil-bound matt paint. When dry further trimming to shape is carried out, so that it is ready to receive its foliage.

FOLIAGING

Right: a very inexpensive tree made from dried yarrow, dipped into varnish and covered with foliage material.

There is a wide range of foliage materials available on the market, ranging from wood chips, flock, granular cork, rubber and foam, all pre-coloured. 'Woodland Scenes' also produce matting. Apart from wood chips, in my opinion these are all ideal foliage materials. The 'Woodland Scenes' mat is the simplest of all to use as it is simply pulled apart and laid over the branches, using a small blob of glue to secure into position. When the foliage of the tree is finished, scissors are then used to trim off the untidy bits.

The 'Woodland' scenic material is a textured pre-coloured material ready for use. It can also be used in many other ways, for instance low ground cover, hanging foliage on walls or over rocks, etc. A similar home-made matting material can be produced by using wire wool teased out and cross-laid or rubberised horsehair. The basic material is sprayed in the appropriate colour then clear varnish sprayed over it to form a sticky surface (oil-bound varnish is used as it remains sticky longer). On top of this sticky surface is sprinkled the coloured texture materials, cork, rubber, foam, etc.

The clear varnish acts like glue and bonds it to the base material. When dry the excess foliage material is removed by shaking. This same technique is also used for applying the foliage to trees, the model being sprayed the correct colour for the tree being constructed. Then it is sprayed with the clear matt oil-bound varnish used to bond the foliage in place.

The foliage is sprinkled on with a sieve while the varnish is still wet and a dry paintbrush is used to remove unwanted foliage from the lower branches and the trunk. Since clear matt varnish is used previous colours applied are unaffected in their matt finish. Also, since the varnish is clear it does not stain or discolour the foliage material.

Lichen can also be sprayed and textured, or flock material can be applied to conifer trees to represent the needles, using this spray method. Finally, small trees can be dipped into a tin of varnish, spun between the fingers to remove excess varnish, and then textured. These small trees make ideal hedges for the larger layouts, planted tightly together in a row.

SOFT TEXTURES

The selection of texture forms an important part of scenic modelling as coarse over-scale or under-scale finishes look very wrong, i.e. wood chips have a long spiky texture whilst granulated foam has a soft rounder shape. The colour of the texture is also critical as this controls the overall effect, each colour having to work in harmony with its neighbouring colour to please the eye.

The range of pre-coloured textures is vast but the dyes used to colour the materials leave at times something to be desired. This can easily be overcome by re-colouring the texture. Emulsion paints work extremely well for this. An old tin can with the top removed by one of the modern openers provides a good mixing container, as the sides are smooth all the way down. (Do not use a jam jar as the lip around the top prevents proper mixing of the materials.) This is important as, when re-colouring only a small amount of emulsion paint is used.

The paint is smeared over the surface of the granules by stirring and working the colour in, rather than soaking the granules with paint. This method, by using the minimum amount of paint, prevents the granules from sticking together and

A WORD OF WARNING
Rubberised spray mount is toxic, both in fume and content and it should only be used in an extremely well ventilated place. For personal protection a mask should be worn at all times. As with all pressurised cans, the empties should never be disposed of in an incinerator or burnt on an open fire.

The safer paint to use as an adhesive is matt clear oil-based varnish, which is extremely sticky. Alternatively to spraying, the 'tree' can be dipped into the pot of varnish and spun by the trunk between the fingers.

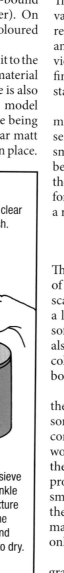

Spray with clear matt varnish.

Or dip into a tin of matt varnish and spin in a second tin.

Use a sieve to sprinkle the texture onto the tree, and allow to dry.

they dry quicker. The drying is carried out on a sheet of newspaper at room temperature.

Textures can be home made by grinding natural rubber foam. Each type of foam will produce a very different type of texture, i.e. synthetic and rubber foam have a very different texture. Polyurethane foam dyed in small squares using cellulose paint becomes brittle and grinds into a dust-like powder, whilst dyed in emulsion paint forms rounder shapes. The round shapes are ideal for small ground cover and the dust texture for grass.

An old mincer or coffee grinder works well for shredding the foam into textures. The mincer's handle is rotated by hand and as the foam emerges from the machine it is sieved through various size sieves so that a selection of granular grades can be obtained. Material, which is still too big, is returned into the mincer for further grinding down. The coffee grinder works in much the same way, but only small amounts can be prepared at a time. Care must be taken in the choice of material to be re-coloured because the 'flock' texturing type of material or some types of 'cat litter' do not re-colour; they only form a sticky mess. Cork granules, sawdust and stone that are non-dissolvable re-colour easily.

HARD TEXTURES

Hard textures like stone and brick are very useful because they are natural materials. This natural look is very difficult to reproduce by painted artwork

Break up plaster as it hardens into pieces and sieve.

Use various sieve sizes, some will need to be home made.

Mix woodworker's 25% glue with 75% water.

Cover area with the thinned glue and apply texture.

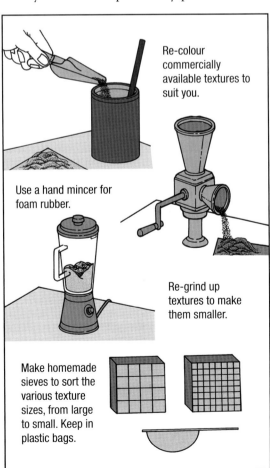

Re-colour commercially available textures to suit you.

Use a hand mincer for foam rubber.

Re-grind up textures to make them smaller.

Make homemade sieves to sort the various texture sizes, from large to small. Keep in plastic bags.

over other surfaces alone. For example, when a surface is painted to represent another material, the addition of the natural texture carefully applied can enhance its appearance. Similarly, a derelict cottage using natural small stones typical of the cottage's construction looks far more convincing than trying to paint pieces of material to look right.

Garden soil, dried out and sieved, provides an easily obtainable material suitable for many applications. The commercial market packages many types of hard natural materials. Certain types of 'Cat Litter' designed for a pet's toilet tray or 'Vermiculite', a material used for insulation, are good sources of small boulders suitable for gluing together or scattering around, re-coloured by painting. 'Vermiculite' has a very good texture, and also compresses so that it can be pressed into shape. Unfortunately neither of these materials are found in hobby shops, like the majority of hard materials. Hard materials are worth gathering and storing in a self-seal plastic bag when making a field trip to a location, so that an example is kept of the soil and stones found in the locality. From these gathered samples coloured paints can be mixed to match the stones and soil colour. The technique is first to paint the area being modelled with a base colour to seal the surface, then apply a second coat, sprinkling on the texture over the wet paint. The wet paint bonds the stones or earth to its surface.

Note: Paint the baseboard the appropriate colours first, i.e. paint green where the grass is to be applied etc. Colour the scatter textures to suit and sprinkle on large pieces first, followed by smaller bits, with the finest last. If necessary spray on further thinned down glue, Allow to dry.

Producing your own granulated texture from natural materials is a long laborious business. Brick dust, for example, is obtained by breaking up bricks with a hammer.
Note: This procedure is dangerous therefore it is extremely important to wear a full safety visor to prevent being struck in the face or eye by flying particles.

Alternatively, a visit to a demolition site could well be fruitful in obtaining this material.

Broken up plaster dyed to colour also works well and is very easily obtainable by crumbling up half set plaster as one works.

These small irregular shapes are suitable for scattering around the bottom of chalk embankments and cuttings rather than using natural chalk, which is very soft and becomes a nuisance rather than an advantage.

Note: Other dried natural tree making materials, (not acid etched or wire armatures) are available but tend to be very brittle and break easily.
The twigs that you get with grapes make natural tree trunks. See page 33 for how odd trees that have been pruned look.

SHRUBS AND FLOWERS

The 'gardening' of the layout plays a crucial role in the visual appearance of the model. Therefore it is well worth spending time taking care with the landscape.

The planting of back yard or garden detail either in tubs or around lawns forms an important detail that not only provides colour but also creates the feeling that the buildings are occupied. Planting flowers and shrubs to look convincing is a surprisingly time-consuming business as a garden can contain numerous plants, all of which have to be modelled somehow.

A lot of time can be saved by using small natural foliage, i.e. grass seed heads dried out and re-coloured look very convincing mixed with yarrow; both grow wild and are easily obtainable. Flowering shrubs can be made by using lichen dipped in clear varnish, first being sprinkled with a small amount of pre-coloured coarse granules to the colour of the flowers, then with green foliage-coloured finer cork granules. By applying the flower colour first, control over the amount of flowers can be obtained. If you reverse this process all the green sticks in place and the flowers fall off! Reeds and other long plants with heads on can be made from single strands of wire, the wire being stripped of its plastic coating apart from a small piece at the top. The reed is painted and the top colour changed to show slightly differently so as to represent the bloom.

Alternatively, using pre-coloured wire a thin layer of glue can be applied along one side of the wire at the top and sprinkled with a flower coloured texture. This technique produces gladioli-type plants which bloom on one side only. Glue all around the wire obviously produces other plants. For plants with larger heads ground-up foam, coloured, to suit can be used by simply gluing in place on a length of wire, other leaves being made from pre-coloured paper cut to shape. The detailing of plants can continue until the complete flower is built up of individual leaves, the sunflower being the biggest and most popular example. The petals are applied around a disc of paper and the leaves applied one at a time along its stalk. An easier way is to go to a dried flower specialist and purchase a selection of dried flowers, and paint them to suit.

For super-detailing of gardens etched plantation is available, or one can make one's own. This involves drawing up the plant's leaves and flowers on a thin copper or brass sheet. The best material is shim brass sheet, which is an extremely thin. The back of the brass sheet will require to be completely painted with acid resistant. The front of the sheet is painted with acid resistant to represent the leaves and flower detail.

All the painted components will have to be linked together so that they sit on a spider's web which holds them in place. (Like the 'sprue' in plastic kit.) The sheet is then immersed in acid, *(available from DIY radio shops for circuit making. Warning: always take great care when using acid.)* and when the acid has etched through the sheet, the sheet is removed and then washed in running water. The resist is also washed off with a solvent. The method is simple, but hazardous, so I recommend that a specialist carry out the etching.

Natural dyed dried foliage, planted in predrilled holes. Vary the colours slightly within a group, and they will look more natural.

Tubing glued to bits of wire to form reeds. Mix with coloured slivers of paper and brush hairs from an inexpensive wall papering brush. Paint after fixing in place.

Paper glued to bits of wire make good flowers, alternately use small real flowers dipped in flower coloured texture. Note: flowers are easier to make at '00' scale than at 'N' scale.

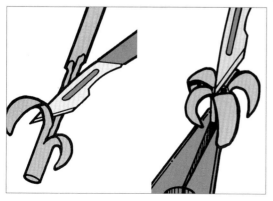

By cutting matchsticks and then reworking the middle long leaved plants and flowers can be made at '00' and larger scales.

I prefer to use lichen, dipped in white glue and sprinkled with flower and leaf coloured texture material, for smaller scales.

PALM TREES

Palm trees are one of the simplest types of tree to make requiring paper, wire, glue, drinking straws and scissors. A real whilst watching TV job! The technique is to pre-coat a sheet of writing paper with UHU® glue, spreading the glue with a piece of plastic to form an even thin coat over its surface. Then you pre-cut lengths of wire and insert them into the tube of glue's nozzle so as to coat their surfaces. This glue-covered wire is then laid down on the paper's surface so that it sticks to the paper, leaving a gap between each length of wire. A second freshly coated piece of paper is now glued in place over the first sheet of paper, trapping the wire in between the two sheets of paper. The leaves are now ready for cutting out with a pair of scissors in a typical palm leaf shape.

Having completed this the leaves are cut across to form the individual leaves typical of a palm, the wire in the middle preventing an accidental cut, from cutting the leaf in half. Keep the cuts close together; the best technique for this I have found is to hold the scissors steady and pass the leaf through the scissors as one opens and closes the scissors, rather than moving the scissors along the leaf. This way you can estimate the amount of cut rather than looking to see how much has been cut.

On completing the leaves they are bent to shape, the wire holding them in position. The stalk of each leaf is inserted into a paper drinking straw with a blob of glue to secure it. The easy way is to force some glue down the drinking straw and push a number of leaf stalks down it (approximately nine to twelve) so as to form the top of the tree.

The trunk of the tree is now covered with further drinking straws, cut along their length so as to open them out. Then cut across completely at an angle, these separate pieces of drinking straw being glued to the trunk of the tree starting from the top and working down, overlapping each one so as to lose the gap formed by cutting the straw in half along its length. This is continued down until the trunk is completed leaving a short length at the bottom for planting into the base.

 A second method for making small palm trees is by using feathers. The feathers are cut to shape and glued into position with car body filler or

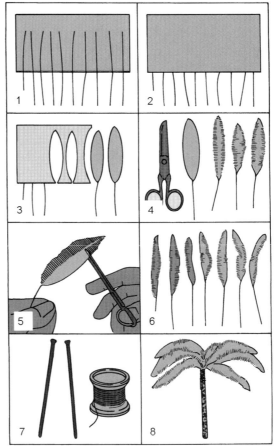

From Top Left:
1: Cut out an oblong sheet of paper and pre-glue by applying a thin layer of UHU® glue with a spreader, and glue wire in place, by inserting into the glue tube's nozzle and fixing in place.
2: place a second sheet on top and fixed in place with UHU® glue.
3: Cut out palm leaf shapes.
4: Using scissors cut the individual leaves to shape.
5: The wire in the middle should prevent the leaf from being cut in half.
6: Make 9 to 12 leaves per tree.
7: Bind the leaves to 2 inch nails or push into suitable tube.
8: Paint leaves and trunk a suitable colour.

Finally drill holes in the baseboard and insert the trees.

Alternatively chicken feathers can be used, cut to shape and glued to the top of a nail with car-body filler.

epoxy resin on top of a large nail, the resin being a thick or stiff glue holds the feathers in place without dropping. Alternatively the feathers can be bound to the nail and the trunk covered with paste to disguise the binding. Finally, metal etched leaves can be used, soldered in place on a length of wire, sleeving being used to thicken up the trunk and painted a suitable colour.

Left: Palm trees growing in people's back gardens are reasonably common in the south of England, because the climate is milder. Back gardens need to have that abused look, whereby only a few actually have a pristine rear garden; most could do with a bit of gardening and a good tidying up. It is also the place to hang the washing out to dry.

Working at '00' scale, the garden can be 'modelled' in greater detail, at 'N' this becomes more difficult, because everything is that much smaller, so go for effect rather than detail.

5. BUILDINGS

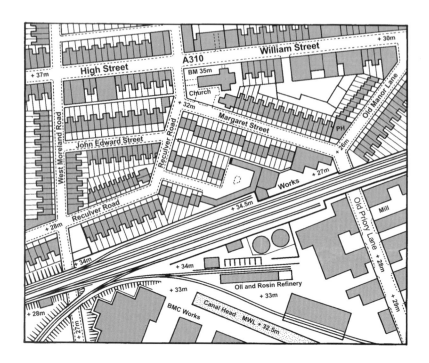

Above: The map shows the roads, buildings and spot heights. The bench mark (+35m) by the church will be carved into the building above ground level.

Below: This shows a typical rear view of a row of terraced houses, which back onto the railway. The various different extensions built onto the backs of the houses could well have been added at a later date.

PLANNING A TOWN BASEBOARD

When a study is made of a town or city map, it will show a random arrangement of roads and buildings. Time has produced this, due to the changing situation of its history over hundreds of years. The original buildings in many cases no longer exist, but the roads or footpaths remain, and in many cases the actual name. For example, 'Moorland Road' could well be found now in the middle of the town, but once it led directly to the moors. By studying the true to scale map shown it can be seen that it contains approximately 200 houses, a selection of shops, offices, factory sites and a railway. Whilst quite a lot of modelling potential, unfortunately for us the size of a moderate town built at 00 scale would be enormous, even at N scale it would still be very big. Just to build the area of the map shown at N scale layout would require a baseboard 6ft by 5ft in size. The railway's layout would also be impractical for our use.

By reducing the town and making the railway curves smaller than in real life, an acceptable part of it can be modelled, the number of houses reduced and the eye can also be deceived allowing the mind to be fooled into thinking things happen that in fact do not. For instance, part of a large station can be built, the roof used to cover a track return loop, designed so that it emerges at a lower level to rejoin the main line which apparently goes into the large station. This redesigned town baseboard now forms a return loop for practical use of the track. The arrangement of the roads and buildings should also be aligned with the baseboard edge so as to avoid as much as possible cutting off buildings in half, yet the roads and buildings should portray the feeling of 'being there first', i.e. before the railway rather than as a backdrop for it.

The redesigning of a township is very much a compromise. Although track radii are variable, as are the widths of roads, paving, and house sizes, etc, there are minimum sizes that cannot be reduced whilst still appearing to look convincing.

Buildings require certain head room inside; also the floor area that they occupy cannot be reduced beyond a certain size. This also applies to roads and footpaths. Towns occupy a lot of space. For instance, 67 houses in a row, each house 15ft wide, equals 1,005 scale feet. Built at N scale (2mm to 1ft) this is about 2m (6ft) in length at model size, yet only portrays reality of less than one fifth of a mile—the length of 14 carriages and one locomotive.

UNDERSTANDING DRAWINGS

When plans of buildings are first encountered, it is like looking at a new and foreign language, and these plans or drawings can be extremely difficult to interpret especially if the design is complex. Fortunately outline architectural drawings are basically easy to read, except when dealing with the finer points such as damp courses etc, and in model form this can be ignored. The information on the basic outline is all that is needed, and this can be obtained in the form of floor plans, sections and elevations.

The floor plans will clearly show the layout of the internal walls and the positions of doors and windows (see illustration). By placing the drawings on top of each other and in the order of the ground floor, the first floor, etc, finally the roof, the planning arrangement can be quickly followed through and understood. By looking at each plan in turn, down through the building, a mental picture of the walls can be formed. Then, by looking at the sections the floor to ceiling heights can be established, together with the thickness of the floor slabs. Finally, one looks at the outside elevations so as to establish the positions of the doors and windows, their heights and sizes, etc, and even the style of glazing.

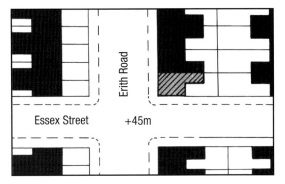

Left, The Street Plan: This shows the outline of the buildings, the pavements, the roads and names plus spot heights.

Below, The Ground Floor Plan: and the front and rear elevations. The elevations are what you see from the road.

Photo: Alms house.

Ground Floor Plan

Right, the First Floor Plan: shows the layout of the internal rooms and the position of the staircase leading from the ground floor, to the first floor. There is no room at the back of the house at 1st floor level and the staircase uses part of the roof space that is fitted with a roof light.

The Roof Plan: shows the tiles and the roof light.

The Section: shows a cut-a-way through the building.

The End Elevation: shows what is seen from the side street.

Below, The Isometric: shows a bird's eye view of the building, and the next door house. The view is from the back and shows how the roof works. It is a typical London roof house, whereby the water gully ran across the house, and the front elevation is higher.

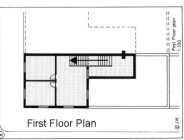

First Floor Plan

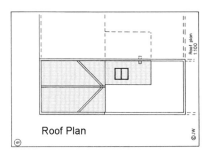

Roof Plan

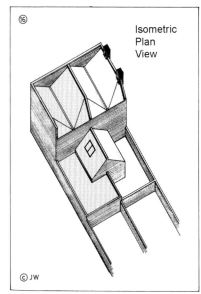

Isometric Plan View

© JW

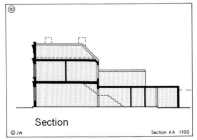

Section

Section AA 1:100

North Elevation   Side Elevation

© J.Wylie Lecturing Service   Scale 1:100

Below: This plan shows handed houses in which the houses are mirror imaged, throughout the length of the building. The advantage with this type of design is the fact that the water, gas, electricity, sewage and chimneys shared the installation costs, making the building cheaper to build.

This type of design also allowed a greater amount of light into the rear of the dwelling.

Below Right: The plan shows a house with the street door to the left of the building, as it is approached. The rooms on the inside are to the right, and so are the chimneys. Each house is identical to its neighbour. Whilst the roof can change, the inside remains the same.

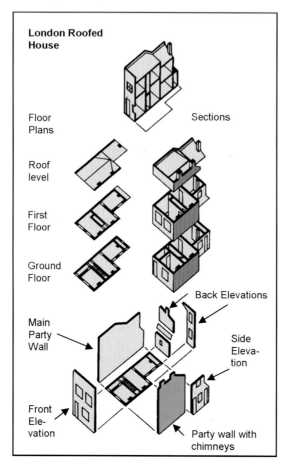

London Roofed House

Floor Plans — Sections

Roof level

First Floor

Ground Floor

Main Party Wall — Back Elevations — Side Elevation

Front Elevation — Party wall with chimneys

The buildings illustrated can be found in many countries and are typical of the terraced design of house. The buildings share a repetitive front, rear and floor design, and the walls each side are shared with the adjoining building. Some of the houses are 'handed' so each alternative house is a mirror image, to form left- and right-handed houses. (See roof plans & elevations below).

By 'exploding' the house as shown in the illustration, it can be seen that the elevations comprise: main building front elevation; main building first party wall and extension; back extension elevation; side extension elevation; main building back elevation; and main building second smaller party wall. In practice, when sections through a building are shown on a drawing, they generally cut through it in a straight line at any point across or along the length of the building, but sometimes a staggered section is shown which can be very confusing.

The illustration below: Shows the handed house 'London Roof House' that has the street doors adjacent to each other, so that the houses are alternatively handed left and right, the length of the building. The rear elevation is also handed.

The illustrations below right: show the arrangement of a 'Right Handed House' whereby the rooms are to the right of the street door as you go into the building.

Note the way the chimneys are arranged, on

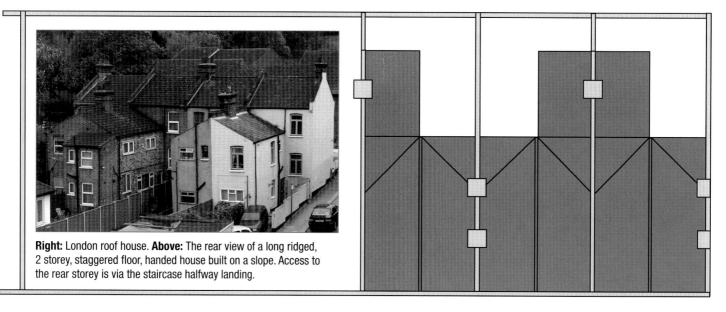

Right: London roof house. **Above:** The rear view of a long ridged, 2 storey, staggered floor, handed house built on a slope. Access to the rear storey is via the staircase halfway landing.

a right handed house, the rooms are to the right of the street door, therefore the chimney is on the right hand party wall, because the passage way runs through the building on the left!

With the handed houses the chimneys are joined together, so that eight chimney pots indicate four rooms in each of the main parts of the building, and commonly referred to as 'two up two down'. Most buildings these days have a rear extension of some form, of either one or two floors (ground and first floor.)

The style of the building will also vary; northern architecture is different from the architecture in the south of England. The internal layout is often the same, but the difference lies within the outside treatment of the building. Architecture is local material dependant, therefore where clay abounds brick buildings are common, as where stone is freely available, the area is saturated with buildings built from stone.

Stone is a very sought after material, so you find that old castles and churches were looted for their stones, and these stones have found their way into other buildings; built at a later date. By good fortune due to the extremely robust nature of stone, and being big and heavy a lot of stone buildings remain, which can be interesting to model and can add a lot of interest to the layout. Houses run by the church for the poor of the parish are generally a good source of interesting

architecture and depending on locality could be build of brick or stone.

But the most common type of dwelling is the house that was designed to house the worker near to their job. The mill towns are typical of basic living accommodation, whereby as many houses as possible were crammed into a small space, because land cost money, and more often than not it was the employer that was paying for the houses. The tenants then became what is known as tied workers, whereby they could not leave their job because they would lose the house.

Below, the long ridge house: (Above the road) This has the peak of the roof running the full length of the building.

The London roofed house: (Below the road) This has the roof's drainage valley running across the building. Both houses use similar floor plans.

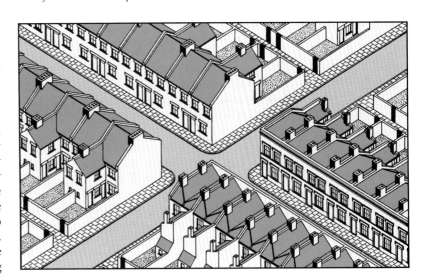

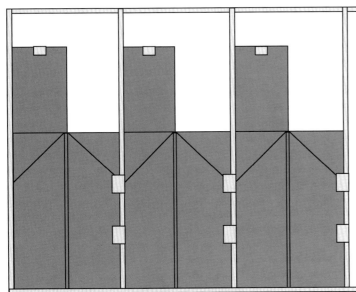

Left: London roof house. **Above:** The rear view of a long ridged, two-storey, staggered floor, non-handed house built on flat ground. Access to the rear storey is via the staircase halfway landing.

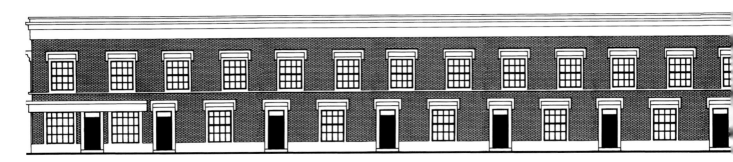

STYLE OF BUILDINGS

The style used in modelling buildings must be consistent. This is very important in order to retain visual harmony throughout the layout. Other points to consider are: The available room on the baseboard; the total number of buildings; the style of the buildings, because as each country has its own form of architecture. The number of repetitive buildings must be considered as this influences the method of model construction, and finally, the number of self-contained or separate buildings.

The next stage to consider is the overall size of each building (i.e. a small cottage or a large factory building); the availability of information to allow a reasonable representation of the building to be made; the availability of suitable materials commercially produced; and finally the modelling style, as the scale of the building influences the amount of detail that it is practical to model.

So as to provide an indication of model size, the illustrations shown are produced to three popular modelling scales.

The top left is at 00 scale (4mm to 1ft). HO scale (3.5mm to 1ft). N scale (2mm to 1ft). The bottom right drawing showing the back, front and section measure: (2mm to 1ft) frontage 13ft 6in, depth 34ft 9in and parapet height 23ft 3in and details a typical London roof terraced house. Six houses of this type total almost the same length as the 'Flying Scotsman' locomotive and tender. Thus it can be calculated quickly that a baseboard of 1,950 mm (6ft 3 in) in length at 00 scale can only contain 36 terraced houses along its length, but at N scale (2mm to 1ft) 72 houses. This is not many when one considers the normal number of houses in a street or road.

The illustration below shows at N scale a typical London roofed house, whilst the photographs show a long ridged roof, and the pitch runs towards the road and to the back of the building. This type of roof is found throughout the UK in many forms, and can be tiled as well as slated. The London roof is shown tiled and the long ridge houses are shown slated.

Above: This shows identical elevations drawn at the three popular modelling scales, 00 @ 4 mm to 1 foot, HO @ 3.5 mm to 1 foot and N @ 2mm to 1 foot. 00 and HO run on the same track gauge, which leads people to think the scales are the same, they are not.

Right: This photograph shows a view of the back of left handed houses.

Bottom: This shows the front and back elevations of a left handed house, plus a section through the house including the rear side elevation.

A plan of this type of house can be found on page 85, including an aerial view.

The internal layout is a traditional design and provides four rooms and a rear two-roomed extension. When the house was first built the WC was outside.

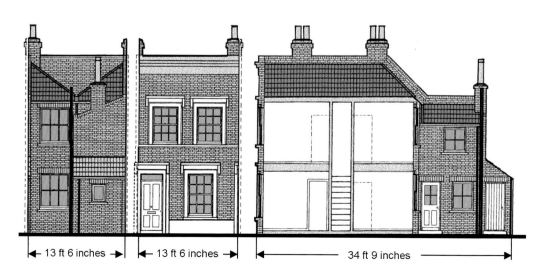

|← 13 ft 6 inches →| |← 13 ft 6 inches →| |← 34 ft 9 inches →|

PAUL JOHN CHARTERED SURVEYORS   018177 44687

25ft @ 4 mm to 1 foot

Above: This is part of a set of survey drawings I prepared years ago and has been re-drawn to the scale of 4mm to 1ft (00 scale). At the bottom of the page is a photograph taken as part of the survey. The six-roomed houses shown were very luxurious for their time, and were complete with a front and rear garden.

The middle two photographs show typical long ridge handed houses, (Plans shown on page 86) and are also 2 up, 2 down and 2 at the back houses. These look far less grand than the houses shown on the drawings, and were similar in size. The houses also lack a front garden, so that the social status of the dwellings were lower than the ones with the front garden. The final photo shows a modern version of the same design.

EXPLORING ARCHITECTURE

Modelling railways provides a great excuse to explore architecture within the landscape. This is because without the landscape you would have no place in which to place the architecture. If you look around us, most of us have little idea of what small but interesting buildings are tucked away within a 10 mile radius of our own homes.

Architecture comes in many forms, be it a bridge, a home, a place of work or a place of interest; we are surrounded by it. Architecture and landscape go hand in hand, and a journey on the railway carries its passengers through it, therefore the landscape generates the environment in which the railway is located. Buildings are associated with a place to live or to work in, engineering is associated with bridges, roads etc. The viaduct sits onto the landscape, with its embankments lost under a covering of trees and shrubs, whilst the buildings nestle into a valley, and the street corner providing a turning point from one view into another.

The architecture of this country has a style that can only be classified as 'British' and it varies between the 'North' and the 'South', with the architecture in the north being more rugged through the use of natural stone, whilst in the south it is clay based brick. This in turn varies with the type of clay, so that we have red or yellow bricks.

The buildings at the start of the chapter show typical 'London' architecture, whilst on this page the viaduct is in Kent, and the valley and house is located on the Yorkshire/Lancashire borders.

I now use the internet rather than books for research, because it is easier to locate buildings of interest, i.e. maps are available that also link up with aerial photographs, that cover the British Isles, so you can find a building and then find out where it is on the map!

Whilst buildings can be located this way you will still need a site visit, which is best undertaken during the winter months when there is no foliage on the trees.

Opposite top: The brick built viaduct is a common architectural feature of all railways.

Opposite middle: The bird's eye view of a small group of houses tucked away in a deep valley in Lancashire.

Opposite bottom: This small house formed part of an estate built by a company to house its workers.

Left: The yellow brick, the deep red and the varnished woodwork work in harmony and give the building character, only spoilt by the lump of concrete that forms part of the Thames flood defences.

Below: A dwelling that time forgot perched on the top of a hill. It is a good example of a stone built house in the style of the cart shed and grain store found on pages 94 and 105.

The problem with all oval layouts is what to do with the centre part of the model. To overcome this on the multilevel oval layout the design uses the terraced houses, the road and the stream as the central feature of the model's landscape. The top of the hill at the main road is above the track level, at the goods depot the road and track are at the same level and the road is below track level at the railway bridge. This represents a 60 foot change in road's ground level from one end of the layout to the other end.

The amount of detail that can be shown is relative to model size, the smaller the model the more difficult it is to make. The photographs show on page 92 'N' scale buildings and on page 93 '00' scale buildings. The choice of scale is difficult and relates to available space and how you want to run the layout. Below: For the modeller who prefers to purchase ready made buildings the Scenecraft® range by Bachmann® is ideal.

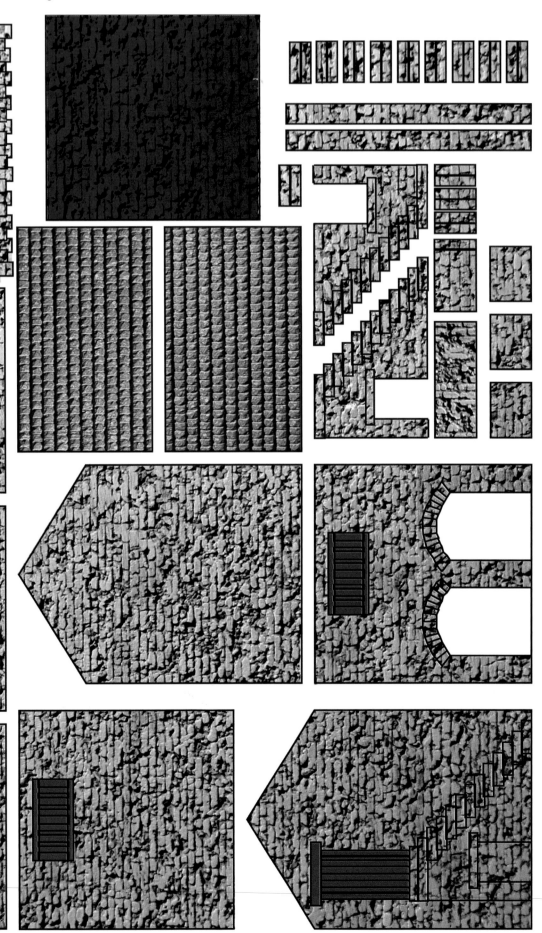

SIMPLE BUILDINGS

The easiest and quickest building kits I found to construct were the Graham Farish N gauge range, (shown in the above photos.) which the only tool needed was a pair of scissors. These are no longer available but can be easily simulated using card house shaped cores covered with homemade computer generated self-adhesive elevations. (See pages 110, 111, 114 and 115.)

The next range is Super-Quick 00/HO scale card buildings which are built up using the hollow construction method. This is far more time consuming as the 00/HO scale cardboard buildings are printed on medium thickness card, so that they have to be cut out if they have not already been pre-cut. As always, the kit's instructions should be thoroughly studied before starting construction.

A most important point is: Do not remove any components from the pre-cut sheets until required because pieces that look like scrap are often used as bracing and corner strengtheners. After reading the instructions detach each component as required using a very sharp knife and trim as required. *(Swan Morton® produce excellent scalpel knife handles which have replaceable blades suitable for modelling)* Cut along a steel rule so as to keep the line straight, and always cut out on a scrap piece of card placed on top of a piece of hardboard, so as to protect the knife blade's tip and the table's surface. Assemble the building on a flat piece of chip or block board, which should be sufficiently large to also allow the use of metal engineer's squares, so the walls of the building can be held upright whilst the glue dries. (Alternatively, use cardboard squares).

Start construction with the largest wall and corner first. Pre-glaze the windows during construction and do not forget to touch-in the bare cut edge of the cardboard around the windows etc., with a colouring crayon of a suitable colour. Ideally purchase the water-soluble type which is like a colouring pencil but turn into water colours with the aid of a wet paintbrush.

The window glazing only needs to be lightly tacked in place, which will prevent excess glue smearing the window glazing. This also applies to the main corner joins, as I have found that to use a lot of glue on a corner makes a messy join. I now prefer to tack join the corners and brace them using a small square strip of balsa wood to form a fillet which strengthens the corners. After the glue on the first corner has dried continue construction by adding the other walls. If the walls are long and without further support (i.e., kerb or base) it is best to fix further balsa strips to form internal bracing along the inside of the building, continuing the construction in this way until the model is completed.

The choice of glues for construction is important, my own preference being a mixture of white PVA woodworker's glue and clear Universal® UHU. PVA glue is easy to remove with a damp cloth should it accidentally come in contact with the printed elevation and is ideal for applying the balsa strengtheners. UHU® is used very sparingly for general construction and window glazing, also for laminating card together when the use of PVA (which is water-based) would warp the card.

Above: Graham Farish buildings were very easy to make and look very realistic. The photograph shows the single track level oval base during and after construction. The main visual difference clearly seen is the fact that the image on the left has trains, cars and people.

Below: One of the many traditional cardboard kits available on the market. The photograph shows just the front part of the kit, prior to the windows being added. All glazing should be fixed in place prior to fixing the elevations together.

Opposite page: Photocopy this simple card building and make. See p115.

ADDING DEPTH & DETAIL TO ELEVATIONS

The landscape and buildings are an integral part of railway modelling. No layout would be complete without its setting. Therefore it is a love hate relationship between some modellers, some love making the landscape others hate it.

By good fortune I enjoy making the buildings and the landscape, because it brings the model alive.

The building above is a mixture: Graham Farish® buildings totally changed to make a new building by fixing the self-sticky elevations onto card (7 identical tops) and then using 2 Post Office fronts plus 5 other shop fronts, fitted with different names, cut from magazines, and junk mail.

These days it would be easier to go out and photograph the shop fronts, manipulate the print to fit the elevation, and print on good quality matt paper. This opens up the possibilities of making scratch built basic cardboard buildings that much easier and less expensive, for making repetitive buildings.

The thin card on which cardboard kits are printed is much too thin at 00/HO scale to represent the thickness of the walls, and much the same applies to the N gauge range of buildings. By carefully selecting additional cardboard backing, these elevations can easily be made thicker and truer to scale.

The earlier Graham Farish range of N gauge buildings are among the easiest to upgrade, using homemade elevations produced on a computer. To add depth to the elevation, the modeller simply applies the new self-adhesive elevations to a sheet of suitable thickness cardboard. The technique is first to cut out the windows and doors, leaving in place the backing that protects the adhesive. These doors and windows are now placed to one side, then the protective backing to the elevation is removed and the cut-out elevation is stuck on to a sheet of card, being careful to avoid wrinkles. This now forms a thicker laminate. Carefully apply double-sided sticky tape to the back of the card, again taking care to avoid wrinkles. You now have a thicker elevation with an adhesive on its back.

Cut out the window and door openings again so as to remove unwanted card and paint the exposed card edges to suit. On completion, stick the elevation in place on its plastic blocks by removing the backing to the double-sided sticky tape. This gives you an elevation with a recess around its windows and doors. Remove the protective backing from the previously cut-out windows and doors and replace them in position in the deeper door and window openings.

Repeat this around the building as required, disguising the cardboard's edge by using spare brickwork saved by using sticky labels to fix the blocks together on adjacent walls of buildings that join next to each other, or paint to match. Do the same to the roofs and paint the edge as required. Finally, paint thin strips of card pre-backed with double-sided sticky tape for the protruding window sills and place them in position. This all produces a building with depth to its elevation.

Normally the cardboard kits produced have their detail printed flat on their surfaces so that window sills are non-existent in three-dimensional form. This unfortunately looks wrong when viewed from any angle other than square-on as there is no recess around the window or a protrusion from the window sill.

Other manufacturers' kits can be modified as described but are more complicated to undertake as they are produced as hollow models. The technique for these is to use thick card or balsa wood to back the thin cardboard elevations. This must be done very carefully, so as to avoid complications in the later part of the building's construction, unless one is good at mitring corners. (Mitred corners are produced by cutting a 45 degree angle cut along the two corners to be joined together.) Once perfected this method can actually speed up construction but the beginner is recommended to keep to straight square cuts using a metal ruler or metal engineer's square, and cutting the backing card less its thickness at certain points (see illustration), so that it does not interfere with the construction of the kit.

Start by pre-coating an elevation on its back with glue, UHU® is ideal as it can be spread out thinly across a surface. Then, by pre-coating the second cardboard/balsa wood surface, the two surfaces can be joined as if one were using an impact adhesive. Since the bond of the join is made on contact, great care must be taken to correctly align the surfaces before pressing them together; because you cannot rely on sliding the pieces into final position.

Note, do not use water-based glues such as PVA for laminating or it will warp or twist the cardboard.

Having completed the first layer of the elevation, cut out the door and window recesses as required. If the model is a Tudor type of building, cut out additional overlays of thin card and apply these over the timber areas so as to raise these from the main surface (as would happen in reality). Alternatively, purchase two identical kits, cutting one up to provide these timbered overlays. Cover the back of the second kit with double-sided sticky tape and after removing its backing, place in position over the original kit's timber framing. Alternatively, to avoid having to buy a second kit, carefully cut out a piece of card to the size of the elevation then copy the timber framing, using tracing paper and redrawing by using carbon paper to transfer the lines on to the card. Glue down using double-sided sticky tape. If this method is used the entire back of the card should be covered.

The use of double-sided sticky tape has an advantage over the conventional types of glues in this particular situation: because with a lot of small joins on one piece it is difficult to apply the glue in such a way that it has not dried at one end whilst you are is still applying the glue at the other end. An alternative to double-sided sticky tape is to place the cut-out elevation face down and spray it with display mount so the back receives an even coat of adhesive in one application. Then, when the overlays to the elevation are completed, colour around the window and door recesses with the appropriate coloured paint.

During construction always glaze the windows before assembling the elevation, because you will find that they cannot be conveniently reached when the building is completed. Curtains can be made by using coloured photographs from magazines cup up and folded to suit (see illustration). Repeat as required, by working around the building and assembling each elevation as required. Remember

to cut the backing card to suit for width and length as necessary, so that the kit's true elevation size is not distorted. Brace the building internally as necessary to strengthen it and also fix a baffle or floors in the middle of the building; otherwise you will be able to see through the building. Finally add the roof and chimneys as per the kit instructions to complete the building, and weather repetitive buildings so that they do not look identical.

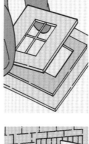

Left: Early Graham Farish building elevation, with the windows cut out. The elevation was fixed to thicker card, using double-sided tape. Re-cut the elevation out using a sharp knife. Paint exposed edges wall colour as required. Leave the windows as a single layer and fit back into windows. Apply other detail to suit.

The card kit building had the window openings thickened by gluing the printed card onto thicker card and cutting through both the layers.

Floors and internal walls were added to stop being able to see through the building. If the model is at the front of the layout paint the rooms different colours and dry brush the back of the clear glazing so that it looks like net curtains. Fit colour coordinated curtains with some partly closed, to add interest. Place a figure on the inside of the building by the window or in an open door in some houses, to add interest. Build up the thickness of the elevation using home made overlays, printed out using a computer. Alternatively, find suitable details from books and magazines.

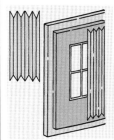
Mark around the elevation and the windows with a fine pointed pencil.

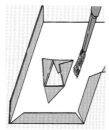
Apply brick printed paper to the card elevation and wrap edges, or alternatively paint edges.

Mark out the clear acetate windows using thin self sticky strips, and fix in place.

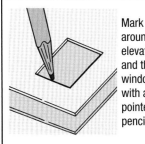
Fit curtains top and bottom from behind the glazing. Fold as shown.

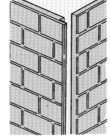
Take care to overlap brick paper on the edges to minimise the join. Use a good sharp knife for cutting corners.

Add brick lintel and windowsill to each window. Apply weathering using water colour pencils and dampen.

Right: The Wills signal box is a typical high quality plastic kit which has all its components pre-moulded to shape and all the modeller has to do is to assemble the pieces. *(This kit with some added internal detail makes into a magnificent model.)*

By assembling the components using liquid glue, the pieces can be fitted into place and the solvent applied with a brush.

I prefer to assemble the building (glazing added later) before painting, and then to paint the various components. The reason for this is when you paint the components on the sprue, and then try to assemble the bits, the bits need scraping along the join line, otherwise they don't stick.

Alternatively the adhesive spoils the painted surface.

The Wills Craftsman series shown on the opposite page requires the modeller to undertake more of the cutting and shaping of the components that make up the building. This really is the beginnings of scratch building rather than assembling a plastic kit. Unlike a conventional plastic kit, it leads to easier alterations or conversions to make another building, similar to the one shown in the kit.

This is very advantageous because it is easy to build a row of houses using the external detailed elevations and plain plastic sheet for all the internal walls.

Note: Internal walls and floors stop the viewer from seeing through the building, which looks unnatural. The internal walls etc, do not need painting black.

BUILDING PLASTIC KITS

The assembly of plastic kits is very much like that of the cardboard kits, in the sense that everything is pre-made, and in many cases pre-coloured, and contains a set of instructions that should be followed. The real difference is the method of construction and finishing, because the plastic will accept various types of paint on its surface. The surfaces of plastic kits also contain raised or applied moulded detail, which can be picked out during painting, so in this sense the plastic kit is very different to the cardboard variety, as the cardboard kit has its detail printed on its flat surface.

Plastic kits are manufactured by the injection-moulding technique, which uses a sprue to feed the molten plastic first into the mould and then into the components that make up the kit. These components are numbered, generally in order of assembly, so they should not be cut off the sprue until required.

The approach to building plastic kits varies, as some modellers prefer to make up the entire kit and spray it with a primer, then repaint all the detail by hand. Other modellers prefer to part assemble the bulk of the kit and paint it, painting the remaining parts whilst they are still on the sprue, and then continuing with the assembly of the kit. The latter method is suitable for difficult small pieces with fine detail, but the down side is the paint has to be removed in places to make the component stick.

There are various glues and solvents available on the market. Tube glues are the most difficult to use, although they form a sounder join than do the liquid solvent types which only weld the plastic together where the two surfaces touch (i.e., they do not have any gap filling qualities). Whilst a solvent

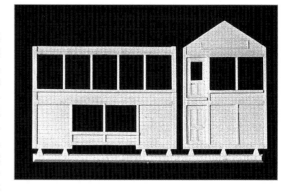

is quicker and cleaner to use, it requires a good fitting join to work efficiently. To overcome this problem the building can be glued together using solvents and then the hidden joins (e.g., corners inside the building) strengthened with glue from a tube which has gap-filling qualities.

The technique of building plastic kits is to carefully cut from the sprue each component as required. Clean by filing and scraping each component, so as to remove the 'flash' that is sometimes formed by the mould join and to reshape edges or round mouldings, etc. Use a very sharp knife for this in a scraping action, so that the join of the moulding line is cleaned off. Round objects generally are the worst offenders, sometimes being moulded slightly out of alignment and needing to be re-shaped.

Begin assembly of a kit by first cutting the base and then adding the first two adjoining walls, gluing all three together in one go. This ensures that the two walls are upright. Next cut the remaining walls and assemble, so they form a basic box, adding detail to the elevations as supplied. The roof can be joined in the middle along the roof ridge line and allowed to dry, then removed for painting separately if required. The same applies with other components still left on the sprue.

The solvent or glue will attack all surfaces it comes into contact with, so care must be taken not to place fingers over a join whilst applying glue or solvent as fingers tend to smudge glue and attract solvent through capillary action, causing damage to the plastic's surface. This is particularly important when you are going to leave the kit in its natural plastic finish.

Plastic kits readily render themselves to converting or extending by adding, for example, two or three kits together. Engine sheds are a particularly good example as many manufacturers design their kits with this in mind. When several kits are joined together the pieces that are left over (e.g., spare walls and windows) make ideal starters for the construction of part kit, part scratch-built buildings; because pre-moulded sheets of brickwork, windows and doors are available, the bits left over can be readily used in the making of a different building based upon the spare components but adapted to suit a particular situation.

The Wills house kits are a typical example of a kit that needs the modeller to build, rather than assemble because the windows and the walls need to be cut to shape. In some ways they are like scratch building because you work from a plan and elevations, and you cut the components out as you need them. These kits are really for the advanced modeller.

The two house kits shown are produced by Wills and are really the start of advanced modelling, because of the amount of work the individual has to do. The signal box is a typical plastic kit that you simply assemble and paint, which is ideal for the inexperienced modeller to make.

Any model building I feel needs some form of texture to make it look a little bit more realistic. Wills® for example produce an excellent range of moulded building accessories, suitable for the scratch modeller. *(The term 'Scratch Modelling' refers to making something from the very beginning. Hence to start from scratch!)* The easiest starting point for the beginner is to repaint a building using a texture over the existing walls of a plastic kit.

For example the top half of the building could have a texture and the lower half remain as a brick finish, or a end wall could have a cement rendering, to make it waterproof. Experiment with the various methods of obtaining finishes.

SPECIAL WALLS AND ROOFS

Special walls can be made in a number of ways by using water based fire clay cement, 'Das' modelling clay, Plaster of Paris or Polyfilla®, to name a few, (available in premixed tubs). These materials are ideal for spreading on wood or card surfaces, but not plastic because it falls off when dry. This fact can be used to an advantage, i.e. spread fire clay or a thin layer of plaster onto a thin sheet of plastic. Allow it to harden to a semi-solid state, and then scribe through the thickness into predetermined sizes. When it is completely set, remove by cracking off from the plastic. Depending upon their size, these chips can then be used for bricks, rough stone walls or paving slabs.

The Plaster of Paris left over when mixing up can also be broken up into small pieces as it sets, providing small rocks which can be sieved out to a selected size. Later these are embedded into a thin layer of newly cast Plaster of Paris, sprinkling the chosen material through a sieve, to spread it out evenly, and then pressing it down into the plaster, before allowing it to harden.

Peel the casting off the plastic sheet and examine it; if the texture is too coarse, make up a runny mixture of Polyfilla® and brush in to obtain the desired effect, and then allow the mixture to set. Mark out, and then cut to shape using a saw. For the window openings drill through as required, file and sand to shape, then repeat for other walls.

Note: All examples produced by Wills®.

Left: Typical flat roof tile, used on modern houses, normally cast in coloured concrete.

Right: The traditional wire cut clay tile that normally has a slightly rounded edge shape.

Left: Typical curved 'Roman' style clay roof tile, generally used on traditional style properties.

Right: Wall hung tiles come in various patterns and styles. They even come in brick sizes and look like a brick wall!

Left: Typical wavy edged wooden cladding has been used for hundreds of years.

Right: Traditional York stone random paving slabs; modern paving uses standard sizes and are a lot smoother.

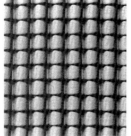

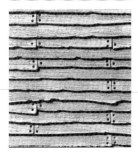

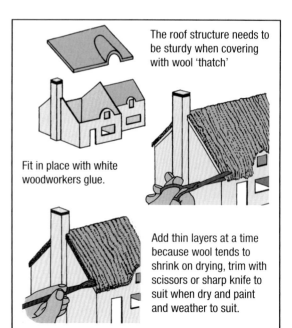

The roof structure needs to be sturdy when covering with wool 'thatch'

Fit in place with white woodworkers glue.

Add thin layers at a time because wool tends to shrink on drying, trim with scissors or sharp knife to suit when dry and paint and weather to suit.

For a garden wall, both sides of which will be seen, stick two pieces together, file and make good the top and the corner joints. The effect obtained gives the appearance of random stone walling, ideal for old cottages etc.

Stucco Walls And Pebble Dash: To make stucco and pebble dash walls, first cut the cardboard or balsa wood elevations to size, assemble the walls of the building and brace them well, then seal with an oil bound paint. When dry, sponge PVA woodworker's glue on to the elevations and sprinkle on Polyfilla®, using a sieve. Tap off unwanted material and allow to dry, and then brush off any further unwanted material and paint. This gives a pebble dash effect, which can be sanded down slightly for a stucco effect.

Tile Roof Surfaces: Since there are many roof surfaces already commercially made, in most cases it is not practical to make one's own, but in some instances there is no choice. The smaller the scale the more difficult it becomes to model specialized 'Roman' or 'Modern' clay tiles, as they are laid out very precisely and in a repetitive way. The method I have used is to make a tool the shape of the tile, and then using the 'Ploughed Field' method produce a strip of tiles, moulded in car-body filler. This was then cut into strips across the ridges, and fixed together at an angle to give the tile edge effect. This was then trimmed and mounted on a board and a rubber mould was made followed by casting the roof tiles, which were cut to size. See Chapter 6: Casting & Moulding.

Slate Roof Surfaces: To model roof slates, carefully mark out the roof both horizontally and vertically. Then emboss card or score plastic sheet vertically, making the length longer than required, and cut it across into strips. Lay these strips starting from the bottom of the roof, using the lines drawn as a guide. Lay the next row on top but half overlapped so as to stagger the tiling. Cut and trim the roof when finished or as each length of tile is laid. Use as little solvent or glue as possible to avoid warping the roof on a modern building, but don't worry too much on a period cottage as these are often heavily warped in reality, and you may wish to create this effect deliberately!

Finish the roof with a capping strip to form the ridge tiles on small-scale buildings or use individual ridge tiles on larger-scale buildings. To add a decorative ridge on small-scale buildings glue micro rod in place; on the larger scales glue the rod in place first then cover with the ridge tiles, crimping the tiles with bent flat ended tweezers.

For older roofs, to add variety the pre-scored tiles or slates can be further worked upon, by cutting the material used through and re-cutting the ends to a random length, with the odd long tile inserted or a tile missing.

Thatched Roofs: Thatched roofs are a traditional style made of straw or reeds, which give a house character. In model form wool or horse hair is suitable, but you will need a stout support for the material as a lot of glue is used. Soak lengths of wool in water and detergent to reduce their oil content then unwind the twists in the strands so that they lay straighter and blot off excess liquid in newspaper. Lay them on to the roof after precoating it with PVA glue and then sparingly drip thinned PVA glue on top of the wool so that it soaks into it. Sprinkle on flock grassing material and Polyfilla®, then brush in the direction of the lay of the roof, from top to bottom and allow to dry. Finally trim with scissors or a sharp knife to shape and texture the ends and paint in the chosen colour, new thatch usually being yellow and fading to a dull greyish tone with age. Make the thatch darker under the eaves.

Corrugated Iron Roofs: Small-scale corrugated iron roofs can be easily made from thin aluminium foil of the type that builders use, scored with a rounded scriber (see illustration elsewhere) on top of very soft card. The second method is to make a jig by gluing a series of round metal rods on to a strip of ply or chipboard, then placing the foil on top, covering it with a strip of soft card or pulp board and squashing it in a vice, the pressure shaping the foil over the rods into corrugations which can be repeated very quickly. By precutting the foil to size you avoid damaging the corrugated shape. A non-scale method is a crinklier, purchased from a craft shop, and is used in making cards.

Asphalt And Lead Roofs: Asphalt and lead roofs can be quickly made laying masking tape or sticky labels in strips. To show a rolled join glue micro strip or thin string to the roof structure first, then cover with the masking tape, pressing the tape into the ridge shape of the raised lines formed by the string. Paint to suit.

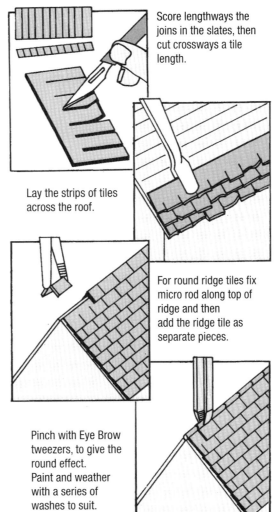

Score lengthways the joins in the slates, then cut crossways a tile length.

Lay the strips of tiles across the roof.

For round ridge tiles fix micro rod along top of ridge and then add the ridge tile as separate pieces.

Pinch with Eye Brow tweezers, to give the round effect. Paint and weather with a series of washes to suit.

Depending upon the type of roof that is modelled, and the scale as to the choice of material suitable, for '00' scale then the material needs to have a texture and show individual tile or slate joins. At 'N' scale the tile joins are finer, and more difficult to model.

For the modeller who prefers to 'Make the Environment' rather than 'Run a Layout' the larger scale has all the benefits of a nice scale to work too, whilst 'N' scale in comparison is small and fiddly.

The building being re-roofed shows that the roof trusses have been boarded over and then covered with a waterproof membrane, held in place with wood batten, on which the roof slates are fixed with either 1 or 2 nails, working from the bottom upwards. Note the rock on top of the slate caps of the chimney, to help hold it in place.

6. ADVANCED ARCHITECTURAL MODELLING

Vanishing point

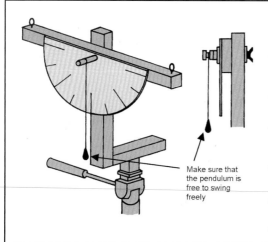

Spire set back

45 Degree Angle

Same length

Same length

Measuring Pole

Height finders height

Measured the distance from building on the ground

Height Finder
This method uses basic maths: measure a 45 degree angle, and the height equals the length.

Available in the market are various commercial laser measuring devices which makes the surveying of buildings a lot simpler.

When surveying make allowances for buildings when the measuring point is set back.

Left: This simple homemade measuring device fits onto a camera tripod. The device is set at 45 degrees and you walk away from the building. When the top of the building aligns through the sight, realign the sight with the measuring pole, and take a reading. When on flat ground the reading should be the same as the height of the measuring device above ground level.

Make sure that the pendulum is free to swing freely

SURVEYING

The recording of information on a warm sunny day is one of the delights of surveying. The equipment required need not be expensive – pen and pencil, a rubber, a tape measure, a few sheets of graph paper, a straight edge and a good eye for counting bricks will suffice, but in addition I have found useful a measuring pole. This pole I stand alongside the building when taking photographs. It is marked out in feet on one side and metres on the other and is 10ft long when unfolded, and is made from three pieces of 75mm x 24mm x 1.07m long (3in x 1in x 3ft 6in long) wood, hinged using bolts fitted with wing nuts so as to allow it to fold down and be easily carried.

Traditional Surveying Method: The traditional method of surveying (see illustration left) is by using the measuring pole and to photograph the building at an angle of 45 degrees to the eleva-tion to be measured. Then on the print draw a set of lines to find the vanishing point, followed by placing a suitable scale rule vertically and drawing a line at the point it aligns with the known height; other measured heights can be obtained directly from the photograph.

The illustration shows the 10 ft measuring pole and the lines going to the vanishing point, (the point at which the top of the building and ground lines cross) and the line from the top of the measur-ing pole meets the vanishing point. (The building scales 18ft high and the brick count confirms the pole to be 10ft high at four bricks to the foot).

Note: Railway Modelling scales by tradition are at millimetres to the foot, therefore it is easier to work in imperial measurement than convert to metric i.e. 4 bricks to the foot at 00 scale would equate to 13 bricks to 1 metre (3ft 3 in).

Height Finder: This method uses basic maths: measure a 45 degree angle, and the height equals the length.

Although the height finder (see illustration) looks difficult to make and use, it is in fact very simple and it fits onto a camera's tripod. It is fab-ricated from a length of 1 in square hardwood fitted with two screw eyes, which form the sights. In addition to this is fixed a big home-made pro-tractor used to measure the angle. Finally there is a bolt passing through the centre, on which a piece of wire is free to swing (because gravity is used to keep the sight line wire vertical so that various angles can be read off from the protrac-tor) with an eyelet at one end and a fishing weight at the other, secured with a nut and locking nut then a washer.

The bolt then passes through the 1in hardwood and protractor and a second washer is fitted. The bolt continues through the support followed by a third washer and a wing nut. This final wing nut is tightened against the support to lock the device.

By setting the height finder at 45 degrees to the wire, then moving away from the building until the sight aligns with the top of the building, you can easily measure the distance. i.e. the distance away from the building equalling the height.

If the building has a flat elevation calculating the height is easy, it is when the top sets back that it becomes complex. Church steeples set back from the tower, so measure the tower and half the distance and add this to the ground measurement.

The next stage is to find the horizontal level by taking a reading from the measuring pole and add or subtract the amount shown from the height marker on the pole of the height finder's setup level. For example, it reads 5ft 6in above ground level on the pole. If the height finder is 5ft 6in above the ground, add 5ft 6in to the distance away, and add or take away the discrepancy as necessary. Measure and draw this out on graph paper to scale then take intermediate angle readings and project these across at the indicated angles given on the height finder. These supply further heights. Re-check these dimensions and angles from a second position in the same way, averaging out any minor differences.

I find this method works extremely well for large tall buildings, when the brick-counting method cannot be used.

Brick Counting: Finally, you can use the brick-counting method either from photographs or reality. Just count the bricks but be careful of the way they have been laid, because there may be cut bricks in the courses. Ideally you will still need to measure the length of the elevation, door and window widths, then count the bricks up from the floor at 4 bricks to the foot full-size. Since the vast majority of buildings are pre metric, you will find windows and door openings revolve around brick sizes i.e. 4 bricks lengthways equals 3ft, a door size.

Modern Method: The modern method uses a digital camera to photograph the front, the sides and the back elevations (whenever possible) of the building. These photographs should be taken at 90 degrees (square on) to the face of the building, so that the perspective within the photograph is minimised. The photographs are downloaded onto the computer and using Photoshop® manipulated using the commands, Scale, Skew, Distort and Perspective until it fits into the height and length measurements predefined by earlier measuring.

Low Relief Buildings: The measuring overlay can be removed and the sized photograph printed on matt paper and fixed directly onto a sheet of cardboard. The windows and doors can be cut out, the edges painted and then fixed onto a second print, that has been fixed into card. If the second print is on glossy paper it looks like the windows are glazed and the door has a coat of glossy paint!

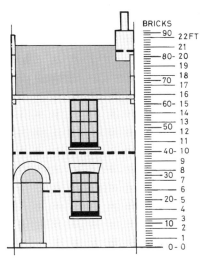

English bond brickwork.

Flemish Bond, showing a cut brick in the centre course.

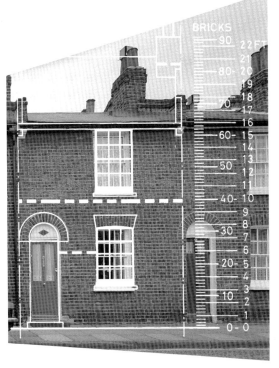

Above Left: The brick counting method has been a long and established method of surveying buildings. Whilst it is very reliable for calculating heights, it can be very unreliable for calculating lengths because some brick courses are not laid with full length bricks, i.e. half or quarter bricks are used.

Left and below: Digital photography and computers have changed surveying methods, because all that is necessary is to know the height and the width of the building, and then the photograph can be scaled to fit.

The top illustration was reversed out so that the black became white, and overlaid onto the photograph of the building. The image of the building was then manipulated to fit the drawing. When you consider that the drawing and the photograph were printed in the original book and was only recently brought together through modern technology, it shows the method works and is very accurate.

One of the nice things about scratch building is the fact you can please yourself what you model, you can look through books and magazines, go on the web and download all sorts of weird and wonderful buildings.

The sketches show a classic style country house and a modern church based on traditional design.

Both are reasonably small, therefore it makes them suitable for installing on various types of layouts.

SCRATCH-BUILDING IN CARD

Scratch-building in card is the natural extension of card kit modelling, but this time the modeller has to prepare their own detailed elevations. By copying the construction of a kit, many of the techniques as to the way the components should be designed and overlaid with colour can be learned.

The skill of card modelling lies within the ability to make things from scratch and to be able to improvise as required.

For example the stone built cart shed and granary store is a delightful little building to make, but there is only one view of the building. Therefore we must assume that the back wall is solid at ground level, and has no windows, but upstairs the window we can see on the front is probably repeated at the back, because it would allow the air to circulate through the building. The chances are it would have a wood floor, and wooden rafters, to support the roof. The tiles look like split stone, but in earlier time it may have been a thatched roof, because thatch only lasts for around 50 years, and this building could now be 300 years old.

METHODS

Cutting card requires a very sharp knife, a flat cutting board covered with a layer of card, a steel ruler and an engineer's metal square; also a draftsman propelling pencil, which uses a 0.05mm lead, to give a fine line to work to. (Don't use a biro or the ink will bleed through the paint.) Mark out and then working against the steel rule or the engineer's square, cut the card with a series of light strokes, making sure the corners are cut and re-sharpen or replace the blade when the point becomes blunt or broken.

The engineer's square should be held firmly against the bottom edge of the card, so that the cuts remain vertical, as with the steel ruler, all cuts should remain in line, so that window openings do not wander up and down along the row.

The use of floor slabs and internal walls form a core on which to fix the elevations, and this makes a row of terraced houses easier to construct. The core will also prevent the light from passing through the building.

Figure 1: Mark and cut out the elevations and note how they are aligned by deliberately marking one out upside down. Complete each elevation's detail such as glazing and curtains before fixing it to the centre core. The length of the elevation will depend upon the number of houses that are modelled and its height upon the number of floors.

Figure 2: Make the core of the building (floor slabs and walls) and a second technique is to cut out the doors and window openings, but not to glaze the windows at this stage, and to assemble the shell of the building, leaving the roof and the ground floor off for access for the time being. Paint all over by spraying or using a brush, so that the building has its finished colour, and then apply glazing and curtains.

Figure 3: Fix ground floor and top floor ceiling in place. Now cut the roofs to shape, supporting the roofs along the party walls as necessary and fixing them in place.

Figure 4: Finally cut out additional pieces of card to thicken the walls which show above the roofs. Paint or cap as necessary to form ridge tiles, etc. Finally add the chimney stacks, painted complete with rolled paper chimneys, the guttering and down pipes. The last stage is fitting the building into the landscape.

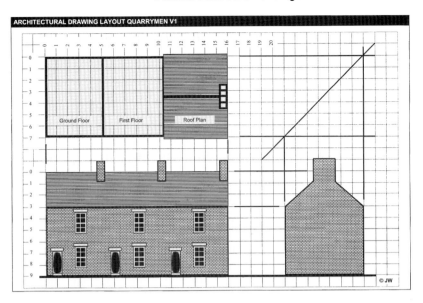
ARCHITECTURAL DRAWING LAYOUT QUARRYMEN V1

Ground Floor First Floor Roof Plan

© JW

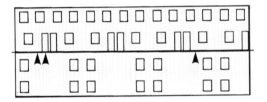
Figure 1

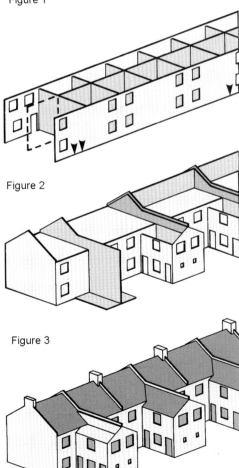
Figure 2

Figure 3

Figure 4

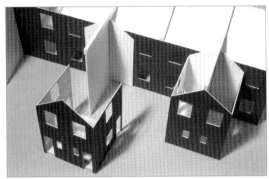

Further details
page 94

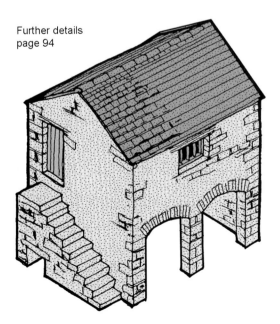

Above: This shows a typical plan, side and end elevation, which will need to be drawn to scale. **Note:** The grid on the drawing is marked out in 1 metre squares, and not feet and inches.

Far Left: This shows the construction stages of a row of terraced houses constructed using cardboard. This starts with the marking out of the front and rear elevations, as a pair so that they align, and continues with the making of the internal walling, and floor slabs. The next stage is to add the rear party wall, end walls and roof supports, followed by the main roof and the roof to the rear extension. *(Don't fix the roof in place until the windows are glazed, and make the rear extension detachable so that windows can be glazed!)* The roof tiles are then added as a separate layer, from pre-made roofing material. Finally the remaining party wall is fitted to the roof. The building is now ready for painting if not previously done.

Left: The stone built cart shed and grain store is a very simple project to start with and measures about 21ft x 30ft x 27ft high.

One manufacturer who encourages a mixture of scratch-building and kit building in H0/00 is 'Linka', who produce component pieces which interlock. Linka market a series of moulds from which you cast your own sections of brick, stone or windows. This is an ideal way of starting scratch-building as more and more hand-built pieces can be added until the building becomes completely scratch-built.

To take the hard work out of constructing a street scene think what repetitive units does it contain. I.e., the front elevation has repetitive doors and windows, so we can make a lot of doors and windows, and cut holes in the brick textured plastic sheet, one at a time, for the doors etc.

Alternatively you could say that there are two repetitive handed houses, containing two street doors and six windows, which could be cast, so that six houses could well be reduced to three castings. Apply this logic to all the elevations and roofs, and you are beginning to assemble your own house making kit.

The methods used for the making of the masters for castings need to move away from the cards and foam, to materials more solid and robust, because you remove sturdy masters from the mould without breakage.

Right: Most professional model makers prefer to work in Perspex® because the material is easily worked with power tools and gives a durable model that will last for many years.

CUTTING MATERIALS

Available on the market are various modelling materials, ranging from brick papers to plastic moulded windows. Not all of the materials are sourced from the local hobby shop, because textured papers and card could well be found in an art shop, along with a wide range of paints and brushes. What the art shop will not stock are the specialist materials, e.g. moulded or vacuum-formed random stone walling or the embossed card sheets.

The down side is the size of the sheets available but it is very easy to manufacture one's own texture by scoring card or plastic sheet. For example, a pebble dashed effect can be simply produced by using paper which has been pressed onto

sandpaper using a rubber roller. (Note: Sandpaper very quickly blunts the edge of the knife.) The brick walls commercially manufactured either in card or plastic sheet, although not producing quite the same effect as individual bricks, do portray a brick texture. Pre-printed brick papers are also available and are fixed onto the surface of the elevation and the windows cut out. The best method for window opening is to cut an X, the cuts running from one corner to the opposite diagonal corner so that four flaps are formed. These are then glued through the opening of the window onto the back of the elevation, covering the edges of the window.

Plastic vacuum formed brick sheet needs to be firmly fixed to a backing of thick card or plastic and then cut out using either a very sharp knife (if cardboard backing is used) or a fretsaw if plastic sheet is used. The edges of the windows are filed square afterwards and gaps between the plastic and its backing filled (carpenter's 'Brummer' paste or car body filler being ideal for this) prior to painting in the brick detail in the recesses. The windows are fitted after the painting is completed, thus avoiding the task of masking them.

Doors can be produced in much the same way by overlaying a series of oblong plastic or cardboard panels and painting them to suit. To add extra realism to the scene don't show all doors and windows in the closed position but pre-plan some to be open. In the case of doors a group of people can be arranged outside as if a neighbourly chat was in progress (e.g., the milkman calling) or somebody was entering or leaving the building.

Roofs can be modelled in much the same way using pre-printed card or moulded plastic. The slates can be very easily modelled by scoring a sheet of thin card or plastic. This is then cut into strips across the scored lines and applied, starting at the bottom of the roof and overlapping as described earlier. There are several methods of scoring and which is used depends upon the material: for example, to scribe on paper a blunt scriber is used similar to a dried-up ball point pen. The paper is laid over a sheet of card and the scriber pressed hard on the paper, guided by a steel rule to form a straight line. By carefully choosing a paper with a texture a terracotta tile effect can be obtained. The paper is then cut across the ridges to form strips of tiles and laid on the roof. The same method can be used on thin aluminium sheet cut into strips, but in both cases care must be taken not to flatten the ridges when cutting and gluing into position.

For cutting cardboard the knife blade should be sharpened on one side only so that the steel ruler keeps the wanted side of the cut flat. If you use a thick steel rule the edge of the blade can be held against it to keep the cut square and clean.

When scribing plastic a different technique is used as the back edge of the blade is used to remove a portion of plastic each time a cut is made. At the same time take care to avoid burning the edges of the cut. Ideally the scriber should be ground and sharpened to the shape shown, the idea being to groove the plastic with a clean V cut so that the plastic is weakened and then when a bending pressure is applied at the point it snaps cleanly along the scribed line.

Alternatively the scriber is ground with a flat tip. This flat scriber is ideal for brick scribing or filling with paint as the width of the blade used forms the width of the scribe line. This always remains constant irrespective of the depth of cut (The flat-tipped scriber is only useful for groove scribing and not for breaking along its line). A 1/8in (3mm) chisel is also useful for scribing weather boarding on styrene sheet; simply remove the unwanted styrene with a scraping action along a steel rule.

Another method is to fretsaw out the overlay, especially in the case of plastic injection moulded brickwork or random stone walls. *(e.g., Slater's® or Wills Finecast® materials)* The method is to redraw the elevation's detail on to a sheet of tracing paper and fix the tracing paper in position with double-sided sticky tape (work from the front).

Then drill a small hole in the middle of the window and fret out the openings for the windows and doorways. Trim the openings to size and square up with a sanding stick or flat file. On completion place the overlay on to the sheet of clear Perspex® and mark out around the openings with a pointed scriber so as to transfer the positions of the windows on to the clear Perspex®. Follow this by ruling the windows' glazing bars to fit these marks. Alternatively, use glazing bars from a commercial manufacturer. If this method is to be used check the fit of the pre-made windows into the openings and allow some tolerance around them for the thickness of the paint.

Since plastic or metal etched windows are difficult to mask, they are applied afterwards. The clear Perspex® is masked up only, and on completion of the building and after spray painting, the window glazing and bars are finally applied.

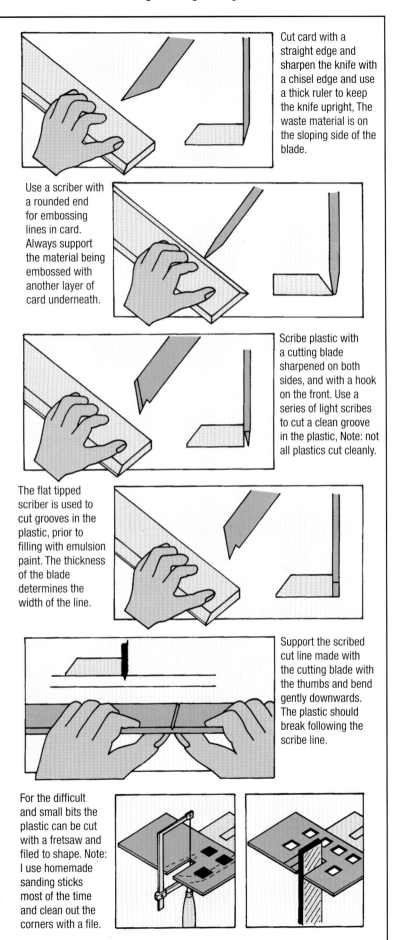

Cut card with a straight edge and sharpen the knife with a chisel edge and use a thick ruler to keep the knife upright, The waste material is on the sloping side of the blade.

Use a scriber with a rounded end for embossing lines in card. Always support the material being embossed with another layer of card underneath.

Scribe plastic with a cutting blade sharpened on both sides, and with a hook on the front. Use a series of light scribes to cut a clean groove in the plastic, Note: not all plastics cut cleanly.

The flat tipped scriber is used to cut grooves in the plastic, prior to filling with emulsion paint. The thickness of the blade determines the width of the line.

Support the scribed cut line made with the cutting blade with the thumbs and bend gently downwards. The plastic should break following the scribe line.

For the difficult and small bits the plastic can be cut with a fretsaw and filed to shape. Note: I use homemade sanding sticks most of the time and clean out the corners with a file.

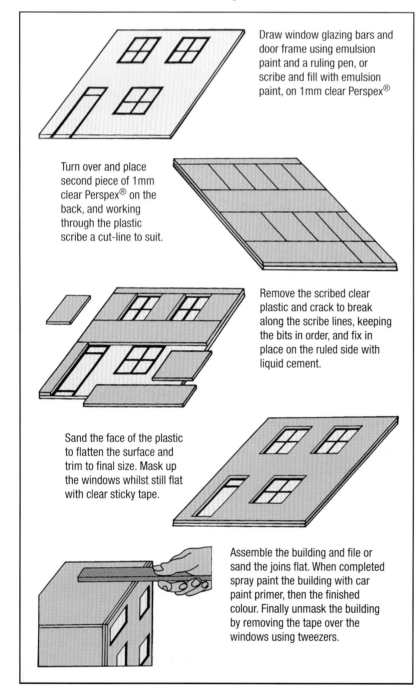

Draw window glazing bars and door frame using emulsion paint and a ruling pen, or scribe and fill with emulsion paint, on 1mm clear Perspex®

Turn over and place second piece of 1mm clear Perspex® on the back, and working through the plastic scribe a cut-line to suit.

Remove the scribed clear plastic and crack to break along the scribe lines, keeping the bits in order, and fix in place on the ruled side with liquid cement.

Sand the face of the plastic to flatten the surface and trim to final size. Mask up the windows whilst still flat with clear sticky tape.

Assemble the building and file or sand the joins flat. When completed spray paint the building with car paint primer, then the finished colour. Finally unmask the building by removing the tape over the windows using tweezers.

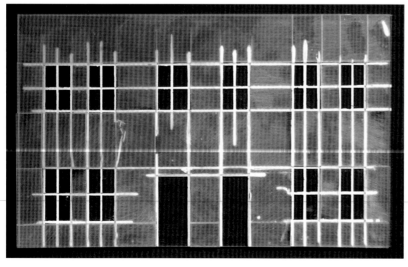

SCRATCH-BUILT BUILDINGS IN PLASTIC

By referring to earlier chapters it can be seen that buildings consist of a series of walls, doors, windows and roof, and come in all shapes and sizes. Therefore it is impossible to get a plastic kit or cardboard kit of every type of building. This will leave no alternative but to build your own version of a particular building.

One of the advantages of kit buildings is the repetitive way in which they assemble, each house being modelled exactly identical to its neighbour, and with the windows, etc, painted in the same colours, makes the building look part of an estate. To counteract this each house needs to be customized. That is to say, each house is made into an individual, even on a new estate for example. The houses, although basically identical, are made individual by varying the gardens and curtains. As houses become older, external repair work will have been carried out. Older houses in the same street can well have old dirty brickwork; pebble dash finish left in its natural colour, painted brickwork or painted pebble dash. The roofs will have been repaired or replaced with new slates or tiles, and finally the windows replaced so that in the end each house, although identical in its overall shape to its neighbour, becomes an individual dwelling through numerous detail changes.

The most popular dwellings found in a town (United Kingdom) is the terraced house and since it is impossible for me to describe every type of building in detail, the book contains a lot of information that explains just one type of building. The problem is that buildings are infinitely variable. Not only do they change throughout the length of a street, but from area to area and finally from country to country.

Plastic Clear Material: *(Note: Perspex®, Oraglass®, Plexiglass®, etc. are registered trading names associated with a particular type of clear plastic. The material is not the same as clear styrene sheet and does not craze or disfigure when solvent is accidentally applied to its surface. The material also machines, moulds and snaps in a very different way.)*

Whatever method of construction is chosen, using either Perspex® or vacuum formed, or plastic injected walling material, you will first need a drawing to work from showing in detail each of the elevations. This should preferably be drafted out to the modelling scale, because the majority of construction mistakes occur through incorrect rescaling, and unlike a drawing a mistake in the model's construction is often very difficult to rectify.

Construction Methods: The drawn elevations are overlaid with 1 mm clear Perspex®, Oraglass®, or Plexiglass® etc. (not clear styrene) and ruled up on their faces with emulsion paint to represent the windows' glazing bars (see illustration). When the paint has dried, turn over the clear ruled Perspex®

and overlay it with a second piece of clear Perspex®. Now, by aligning a steel rule or square, scribe the window pattern out by looking through the clear Perspex® layers carefully. This forms the overlay (see illustration). When completed crack out the unwanted window areas by applying pressure on the back of the 'V' scribe cut line and as each piece breaks off place it back into position, this time on to the ruled side of the clear Perspex® (face) ready for gluing into position.

By cracking the overlay in the horizontal direction first (see illustration) and then in the vertical direction the windows will remain horizontally in a straight line. This is important as the eye can see straight lines running horizontally very well, and will quickly spot a window that is higher than the rest. When you have completed the 'cracking-out' of the overlay check its alignment with the window glazing lines and touch in any discrepancies in the ruling with a glazing bar colour to suit. Finally fix the overlay carefully in position (use liquid solvent applied with a fine tipped brush). Since the scribing for the overlay has been completed on the back of the sheet of Perspex®, the join should now be virtually invisible and require the minimum of sanding and filling. The elevation is now ready for masking.

There are a selection of masking materials available on the market and clear sticky tape is ideal, but you first need to check that it does not leave a sticky mess behind when it is unpeeled from the Perspex® and that is does not react with the paint that is used, by shrinking, etc. (Note: the paper tape manufactured for general masking does not give the same crisp line as the clear tapes and is more difficult to use.) This completes the first elevation detail ready to be trimmed to size. Repeat this on the other elevations around the building as required.

Additional detail can be added such as weather boarding, which can be made from thin card, or preferably thin styrene white sheeting, cut in thin strips to suit. The method of cutting thin strips is to use a very sharp knife and not to start at the very edge of the sheet, but about 1 cm in from the first edge and to stop about 1 cm from the other end. (This stops the strip from curling as it is cut, and holds them all together.) To cut even strips and all of the same size I use a ruler that has been scanned into the computer and printed out to the required size. The print of the ruler's edge is then fixed onto the styrene sheet with double sided sticky tape at each edge of the sheet, and a steel rule bridges the gap, which is used to obtain a straight cut. This is far more accurate than measuring each side and making a mark with a pencil.

The photographs show, starting with the one on the left a elevation that has just been assembled using the scribe and crack method, and sanded smooth to lose the joins. Because you can see through it, it looks messy. The one on the right has had 'styrene' weather-boarding added, has been painted, and awaits the application of window sills, roof and door, and when finished will form part of a background low relief building.

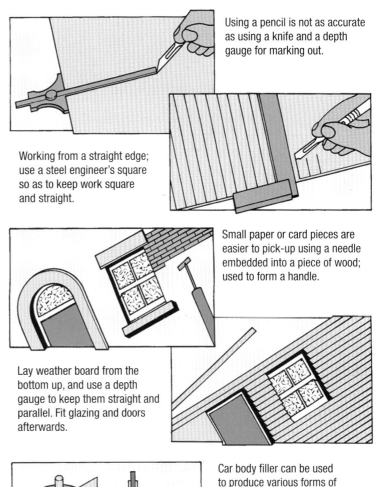

Using a pencil is not as accurate as using a knife and a depth gauge for marking out.

Working from a straight edge; use a steel engineer's square so as to keep work square and straight.

Small paper or card pieces are easier to pick-up using a needle embedded into a piece of wood; used to form a handle.

Lay weather board from the bottom up, and use a depth gauge to keep them straight and parallel. Fit glazing and doors afterwards.

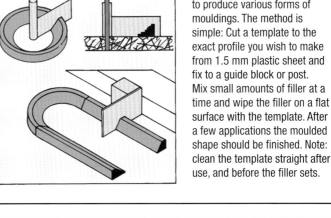

Car body filler can be used to produce various forms of mouldings. The method is simple: Cut a template to the exact profile you wish to make from 1.5 mm plastic sheet and fix to a guide block or post. Mix small amounts of filler at a time and wipe the filler on a flat surface with the template. After a few applications the moulded shape should be finished. Note: clean the template straight after use, and before the filler sets.

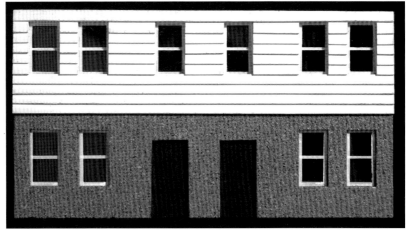

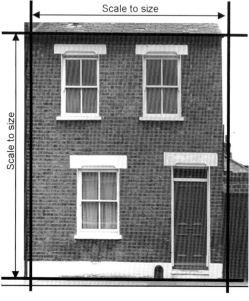

Scale to size

Scale to size

Above: The photograph will need the verticals correcting and scaling to size, as shown on the right.

Top right: Part of the wall photograph that formed the master by stitching a number of photographs together.

English Bond and Cavity Walls.
Brick Counting: High
 3 ft = 12 bricks
 6 ft = 24 bricks
 9 ft = 36 bricks
12 ft = 48 bricks
15 ft = 60 bricks
18 ft = 72 bricks
21 ft = 84 bricks
24 ft = 96 bricks
27 ft = 108 bricks
30 ft = 120 bricks

Brick Counting: Long
 3 ft = 4 bricks
 6 ft = 8 bricks
 9 ft = 12 bricks
12 ft = 16 bricks
15 ft = 20 bricks
18 ft = 24 bricks
21 ft = 28 bricks
24 ft = 32 bricks
27 ft = 36 bricks
30 ft = 40 bricks

Right: Visualise the building as a series of boxes, what is shown on the front is shown on the back. The ground floor boxes can be swoped around, so that the door is on the other side.
The windows can be changed in size and shape, and more often the windows at the front are more elaborate than the ones at the back.

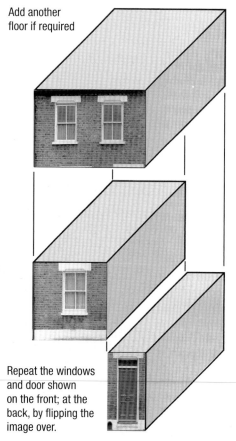

Add another floor if required

Repeat the windows and door shown on the front; at the back, by flipping the image over.

COMPUTER GENERATED ELEVATIONS

The dream of just pushing a button and a model building pops out of the other end of a machine has long been a reality, but few of us have the access to such a machine. But many of us have access to a home computer (PC), which with the aid of a digital camera can be used to produce printed elevations that are ready to be fixed onto cardboard, and made into buildings.

The method used is quite basic, first a brick wall is photographed; that has the minimum of blemishes or repetitive marks. It is photographed square on (90 degrees to the face) so as to minimise distortion. The photograph should be about 20 bricks long and about 48 high, (15ft x 12ft high) to allow a good overlap when joining the photographs together on the computer. Photograph a number of end walls, so as to have a small selection to pick from when producing the various elevations. For example, old yellow London stocks, cleaned London stocks, old and new red brick etc., to name a couple of the most common bricks found. Join nine single photographs together to make a larger panel of bricks, which will form a master (see right).

The technique is to square the photograph up in Photoshop® or any other image manipulation programme, so that the brick courses run vertically and horizontally, and are to scale. For example a brick measures with cement approximately 9in x 3in x 3in. Therefore at the scale of 1mm equalling 3 inches ('00' 4 mm to the foot scale) 10 brick lengths measure 30mm. The same applies to the height, 24 bricks measure 24mm. The first photograph is scaled to these proportions, and it does not matter if the photograph contains more than 30 x 24 bricks. Having done this open a new blank page 3.5 times higher and wider than the original image and at the same resolution as the existing image, and copy and paste the original over. This is the first layer, which needs its edges softened by using the Photoshop's 'Polygonal Lasso Tool' by five pixels. Copy and paste the original to make a second layer, and flip the image horizontally, so that the same edges join, and slide together so that the join disappears. Paste a third image to form the third layer, and join. When satisfied flatten the image and copy and paste what is now a long bit of wall underneath the upper image and join. Do the same with the last layer. When satisfied save as a PSD file to preserve the layers and then flatten the image, crop and save to a TIFF file. This is your master wall file. Open and rename and then insert the photograph (Photo 2) of your choice that has the doors and windows you wish to copy. Size the photograph so that the bricks are the same size at the master wall, and square up etc. Having done this copy and paste the windows and doors over by using the Polygonal Lasso Tool, and position in place on the master wall, as required. When finished discard photo 2 by depositing the layer into the waste bin. Repeat on the other walls as required, to finish the building.

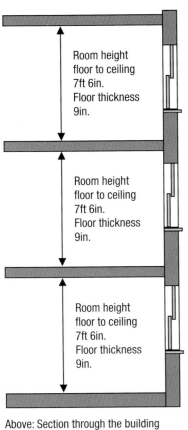

Room height floor to ceiling 7ft 6in. Floor thickness 9in.

Room height floor to ceiling 7ft 6in. Floor thickness 9in.

Room height floor to ceiling 7ft 6in. Floor thickness 9in.

Above: Section through the building

9 ft 3 inch

17 ft

Above: The finished elevation

Above: The original elevation

Above: The shop building as purchased.

Left: After re-painting and adding 'photo' shop windows.

Below: General views over the layout.

Local stone or other locally available building materials are normally used to cut down costs. Therefore in an area with a rich supply of local stone, just about everything is built using stone and bricks are a rarity . **Bottom photo:** Note the use of stone for the embankment walling etc!

Left: The castings are cut to size and fixed together, (see page 116 & 118 for making masters and moulds) holes filled, cement fills, lead flashing and ridge tiles (see page 101 using paper strips) fitted as required.

Below: The building is then primed using car spray paint and further holes filled.

Far left: The building is given a thin coat of grey household matt emulsion paint and allowed to dry. A second coat is applied picking out groups of stones with darker colours so the effect is slightly mottled and allowed to dry. The detail is then picked out with individual colours and a series of washes are applied to suit.

Building drawn at 2mm to 1ft
('N' scale)

Inside wall
at roof level

MODERN TWO STOREY TOWN HOUSE

Capping strips for walls
and roof.

Basic artwork of a building produced on a
computer using a simple drawing programme.

Above: Artwork has a flat un-textured surface **Below:** This building uses a textured surface

LOW RELIEF BUILDINGS

It has been established that simply photographing a building and then turning the photographs into a model is not a dream but a practical method of model construction, which saves a considerable amount of time. It does have its limitations in that it relies on the individual's skills with a camera and knowledge of computers, but again there are lots of courses available to learn image manipulation programs such as Adobe Photoshop®.

The illustration shows that the building consists of six elevations, three of which will need windows and doors. The other three elevations have no doors or windows. It will also depend on whether the building is part of a row and alternately handed as to whether elevations 1 and 5 are seen, except for the end of terrace buildings.

Let us assume that 12 prints have been made, one set of six for the elevation overlay and one backing set. Using the method detailed on page 97, the first set is fixed onto card and the windows cut out, and then fixed on the backing sheet so that the doors and windows align. The difference this time is that only the elevations seen are detailed in this way, because the elevations facing the backing board (sky) will not be seen.

Computerised Building Designs: The illustrations on page 111 and on 114 show buildings drawn at 'N' and '00' scale. These are designed to be colour copied and made as part of the introduction to card modelling, as well as introducing computer-aided artwork using Photoshop® and Microsoft Publisher® programs. The building need not be constructed from card, but could be made from plastic using the drawings as templates.

The cart shed and grain store is a very simple building to make, except the external steps will cause some difficulties! The technique is to fix all the elevations onto photo-mount card, but not the flagstones (bottom corner right) and the corners (top right) which are fixed later when the steps are made. (Build separately using extra pieces of card to form the steps etc, on the inside, which are covered with the flagstone bits saved earlier.) Having made the steps continue with the main building by cutting out the back (1) and side (2) elevations including the window, the back and side inside walls and the floor. These are fixed together by gluing the inside to the back wall and then the side wall, the internal side wall and the floor.

Note because card varies in thickness some trimming will be required to achieve a good fit. Repeat with elevations 3 and 4 and cover the corners with the corner stone pieces to lose the join. Fix some scrap pieces of card into the corners of the top floor and fix the roof in place.

Much the same technique is used on the building shown left, but you will be required to make your own floors and internal walls etc. alternatively make the building as if it is being built.

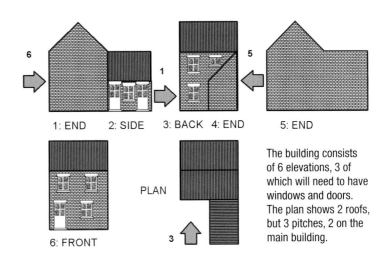

1: END   2: SIDE   3: BACK   4: END   5: END

6: FRONT   PLAN   3

The building consists of 6 elevations, 3 of which will need to have windows and doors. The plan shows 2 roofs, but 3 pitches, 2 on the main building.

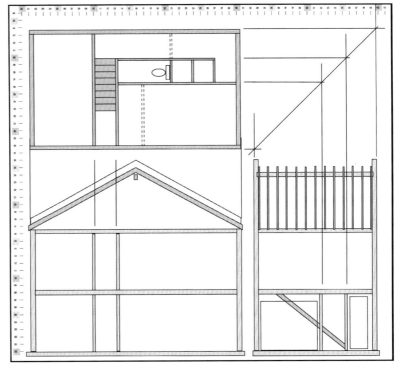

The masters can be made by using any of the methods described and the place to invest time is in making the masters perfect, because any damage or flaws will repeat on every casting. For the same reason details such as damaged bricks or tiles should be added on the castings, not on the master, to prevent each casting having identical characteristics that are easily identifiable.

The cutters used are of the carbon tipped type, but I also make homemade ultra-fine cutters from brass rod and Obo® nails suitably ground to shape. This saves a lot of expense.

Note: *The cutting equipment shown has had the clear guards removed for the photographs, so that the cutter and the block being machined could be clearly seen.*

Disclaimer: *All the machining methods shown in this book are for information only. Therefore the methods do not constitute any form of training in the use of such equipment.*
If you wish to gain knowledge in the correct use of such equipment I recommend that you enrol on any of the approved engineering or model making courses that are run by any of the various educational establishments.
All power and hand tools are governed by a code of safe practice, of which it is your own responsibility to implement such safe working practice as deemed necessary, and you are also responsible for those around you when using such equipment.

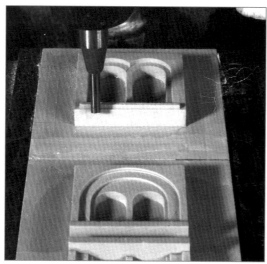

MAKING MASTERS

In the professional world of model making the model maker has to be a highly skilled craftsman, proficient in using a wide range of hand and power tools. They also have to be extremely adept at improvising various methods of achieving the desired effect: whereby the old model maker's statement remains the true 'anything under a coat of paint will do' which when considered is basically true. Take for example rock faces made from plaster or buildings made from plastic – all looking realistic when captured on film or as seen by the naked eye.

The art of making a model look convincing is in the quality of the workmanship; therefore it is very necessary to produce everything to the best of one's ability. The outcome of this is that at times machine tools rather than hand tools have to be used.

The router table shown is a homemade version of an expensive computer navigated cutter, or milling machine. Whereby two 'X-Y' vices are used to provide the horizontal cross cut and the vertical axis movement. The first vice shown in the photograph provides the left or right, (the 'X' travel) sideways movement and also the towards and away (the 'Y' travel) from you cutting movement. The second vice behind the router provides the up and down (the 'Z' travel) movement of the cutter. There is one more movement left on the second vice and this is used to extend the travel of the left and right travel of the cutter.

The photographs show one of the window masters being produced for the 'Rochester Castle Model' which was built to the scale of 1:100 (approx 3mm to 1 foot scale) This scale was chosen because the model had to go up one of the spiral staircases in the actual castle!

The method used is to secure a block of Urial® in the lower vice and to make the first dressing cut using a large cutter and then to turn the block over and dress the block the other side. The block is then removed from the vice and marked out using an engineer's square and knife.

Note: Urial® replaces the use of plastic etc., and is a resin bonded block of what appears to be fine plastic granules that has superb machining, gluing and stability properties. It is probably available from pattern making companies in small amounts.

The block is then fixed back into the vice and the outside cuts around the windows are made. The cutter is then changed to the smaller cutter which will cut the two arched windows, followed by the larger cutter that spanned the two arches and finally the cutter that produced the biggest cut over the top of the window. The window sill was cut as a separate piece and glued in place and machined to final shape, the entire process taking about 15 minutes to machine.

The lower photograph shows a mixture of methods that uses machining as described, plus lathed components and other separate components fixed together to make the master.

Random Stone Walls: The production of a random stone wall starts with mixing up a small amount of fine quick setting plaster, (Plaster of Paris) which as it is setting it is broken up into small pieces between the fingers. The hardening plaster will then need an old rolling pin to crush the setting plaster and finally a hammer when it becomes very hard, to break it into pieces.

The pieces of plaster are then sieved, using various wire meshes to produce various 'granule' grades (3 or 4 grades). Having done this a piece of MDF (30 x 30 cm) is prepared by priming the surface to be used with oil-bound household paint, to make it waterproof. When dry it is then thickly coated with PVA white woodworker's glue, and the brush marks evened out using a piece of sponge, (old washing up pot scourer/sponge is ideal) and don't worry about the bubbles!

The glue is then coated with the larger grade of plaster granules, applied using a sieve. When covered with granules, carefully turn over and lightly tap the back, to dislodge the granules that are not stuck in place. The procedure is repeated with the finer grades, and each time the back is tapped to dislodge the granules of plaster that have not glued in place.

Finally sprinkle pure plaster powder over the lot, turn over and tap, turn back over so that it is face up and allow to dry (24 hours). In effect what you have done is to apply lumps of plaster, and to fill in the gaps between the lumps with smaller and smaller pieces of plaster until finally powder is applied to fill in the remaining gaps. The next stage is to gently sand the dry surface of the plaster, constantly turning over to clear the dust away to view the effect.

When acceptable, the surface is scribed horizontally using a flat ended scribing tool. The gap between the lines will depend upon the scale being modelled. Having done this the vertical lines are now scribed by hand, picking suitable gaps etc. between the texture of the wall, and as you scribe the stones bits will break off and this will add to the effect. Repeat the procedure of scribing horizontally, vertically, sanding and cleaning until the desired effect is obtained. Having achieved the desired effect seal the surface with car primer spray paint. Finally mount in a box ready for the rubber mould to be made.

Brick Walls: The best method I know for producing brick walls is to make a master on the computer and have the artwork acid etched to size. Unfortunately it is a very expensive process, even to produce just one master. Alternatively just the horizontal cement course between the bricks could be very carefully scribed. For 'N' scale I have used extremely coarse sandpaper, fixed as a thin strip on a solid square block, and run this along the face of the building. This scratches a series of horizontal grooves along the face of the building that looks like the horizontal brickwork cement lines.

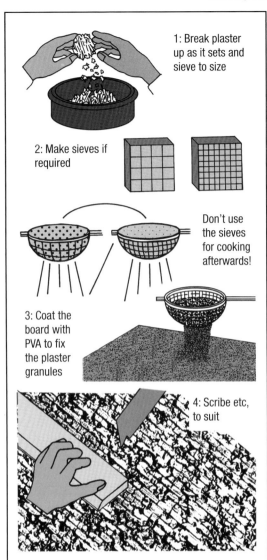

1: Break plaster up as it sets and sieve to size

2: Make sieves if required

Don't use the sieves for cooking afterwards!

3: Coat the board with PVA to fix the plaster granules

4: Scribe etc, to suit

1: Break up plaster as it hardens and sieve into various sizes of granules.
2: If necessary make your own sieves using different sizes of wire mesh, as well as the type found in the kitchen. (Don't use for cooking afterwards).
3: Apply various sizes of plaster onto a board coated with PVA that has been previously primed with oil bound household undercoat. (This stops the water in the PVA from warping the board).
4: When dry sand, scribe etc to achieve the desired effect.

Below: This photograph shows part of the multilayer layout, using stonework produced using the method as described to make the master. A casting was made from the mould, trimmed to size, doors and windows cut out and fixed to a wooden block.

The windows used the traditional photographic method which is now superseded by the computer method of producing windows.

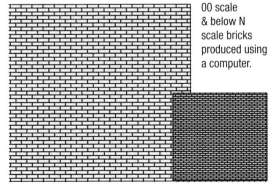

00 scale & below N scale bricks produced using a computer.

N & 00 Scale brickwork is almost impossible to produce by hand, I have seen some very near '00' scale bricks produced using computer paper sprocket hole chards, but they are a bit big! The best way is to produce an acid etched sheet, and use that as the master.

The fibreglass panels made from fibreglass moulds are ideal for the large outdoor layout when buildings need to be made water and frost proof.

Glass Fibre Moulds

1: Make a master using suitable material, wax it, and apply a coat of PVA release and then wax again.

2: Apply a gel coat, which is thicker, so it does not run on vertical surfaces.

3: Cut squares of thin matting and stipple the resin well in, whilst avoiding the trapping of any air pockets. Allow to almost set hard and apply a second layer.

Trim the edges whilst still part set.

4: When set remove the master and clean the mould. Repeat the procedure to make the moulding.

Rubber & Plaster Moulds

1: Make a wall around the master and coat the master with latex moulding rubber, Vinamould® or cold cure rubber.

2: When set cover with plaster, so that the box is filled and allow to set.

3: When set remove both the rubber and the master from the plaster and remove the master from the rubber. Carefully replace the rubber back into the plaster backing.

4: Cast your first moulding. When set remove and clean as required.

Solid Rubber Moulds

1: Make a wall around the master and fill with 'cold-cure' mould making rubber.

2: When set remove the master.

Fill the mould with casting resin and cover with waxed plastic sheet.

4: Clean the casting and make as many as required.

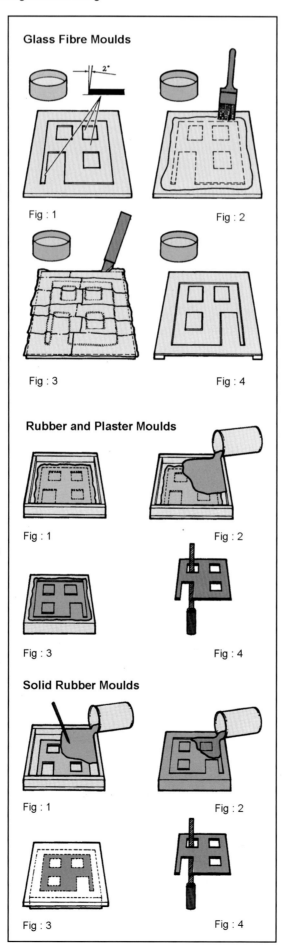

Glass Fibre Moulds

Fig : 1   Fig : 2

Fig : 3   Fig : 4

Rubber and Plaster Moulds

Fig : 1   Fig : 2

Fig : 3   Fig : 4

Solid Rubber Moulds

Fig : 1   Fig : 2

Fig : 3   Fig : 4

CASTING AND MOULDING

Having established that roads and streets do tend to have a lot of repetitive buildings along their length, and because a large number of model buildings are required to make a town setting, some form of mass production system is needed to speed up their construction and reduce the time and effort involved.

The technique described is suitable for all scales although details vary. For example, on an outdoor layout the materials used need to be waterproof, so they do not deteriorate under the extremes of weather conditions, but buildings on a smaller indoor layout, being protected from the weather only have to be sufficiently strong to withstand general usage. Size also needs to be taken into consideration. Small N gauge buildings can be cast in one piece; HO and 00 models can use elevations moulded in plaster, resin or plastic, but the 0 gauge outdoor layout requires resin and glass fibre or cast concrete, complete with wire reinforcement. The common factor is that in each case a mould is needed from which to produce the castings.

Since the buildings will have to be rigid, the moulds must be designed so as to enable the castings to be released easily. Although rigid moulds can be used for large glass fibre castings they will require release angles and release waxes and films. For all large-scale mouldings I recommend the use of the rubber and plaster backing method, as this allows more detail and undercuts to be made on the master. For smaller scales the solid rubber mould is best. Since the rubber is flexible it allows undercuts to release, unlike a rigid mould which will lock an undercut firmly into place, making it completely and totally impossible to separate.

There are a variety of moulding materials available on the market, air drying latex rubber being one. This is applied in a series of thin layers so as to build up the required thickness and is one of the most economical materials to use, as the rubber is backed with inexpensive plaster. This method therefore requires very little of the latex rubber, compared with casting a solid mould using a cold cure casting rubber. This second method, although more expensive, allows flat moulds to be produced, which are very convenient. The same applies to the hot re-usable casting rubbers. This time the disadvantages are that the master pattern must be heat-proof and that this type of moulding rubber does not give the same fineness of quality in its reproduction as the cold cure rubbers. On the other hand, since it is re-usable you can save money, if you are prepared to accept the loss of quality.

The master pattern is without doubt the most important component. For hot casting rubbers it can be made in card, resin or metal, as they are heat-proof, whilst for the cold cure rubbers, plastic or plaster can also be used. The air drying latex rubbers can be applied over all these materials, including Plasticine®, modelling clay Milliput®

or wax masters. This provides a choice to suit the requirements of the job in hand, and the individual.

The basic method with all casting rubbers is to flow the rubber from one corner of the mould, allowing it to slowly spread over the surface of the master, so that it does not trap air. Latex rubber has to be brushed on in much the same way, again being careful to avoid trapping air in the mould. The same applies when mixing cold cure two-part rubbers. Don't beat the rubber into foam when mixing, but stir the hardener slowly into the rubber, avoiding as much as possible aerating the mixture.

When pouring from the mixing vessel, pour in a thin stream close to the mould's surface, again to avoid trapping further air in the mixture, because air bubbles are a mould's worst enemy. (Ideally the rubber should be degassed in a vacuum tank to remove all the bubbles.)

To prevent the rubber escaping from the master, build a wall around it, using a suitable material compatible with the rubber, and fill to the top of the walls, then cover with a flat piece of plastic so as to produce a smooth back. This is necessary so that when the mould is turned over it remains flat, and the same applies when backing a latex mould with plaster. When the rubber is set remove the master by bending the rubber mould.

Casting Material: The material used for casting again is the modeller's choice. Fine casting plaster is easily available in hobby shops and in some ways is easier to use than the casting resins, although these are much stronger. However, some of the casting resins generate heat as they cure which can destroy the re-usable rubber moulds. A good casting mixture can be made from car body filler mixed with glass fibre resin, which is used to thin it so that it flows. The hardener from the car body filler pack will cure this mixture but requires careful mixing to avoid trapping air bubbles. The mixture should

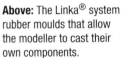

generally set hard without a sticky surface, but if this does occur, reduce the amount of hardener. If the casting resin becomes warm in the mould (through chemical reaction producing heat), the resin and rubber mould can be immersed in cold water to dissipate the heat generated (immerse when the moulding resin is just beginning to set). This method of underwater curing will also reduce the shrinkage of the casting.

So as to obtain a flat back to the casting cover the resin with a piece of release-wax coated plastic. This applies when casting plaster since it also requires a flat back, but don't immerse in water! If, when using casting resins, a sticky surface accidentally appears on the moulded surface, it can be scrubbed off with a household abrasive powder of the type used for cleaning pots and pans (pumice powder is ideal). It is a bit difficult to remove so a lot of scrubbing with a stiff nail brush will be required. Alternatively use a good quality casting resin, which will produce excellent castings, but comes at a price!

Above: The Linka® system rubber moulds that allow the modeller to cast their own components.

Below: One of the many typical terraced house street scenes that can be produced with the Linka® system of casting individual components. The buildings produced look acceptable on a '00' scale layout, and have been painted in different styles to make them look slightly different. A typical terraced house could well be over 70 years old and housed a number of occupiers. Therefore it depends upon the love and care that was bestowed upon the house as to its present day condition, or as to the present day owner, who could have repaired the building.

Caution Copyright Infringement: You cannot make moulds from other people's products without infringing the manufacturer's copyright, and therefore always make your own masters.

There is no single way of producing castings or mouldings that is suitable for every occasion, therefore use the method that suits the job in hand. Sometimes it is quicker to set up a template and machine components rather than mould them, when you take into account the time spent in producing the mould and clean the castings etc.

MASS PRODUCTION AND MOULDING

The biggest problem in mass production is finding a way in which components can be made quickly, accurately and with the minimum of finishing. Casting from rubber moulds in epoxy or polyester resins becomes a long process, especially if a lot of cleaning up is required. The plaster method is ideal from the cost point of view, but still requires a considerable amount of time. Also, after the castings are made they will require time to dry out before use. They are also brittle and easily damaged, again a problem. If you add PVA to the plaster they set like cement and are unworkable!

This method is very good in the fact it produces plastic mouldings that can be fixed to other plastic components, using a solvent, but this method again has its limitations. The technique is to make the master in the usual way (i.e., in Plasticine®, modelling wax, plastic and styrene, etc), taking care to bevel the sides of each vertical edge (master laid

flat) so as to form a release angle. Then place the master in a box taped into position with double-sided sticky tape and apply a coat of wax, then water soluble release agent and wax again. This time, instead of pouring in rubber pour in a mixture of car body filler and glass fibre resin, mixed up approximately 50:50 so that it is like a cream. Carefully add hardener mixed in much the same way as casting into rubber moulds, and fill to the top of the walls of the box, then cover with a piece of waxed plastic. Check on its setting time and when it sets to a cheese-like hardness, immerse in cold water and leave until it has finally hardened.

Dismantle the box and remove the master from the mould then mount it on to the press as shown in the illustration by gluing to a block of wood; screw into position as shown, make the hinge and spacer, cramp to the edge of a solid table and the press is ready for use.

The sheet styrene (not expanded ceiling tile type) of about $\frac{1}{10}$in (2.5mm) thick is then cut to a slightly larger size than required and heated in an oven on a flat piece of wood until it is soft. Using gloves remove the wood and styrene from the oven, then take the heated styrene from the wood with pliers and place into position under the press. Apply pressure onto the hot styrene sheet via the mould so as to emboss the shape of the mould into the sheet of styrene.

Hold pressure until the styrene sheet cools then remove from the mould. If the mould tends to stick brush a thin coat of neat washing-up liquid on the face of the mould. This washes off the moulding in warm water. This method of hot pressing considerably speeds up production time although the moulds have a limited life of approximately twenty to fifty pressings. However:

An Important Word Of Warning: Always follow the safety code of practice; this means it is your own responsibility to take care at all times of both yourself and of others and to take precautions against fire when working with hot or inflammable or other materials. Work in a well-ventilated place with any material that fumes. Never use or work with equipment that is beyond your skills or knowledge, or that is in an unsafe state or condition, or in conditions or manners that are unsafe. Think always 'safety first'.

This method produces the equivalent of an injection moulded plastic component, and is suitable for the production of complex pieces. The mould does have a limited life of between 20 and 50 pressings, depending upon how fine the detail is and the acceptable quality of the moulding. If a wax master was used then make another mould from a good styrene moulding.
Note: the grooves in the outside edges of the mould are for the excess styrene to easily escape.
The hotter the styrene the easier it moulds, but the shorter the life of the mould. The same method can be used for embossing thin card, by using a male and female mould, but it is limited in its use.

Insert the master into a box and fill with thinned down car body filler.

Remove, wash and trim as required and file grooves in the outside edge.

Fix to the piece of wood that forms the arm.

Bolt the arm to form a hinge in blocks of wood.

Place the heated styrene on a block of wood that forms a spacer and press the mould into the styrene. Allow to cool.

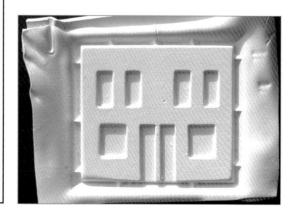

Left: Part of the 'Tuscan Rock' layout built by Lee Clark. This finely detailed model depicts the narrow gauge 'Rio Grande Line' and is built at the American Hn03 scale, which is equivalent of the British HO (3.5mm to 1ft) scale. America uses vast amounts of timber in the construction industry, and this trestle bridge is no exception. If you study the layout you will find that most of the buildings etc. are made from wood.

MASS CUTTING AND SANDING

Bridges and other large wooden structures generally require hundreds of identical sized pieces. If these are produced individually, it is very difficult to maintain an exact consistency of size, and this then causes construction problems.

This method is also very time-consuming, compared with the careful setting up of a series of jigs which cut the piece exactly to a given length or an exact angle.

Surprisingly, the method for setting up jigs for cutting is very simple, only requiring scrap pieces of timber. These should be of a hard wood so that they are sufficiently durable, and one and a half times the thickness in height and width of the material being cut. This extra thickness is required so as to start the edge of the saw in the grooves of the jig, so that the cut is made in the right place.

The wood that forms the guide is nailed into position on a scrap piece of block or chipboard. Then the master groove is cut using a steel square to guide the cut, so that it is true both across and vertically. Use double-sided sticky tape to hold it into position for trial cuts and when it is sized properly fix into position, so that it is not accidentally moved. A gap is left between the end of the jig guides and the stop so that dust from the sawing can be removed easily and to prevent it from interfering with the jig's sizing. For the next size of cutting a second jig will be required, made in the same way, so that in the end a series of jigs are made which are kept until the model is complete. This method becomes especially convenient when it is difficult to calculate the exact number of same-length components required. When the number is known the jig's stop can be clamped in position.

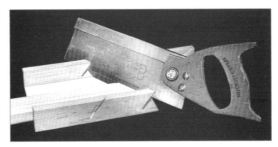

Cut timber will also be required to construct the baseboards so use a tenon saw for cutting large pieces and a razor saw for cutting smaller pieces. Do not use a knife because the pressure used will probably snap the blade, which is without doubt extremely dangerous if it was to fly up into the air. Wrap all blades on scalpels with clear sticky tape to prevent this happening.

Left: The simple cutting jig can speed up the construction time because the cuts will be accurate. Cover the assembly jig's surface with masking tape or wax because this helps prevent the glue from sticking to the jig.

Below: The finished building which used the hot press method to produce the elevations. The windows were produced using a photographic method now outdated.

The technique for ruling glazing bars is quite simple as a draughtsman's spring pen is used. This is filled with paint of a colour to suit, which should be sufficiently thinned to allow it to flow, but not run. The Perspex® should be pre-washed using washing-up liquid and thoroughly rinsed and dried on a kitchen paper towel, taking care not to scratch its surface, so that the clear Perspex® or plastic is free from grease. One simply rules the paint on to its surface using a steel rule or square to keep the lines straight. Horizontal lines of brickwork can also be ruled in this way or scored into the plastic or card.

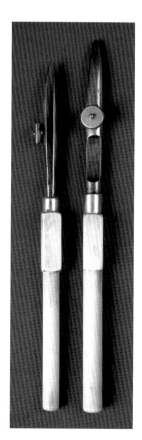

Above: Using a ruling pen the door or the windows can be drawn several times larger than required and then scanned. The scanned image can then be scaled to the final size required. Household emulsion paints are ideal for use in a ruling pen.

THE RULING PEN

The old fashioned draughtsman spring bow ruling pen has adjustable settings so that the lines they draw can be varied in width. Also, since the pen's nib is made from metal, it can be used with all types of paint without damage and easily cleaned with thinners or by scraping with a knife.

The secret of using this type of pen lies in mixing the paint. If it is too thin or the nib is over-filled then it blobs, if it is too thick it will not work at all: So it requires some trial and error with each paint mixture to get the mix right. Fill the pen using a paint brush and take care not to paint the sides of the pen, so that clean smudge-free lines can be drawn. To help prevent paint creeping under the ruler support the ruler on a strip of thick card taped into position with double-sided sticky tape about 3 mm back from the edge or make a bridge ruler, supported on blocks at each end. This is ideal for working over wet lines to speed things up.

By ruling a darker tone over a colour, shadow can be formed on a flat surface. Street doors, for example, can be made very quickly this way by ruling a series of lines. The technique is first to paint the main door colour over a piece of card, then to rule in a series of darker tone lines horizontally and vertically using the same base colour but with black added to represent the panels.

The technique is to draw the top and one side of each panel in a dark line and the bottom and the opposite side in a lighter line. Always keep the dark lines to the right and the light lines to the left (or vice versa) so that as a series of doors are made over a period of time they always match. Brickwork can also be ruled up in the same way but this is very time-consuming. Whilst most of this can now be undertaken using a computer, computers cannot draw road markings, line locos, and edge colour buildings!

The Computer: Small lettering on shop signs, etc, can now be easily produced using a computer and replaces many of the photographic techniques once used. One technique is to use Microsoft Publisher® and to draw at about four times scale size. The illustration on the right shows a typical street door, 8ft 3in high by 3ft 0in width (33 bricks high x 4 bricks long) set in a 4 x 3in timber frame, that has a wired safety glazing at the top.

The method used was to draw a scale ruler using the rule at the edge of the window, at say 1 mm equalling 1 inch, or 1 mm could represent 2 inches model size. This becomes our master ruler which is set at the edge of the page. (Lock the layers by grouping.) A copy of the ruler is made and flipped sideways, and placed at the bottom. Using the scale a rectangle to the outside edges is drawn (8 ft 3 in x 3 ft 0 in), and fill with white. The door is then drawn 6ft 9 inch high, to fit inside with a 3 inch surround, bottom and sides. The window is then added above the door with a 3-inch surround. The door panels, the letter box, door knob and keyhole are also drawn as required.

1mm = 1 inch scale	
1mm = 1 inch	12mm = 1 foot
2mm = 2 inches	24mm = 2 feet
3mm = 3 inches	36mm = 3 feet
4mm = 4 inches	48mm = 4 feet
5mm = 5 inches	60mm = 5 feet
6mm = 6 inches	72mm = 6 feet
7mm = 7 inches	84mm = 7 feet
8mm = 8 inches	96mm = 8 feet
9mm = 9 inches	108mm = 9 feet
10mm = 10 inches	120mm = 10 feet
11mm = 11 inches	240mm = 20 feet
12mm = 1 foot	360mm = 30 feet

00 Scale sizes	(4mm to 1 foot)
1mm = 3 inches	28mm = 7 feet
2mm = 6 inches	32mm = 8 feet
3mm = 9 inches	36mm = 9 feet
4mm = 1 foot	40mm = 10 feet
8mm = 2 feet	80mm = 20 feet
12mm = 3 feet	120mm = 30 feet
16mm = 4 feet	160mm = 40 feet
20mm = 5 feet	200mm = 50 feet
24mm = 6 feet	300mm = 75 feet

N Scale sizes	(2mm to 1 foot)
1mm = 6 inches	20mm = 10 feet
2mm = 1 foot	40mm = 20 feet
4mm = 2 feet	60mm = 30 feet
6mm = 3 feet	80mm = 40 feet
8mm = 4 feet	100mm = 50 feet
10mm = 5 feet	120mm = 60 feet
12mm = 6 feet	140mm = 70 feet
14mm = 7 feet	160mm = 80 feet
16mm = 8 feet	180mm = 90 feet
18mm = 9 feet	200mm = 100 feet

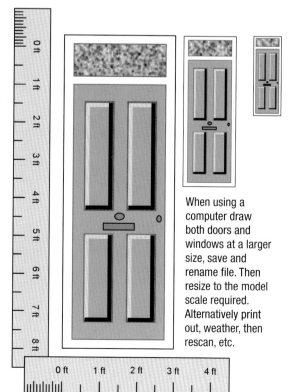

When using a computer draw both doors and windows at a larger size, save and rename file. Then resize to the model scale required. Alternatively print out, weather, then rescan, etc.

FITTING THE BUILDINGS

The correct axis of a building upon a baseboard is one of the most important points of a layout, because a leaning building looks most unrealistic. The easiest method is to arrange the foundation of the building to be flat. Unfortunately this is not always possible. On a flat baseboard it is a case of making the building to ground level, but on a contoured base this is not possible so the buildings have to be made to extend below ground level as well and placed on a flat platform inside a hole; which is cut out to the shape and size of the building's base, and the building has to fit inside without leaving any gaps around it.

For a series of buildings going up a hill the ground can be twisted to suit the buildings by using the front and back garden and placing the buildings on the 'flat' formed by cutting and twisting the ground level. The differences are disguised by using walls which cover the change in levels. Alternatively, the buildings can be placed upon a raised level and the ground shaped to meet the road and surrounding area.

Many houses are built in this way, to the extent that at the rear of the building the garden level could well be above the street level at the front, and the building may require retaining walls and steps leading up to its ground floor level. But for the high street, or houses without front gardens, you have to make a hole in the baseboard which is packed up to a convenient height, and the building extended below ground level. The important part of fitting buildings on a slope is to make sure that the doors are at ground level, because a 3 foot front step or a low 4 foot rear door looks rather strange and far from realistic.

Fortunately the rear of the building generally can be built on the flat and the change in levels being hidden by walls, other buildings etc.

Unfortunately there are times when the slope around the building is diagonally across the site and there are no walls to disguise the change in levels. This calls for careful cutting out of the base's overlay using a razor saw and carefully sanding to match the shape of the building, then packing up to suit the building's level. Paths and planting, etc, can then be added around to help disguise the join line.

Depending upon the model's construction wherever possible I prefer to use a method of securing the building in place that is also removable. Double sided sticky tape is useful, and so is a wooden block fitted inside, so that a wood screw can be used. Fixing with glue is the last resort!

In real life most houses back onto the railway line, which leads to all sorts of peculiar situations as small plots of land are built on adjacent to the track. The same applies to when the houses were built first and the track has been threaded through the gaps in the houses. The Continent is strewn with situations whereby trains run along the high street, share road bridges with cars and people, etc., small branch lines tend to do this!

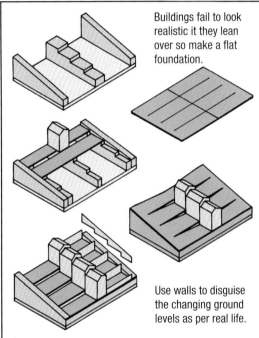

Buildings fail to look realistic it they lean over so make a flat foundation.

Use walls to disguise the changing ground levels as per real life.

Above: The 'High Street' is on a slope therefore each of the buildings are propped up to suit the ground outside its frontage.
Left: This shows how the ground can be arranged to suit a sloping site, so that the buildings sit on a flat foundation.
Below: The buildings on the multilevel layout are situated on various pieces of sloping ground, and the picture clearly shows the sloping road and pavement and the flat foundations. The gardens at the rear of the building are also on the flat, so walls are used between the levels of each garden.

Right: The oval layout portrays a small town setting, with a mixture of buildings and open spaces. The construction of the base is in one piece, except for the two hatches (trays) that allow access to the track level under the hillside.

Below: The multi-level oval layout, whilst still self contained in the fact that the track is fixed, is built using removable trays (hatches) that permit not only access to the lower track levels but the opportunity to replace the trays at a later date with a new version, so that the appearance of the layout can be changed.

Bottom: The station tray under construction, using wood blocks dressed with Perspex® elevations, prior to being painted.

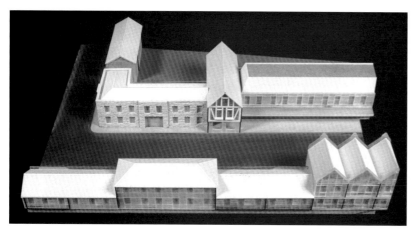

BUILDINGS: THE SETTING

In the previous pages in this chapter I have described a wide variety of ways to model buildings. This is because each building is an individual and will have its own modelling problems; therefore each building will require a mixture of modelling techniques.

A wide variety of buildings will be found in even a small area of most towns, so you can choose which types to model to suit your inclination and skills. The beginner can thus choose to start with simple block-like buildings, the expert complex ultra-detailed buildings which will stretch one's modelling skills. But it is the finer detail that will add not only the feeling of scale, but the feeling of reality. Street signs, traffic lights, lamp posts and cars, etc, commonly known as 'street furniture', and finally the people themselves, all add scale and life to the setting.

It is quite surprising just how many cars and people are needed; for instance, a busy high street can be full of traffic and the pavements absolutely crowded with people going into and out of shops, crossing the road, etc. A road crossing forms a good focal point for people and by using the crossing to stop the traffic, some explanation is given to the eye as to why the traffic is stationary. Thus the scene in the end can become like a still photograph, fooling the eye into believing it is reality.

Model people generally look very static unless they are particularly well sculpted, and due to technical reasons in mass production figures can look rather lifeless. This impression can be overcome by arranging figures with static postures at the edges of roads as if waiting to cross, in queues at bus stops or in groups apparently talking to each other, generally positioned in the most awkward of places which causes considerable pedestrian congestion!

Shops themselves will contain all sorts of advertising and signs adding colour to the scene. All the buildings will be in various states of repair, some newly painted in fresh colours and of modern design, whilst others will look weathered, worn and in need of repair, all again adding character to the street.

A good source of street planning is to obtain one of the many books showing aerial views of our towns and cities, the internet also as to be a good source but the sources of aerial views have degraded their images to a low resolution factor; which means that most images have now become useless for our use, because you cannot study cars and people.

The average high street is normally extremely busy during shopping hours, hectic on Saturdays and deserted on Sundays. The side streets follow a similar pattern, with shoppers' cars parked more densely in the roads near the shops, to a few cars parked further away. Pedestrians are the same, the nearer to the shops or train station the more people gather, so show this on the model.

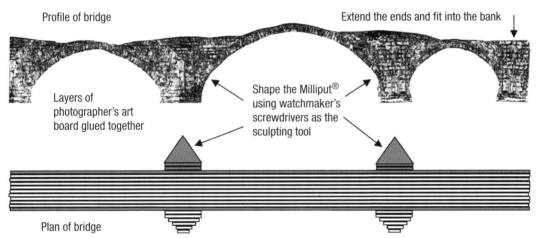

Profile of bridge

Extend the ends and fit into the bank

Layers of
photographer's art
board glued together

Shape the Milliput®
using watchmaker's
screwdrivers as the
sculpting tool

Plan of bridge

Above: The old foot bridge across a wide stream that is very shallow during the summer months, but becomes a raging flood during winter. As a model it would be easy to make from a series of cardboard layers covered in 'Milliput'® which is a 2 part epoxy modelling clay that is mixed up in small quantities because it sets rock hard in a few hours.

PLANNING FOR CHANGE

Most layouts are built in one piece, and the landscape forms an integral piece of the baseboard, therefore any change involves removing all existing work within the area of change. The alternative method is to build the base as a collection of removable 'trays'. The method of building the layouts using a series of trays is not new, and is in many ways superior to that of building the track and the landscape in one piece. For example, I recently discovered an old foot bridge, as well as a small castle, both of which I would like to model. If I had built the new oval layout in one piece as per the old oval layout, any changes would be difficult; but because it is built using trays, it is a simple case of making a new one. The main layout has only two removable hatches (trays) which could easily be replaced with a new landscaped section.

The multilevel oval layout has been designed from the start as a series of 'trays' on which is modelled a selection of themes and these trays are replaceable with a new idea that upgrades

the layout; because modelling is a progressive skill that grows over the years. Therefore the oval layout whilst its track-work remains the same can be revamped many times over and appear in many guises. I am already thinking how one of the 'trays' can be replaced with a new one that contains the remains of a small castle and bridge over the remains of a moat partly filled with water!

Below: The base 03 has two removable hatches (trays) that could be easily replaced with a new 'tray' containing a very different landscape. For example the field on the left could now contain a new housing estate!

7. PAINTING AND WEATHERING

We are surrounded by weathered buildings and landscape. Trees are weathered, i.e. they are greener on the mossier Northern side than the Southern side, because the South side is drier. Buildings are the same, the Northern side is the damp wall, therefore the moss flourishes, and the wall looks greener than the dry South side. Old buildings tend to be dirty, especially in the industrial areas, whereby years of factory smoke has discoloured the building.

WEATHERED SCENERY

First impressions count: Painting and weathering complement the landscaping in creating an immediate impact, because the eye views the overall scene and makes a lasting judgement before inspecting the detail of the model. It is well known that the first impression is the lasting impression of the model, and that a poor model well presented can look far better than a good model spoiled by poor landscape and painting.

Landscaping the country scenery on a baseboard is best started with the roads, by applying basic colours depending upon the road's surface. Tarmac, for example, is a very dark brown-black, roads surfaced with slate chips are a light grey whilst natural stone chips are a biscuit colour. I have found that the best type of paint to use is matt emulsion. On top of this base colour is added the weathering, caused by passing vehicles' tyres which tend to keep certain parts of the road clean, whilst depositing dirt and dust in other parts, especially the edges. This changes the road's colour in places and is particularly noticeable on single width country roads where the traffic is forced to use the centre part of the road only.

WEATHERING ROADS

To represent road dirt colour mix up matt emulsion paint using white, brown and black plus the soil colour of the adjacent fields. Mix all the colours together in approximately equal amounts so that they total about an egg cup full of colour. Then thin with about 65 per cent water and about five per cent white PVA glue so as to form a thin dirty wash of colour. Apply liberally to the road's pre-coloured surface then, using a soft camel or sable haired brush which has been partially dried on household kitchen roll, brush along the part of the road that the vehicles travel along, so as to dry it. Finally sprinkle on some very fine dirt and dust that has been sifted through a nylon stocking on to the remaining wet areas, so as to form a dirt texture deposit by the edges of the road. Use very little as the diluted glue/paint mixture has very limited gluing capabilities. Just enough is needed to form a dusting of texture. When dry, clean off any unglued texture with a vacuum cleaner and soft brush.

WEATHERING GRASS

Paint the grass side edges of the road/paving with soil colour, using household matt emulsion paint, 25% mixed with PVA woodworker's glue, 25% diluted approximately 50% with water, and paint this mixture on to the pre-coloured base, and texture on top of the wet mixture with the fine dirt texture and grass colour; spraying large areas with water to make these easier to work. Use a series of textures, starting with various shades of grass colour. Begin at the edges of the road as these tend to be a dirty colour compared with the grass a few feet away from the edge of the road. Constantly mix the grass colours by sprinkling using your finger and thumb (see illustration) to give finer control over the amount of texture applied. Allow some bald patches of grass by sprinkling on soil texture, again sieved through a fine mesh, and finally on top of all this sprinkle through a sieve the main grass-coloured texture chosen and allow to dry.

Remove unwanted texture with a vacuum cleaner fitted with a tube, to which the toe part of a nylon stocking has been knotted so as to form a small fine mesh bag taped in place in the tube. By using this method the unglued texture sprinkled on the baseboard can be carefully salvaged for re-use but any smaller dirt particles disappear into the vacuum cleaner itself so that the grass texture remains clean.

BUSHES AND TREES

On top of the grass texture now glued in place add ground cover in the form of small bushes, etc, made as described in Chapter 4, and build up height to the sides of the road with foliage or hedging, fencing, etc, to denote changes in land use or ownership.

Grass changes colour according to its environment. When it is near water, inside dips and hollows or other sheltered places, it will be a rich green colour. When exposed to strong sunlight, on stony ground, it will be bleached, i.e., browner and slightly dried out. Alongside footpaths, or in front gardens where the grass is well looked after, it will be a rich colour, but where it is a nuisance it should be straw coloured as if being treated with weed killer. Constantly change the grasses' colour and texture so as to represent well-kept short grass and rough unkempt long grass. Allow thin patches of grass to show the soil underneath. This is particularly important at gates and openings into grassed areas so don't cover the baseboard with a single solid texture. Remember grass is a living plant of a constantly changing colour, which wears out with heavy foot traffic so that 'bald patches' appear and therefore the bare earth shows; it's been weathered!

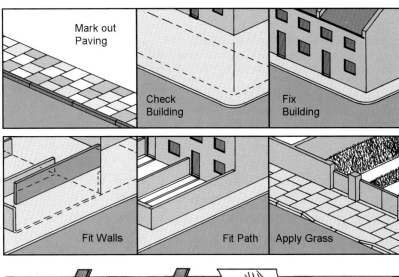

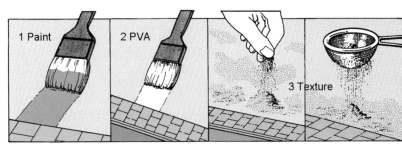

Top: Paint the roads and paving in a series of colours, by picking out individual paving stones etc. Followed by fixing buildings and walls in place before adding the grass texture.

Left: Use a mixture of grass colours, then add planting by drilling holes in the base and inserting bushes, trees etc. glued in place.

Below: (See pages 124 and 193) The removable ivy covered wall in place that allows access to the lower track on the multi level oval layout.

Right: 1. Having wired up and everything works spray the track a basic colour. **2.** when dry pour dry ballast over the track. **3.** using a paint brush carefully spread the ballast between the sleepers. In places mix old and new ballast to provide the appearance the track has been re-laid. **4.** Using an eye dropper, plastic bottle etc., drip thinned PVA woodworker's white glue onto the ballast and allow to dry.

Photos: Ballast is smaller than a clenched fist, therefore 'N' scale ballast shown below is always slightly over scale, but looks better at '00' scale **(right)**.
Bottom: Tracks are not always weed free, therefore some little bits of green mixed with the ballast is acceptable. Apply more on disused lines.

BALLASTING THE TRACK

Having completed the wiring and everything works the track is ready for ballasting. The first stage is to paint the track's sleepers and rails a basic colour and then apply a wash coat of rust colour over the sleepers, so as to weather them.

The track can be ballasted using two different methods, because each is suited to a particular situation. The first method is for laying long uninterrupted lengths of track. The baseboard is first painted ballast colour over the area where the track is going to be laid, i.e., over the cork underlay, then each side of the track is landscaped up to the painted ballast edge. The track is then positioned and dressmaker's pins pushed in alongside the outside rails so as to show their location, as the track is now removed and PVA glue is applied to the area where the ballast is going to be applied. The track is then repositioned using the pins to locate it on top of the wet glue. Check it for alignment, then apply the ballast directly on top of the wet PVA glue and track and allow to dry.

When dry the ballast is removed using a vacuum cleaner fitted with a nylon stocking in the tube, leaving the track and ballast firmly fixed in position. I have found that this method considerably speeds up track laying and ballasting on the easy lengths of track.

For the difficult parts of the track such as curves and points the track is laid and permanently pinned

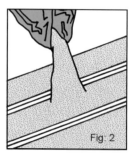

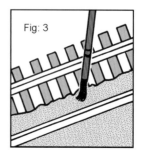

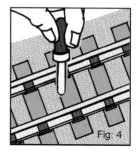

into position on the pre-painted cork underlay, and the landscape is completed each side of the ballast area. The ballast is then applied on top of the dry pre-coloured underlay very carefully, by brushing so that it is precisely in place. Glue watered down 50:50 is then applied to the ballast between the sleepers using an eye dropper or syringe, taking care not to touch the ballast but allowing the PVA glue to soak into it and hold it in position. Allow to thoroughly dry and spray the ballast a rust colour to suit.

Points: The points or other moving parts of the track must be kept free of ballast and glue leaving just the pre-painted underlay showing. This should obviously match the colour of the ballast being used. Finally, when dry thoroughly vacuum off loose ballast from the track, as ballast is generally made from a grit which tends to get into the working components of the rolling stock, causing unnecessary wear. This factor also applies to all the textures used so after construction clean and remove all unfixed textures that are not wanted.

EMBANKMENTS AND ROCK FACES

The basic construction for rock faces, embankments and cliffs has been explained in Chapter 4 but it is the painting and texturing which creates the final effect. Unfortunately, like the basic construction it is also something of a messy procedure.

For painting and texturing this type of natural topographical formation I have found over the years that emulsion paint is again best suited as it has so many advantages. There is a good range of colours, it can easily be mixed with acrylic or poster paints to change its tone or colour, it dries matt, it can be thinned and is waterproof when dry; the brushes are easily cleaned under the tap in running water, and it is reasonably cheap. Most important of all though is the fact that it can be used in the way one uses water colours, by applying washes, but it also successfully dry brushes and mixes with white PVA glue which is also water-based. This is a very useful point to remember as by increasing the glue percentage a matt paint can become a semi gloss, ideal for painting odds and ends that require a slight sheen when gloss paint is too shiny.

The technique for painting rock faces and embankments is first to apply two coats of paint to the plaster, cork, coal or whatever has been used for the foundation of the face. The first coat is a priming coat and is applied straight from the tin. This seals the surface and, because of the nature of the material it is being applied over, quickly dries. The second coat is a texturing coat in which mixtures of colours are applied 'wet'.

Thin the paint on the surface of the rock face by flicking with water from a large household wallpapering brush. This causes the mixture of colours to run into each other and also down the surface of the rock face. Whilst the paint is still wet strong un-thinned colours are applied as necessary to highlight points and are again allowed to mix on each side with the earlier coats. When the desired effect has been reached allow to partially dry so that the exposed protruding parts of the rock face are dry but the cracks between are still wet. At this

point texture the surface with a mixture of grass colours by literally throwing the texture at the surface of the rock face, forcing it into the cracks. Allow to dry thoroughly, and then clean up the baseboard using the vacuum cleaner method to regain unused and unglued grass texture. Use a soft paintbrush over the rock face surface so as to dislodge texture material that has not properly glued in place. Then dry-brush high points of the rocks so as to further highlight them. Add indications of bird droppings, etc, to give the impression of wild life existing on the rock face. The final effect is provided by planting small shrubs and flowers in some of the nooks and crannies of the surface. By using the wet paint and PVA glue method additional texture can be added as required without showing glue lines until the final overall effect is reached.

Above: This is part of a quarry that provided sandstone that was used to build local houses. The stone has been cut in horizontal bands ready for vertical cutting. Therefore the face of the stone is straight. From the modeller's point of view it is easy to carve from spray on expanded foam (used to seal gaps under the eaves of a house) that has been covered in plaster and painted. Whilst the paint is still wet, it is sprinkled with grass texture. The rock face has plenty of ledges, which are normally the home to birds; which leave their trademark! The method used is to paint the rocks a basic colour using emulsion paint and then add a series of washes of similar colour, followed by lots of white flecks flicked from a tooth brush and dry brushed to smear.

Far left: Adding the grass texture.

Left: The North facing tunnel portal is covered with mosses, and the embankments are covered in undergrowth.

It is well worth investing in a small lightweight digital camera for capturing photographs of the places you visit. The colours rendered in the photographs will not be 100% accurate, because of variable factors, but in most cases will be sufficient to meet our needs. The black and white photograph shown right, shows the tones of the image in greyscale. The tones we expect to run from black, through shades of grey to paper white. The same applies to colour, we expect to see a black and white. On the model we use a dirty wash to provide the black and white tones because on the model the colours need to be dulled to look realistic.

Colour photos: These portray a series of simple snapshots that could be taken on your travels, whilst you gather detailed information as part of your research.

Above: This black and white photograph shows the long grass leading down to the stream and was taken from a public footpath.

Colour opposite page: This shows weeds growing out of the mortar joints of the ornate buttress.

Rye signal box, looking disused with ivy growing up the side. This brick built viaduct has salt stains discolouring its surface. This photograph shows a close up of rust coloured ballast, notice the size of the ballast; about 8 stones span the gap between the sleepers. The final photo shows a general view down the track, which is extremely discoloured by rust.

CHOICE OF COLOUR

You have to be very careful in choosing colours and textures so that they remain in scale and harmonize together. Be wary of using colour photographs as a guide as at times these are inadequate in their colour rendering and can be very misleading due to the way the camera records colours. The reasons for this are the colour temperature setting, saturation of the image, filters in front of the lens and print processing. To the photographer this means that the digital camera on an overcast day will produce dull coloured photographs, whilst on a bright sunny day the colours will be enhanced. Finally, if a photograph is taken in the early morning or evening on a bright sunny day it warms up the colours.

Digital Cameras: Digital cameras have several colour settings, i.e. auto, bright sunshine, overcast, night-time and indoor. The camera also has other settings, i.e. Auto, Aperture, Shutter and Manual. I advise that unless you understand how to use your camera, you leave it in the auto settings throughout.

Exposure affects the colour density of the finished photograph, irrespective of the light available. An underexposed image is dark and dull, whilst an overexposed one will have its colours burnt out.

Inkjet Printing: The same applies with the filtration used in printing, i.e. the colours produced on inkjet photo paper are richer than those printed on plain paper; therefore this has caused a colour change.

The choice of how colours are finally picked is very much up to the individual. Colour is used to enhance or create atmosphere within a layout. In the age of steam, colours very quickly became drab due to smoke and grime in built-up town and city situations, whilst most of the country stations remained considerably cleaner. But this was with the aid of the local station master who took great pride in his station. This still applies today, but to a lesser extent.

A cutting which has brick walls built up on each side and has a heavy flow of rolling stock passing through quickly weathers. (The term given to describe natural discolouration.) The grime is deposited from the trains' and cars' exhausts, by smoke from factory chimneys or by steel particles from the trains' wheels which settle on the walls and then rust, causing a dark brown discolouration. Much the same applies to the ballast of the track, as oil and grime settles upon it so that viewed from a distance the track becomes a rusty brown colour intermingled with new cleaner ballast at the points where the track has been re-laid or adjusted.

The same applies to the embankment where the grass has been cut or sprayed with weed killer, causing brown dead grass along the sides of the track intermingled with the fresh green of the newly cut grass, or grass that is re-growing.

The time of year also plays an important part as it influences colour too. Spring brings new fresh plant growth which is lighter in colour. In mid-summer the leaves are a rich mature colour, whilst the autumn brings forth a rainbow of colours as the leaves go through their final change and prepare to fall from the trees. This is the most colourful time of all.

Grass also changes colour from rich green to straw colour, depending upon the amount of moisture in the ground, so that within a very short distance the grass will vary from yellowy-brown to a rich green. This especially applies along waterways where moisture will have soaked into the soil along the edge of the water, but the top of the embankment will have remained dry, causing the grass to discolour. This constant change in colour, when properly used on the layout, creates a natural feeling to the scenery which is much better than using one colour for the grass, one colour for the ballast and so on, which is most unrealistic.

WEATHERING BUILDINGS

Scenecraft® by Bachmann® in 2008 released a new series of resin cast super-detailed buildings which are ideal for installing straight from the box and onto the layout. The 'Market Hampton' country station is made up from several buildings that are joined together using spacers.

Below: I chose not to join the buildings together using the spacers, but to remove the ends of the roof using a saw and these ends I will use later.

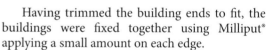

Having trimmed the building ends to fit, the buildings were fixed together using Milliput® applying a small amount on each edge.

When set any gaps were filled with woodworker's Brummer® and smoothed as required whilst wet.

Thin paper gullies were then added along the corners of roof tiles; to represent lead flashing and painted to suit. The roof and walls were then given a thin wash to provide a matt finish to the building.

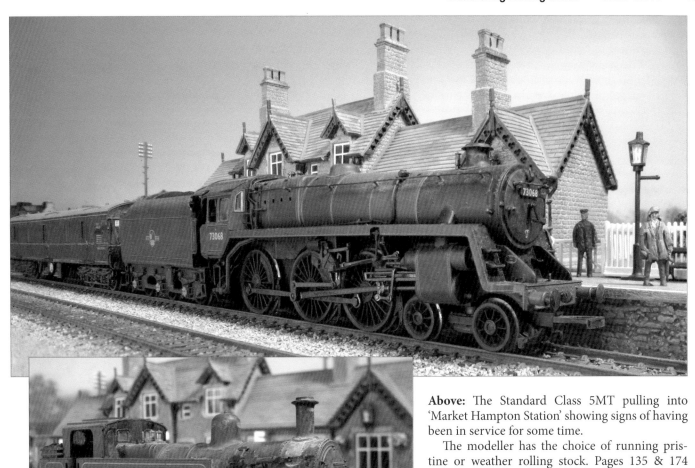

Above: The Standard Class 5MT pulling into 'Market Hampton Station' showing signs of having been in service for some time.

The modeller has the choice of running pristine or weather rolling stock. Pages 135 & 174 show painting methods that can be used, but the dirt effects are copied from photos shown in books i.e. *BR Steam Portrait* by P H Wells, or *British Railways: Steam & Traction in Colour* by Colin Boocock & Brian Morrison; the latter book is very good because it shows trackside locations and settings. Old books can be sourced on the internet at reasonable cost.

Above and Right: The 0-6-0T 'Jinty' engines have been given a thin wash of matt dirt coloured emulsion paint, followed by a thin wash of very light grey, which has been allowed to run and blend into the dirt wash. To represent oily dirt around the wheels a sheen paint has been used. Clean the name plate and give the number a polish!

Left: The dirt on the diesel engine has been applied using paint flicked from a tooth brush, which produces a coarse speckle, after the application of the dirt wash.

Note: Thoroughly clean the rail top and wheel rims for smooth running!

Right: The ground contours of the multilevel layout constantly change, as does the ground in reality. The same applies to whatever man has made, over time it will change.

The track ballast is a typical example of colour change, from old to new ballast. But both are blended by dust, which depends upon the area as to its colour.

For example lower right is the coaling area; therefore the ballast is mixed with coal dust. This dust spreads to the adjacent track. The siding has been recently re-laid, and therefore cleaner. Towards the station and the tunnel the ballast is older and therefore dirtier.

Soot, oil and rust are materials that create their own colours. Most stations are no longer the overall dirty soot colour they used to be, but the centre of the track is still stained a dark colour caused by oil from the passing diesel engines.

Rust can be found a reasonable distance from the track and is caused by the tiny particles of steel that are generated as the track and the rolling stock's wheels come in contact with each other. Add some water and the steel rusts causing brown stains to appear that are partially noticeable on white paint. (See page 33).

The rails also rust, but not everything is a standard colour. For example in the sidings and marshalling yards quite often the track is a dirty oily black, but in the area of the ash pit the track is almost white. It also depends upon what the hopper wagons carry and what they lose!

PAINTING BUILDINGS

Buildings require a series of different painting techniques ranging from paintbrush to spray gun use. Each method produces a slightly different finish. For example, dry brushing gives a different finish to spray painting a dirt and grime effect. This is because the paintbrush is used to apply colour in solid form or as a wash rather than dusting paint onto the surface as with a spray gun. Rolling stock moves and buildings do not hence they weather very differently; therefore different methods of painting are used.

The first stage in painting any surface is to apply a primer coat of paint suitable for the material it is being applied over. Sheet styrene and plastic kits are noted for their dislike of cellulose paint, because the paint's solvent attacks the surface, so this material is best primed with an acrylic or oil-bound paint.

This forms a key for further applications of paint. The primer coat should be sufficiently dense to make the building appear 'solid'. This is very important when using clear Perspex® *(Note Perspex can be sprayed with cellulose paint)* as it is a material that tends to glow if insufficient paint is applied, since being transparent it allows light to pass through it.

Cardboard is best first sprayed with cellulose primer or brush-painted with oil-bound paint to seal the surface, before using water-based paints. This is because water based paints would be absorbed by the cardboard, which would tend to warp it. Castings will again require priming, cellulose being ideal in the majority of situations, but if in doubt test a small piece first. Plastic kits *can* be sprayed using modern acrylic car body repair paint, these sprays are ideal because the paint mixture in the can is extremely thin and quickly dries, so it has little time to attack the plastic surface. By virtue of the paint being thin it does not hide detail, but it does easily run if too much paint is applied.

On top of the priming coat apply the first of the many layers of paint using a brush. Emulsion or acrylic water-based paints applied in several thin coats produces a far superior finish than one thick coat. The hobby oil-bound paints available tend to be slightly thicker than required so they should be thinned down as required, using the manufacturer's matching thinner. If you use ordinary white spirit or turpentine as thinners there is a tendency for the paint to harden in the tin or separate out if stored for a period of time. White spirit is, however, perfectly suitable for cleaning brushes when changing colours or as a pre-wash prior to finally cleaning the brush with soapy water at the end of the painting session. On the last water rinse of the brush always use hot water and flick the brush so that the hairs form a point, then store it away. *(See page 138 for more details)*

The use of a spray gun produces a very different type of finish as a series of colours can be applied over each other by using a low pressure and a speckled technique. The paint is applied as a series of small blobs, rather than as a fine mist as one normally associates with spraying. The size of the blobs can be varied by increasing or decreasing the airline pressure and by controlling the spray guns trigger movement. By using this speckled technique several colours can be applied over each other so as to form a texture of colour rather than a solid colour. This is ideal for representing brickwork, etc.

The technique is to first spray on the basic brick colour, then to speckle it with a lighter colour and then a darker colour, finally repeating with the base colour. Repeating this process until an even speckled effect has been obtained, increasing or decreasing pressure as required thus varying the size of the speckles. *(See page 140 for more details about spray painting.)*

Take for example six adjoining buildings, each with different owners. Because of circumstances and time, the owner of each of the buildings will have carried out work on the building's front and back elevations, thus changing their appearance, but due to time they will then have changed again, because they have been exposed to the elements. Weather builds up dirt and grime on the surface of the building, rain and damp erode the surface, the heat of the sun fades and discolours it, and through time the building deteriorates with flaking paintwork, rotting woodwork and dirty windows. The building will now look very different from the time it was new and freshly painted.

The buildings shown above are a typical example of a row of buildings found in the 'South of England' and the architecture is different to that found in the north or west of the country. But the same applies, the buildings change in appearance, with buildings far dirtier in the industrial towns than dwellings found in the countryside.

Station buildings are the same, in the age of steam they were soot splattered, This really showed in the days of steam when the track passes under a bridge, because the bridges were totally covered in soot, along with any pedestrians that were unfortunate enough to be passing at the time a train passed!

Today buildings are far cleaner, but not all have been cleaned, therefore showing this on the layout adds interest.

AGING BUILDINGS

Nothing made or grown retains its original appearance for long. Deciduous trees are an obvious example as through the seasons they grow leaves, being bright in colour, then become darker as the leaves mature during the summer months, then change colour again during autumn producing a wide range of colours. Finally, during winter they lose their leaves completely, so the tree has changed its appearance 4 times throughout the year.

Paintwork does exactly the same; it changes in its appearance. Once exposed to the elements it soon becomes dirty unless regularly cleaned and polished. A car is a good example, always requiring cleaning each week to maintain its high glossy finish. In many cases a weekly cleaning is not possible. On a railway bridge or building, for example, the shiny gloss-painted surface soon becomes dull, because of dirt and grime (which has a matt finish) sticking to its surface. For this reason it is wrong to use a high gloss finish on painted surfaces that are exposed to the elements; which would not be cleaned regularly.

Take the above row of fictitious houses, and from left to right the owner of the first building could well have painted the woodwork some years ago and his wife regularly cleans the windows, so that the front of the building looks brighter, but the brickwork is dirty.

The second owner may have done this many years ago and the elements have badly weathered the paintwork, and he has not washed the windows therefore the building looks dirty.

The last and third building owner has just acquired his property and has stripped the building and put on a new roof, new windows, etc, cleaned the brickwork of the building and then repainted it in a modern colour, so that the building looks new.

From the modeller's point of view, identical kits can be purchased, each being changed slightly, involving very little work, but being painted differently to its adjoining neighbour. This is a process that can be expanded along an entire block of independently owned buildings so that each individual building making up the block becomes different in appearance, although it is the same basic structure, but through time each building has changed its appearance. (Another view of these houses can be seen on page 106.)

Cardboard kit built buildings are far more difficult to weather because the water based paints tend to warp the card, whilst oil-based do not distort the card, (I find oil based paint more difficult to use.) The same applies to the computer based printed elevations; the water softens the paper's surface which means that it can be easily damaged. But if the elevations are all pre-printed as being weathered, the row of identical buildings look wrong.

Just to add to the confusion, local council or housing associations tend to use the same colour scheme throughout, so that the block of houses all look the same, even down to the front door colours. But each of the dwellings will have different coloured curtains!

What is needed is a study of the locality that the layout represents, and a detailed study of the types of buildings found, i.e. is it the posh end of town that is being modelled or the other end! Is the locality in the north of England or in the south or west? Are the buildings stone or brick built, are the buildings new or old? Can you get a kit, or a pre-painted ready built? Can you change its appearance?

Time is a key word and a simple example and justification for a glossy finish is a man painting a fence, the job being half completed. In front of him the fence will be the old discoloured, dirty and weathered paintwork, but behind him, the newly gloss painted fence which now looks entirely different. It is a point in time, and by applying this point in time on the model it can be made to look more interesting.

The above photograph shows a typical street scene. The buildings are dated and some look run down, except for the house on the right which has recently had its brickwork cleaned and windows and doors painted.

But whilst the windows have curtains, there are no nets up at the windows, so the buildings have that disused look, almost as they are about to be pulled down, to make way for a new development.

GRIME COVERED ROLLING STOCK

This is a very individual thing and is achieved in two ways, the first stage is by using the spray gun, the second by using brush. The first thing I do is to use the airbrush to paint in and around areas on the rolling stock where rust appears, caused by metal particles that come off the track and wheels and then oxidize. Rust forms on the lower part of the running gear, particularly around wheels and the lower chassis. This is sprayed in an upward direction, along the direction of travel.

Dirt colour is then applied from the top in a downward direction to give the impression that dirt has settled on top of the subject. Individual pieces are picked out and painted by brush using a very thin wash of colour, particularly around areas where steam emerges which are given a thin white coat painted to form a run in a vertical direction. Whilst the paint is still wet add a rust colour and allow this to run down in the white paint so that the two intermingle.

Areas that are well handled remain comparatively clean so use a cotton bud to remove the dirt and rust colours, or alternatively paint as if the original paintwork has been worn away to expose bare metal.

The choice of weathering colours should match the location of use, as dirt can vary. A classic example of this is when the rolling stock belongs to a cement works, the cement powder colour dominating the natural dirt colour. However, the locomotive collecting these wagons could be from a pool service, used up and down the country, so that its dirt colour will be completely different.

Painting rolling stock to look either new or old is an acquired skill, as is the paint choice used. Some modellers use oil based paints, because this is the type of paint the model shops sell, others use acrylic paints which mix with water but are waterproof when dry. I use household emulsion water based paint, because as a professional model maker I use a lot of paint.

I also use cellulose paints, (traditional car body paint) which are solvent based and highly inflammable.

The advantage with the latter paint is the drying time, which is considerably shorter than oil based paints and they dry harder. This can be a disadvantage because hard paints also chip, and being spirit based can attack some plastic finishes. Oil based paints are safe to use on most plastics. Water based paints tend not to stick on bare plastic, so that a primer has to be used first. Water based paints are rarely available in gloss finish, but have a superb matt finish.

Above: Brush painting was used throughout the creation of this scene. For example the grass was given a foundation of green paint, as were the walls painted a stone colour. The same applies to the road colour, the paving etc. On top of the basic colour a series of similar colours are used, to break up the flat overall tone. On top of this a dirt colour wash is applied which ages the colour.
Right: because it can be messy applying the wash I use a tray made from a cardboard lid and lined with tinfoil.

Below: Ready made and painted buildings look far too 'new' and need to be aged so that they blend into the landscape.

BRUSH PAINTING

The scene above used brush painting throughout because painting buildings, roads and rolling stock when using a brush is very much like an artist painting a picture, you have complete control. A single colour is never applied to represent the brickwork, roads or roof, etc, but a series of colours are used, all similar in their tone, so as to form a texture. A brick wall, for example, contains several tones, as each brick is an individual with its own but similar colour.

It is very important to buy good brushes, as the coarse-haired cheap types really do prevent fine workmanship. I have found through practice that it is very worthwhile to invest in a selection of good quality fine-haired artist's brushes of the sable and the Daler® 'Dalon' nylon type, which if properly looked after will last for many years.

These types of brush have a very long life when using oil-bound paint, but their working life is considerably reduced when using emulsions, which is the type of paint that I prefer. *(Non-flammable and are odour free.)* Therefore I always clean the brushes properly after use and store so as to protect their points.

The choice of bristle length is also important, as short-haired brushes carry very little paint. The

longer-haired brushes still come to a point but carry much more paint, and I find them easier to use as one is not constantly recharging the brush with paint. This is particularly important when painting edges and straight lines. Chisel-pointed brushes are also useful as these allow you to paint up to an edge, by using an upwards stroke into the edge or recess rather than trying to paint along it.

When brush painting, the building should be constructed in such a way as to make it easier to paint. For example, the doors and the window frames, glazing etc, should not be fixed in place, because the plastic pre-moulded window bars are much easier to paint without the clear glazing in place. When the ruled line window method has been used using clear plastic, the complete window can be masked, as the windows' surfaces are flat. The applied strip window glazing bar method is always difficult, requiring utmost care when painting, as this method relies on the glazing to hold the glazing bars in position. The best method is to pre-paint the building and then fit the glazing strips and touching in as required.

The example shown below is a ready made and painted Hornby® building which is far too clean in its present condition to blend into the landscape. To dull the colours a wash colour is made up using

water and emulsion paint, mixed to a dirt colour, and applied with a large sable-haired brush and allowed to dry.

For scratch-built buildings the technique that I use is first to prime the surface using a can of spray primer or household oil-based undercoat, thinned down 50:50. When dry I add a series of further colours, using hobby oil-bound or household emulsion paints. I also tone the colours by adding black or white to the basic colour. Apply several thin coats to build up the colour rather than one thick coat.

By adding texture to the paint (e.g. fine pumice powder) further effects can be obtained by sanding the surface when the paint is dry (ideal for platforms). Unfortunately this type of mixture in the paint quickly destroys sable haired brushes, so use the nylon types. On top of this then is added a series of very thin dirt and grime coloured washes, by mixing up brown, black and white emulsions to form the required colour. *(I use 35 mm film plastic film pots or glass miniature jam pots because they can be resealed for future use.)* Some of the dirt colour is then considerably thinned down (90 per cent water) in a second pot, which is then applied to the building, now placed in its normal upright position so that the wash runs down the building. Again use a large sable brush, and as the wash colour runs down the building brush undiluted colour under the window sills and other places where dirt collects. Wash down the thinned paint as it is applied; this darkens selected areas and excess wash is then removed with a drier brush. Keep cleaning areas with clean water until the desired effect is obtained. When dry the detail of some of the building can be picked out with fresh paint to represent newly painted areas.

The reason for laying the elevations either flat or vertical is to control the wash's flow; because when the elevation is laid flat the wash stays in cracks or score lines, when they are vertical the wash runs out of the score lines and downwards.

Final detail is now added to the building such as glazing, curtains and doors, some window glazing being given a dirty wash to make it look unclean, the centres of the windows then being dry rubbed clean with a cotton bud or piece of cotton wool on a cocktail stick to give the appearance of careless window cleaning.

CHOICE OF PAINT

The buildings' construction is also important as this influences the type of paint that can be used. Card buildings as noted earlier absorb moisture so they need to be primed with oil or cellulose paint before using water-based paints. Oil paint at times does have an advantage over water-based paints, because they do not warp card, and because they stay wet longer, and textures can be sprinkled on to the paint's wet surface rather than mixing textures with the paint. Use Polyfiller® powder filtered through a nylon stocking stretched over a wire frame to form a sieve, or a tea strainer. Carefully tap the sieve or tea strainer so as to apply very little texturing material, removing excessive material

when the paint is dry. After applying the texture repaint with a suitable colour and again allow to dry to secure the texture into position.

FLAKING PLASTER

To create the impression of flaking plaster, first cover a piece of plywood with polythene sheet, fixed in place using masking tape and thumbtacks. Continue by brushing on about six coats of matt emulsion paint. When dry a layer of brittle paint will have been made, because the paint layer can be peeled off. This thin layer of paint is then laid on a piece of card which is supported on a soft surface.

By applying pressure with a finger or blunt instrument it can then be broken up into pieces, but kept in order. This is important as each piece is glued to the front of the building as it is broken up. By leaving some areas clear the brickwork remains exposed, creating the effect that some of the plaster has fallen off. This can be further enhanced by painting.

Above: The turntable was painted a basic colour and then flooded with a dirty wash colour, which was stippled to make it form pools of dirt. The white edging, which is in fact a grey was applied after, so that it looked as if it had been recently painted.

Below: The Hornby® building has had a dirty wash applied, so that the building is now 'matt' and has lost its 'sheen'. Notice the dirt under the platform and even the rails have had a dirt wash colour applied!

AIR BRUSHING

PAINT VISCOSITY
Paints' thickness is completely variable and will depend upon type, make and use. Each particular batch of paint will have to be mixed to match the job in hand and its viscosity established through trial and error to match the equipment being used.

All air brushes and spray guns require a supply of compressed air and can be in the form of a liquid propellant. Unfortunately liquid propellant has a disadvantage, because it drops in pressure when used for a period of time. (Warm in a bowl of lukewarm water to restore the pressure.) Also, cans of liquid propellant run out.

The compressor is the most efficient way of supplying air to both the spray gun and air brush. A compressor also supplies air at a higher pressure (between thirty and sixty pounds per square inch). Although this is not always needed it is handy to have when cleaning out equipment. Spray guns also need higher pressure and a higher volume of air than an air brush.

To control air pressure and air flow a regulator is used because you only require sufficient pressure to atomize the paint into a mist. Over-pressurized spraying pre-dries the paint and blows dry particles on to wet areas to form blowback, which looks like sprayed sandpaper and much the same effect is formed if the paint is too thick.

A problem to watch when using compressors is water in the airline. This results in water droplets coming out of the spray gun or airbrush nozzle and on to the surface being sprayed, with very disastrous results. To overcome this problem a moisture trap should be fitted in the last piece of airline between the spray gun and the pressure storage vessel or compressor outlet.

The pressure regulator and the water trap on a compressor are generally combined, but on a propellant can there is just a regulator valve, as the gas does not generate water. The regulator valve controls the volume of air allowed to pass through and into the airline. This can cause back pressure to build up in the air line between the valve and airbrush, causing momentary high pressure spraying before the required low pressure is reached. A diaphragm regulator valve overcomes this problem, but will be more expensive to purchase.

Masking: Masking material is used to cover areas on the model, so that they are protected from unwanted paint. Two types are available. The first is in the form of a tape, the second is a fluid which when dry forms a protective layer that can be peeled off later. The first material is available in rolls of various widths, and of different types. Paper tape is the most commonly used for masking but does not provide a crisp edge, since the paint creeps under the paper folds. This is because the paint viscosity that we use in modelling is considerably thinner than that used for industrial purposes.

Clear sticky tape is better for our use, and is available in high or low tack. High tack is the sort of tape, such as Sellotape®, most normally found in the stores. Low tack is for special purposes, such as artwork when high tack would stick to the paper too well and spoil its surface on removal.

Low tack tapes are used for masking painted polystyrene, because it has low paint adhesion properties. Alternatively, normal tape can be used provided that its stickiness has been reduced by passing it between the fingers a few times. The secret of successful masking really comes down to using a sharp knife; using tape for flat areas and masking liquid, which is simply painted on the difficult bits.

Spraying Distance: The distance from the nozzle to the subject is important and will vary depending upon the equipment used. A recommended minimum distance will be found on spray cans, which also need to be well shaken. This is to mix the

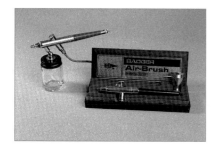

colour up and to mix the propellant into the paint. The minimum spray distance is to allow the propellant to dissipate into the atmosphere, so that paint only reaches the surface of the material. There is no such minimum distance when using an airbrush or spray gun, so the distance can be varied over a wider range. The spraying pressure and the thickness of paint can also be changed to suit the job in hand.

Airbrushes are used at a very close range, from around an inch (25mm), and with much thinner paint than spray guns. The size of the gun and its nozzle pattern determine the distance. When a large pressurized gun is used the paint is very thick and is forced out, the spraying distance needing to be around eighteen inches (450mm). With a small gravity-fed gun it is around six inches (150mm). These minimum distances are for general spraying at normal pressure, but can be increased or decreased along with the pressure and the thickness of the paint. If you wish to achieve a speckled effect, for example, the pressure should be lower than normal and spraying distance two to three times further than the minimum.

Spraying Technique: Having prepared for spraying it is good practice to test the spray on scrap material first, preferably of the same shape to be sprayed and of the same type of material (an old kit is ideal). Start by blowing the dust off the subject with a dry gun and use a clean dry paintbrush to remove stubborn bits. For high gloss finishes overlap the spray area slightly. Start with the nooks and crannies, working each one in turn and carefully checking the surrounding area for wet paint build-up. When this is completed continue with the easier areas, finishing with the largest areas, working through the primer coats and then the finished colour coats. Allow the paint to completely dry before re-masking other areas. On very small areas it will often be found more practical to mask and paint by hand.

Painting & Weathering Rolling Stock: The model should be masked for the first stage of colour, working preferably from the lightest colour. The reason for this is that darker colours have greater covering power. Pigments used in paint are also of different densities: yellow I have found to have the least covering power, so for this colour I use a white undercoat. Red should be one of the last colours to apply as it tends to bleed through, especially if white is required and when cellulose paints are being used. *(Note: Never use cellulose paints on polystyrene as they dissolve it.)*

The paint thickness should be kept as thin as practical, so as to retain as much detail as possible. The term 'a coat of paint' does not refer to a single layer applied in one go, but to a series of very thin applications, sometimes up to five layers to build up the density of colour. It may at first seem stupid to have this many layers, but each is so fine and thin that it barely covers the surface, and since it is so thin it dries very quickly. This prevents the paint

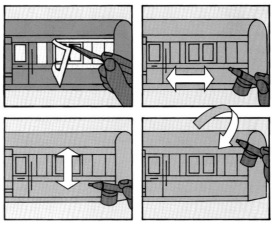
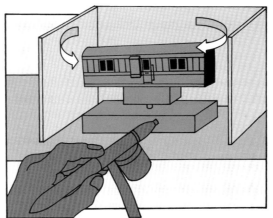

SPRAYING
So as to contain the mess that can be made whilst spraying, a cardboard box may be used with the front and top removed. For convenience the model should be mounted on to a support for handling. A rotating base has advantages, as the subject can be easily moved into a new spraying position without fear of knocking it over.

running into thick streaks and forming tidal waves, associated with wet and heavy spraying or spraying too close. Spray cans are particularly prone to do this as the pressure cannot be varied. Thus, when a small component needs to be painted; most people hold the component too close to the nozzle; the result is that it becomes swamped with paint, which runs all over the place.

Lining: The best method for lining is to use a draughtsman's ruling pen filled with paint using a paintbrush. Do not over-fill the pen as this will cause it to blob. Support the pen and hands well by using a jig as shown in the illustration. Rule the straight lines first and fill the radius corners in by using a fine-tipped paintbrush. Wider lines can be achieved by ruling in two lines and then filling in the gap between by brush painting.

Opposite bottom:
Airbrushes are available in various types and prices. The cheapest normally are more difficult to control, because they have to suck the paint up from the glass reservoir, unlike gravity fed guns which respond the moment the trigger is moved. Unfortunately spray guns tend to be a lot bigger therefore cannot produce such fine work.

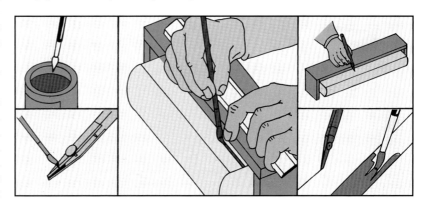

8. TRACK LAYING, WIRING AND SIGNALLING

INTRODUCTION

The importance of taking care in laying and wiring the track cannot be stressed too much as without this functioning properly the layout will never be successful and a joy to operate. This means that the track must be firmly fixed on to a smooth surface, and that curves must be progressive bends starting with a large radius, reducing into a smaller radius, and ending with the required radius, so that sudden direction changes are avoided.

The joins in the track should be as smooth as possible and the alignment of the track at the baseboard's edge should be parallel, so that both wheels of the rolling stock encounter the join at the same time.

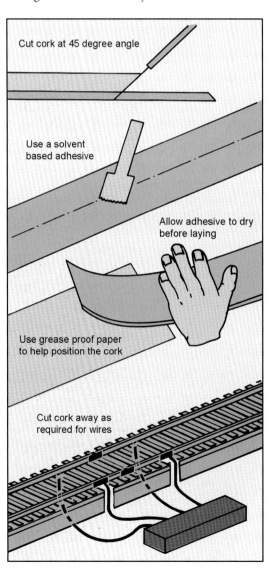

Cut cork at 45 degree angle

Use a solvent based adhesive

Allow adhesive to dry before laying

Use grease proof paper to help position the cork

Cut cork away as required for wires

The mechanical-working components which help the tracks' use should also be easily accessible, just in case of a malfunction. Finally all wiring should be tagged and carefully secured to help prevent accidental damage. Gluing a wiring diagram to the underside of the layout helps in the location of faults. Remember, if it is easily accessible, it is easier to repair.

Laying The Cork Underlay: Having assembled the base and planned precisely the position of the track, mark out the track's ballast outline by drawing directly on to the top of the baseboard, using the track's exact position. Two methods can be used: the first is to trace this out using tracing paper and re-mark out on to the cork to be used as an underlay (this helps reduce running noise). The second is to cut the cork in long straight strips half the ballast width, with one bevelled edge and one square cut. The square cut edge is made to follow the centre line of the track along the straights and curves by bending the cork as necessary. The reason for cuffing out the cork with a bevelled edge is so that it looks like ballast raised above ground level.

The cork is glued on to the base's plywood top with one of the contact types of adhesive, i.e. Evo Stick® or Thixofix®, coated on both surfaces and allow to dry. (Contact adhesive is used as it does not wet the cork and expand the materials, as would water-based adhesives.) Place over the dry contact adhesive a sheet of greaseproof paper and position the cork, slowly removing the paper and pressing the cork into position (see illustration).

The Track: The track performs two functions: it guides the rolling stock and it supplies electrical power to the driving motor. This means the track must be wired up to a safe 12 or 16 volt power source. This unit is called the transformer and is frequently built into the controller.

For a simple single-track oval layout, running one train only, this is very easy, as it just requires two wires leading from the controller's terminals, one to each of the rails. It is not even necessary to align the polarity of the power, as this is reversible via the controller. To run two trains on a single line oval, however, it will need to be divided up into three separate electrical sections, each independently switched on or off from the one controller, so that power can be selectively supplied to any section of track at any time or leaving sections without power.

On layouts using DCC or any of the two-wire microchip systems the sectioning of track does not apply, as the system supplies coded signals to every part of the track, the locomotives on the track responding to their own code via a built-in microchip circuit. This system is without a doubt the easiest to wire, but is at present only available at reasonable cost for HO, 00 and larger scales.

Note: Dividing the track into sections is for powering conventional rolling stock built without microchips or coding devices.

Refer to the illustration showing the sectioned oval. The first locomotive (1) on section (A) of the track is stationary, whilst the second locomotive (2) moves from section (B) on to section (C) where it is stopped. This clears the (B) section of track, and the power to the (C) section on which the locomotive now rests is switched off. The power is now switched on to the (A) section of track, for the first locomotive (1) that has remained stationary. This can now be moved forward on to the cleared section of track (B) and it is stopped on this section of track. This then clears the section ahead for the second locomotive and the procedure is repeated over and over again.

To enable this to work the track has to be electrically broken into three sections. The rails of each section are joined with nylon rail joiners, which unlike the metal joiners do not conduct electricity. Thus the rail is mechanically but not electrically joined. Since there is no longer a continuous electrical link, each section of track will have to be wired, back to the controller via an on or off switch, and this is the basic procedure for the conventional type of wiring.

The passing loop layout with sidings is a good example of the use of two controllers, which allow independent control over all sections of track. The rolling stock is passed from the first to the second controller, when necessary, allowing two people to operate the layout.

The track arrangement of the new multi-level oval base shown in a later chapter provides wide scope for various running schedules which could be built on a flat baseboard, ignoring the lower levels. (See the track plans on the previous page for the one piece oval layout.) The new multi level layout is capable of handling 12 locomotives plus goods and passenger rolling stock. The track has two continuous loops and by sharing part of the line with other rolling stock a logical reason for having stationary rolling stock is suggested. The track layout consists of two basic ovals with two passing loops, one waiting loop and three sidings, plus coaling etc. It also has three storage loops hidden from view, which can store nine trains. It is serviced by 28 sets of turnouts (points), and to start with I would suggest that these are initially installed in the manually-operated mode. (Install the point motor etc, but do not wire up until everything works). This is to reduce the wiring of the layout for problem solving; because it can be operated from one controller plus a number of switches to switch on or off individual sections of the track.

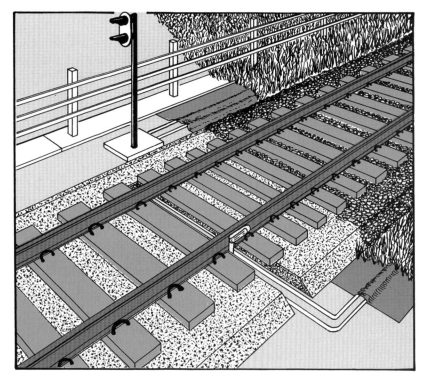

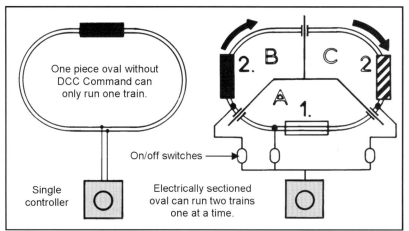

One piece oval without DCC Command can only run one train.

Single controller

On/off switches

Electrically sectioned oval can run two trains one at a time.

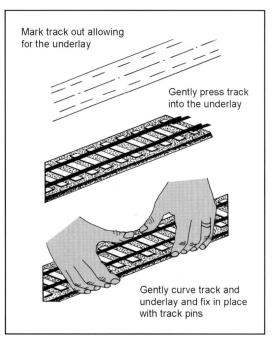

Mark track out allowing for the underlay

Gently press track into the underlay

Gently curve track and underlay and fix in place with track pins

Top: Cut slots in the cork to enable the wiring to pass underneath the track and only ballast after everything is working.

Middle Left: The basic wiring of the simple oval layout using a conventional controller

Middle right: This shows the track broken up into separate electrical sections.

Left: Laying 'Foam Rubber' track underlay that is fixed in place using track pins through the sleepers. Take care not to damage the track with the hammer!

Opposite page: Note not all overhead pickups actually work and those that do will be fitted with a switch that will need to be set as required.

Opposite page, lower right: The non-working oval stumps many a beginner. The problem arises because on a single track return loop (shown in grey) section needs to be electrically isolated and a reverse wiring switch is fitted.

This is the reason why the oval layout shown at the front of the book does not work electrically.

By simply returning the track back upon itself the polarity of the rails becomes electrically crossed, causing a short circuit. (Also see page 146.)

Below: The DCC Bachmann starter set is packed with everything needed to assemble a basic oval.

BASIC WIRING

For the 'HO & 00' modeller the advent of Digital Command Control (DCC) has made wiring easier, because all that is required is to split the track up into electrically isolated sections and power each section. For the non DCC user each of these electrically isolated sections will need a switch, to control the power to each of these sections, and a series of sections powered to allow the train to move along the track, from section to section.

The basics of wiring a layout are reasonably straight forward, because it only progresses into the difficult stage as the layout becomes more complex. Most people start with a clip together layout, and then assemble the wiring to make it work. This is a very simple procedure, because a boxed layout contains everything needed to make it work and it is the same with the add-on track kits. The difficulty arises when the individual decides to assemble the track in a different way to that shown in the instructions, and nothing works!

How the Model Works: Since the majority of model locomotives used on indoor layouts are very small, they use electric motors to provide the driving force, working generally from 12 volts direct current (DC), the same type of voltage provided by batteries. Unfortunately, due to the amperage drawn by the model's electric motor, batteries are soon exhausted of their power.

To overcome this problem on a conventional layout (not DCC) a transformer is used. This works from the mains 240/110 alternating current (AC) and reduces the high voltage mains supply to a

safe low voltage. On no account should the track be wired directly to the mains. The transformer converts the mains voltage into 16 volts AC and then by using a rectifier finally into 12 volts DC. This provides two sources of power, 16 volts AC for point motors and 12 volts DC for the model locomotive's electric motor.

Controlling the Train's Speed: In order to control the locomotive's speed the voltage/amperage is increased or decreased making the electric motor run faster or slower. This is done in one of two ways, either electronically by using variable pulses of full power, (Digital Command Control does the same) which provides greater pulling power at low speeds, or by using a wire wound resistor (old non transistorised Controllers).

The latter method relies on special wire that resists the electricity so that the further the electricity travels down the wire the greater the resistance; the outcome is less power. In practical terms the wire is wound around a former either in a straight line or in a half circle and a wiper presses on to this. The positive (live) side of the electricity is supplied into the resistance wire and taken out at the point of the wiper contact. This is then wired to one of the rails. The second wire is joined to the other rail, so that each pair of rails has either a positive (live) or negative (return) electrical status.

By using the wheels of the locomotive to pick up the power from the rails, electrical continuity is maintained. Each axle for each set of wheels is insulated to prevent an electrical short circuit and so as to provide a good running characteristic several wheels are used. In some cases both the locomotive and tender are used, the locomotive chassis is picking up the positive, the tender chassis picking up the negative. This overcomes the problem of using wiper pickups against the wheels which continues the electrical circuit. From these pickups a pair of wires goes to the motor's brushes which are spring-loaded against the motor's commutator. This is a rotary switch, and as it rotates the segments switch on or off the electromagnets which make up the motor's armature.

The principle is a static magnetic field produced by the permanent magnet. When an electromagnet contained in the armature is switched on it is attracted to the magnetic pole of the fixed magnet.

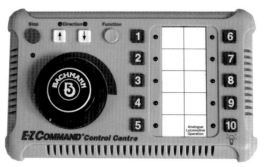

Since the electromagnet is on a drive shaft it rotates towards the pole of the fixed magnet, then it is switched off by the commutator. The commutator then switches on the next electromagnet and the shaft continues to rotate, the procedure repeating itself whilst electricity is supplied. So as to make the motor more efficient, several electromagnets are used on the armature, five pole motors being more powerful and smoother running than three (the poles' being the number of electromagnets contained in the armature).

To increase the power output of the drive shaft of the motor a gear ratio of around 30:1 is used. This means that the motor's shaft rotates thirty times to one revolution of the axle on which the locomotive's wheels are fitted. In theory the axle is thus thirty times more powerful than the motor's drive shaft. Some power is lost, however, but nevertheless it is still a considerable increase in power. The gearing down of the electric motor also makes the locomotive smoother running.

Two types of gears are used. One is a series of gear wheels which provide the reduction necessary. These are generally used on motors which are mounted across the chassis. The second type is known as a worm drive, used on motors mounted along the chassis which require the drive to be turned through ninety degrees.

Remember: since the electricity is supplied to the track, only a single locomotive can be run when the track is wired in a single one-piece circuit (i.e. an oval passing loop with a siding), but by breaking the track electrically into sections several locomotives can be run, as each can have the power separately switched to the section of the track that it occupies (excluding DCC).

This is the basic principle of wiring a layout: each length or several lengths of track is linked via switches and becomes a section independently controlled from the rest. By then switching on adjoining sections the locomotive can be made to travel from one section to the next, being handed over from controller to controller if necessary. The layouts with a working overhead gantry system can use the power supplied by the gantry to operate independently two different trains on the same track. The method is to use one rail as a common return (Negative) and then one track as the supply 1 (Positive) and the gantry as supply 2 (Positive) for travel in the same direction.

Left: A section through a typical locomotive which has its motor mounted 'lengthways' and a worm gear is used to transfer the electric motor's power to the driving wheels The electricity is picked up from the track.

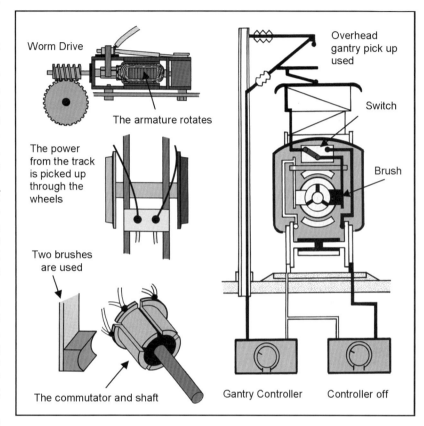

Worm Drive

The armature rotates

The power from the track is picked up through the wheels

Two brushes are used

The commutator and shaft

Overhead gantry pick up used

Switch

Brush

Gantry Controller   Controller off

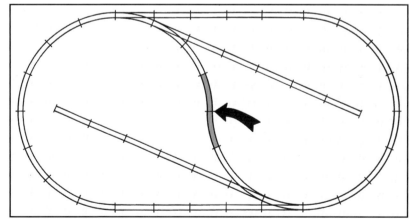

ABOVE: ANSWER FROM PAGE 10
Follow the arrows, the inside rail becomes the outside rail as the track crosses the oval, the fault is that basic! **Left:** A cross mounted tender fitted electric motor.

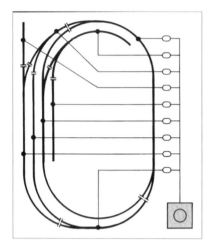

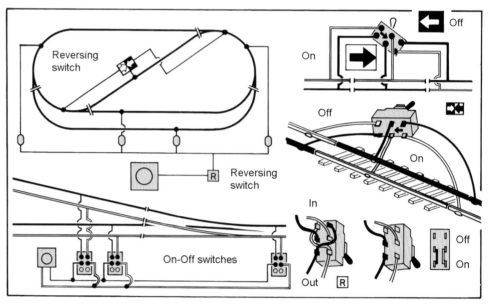

Above: An oval layout operated by one controller split into electrical sections allows several trains to be operated on the layout, one at a time.

DCC COMMAND
Above: The basic oval layout using a single conventional controller will operate a single train. I use the term conventional controller because digital controllers are now available which render much of the switches on the layout redundant, but not the power supply, so these switches could be left permanently in the 'on' position.

Unfortunately it is either a DC 12 volt layout (Conventional) or an AC 16 volt (Digital) layout, but if switched as shown the layout could be used for running both types of models: One type at a time, not mixed. In the foreseeable future all '00' scale models will probably be digitally controlled, but until suitable miniaturised command units can be made for 'N' scale they will remain as 12 volt DC models.

ELECTRICALLY ISOLATED TRACK

The track will need to be split into electrically isolated sections, either by cutting through the rail or by fitting plastic rail joiners. The reason for this is to prevent the electricity from uncontrollably flowing around the track. The most important switch it the reversing switch located in the centre of the oval, which without this the track would electrically short circuit.

I prefer to use double pole switches because these switches control the power to both rails and therefore cause fewer feedback problems when rolling stock electrically bridges the insulated track joins. To prevent steps in the track, when cutting through the rails after the track is laid, stagger the cuts, so that they are not opposite each other.

Types of Switches: The reversing switch used in the centre is a double-pole, double-throw, on-off-on, miniature 3 amp 250 volts rated switch. And the other track switches are double-pole, double-throw, on-off, miniature 3 amp, 250 volts rated switches.

Now let me explain: a double-pole switch refers to the number of internal contacts within the switch, i.e. two individual circuits (4 or 6 terminals). 'Double throw' means the internal contacts are at each end, so that the switch operates on or off in both directions (DPDT). The switch can have a centre off position and be on when the toggle of the switch is up or down (On-Off-On). The next bit is the switches' size classification, i.e. miniature and

the last bit is its current rating, 250 volts at 3 amps *(125 volts at 6 amps or 60 volts at 12 amps or 30 volts at 24 amps)* which puts it well into our operation range of 16 volts at 2 amps. Voltage is like a car without fuel, it's not going anywhere. Amps are the fuel, that propels the car along, and nothing works without both being present.

Old Rolling Stock: The reason for that old engine not working could well be that the modern transformer/controller that is being used to make the model work does not have sufficient amps, i.e. is rated at 0.8 amps before the automatic cut-out applies itself.

The problem is that modern electric motors draw less amps than the old motors, say 0.5 amps compared with the old motors 1.2 amps. Therefore the moment a motor is detected that draws the higher amperage than the transformer can deliver, the transformer goes to the fail safe mode and switches its power off. The same applies as to why two engines on the same track won't work, two 0.5 amp motors total 1 amp, and is above the transformer's fail-safe setting of 0.8 amps. Note not all transformers are set at 0.8 because makes vary in the power outputs.

Stalled & Start Amperage: The electric motor has two amperage figures, the running amps and the stalled amperage rating. The first is its safe running amperage, at which it delivers its maximum power, and could be rated as continuous or intermittent running. The second is the stalled (not running

Right: SPST
ON-OFF
SWITCH
Single-pole
general purpose
switch

Right: DPDT
ON-OFF-ON
SWITCH
Double-pole
general
purpose switch

Right: SPDT
Brief Contact
ON-OFF-ON
SWITCH
Used for
activating 1
or 2 Points
simultaneously

Right: DPDT
Brief Contact
ON-OFF-ON
SWITCH
Used for
activating 4 or
more Points
simultaneously

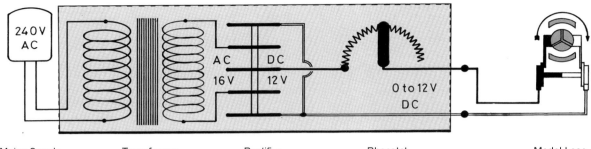

| Mains Supply | Transformer | Rectifier | Rheostat | Model Loco |

because it is jammed) rating, which will damage the motor. Therefore the amperage (say 0.85 stall amps) should not match or exceed this, hence the thermal automatic cut-out set at 0.8 amps. The final amperage figure is the start factor: What it takes to get the motor to rotate from stationary, which could well be 50% of its running amperage i.e. the motor, draws 0.75 amps at starting and drops to 0.5 amps when running. It is for this reason that old transformer/controllers are not recommended for use with modern rolling stock, unless you are aware and fully understand the limits that the model's electric motor has to be worked within. Finally at no time should a transformer/controller be used without an automatic cut-out, because it is a fire risk.

Voltage + Amperage: This is the bit that can hurt you: 250 volts at 1 amp can kill some people, so let us be very clear about mains voltage, it is very dangerous. It is for this very reason some countries use 125 volts as their standard voltage, because it is less likely to be lethal if you received a shock from the mains. The voltage that the model trains operate on is 12 to 16 volts and is considered harmless.

AC and DC: The term AC represents Alternating Current, and the term DC represents Direct Current and they have different characteristics. Batteries supply DC voltage, a generator AC voltage and AC voltage can be converted to DC voltage and vice versa.

In Britain the voltage produced by the power stations arrives at our homes as 220/240 volts AC

at 60 amps: which at the fuse board is distributed to various sources including a 30 amp ring mains. The plug at the end of our model train transformer is fitted with a 220/240 volts at 3 amp fuse. This fuse protects the internal workings of the transformer. The average transformer delivers 16 volts AC or 12 volts DC and is protected with a thermal internal cut-out as mentioned earlier.

This forms the basis of the power supply used to operate our model trains, which like our homes we have to distribute to where it is needed. For all of us new to wiring, it will take time to understand and to master. The illustrations show basic wiring diagrams. Starting with the top right (page 146): the oval and a single controller, split into sections on which two trains can be operated, one at a time. Left: the more complex layout shows the track work split up into numerous sections, each controlled by a separate on/off switch.

The diagrammatic wiring to each of these switches is shown below, starting (left) with the Single-Pole Single-Throw (SPST) on/off switch. The next is a Double-Pole Single-Throw (DPST) on/off switch. The third is a Double-Pole Double-Throw (DPDT) on-off-on switch wired for two controllers, with a single supply to the track, which can be wired as a single controller (right) supplying one track at a time with a centre off to both tracks' switch position. I favour using the double-pole switches because power to both sides of the track is cut when the power is off, unlike a single-pole switch in which half the track still retains power.

POWER SUPPLY

Since the majority of model locomotives used on indoor layouts are very small, they use electric motors to provide the driving force, working generally from twelve volts direct current (DC), the same type of voltage provided by batteries. Unfortunately, due to the amperage drawn by the electric motor, batteries are soon exhausted of their power. To overcome this problem a transformer is used. This works from the mains 240/110 alternating current (AC) and reduces the high voltage mains supply to a safe low voltage. *On no account should the track be wired directly to the mains.* The transformer converts the mains voltage into sixteen volts AC and then by using a rectifier finally into twelve volts DC. This provides two sources of power, sixteen volts AC for point motors and twelve volts DC for the locomotive's electric motor.

SWITCHES

These control the supply of power so that several engines can be on the layout, but only one engine will work. By supplying sections of track a predetermined route can be followed by the engine without the others moving.

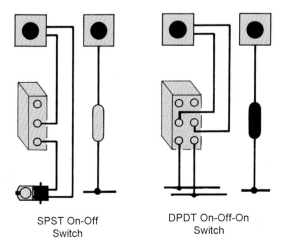

SPST On-Off Switch   DPDT On-Off-On Switch

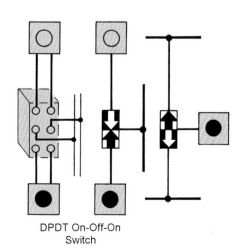

DPDT On-Off-On Switch

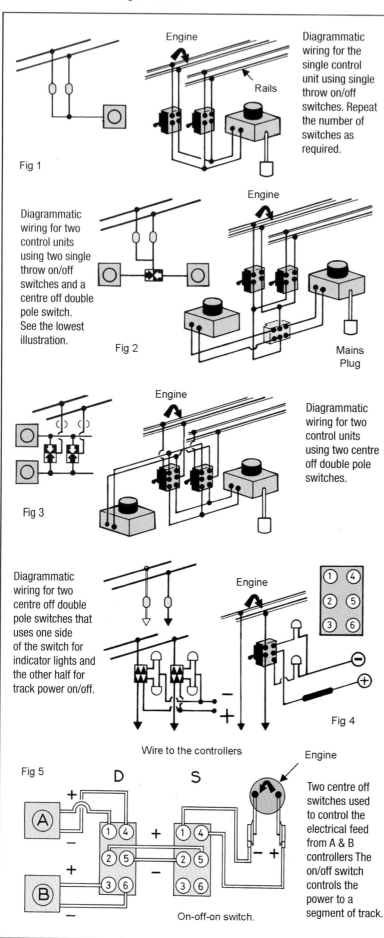

Diagrammatic wiring for the single control unit using single throw on/off switches. Repeat the number of switches as required.

Fig 1

Diagrammatic wiring for two control units using two single throw on/off switches and a centre off double pole switch. See the lowest illustration.

Fig 2

Mains Plug

Diagrammatic wiring for two control units using two centre off double pole switches.

Fig 3

Diagrammatic wiring for two centre off double pole switches that uses one side of the switch for indicator lights and the other half for track power on/off.

Fig 4

Fig 5

Wire to the controllers

D   S

Engine

Two centre off switches used to control the electrical feed from A & B controllers The on/off switch controls the power to a segment of track.

On-off-on switch.

Engine
Rails
Engine

UNDERSTANDING THE WIRING OF SWITCHES

For the railway modeller there are three basic types of double pole switches used. The first is the on/off switch, the second is the centre off switch and the third is push to make contact sprung loaded off. (Like a bell push and used for points/turnouts.) The words 'double pole' means that both sides of a circuit can be controlled by one switch. The first illustration (Fig:1) shows the wiring using a pair of on and off switches, the two wires departing from the controller through these switches and then being connected to the track's rails. The backs of the switches have six connections and are split into two sides, the terminals reading one, two and three for one electrical side of the switch, called a 'pole' and four, five and six for the second side. To wire the on/off switch, terminals one and two are used for one side of the wiring and four and five are used for the other side. Terminals three and six are not used.

The second illustration (Fig:2) shows the use of a changeover switch, for use with two controllers. This is inserted between the controllers and on/off switches and provides the choice, one at a time, of the controller to be used. This time the on/off switch uses all six terminals, terminals three and six are connected to the first controller, terminals one and four connecting to the second controller's terminals. Terminals two and five are connected to the second on/off switches' middle terminals.

The third illustration (Fig:3) shows the use of two controllers, using double pole centre off switches. This provides the choice of either controller or also whether the power is on or off to each track. The wiring to these is much simpler, because it does away with the second switch and its wiring. This time the power departs from the controller into terminal three and out at two, into the track, through the locomotive's motor and back into the track, into terminal five, and out of six, back to the controller.

This method uses the centre terminals of the switch to go to the track, the two outside terminals in each case going to the controller. Since the switch has three positions, it provides an on and off setting to controller 'A' or 'B', which is designated by the switch's 'toggle' setting.

The fourth illustration (Fig:4) shows the wiring of an on/off double pole switch, that uses diodes as an indicator to its settings. This system splits the electrics of the switch into two. The first half is used for the track and the second half for signaling. To make this possible requires a permanently connected wire from the controller to the track (Common return). The second wire has part of the switch inserted between the controller and the rail. Since the track has built in electrically separated sections this is a perfectly acceptable procedure. The electrical power to the track uses terminals one and two, the power to the LEDs uses four, five and six. The positive side goes to terminal five and departs out of either four or six, depending upon

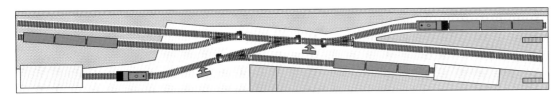

Left: Using Digital Control Command (DCC) only two electrical feeds are required to power this layout.

the switch's setting, then through the LEDs and back to the negative terminal. A resistance is used within the circuit to reduce current and prevent the LEDs being damaged or burnt out. By wiring in this manner the LEDs can be wired back to the control panel and to signalling lights. This, of course, provides an instant visual as to settings on the control panel as well as looking realistic on the layout.

Look at Fig:5 which shows double pole on/off switches. In practice this means the 'positive' side of the electrical circuit is marked with a cross or plus sign and departs out of controller 'B' and into terminal D3, through the switch and out of terminal D2 into S5, out of S4 and then into the track. It then passes through the locomotive's electric motor. Having done this the electricity is now on its return journey, and is marked with a 'minus' sign to denote it is on the 'negative' side of the circuit. It continues back into terminal S1, coming out through S2, then into D5 and departing out of terminal D6, so that it finally returns back to the 'B' controller. This electrical circuit provides the choice of controller 'A' or 'B' and whether a particular track is switched on or off, the electricity making a 'positive' journey outwards, and a 'negative' return, these being the two 'sides' of direct current electricity.

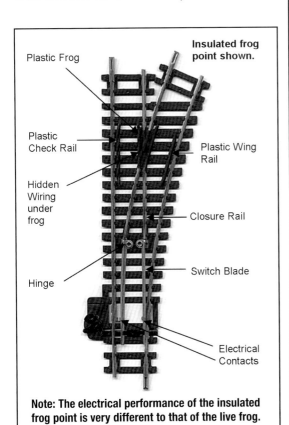

Plastic Frog

Plastic Check Rail

Hidden Wiring under frog

Hinge

Plastic Wing Rail

Closure Rail

Switch Blade

Electrical Contacts

Insulated frog point shown.

Note: The electrical performance of the insulated frog point is very different to that of the live frog.

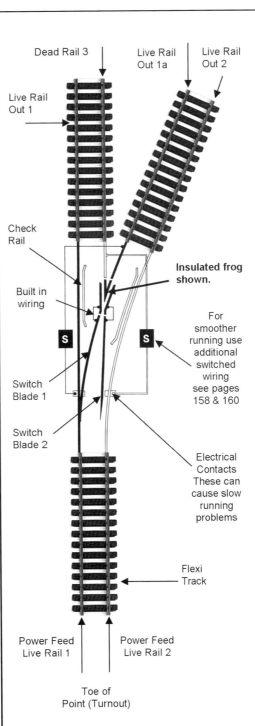

Dead Rail 3

Live Rail Out 1a

Live Rail Out 2

Live Rail Out 1

Check Rail

Built in wiring

Switch Blade 1

Switch Blade 2

Insulated frog shown.

For smoother running use additional switched wiring see pages 158 & 160

Electrical Contacts These can cause slow running problems

Flexi Track

Power Feed Live Rail 1

Power Feed Live Rail 2

Toe of Point (Turnout)

Note: Because the electricity travels around both 'Outside Rails' of the point (Live out 1 & 2) this can cause problems elsewhere. Therefore to resolve any electrical feed back, it is very advisable to split the track up into electrical isolated sections even with DCC layouts.

THE INSULATED FROG POINT (TURNOUT)

Below: The point is shown in diagrammatic form, so that how the electricity flows along the rails can be studied.

The electrical left hand 'Power Feed 1' enters from the toe of the point (turnout) and flows along the track in a straight line, through the point and continues in two directions.

The first is straight across, the second follows the curved track, (Switch Blade 1) and out of the point: Both are shown as 'Live Rail Out 1'.

The right hand power feed at the toe of the point (turnout) is shown as 'Power feed 2' and the electrical power follows the curve until it reaches the end of the rail 'Live rail Out 2'.

Because 'Switch Blade 2' is not in contact with the right hand rail, no electrical power passes down the rail, and is known as a dead rail (no power) shown as 'Dead Rail 3'.

When the point is reset, to 'straight ahead' the switch rails move and 'Switch Rail 2' now touches 'Live Rail 2' and the power now flows into the dead rail, and 'Live Rail 1a' now becomes the dead rail because 'Switch Blade 1' is no longer making contact with 'Live rail 1'.

PROBLEM SHOOTING

Because most modellers 'weather' the track by painting the sleepers and rails, the electrical contacts also get painted. This for obvious reasons prevents them from working, and the train keeps stopping on the points. Remedy, don't paint the contacts and also keep them clean!

Top left to right: The Peco Insulfrog point restricts the way the electricity flows around the rails.

The Electrofrog short circuits one track by allowing the positive pole of electricity into both left and right hand rails of the track, (straight ahead) when the point is set for the train to travel around the curve. When the track is set for straight ahead, the curve now becomes short circuited. This is not a fault, the point is designed to do this.

Lower illustration: Whilst the electrical flow does not short circuit when using insulated frogs, irrespective of how the points are set in relation to each other, the moment a train passes over the track a short circuit can occur.

Therefore both rails of the track will need to be segregated into individual electrical sections.

UNDERSTANDING POINT WIRING

The type of point that we install on the layout will determine the way in which the layout is wired, therefore we must choose carefully between the insulated or live frog type of point; because electrically they are very different.

The most popular make of track purchased in this country is probably produced by 'Peco'. The company produces two types of point, the 'Insulfrog' and the 'Electrofrog'. The Insulfrog type is probably the easiest to wire, because of its built in switch that electrically switches on the chosen path, whilst electrically isolating the unselected route. The Electrofrog is very different, because whilst this electrically switches on the chosen route, it also short-circuits the unselected route. Therefore without using electrical isolation gaps in the track, the entire layout can short circuit at the change of a point. It is for this reason that most ready to run train sets contain the insulated type of point.

The choice of point has always been a matter of hot debate, between modellers; although in reality providing they are kept clean there is not much to choose between them. The efficiency of the point is dependent upon its wiring; therefore its power feed should in theory always be supplied at the toe. (See illustration at the top of the page and below.) Unfortunately feeding the power solely from the toe is not always electrically reliable. Therefore it is not uncommon to back feed the point, using an independent switch (page 158).

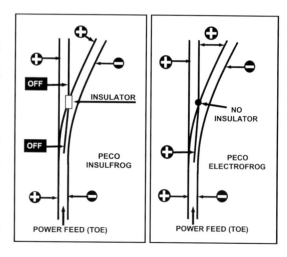

For the beginner I recommend using the insulated frog point, because with the advent of DCC 16 AC voltage layouts these I feel will be easier to wire, because the vast bulk of the track work is 'Live' at all times, unlike the DC 12 volt operated which relies on electrically segmenting the track, so that only the path of the chosen train is powered.

Below: The simple live frog arrangement using two points works well until one of the points is changed which causes an electrical short-circuit. To resolve this problem and others all track work will need to be split into electrically separate sections, and each of these sections independently controlled through switches.

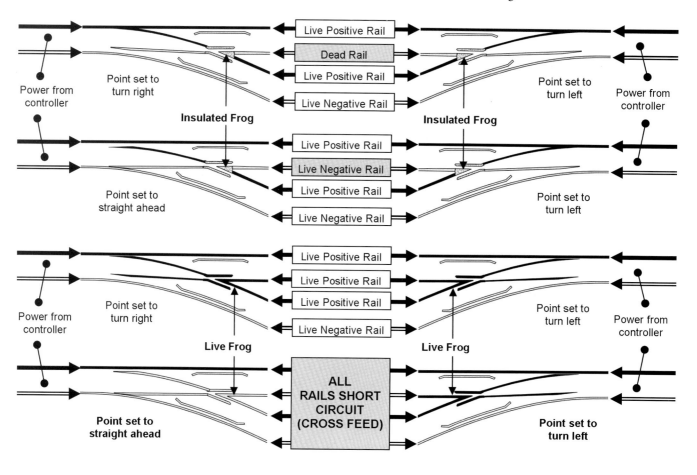

BACK & FORTH 00 SCALE LAYOUT

The baseboard is constructed as shown on page 49 base 01, using 9mm (3/8 inch) MDF and 25 x 50mm (2 x 1 inch) batten. Having assembled the base the circular hole is cut for the turntable and the insert is made using scrap 9mm MDF, and fixed underneath using glue and wood screws. The edge is then covered with wall texture material and the paving top edge is added. The rear base board edge is then temporarily fixed in place, and the upper levels that will form the tunnel are made, together with pulp-board filler cut to size. (See page 70 for more details.) When satisfied with the contours along the back edge, mark out and cut to size, check and then permanently fix in place, followed by the pulp board, walling material etc.

Temporarily fit the track in place, mark the track position and cut the holes for the point motors (see page 161). The track underlay is then fitted using plastic foam wood flooring underlay, fixed in place with double sided sticky tape, trimmed to size with a bevelled cut after the track is laid. The next stage is to use the holes drilled for the dressmaker's pins to locate the track's position (fix track in place using other drilled holes and track pins) and wire the power supply as required.

Fit the remaining pulp board contour levels in place (see page 70) as required. Check everything before sealing with a mixture of woodworker's white glue (25%) and emulsion paint (75%).

Note: The colours of the photographs will vary because different cameras were used at different times under various lighting conditions, together with the problems of colour matching reality with what can be captured digitally and then printed within the book.

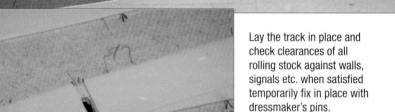

Lay the track in place and check clearances of all rolling stock against walls, signals etc. when satisfied temporarily fix in place with dressmaker's pins.

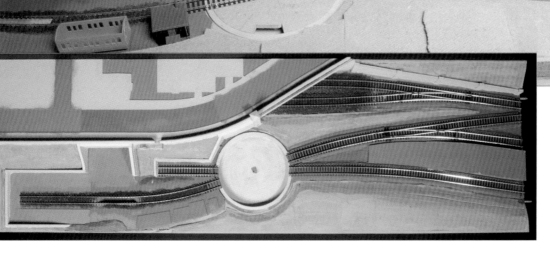

The walls are primed with car spray paint, followed by using household water based emulsion paint. Note; I normally purchase three basic colours, road, paving and grass, in tester pots, as my standard colours, followed by other colours etc as required.

Having fixed the track in its final position, the track is then wired to suit. Because the layout is wired for DCC running and there is not a return loop on the layout, the track is easy to wire.

Note: All tracks are wired together with continuous wiring so that all tracks remain live, which permits any standing engines and carriages to have their lights on whilst stationary.

The bases are now painted and textured, followed by adding small extra detail as required.

The turntable was wired using a continuous piece of wire through a hollow drive shaft. (Replace when it breaks.) This avoids the problem of making wiper contact strips, which can be a source of trouble.

The final stage is the wiring of the point motors, followed by the fitting of the signals with working lights.

Note: Signals with lights are easier to install than working semaphore signals; fit before finishing the landscape etc.

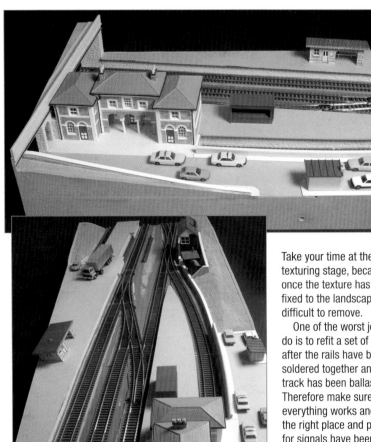

Above: Allow for the platform thickness and the track height (3ft 6in from top of the rail to the platform level) when cutting out the platform supports. Note: The edge of the platform protrudes about 1 foot in front of the wall, and very often is shrouded in cables.

Right: l.5mm thick cardboard paving is added as required to provide a kerb height of around 4.5 inches, fixed in place with woodworker's glue.

Right and below: Views along the base showing how the pulp board has been carved and sanded to suit the landscape. Notice the MDF edging around the base, to form a hard edge to fix the laminated edging onto.

Below: The laminated edging is added before the base is painted. My method of fixing the edging is to use a contact adhesive and trim to shape using a router fitted with a ball-raced trimming guide. (These are commercially available for this type of cutting.) Alternatively use a fretsaw and a file/sand paper block to smooth to shape.

Take your time at the pre-texturing stage, because once the texture has been fixed to the landscape it is difficult to remove.

One of the worst jobs to do is to refit a set of points, after the rails have been soldered together and the track has been ballasted. Therefore make sure everything works and is in the right place and plinths for signals have been added etc, before starting the texturing process. You can add texture on top, but cannot remove!

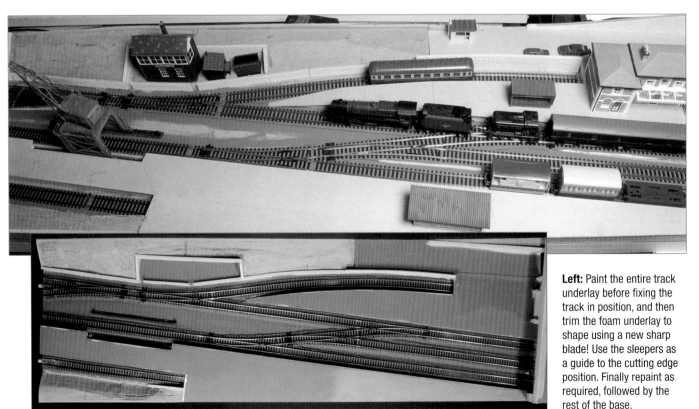

Left: Paint the entire track underlay before fixing the track in position, and then trim the foam underlay to shape using a new sharp blade! Use the sleepers as a guide to the cutting edge position. Finally repaint as required, followed by the rest of the base.

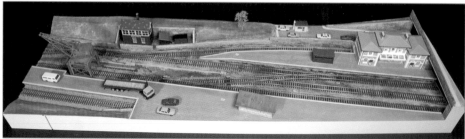

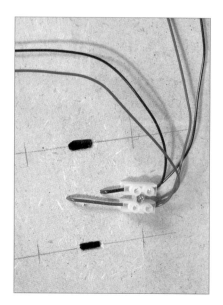

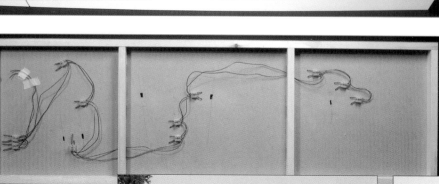

Top: The unfinished Station base with the road and paving colour applied.

Above: The underside of the base showing DCC wiring whereby all the tracks are wired together into a single supply.

Top Right: The wires connect to each other via terminal blocks. The point motors are about to be added.

Right: The view past the signal box and towards the station, showing the toe to toe points, which are wired in the centre as shown in the top right photo.

Far right: The crane in the foreground sets the scene of this busy country station.

Below: The departing passenger train from Wishton Halt station reveals people waiting for the next train, and depicts a typical scene from a bygone era. To bring a model to life it always needs lots of people (120 on this layout) plus lots of cars all positioned to capture a moment in time. The colours used are always muted, with never a pure black or white and I tone down the distant colours.

CONTROLLING THE FLOW OF ELECTRICITY

To resolve the problem of the electricity flowing uncontrollably around the track insulation gaps are cut through the rails and a second power feed added. Like all model making decisions; it is another matter of great debate as to the best position of the insulator gap. There are two choices, install plastic rail joiners (fish plates) on an 'as-you-go' basis or cut them through the track after it is laid. (I prefer to cut them after the track is laid.)

The illustration below shows that by using independent switches, the electrical flow to the track can be controlled and without causing a short circuit when any single point is changed (compare with the illustration on page 150.)

THE RETURN LOOP

This is when the wiring catches modellers out, because it is easy to forget that the rail forms a continuous length that doubles back upon itself. The outcome is a built-in short circuit and is the same situation as shown on page 10, 145 & 146. The only way to resolve this is to use insulated gaps in the track, and use Double-Pole, Double-Throw, centre off switches (DPDT On-Off-On). The method of inserting insulated fish plates on an as-you-go basis

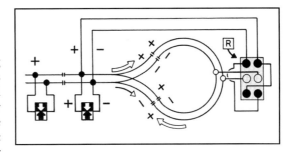

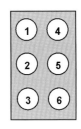

is very simple, instead of using a metal fish plate, a plastic one is inserted in pairs. i.e. one on each rail. The above diagram shows starting from left to right: The incoming track with power supplied from the DPDT switch, followed by track isolators. The track continues with a second power feed, because it is isolated from the first piece of track. This power feed is also wired to a third switch via terminals 1 & 6, 3 & 4. The centre terminals 2 & 5 are wired to the track and the length of track is electrically isolated at each end with plastic fish plates. The train enters from the right, and turns clockwise over the insulation gaps and stops on the loop. The switch that controls the power to the loop is changed, as is the first and second switch, and the train now travels away from the loop and onto the track facing and travelling in the opposite direction. Compare this with the lower illustration.

Below: This shows the same track layout as shown on page 150, but this time insulated fish plates have been inserted between the points. This now has provided us with four electrically separate sections of track, each independently controlled. Because they are independently controlled the power does not cross feed from one track to another, and therefore the track does not short circuit.

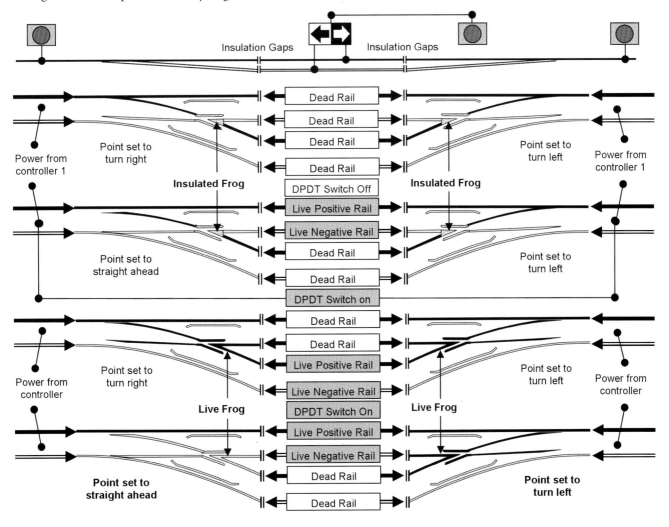

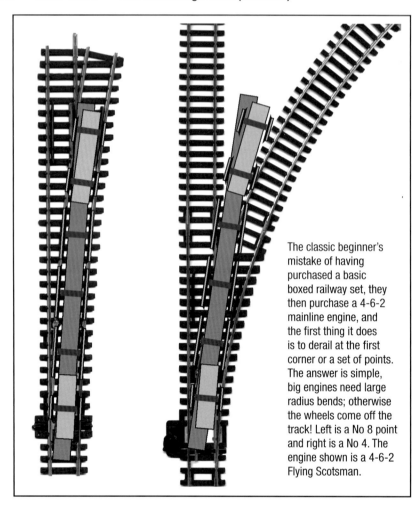

The classic beginner's mistake of having purchased a basic boxed railway set, they then purchase a 4-6-2 mainline engine, and the first thing it does is to derail at the first corner or a set of points. The answer is simple, big engines need large radius bends; otherwise the wheels come off the track! Left is a No 8 point and right is a No 4. The engine shown is a 4-6-2 Flying Scotsman.

FROG ANGLES FOR POINTS (TURNOUTS)

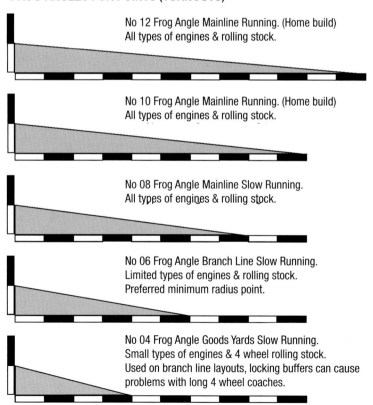

No 12 Frog Angle Mainline Running. (Home build)
All types of engines & rolling stock.

No 10 Frog Angle Mainline Running. (Home build)
All types of engines & rolling stock.

No 08 Frog Angle Mainline Slow Running.
All types of engines & rolling stock.

No 06 Frog Angle Branch Line Slow Running.
Limited types of engines & rolling stock.
Preferred minimum radius point.

No 04 Frog Angle Goods Yards Slow Running.
Small types of engines & 4 wheel rolling stock.
Used on branch line layouts, locking buffers can cause problems with long 4 wheel coaches.

WHAT POINTS (TURNOUT) TO USE

The previous pages have introduced the wiring of the point (turnout) but there is more to it than just wiring, because the mechanical factor will also need to be considered. The first question is: What type of rolling stock will travel over the rails. Will it be mainline or branch line rolling stock? If the answer is mainline then only the frog angles 12, 10 & 8 can be used. But for a factory goods yard using a Class 08 Diesel Loco and short 4 wheel wagons, a frog No 4 could be used.

Terminology: So that the angle of the diverging track can be described in relation to the 'Straight Track' it is given a number. Therefore as in full-size practice these numbers are shorthand for the length to width ratio of the tracks diverging angle. For example a No 12 takes 12 inches to spread 1 inch and a No 4 takes 4 inches to spread 1 inch (see illustration). The measurement can be in feet, yards or metres, the ratio remains the same. In full size practice it is considered that a No 10 is sharp, with No 20, as the preferred size for mainline running. The Number also determines the recommended maximum running speed through the diverging track. For example, No 8, the maximum speed is 16mph, twice the frog angle. Since a scale mile per hour bears no resemblance to real miles per hour, this explains why trains come off the track!

Scale Speed: The British mile is 5,280 feet; dividing by 60 minutes gives 88 feet per minute for 1 mile per hour in real time. If we equate this to 4mm (00 Scale), 88 feet scales to 352mm (approx 1ft 2in) per minute and to the eye this is hardly moving. 10mph equates to 11ft 8in per minute at 00 Scale, and that is not very fast to the eye either! The 10mph speed at 'N' scale (2mm = 1ft) is 5ft 10in per minute! So therefore it is easy to reach a scale speed of 60mph and derail on a 22 mph maximum speed set of points.

Electrical Feed Back: The points (turnouts) of the layout can be operated either by hand or by a mechanical device. In the first instance the operator of the layout reaches over the track and switches the point into the desired setting. For the beginner building a first layout this is ideal as it saves the problem of wiring and cutting holes in the baseboard to accommodate the points motors, etc. But what confuses the beginner is when a locomotive goes over the insulated rail joiner fitted behind the point, and everything stops working.

The problem is due to the fact that most rolling stock picks up its power supply through its wheels, not one wheel but perhaps 6 or more wheels. The outcome is that some wheels are on one side of the insulated track join, whilst others are on the other side, resulting in a short circuit! The return loop shown on pages 145, 146 and 155 that are fitted with reversing switches are particularly prone to this.

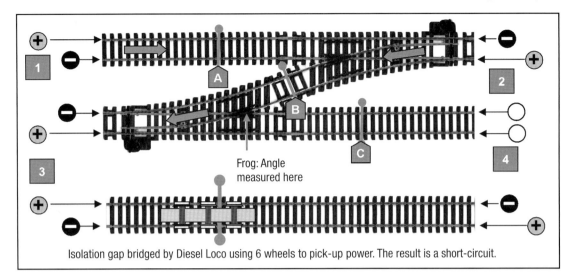

Frog: Angle measured here

Isolation gap bridged by Diesel Loco using 6 wheels to pick-up power. The result is a short-circuit.

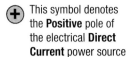

This symbol denotes the **Positive** pole of the electrical **Direct Current** power source

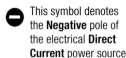

This symbol denotes the **Negative** pole of the electrical **Direct Current** power source

Left: The train arrives from place 1, crosses the insulator 'A' and stops past place 2. Both points are changed simultaneously, by being wired as a pair of points. The polarity is changed over so that the train can now move across the points in the opposite direction and change tracks and to move beyond place 3 (crossing insulator B). The track at place 4, beyond isolator 'C' has the power switched off.

If you follow the top track's polarity between place 1 and 2, you will see that if the isolator 'A' was not in place the track would short-circuit.

Whilst this is not an electrical problem at the moment, if a train passed over the insulator gap, the track would short-circuit.

Most oval layouts using a single controller with a built in reversing switch will not encounter the problem 1 & 2, (shown above) but we will all on numerous occasions encounter this second problem. This occurs whilst the train travels from place 3 to 4. What happens is we forget to switch the power to the track 'on' and the train skids to a stand still as it goes over the isolation gap. The problem is compounded when it is a long train, because it is highly possible that you have to put all the carriages and wagons back in place on the rails! The remedy is straight forward, switch the power on; yes we all do it!

Two Controllers: The 'Multi-Level Oval Layout' is designed to use two controllers; one for the up line (Inside oval) and one for the down line (Outside oval) which minimises the situation of a train short circuiting the layout (Above illustration) when it passed over the insulated track join; to 3 places where reverse polarity could occur. The first is just outside of the station and two more are in the storage loop where trains are handed from the first controller to the second controller and vice versa.

Effectively during the change over a number of things can happen, the first is no power, and the train stops, the second is reverse power, and again the train stops. the last thing is very high power on the track it joins, and the train goes like a rocket, and comes off the track on the first bend! Therefore it is worth taking a few moments to think before transferring from one controller to another.

It is also worth using two identical makes of controller, so that the power out-put is balanced, because there is nothing worse than one controller that needs a high setting, and the other a low setting. This is because in due course you muddle them up, just at the place when a delicate movement of the train is required, and the engine slams into other rolling stock or the buffers.

The same applies to the direction of travel; wire the controllers so that both power settings turn in the same direction, preferably clockwise for left to right and anti clockwise for right to left. Unfortunately, modern and plug in 'hand held' controllers seem only to have a reversing switch, so you have to remember the settings, as well as which controller operates which track!

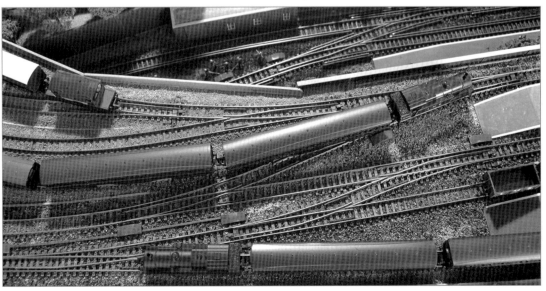

Left: The busy track-work outside of 'Wishton Station' shows its close proximity to the 'Wishton Arms' goods depot, and in the dip the lower 'Wishton Station' can be seen. Electrically the upper level track needs to be very carefully segmented into directional zones, so that one controller powers the up-line and a second the down-line direction. This of course allows two people to independently operate the layout.

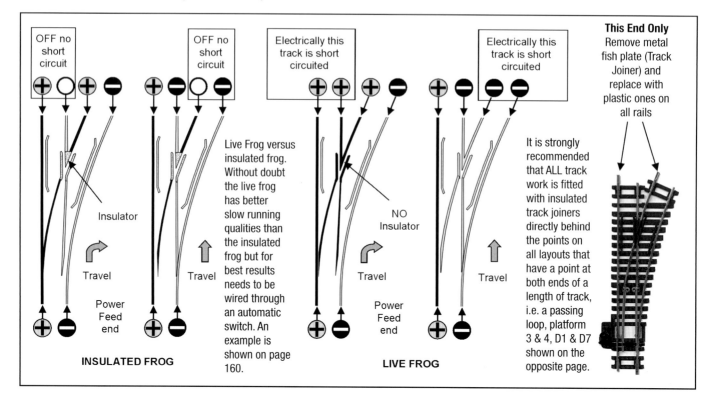

OFF no short circuit

OFF no short circuit

Electrically this track is short circuited

Electrically this track is short circuited

This End Only
Remove metal fish plate (Track Joiner) and replace with plastic ones on all rails

Insulator

Travel

Power Feed end

INSULATED FROG

Live Frog versus insulated frog. Without doubt the live frog has better slow running qualities than the insulated frog but for best results needs to be wired through an automatic switch. An example is shown on page 160.

NO Insulator

Travel

Power Feed end

LIVE FROG

It is strongly recommended that ALL track work is fitted with insulated track joiners directly behind the points on all layouts that have a point at both ends of a length of track, i.e. a passing loop, platform 3 & 4, D1 & D7 shown on the opposite page.

Above: The modeller will need to choose between the insulated frog and the live frog point (turnout) because electrically they have different functions. The insulated frog in many ways is less complex and easier because it self switches the power around the layout without short circuiting any of the track.

Unfortunately back wiring is really for the experienced modeller to use, because it is complex, but is very reliable and provides excellent smooth running, which is worth all the hassle of the extra wiring!

POSITIONING INSULATION GAPS

The position of an insulation gap in the rail needs careful planning, because we must remember the fact that the 'Live frog' short-circuits part of the track, whilst the 'Insulated frog' switches on or off part of the track. The switch part of the point is the moving rail that touches the corresponding rail on the same side to make electrical contact. This is the weakness of the electrical conductivity throughout the layout- because if one of the points is dirty, the section of track fails to work. Note: Do not paint in-between the point blades!

This is when the 'Insulated frog' scores a major victory because it can be back wired. The technique is to take the power feeds to the back of the point, (see illustration below) so that the electrical circuit does not rely on the blade of the moving point to make contact with the rail. Therefore because the blade is already part of the electrical circuit the point is far more reliable. The disadvantage is the fact that the point no longer works as an electrical

switch that isolates part of the track. To overcome this problem the following section of track needs its own separate power switch (see below). Note: The method of back wiring cannot be used with the 'Live frog' because it short-circuits the entire point, unless the point's switch rail contacts are modified so that they cease to work and the inside of the rail that normally touches to make contact is insulated. (A couple of coats of oil-bound paint normally works on the inside of the rails).

The typical mainline crossover that uses 2 points back to back (Page 157 isolator 'B') is a classic example of were it is absolutely imperative to position the isolating gaps. Because if they are not used, the layout will short-circuit with live frog points and could well cause feedback with isolated points. The illustrations show the isolation gaps in the rails opposite each other; but they can be staggered. The advantage of staggering the gaps in the rails is in the fact that having one 'solid' rail opposite a gap helps to align the track. The disadvantage is the gap will need to be cut after track laying. The best method of cutting gaps is to use a mini drill fitted with a grinding disk, some wet tissue to form a heat sink and a jig. The jig will need to be made from scrap wood and shaped to suit the drill, so that it guides the cutting disk whilst producing a straight cut.

Running Procedure: The layout will require the points to be set for a safe journey along the train's path of travel. Finally the power can be switched on for each section, so that the train can pick up its electrical power along the entire length of its journey. The journey might only be short involving two sections, or it could be all the sections that form a continuous loop. Having finished the journey, the

Insulators further down the track and not directly behind the point

On-off DPDT switch

Track has separate section switches

Wiring for use with insulated frog points (Turnouts) only

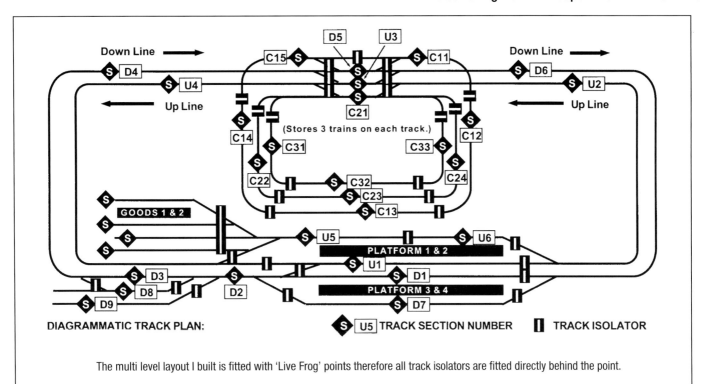

The multi level layout I built is fitted with 'Live Frog' points therefore all track isolators are fitted directly behind the point.

power is switched off, points changed, and a different section of track prepared for running. The technique used for running a layout is in being very methodical. The train stops, the section of track that it rests on is switched off, so that when the next train is started, two trains don't start at once. (Don't worry if this happens, we all make this mistake, the annoying bit is putting all the wheels back on the track, after the derailment.)

The above illustration left shows the power feeds and the isolating sections of the layout. Work on one section at a time, and wire it back to the switches and to the controller, and get each section to work properly, before moving to the next section of track to avoid any confusion. It is also important to identify each piece of wiring with a tag, so that at a future date the wiring can be traced back to its source. Wiring is reasonably straight forward when each section is wired from start to finish in one go. Unfortunately wiring only becomes complex when it has to be done on a bit-at-a-time basis, because of other household jobs; like getting food, cooking, eating, earning money and sleeping, and when you come back to it you have not a clue what you were doing!

The bell crank is used to change the direction of the point motor's movement through 90 degrees.
Fig 1 shows the bell crank moved to the left.
Fig 2 shows the bell crank moved to the right.
The bell crank then pushes/pulls a wire in a tube that in turn is connected to the point's tie-bar. The push/pull action changes the point's settings.

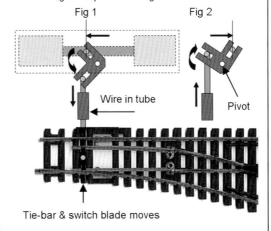

Left: This shows a bell crank used to change the direction of travel of the point motor, (see page 160) and is used on the middle level base, because the point motors could not be mounted under the base. The bell crank is mounted onto the baseboard, as is the brass tube and wire pushrod. The point motor is mounted on a piece of wood above the base and the pin is engaged into the slot in the bell crank. The lower illustration shows how a manually-operated turn-out, uses a push-pull cable within a tube. The pair of on/off switches keeps the track's circuit separate from the LEDs' circuit, used for the indicator lamps.

Note the isolators are not directly behind the point, shown as gaps in the track and are cut in both rails. Using one rail as a common return can cause feedback problems which is best avoided.

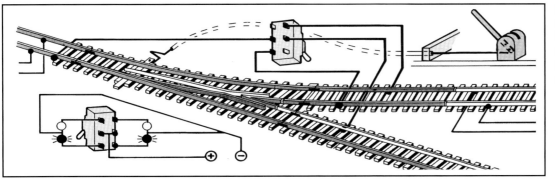

Above: Because the base of the middle level is removable the point motor had to be mounted on top of the base and linked to the point via a push rod. The wiring also had to be surface mounted and lost under a covering of texturing material i.e. ballast and grass.

Below: Instead of using the switch in the Seep point motor for signalling, the switch can be used for controlling the power to the track.

The advantage is that continuity of power no longer relies on the moving rail to make electrical contact, and the running of the layout becomes far more reliable.

Unfortunately it is either signalling or electrical continuity that can be used not both. The choice is up to the individual.

AUTOMATIC SIGNALS AND POWER OPERATED POINTS (TURNOUTS)

There is no end to the amount of automation that can be incorporated in a layout. It is not compulsory, of course, as a layout can be wired to provide the bare minimum of functions. Building-in some automatic features does ease the operation of the layout, however.

There are two basic types of point motors: The first fitted with switches, the other without. The electric point motor itself is a very simple electro-mechanical device, fitted with two solenoids on each end of a bar. These are electro-magnetic coils, powered by 12/ 16 volt Direct Current. The principle of the point motor is that one coil is briefly charged with electricity, which attracts the iron bar into the coil's centre; when the power is switched off the iron bar remains there; when the second coil at the other end of the bar is switched on, it attracts the bar into itself, changing the position. Thus the bar shuttles backwards and forwards in a manner which can be controlled and mechanically linked to the point.

Wiring point motors is very simple as only four wires are used. The middle two link up to form a common return while the other two are linked up to a probe, push button or passing contact switch and then to the power source, so that a short burst of power is applied to the chosen side of the point motor, setting its direction. The advantage in using a motor

fitted with a switch is that it can be used to automatically set the signals, as the point is changed, and to indicate its route settings on the control board.

The various types of signalling combinations are extremely complex as different arrangements are used throughout the world, so some research will be needed. In Britain two types have been common. The first is the semaphore signal which is a mechanical indicator and the second is the light signal which uses a series of coded 'on' lights to indicate 'track clear' (green), 'sections ahead restricted' (yellow and double yellow) and 'stop' (red). The simplest of signals to arrange to work automatically is the red or green indicator lights since the Seep point motor manufacturing company produce a completely water-resistant variable power unit, fitted with or without switchgear and a capacitor discharge unit, which boosts the motor's power and acts as a failsafe by cutting off the electricity.

Semaphore signals will each require an independent motor or solenoid to drive their arms, which increases their cost, whilst the indicator light method uses pea bulbs or light emitting diodes. These require more than simply wiring into the appropriate terminal, as much will depend upon the type used. Pea bulbs (now rarely used), for example, vary in their voltage requirements from 1.5 to 3 volts. 'Light Emitting Diodes' (LEDs) require 1.5 to 12 volts 'Direct Current' and draw very little amperage. This reduction in amperage considerably extends the working life of the switch contacts and the LEDs have a prolonged working life, far greater than a bulb, and they are just as bright without the heat.

Automatic signalling can also be designed to work by using the rolling stock's position on the track. This information is then fed back to the control panel. Two systems can be used: one relies on electrical contact across the track, but unfortunately it cannot sense non-electrical-contact rolling stock. The second system can, as it uses a series of sensors which monitor the passing of the rolling stock. Two methods are used. One method is a photo-electric cell which registers a change through being blacked out. This is then interpreted through a silicon chip into a visual signal change, and as the rolling stock passes over a second photo-electric cell this causes a second signal change. By arranging a series of photo-electric cells along a length of track, therefore, various signal formations can be arranged to suit the layout.

Hand Operated Points: The power to operate the turn-out can be supplied by hand, (6) by using a push/pull cable, either fitted in a tube or via string, eyelets and pulleys. The latter method requires very careful setting up and by its very nature can be a source of trouble, unless fitted with adjusters. If properly constructed, however, it can be a joy to operate as levers can be used on the control panel built into the layout, and moved as per found in real life but only this time in miniature.

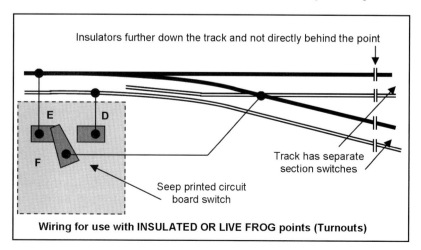

Insulators further down the track and not directly behind the point

E   D

F

Seep printed circuit board switch

Track has separate section switches

Wiring for use with INSULATED OR LIVE FROG points (Turnouts)

Fitting Point Motors (Turnouts): This is a reasonably straight forward procedure, requiring the use of a drill, a file a pencil and the point. The first task is to lay the cork underlay and mark out the centreline of the track. Place the point in its exact position and carefully mark out the line of the switch rod. (1) Drill a row of holes that are at least 4 times the diameter of the wire pin that fits the switch rod. (2) Make the holes into a smooth edged slot using a knife and Swiss file. (3) Check by hand that the point motor works in the slot. (4) Fix the point into its final position and thread the wire pin from the point motor into the switch rod and make a mark on the pin 1mm above the surface of the switch rod.

Remove the point motor and trim the rod to length by using a Swiss file. (File a groove around the rod and snap because the wire is too hard to cut with any wire cutters). File the end of the wire round, for safety reasons. Fit the point motor into its final position using wood screws, (don't glue in place, just in case the point motor fails to work and it needs to be repaired) and wire as required. (5) When the rest of the track is laid and everything works, ballast the track, but keep the ballast and glues away from any rail moving parts and the switch rod (6, 7 & 8). Alternatively the wire in a tube method can be used to operate the points and signals.

Wiring Points (Turnouts) and Signals: The best wiring I find to use is 6 strand telephone cable available from Maplin Electronics® a UK-based specialist electrical dealer. The printed circuit switch plate (9) is marked out with a set of terminals, which correspond to the 6 wires found in the cable. A: Green/white band, point solenoid left. B: Blue/white band, point solenoid right. C: Orange/white band, point common return. D: White/orange band, the negative switched signals return. E: White/green, the negative switched signal return. F: White/blue band, the negative signal common out.

Wiring Light Emitting Diodes: The wiring of Light Emitting Diodes, (LEDs) are voltage polarity sensitive, or in other words: Wire them the wrong way around, they will not work and can be permanently damaged. They are normally indicated as long pin anode 'positive' and short pin cathode 'negative'. They are also voltage and amperage sensitive, therefore they will need to be supplied with a constant voltage and controlled amperage. (An external resistor is used to control the amperage.) LEDs can be used on AC voltages but will need an inline diode fitted, so that only the positive side of the cycle reaches the positive anode. These LEDs flicker at the rate that corresponds with half the mains cycle. A good source of constant electricity are rechargeable batteries, because 1 cell produces 1.2 volts (4 cells 5 volts) at a constant output until the end of its charge. Note: a non rechargeable dry cell produces 1.5 volts when new and the voltage declines with usage until the cell (battery) is depleted.

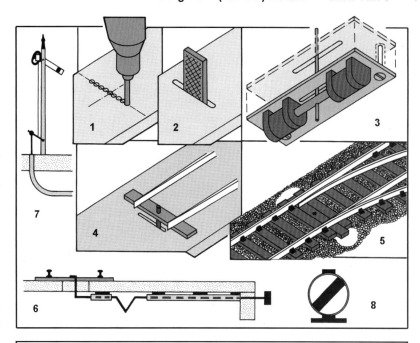

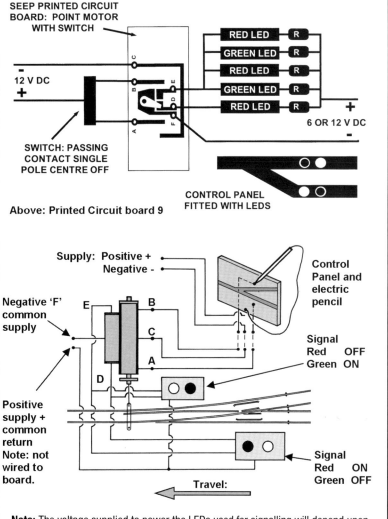

Above: Printed Circuit board 9

CONTROL PANEL FITTED WITH LEDs

Note: The voltage supplied to power the LEDs used for signalling will depend upon the type used. The popular colours are Red, Green, Yellow, Blue and White. The convenient source of LEDs in the UK is Maplin Electronics® Kingbright ® diffused lens 3mm 5v integral current limiting resistor (4 x 1.2 volt rechargeable batteries provides a constant 5 volts). These are useful for '00' scale signals.

Above: The finished middle level base, complete with landscaping, buildings and people.

Note how the third rail is fitted in short lengths and in the station area on the opposite side to the platform. Technically in stations the third rail can be shielded by wooden boards, to prevent them being accidentally touched by rail staff.

Opposite page top: This shows the base prior to laying the ballast and landscaping textures. Notice how the wiring was laid under the track and fixed on top of the base and all wiring is completed and tested before landscaping. There is nothing worse than chipping away ballast to fit another length of wire.

THE MIDDLE LEVEL: THIRD RAIL

The middle level is very easy to wire, because the tracks can be split into two sections (Fig: 3 Top and bottom track electrically separated by insulators) only one power feed is required to each section. (See Fig: 1 below.) The type of points used does not matter (insulated frog advised) for conventional running nor does it need insulating gaps in the top or bottom track (Fig: 3) for this base, but what it will require are end of track diodes (Fig: 2) to prevent the train running out of track.

The distance that the diode is fitted from the end of the track will depend upon the position of the 'engine' in relation to the carriages. When the train arrives engine first, the diode is fitted about two engine lengths from the end of the track. When the train arrives 'engine' last of two carriages, the diode is fitted two carriages and two engine lengths from the end. Note: If you place the train on the track the wrong way round, the engine stops short on one direction, and then crashes all the carriages into the buffers at the other end of the track. The same applies if you do not set the points properly, the train crashes into the other rolling stock!

The wiring for this lower level is via two Gaugemaster Electronic Shuttle Control Modules that fit

between the master controller and the track. This is a very simple procedure to install. Two units look better than a single unit because two trains can move at the same time. A single unit can be wired to control the three trains, on a one at a time basis. Therefore by skilfully changing the points, and the 6 track power switches (Fig: 3) various combinations of different train arrivals and departures can be portrayed. Each sequence will run automatically until the points and switches are changed. The best type of rolling stock is driven from either end units, because visually it does not matter in which direction the unit is run.

Construction: The construction starts by cutting the base out to suit the shape of its location between the upper and lower levels. Because the base has to be removable, the underside must be kept clear of all protruding objects, including cables.

The height of the walls of the base is also critical, because the base fits between two levels; therefore some building parts will need to be removed before the base will be sufficiently low to slide under the upper level. For example the main high wall is part of hatch 3, (Terraced Houses) and the lower section is part of hatch 6 (Public House). The last wall forms part of the main upper level and the removable base butts up against this wall.

Having cut the base to size, mark out the track and fit the cork in place. Start laying the track from the points 1 & 2, inserting an insulated fish plate between them (isolates controller A from controller B) and then fit point 3 using a metal fish plate. Install the point motors on a block of wood and use a bell-crank to change the direction of throw through 90 degrees. The pushrod is then threaded through a brass tube and bent to fit the ends of the bell-crank and point tie-bar (see Fig 4 page 159). Repeat this on the other two points, and when satisfied that everything works smoothly, fix in place permanently.

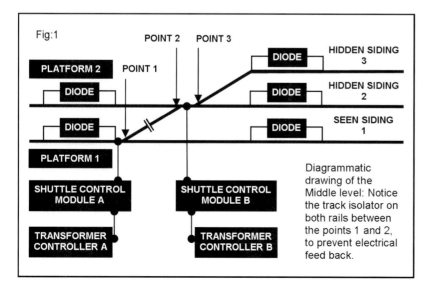

Fig:1

Diagrammatic drawing of the Middle level: Notice the track isolator on both rails between the points 1 and 2, to prevent electrical feed back.

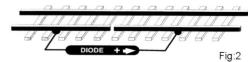

Fig:2

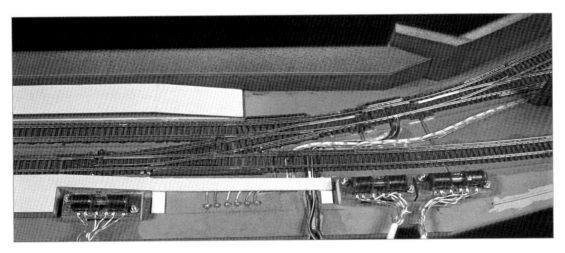

The nice thing about running this prototype is the fact they drive from either end, therefore it is unnecessary to turn the rolling stock around. With modern DCC rolling stock the lighting automatically changes with the direction of travel, and complete with internal carriage lighting looks extremely realistic.

This is made possible because the power to the rails remains constant, unlike conventional layouts that require the power to the track to be switched on or off as required, as each single train is powered so that it can move, from one section of track to another.

Note: the two points that form the crossover must be wired as a pair to avoid derailments.

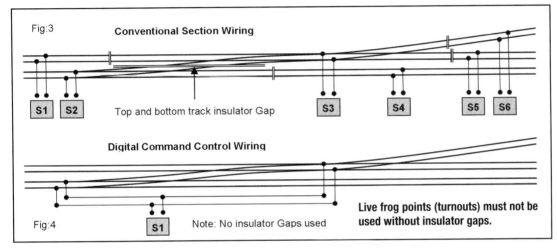

Fig:3

Conventional Section Wiring

S1   S2   Top and bottom track insulator Gap   S3   S4   S5   S6

Digital Command Control Wiring

Fig:4   S1   Note: No insulator Gaps used

Live frog points (turnouts) must not be used without insulator gaps.

Continue by cutting away as required the cork underlay to allow the fitting of the track power cables, (Multi-strand bell wire) at power supplies marked as S2 and S3; both of which are at the toe of the points. ('00' scale DCC layouts minimal wiring) followed by wiring the S1, S4, S5 & S6, insulated sections of track. Finally the insulated sections of track were cut ready for the diodes to be fitted (See fig:2). Having cut through one of the rails as shown fit the diode on a trial and error basis by powering the track, and if the train continues running, the diode is fitted the wrong way round. The train should stop, and when the power is reversed the engine should move off that section of track.

Digital Command Control: This station configuration is an ideal shelf layout design, whereby modern underground trains could be run automatically. To provide additional track length the base could be extended, so that 4 or 6 car units are run instead of just 2 car units. The wiring for a '00' scale DCC layout is extremely simple using insulated frog points (Fig: 4). Remember the track needs to be permanently live, because the trains need uninterrupted power so that they can be instantly called upon to make engine noises, to have the lights on etc. The complex bit of the layout is remembering what to do i.e. to reset the points after one train reaches its destination and another starts its journey.

Third rail made by dismantling a length of flexi track and cutting the sleepers into short lengths and then rethreading the sleepers onto the rail. The track is laid in the normal way and the third rail is fitted along side by inserting the third rail sleepers under the normal track and in-between its sleepers. The third rail is secured in place with the glue used whilst ballasting the track.

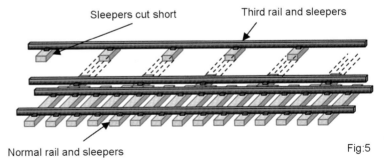

Sleepers cut short   Third rail and sleepers

Normal rail and sleepers   Fig:5

DCC Note: No insulation gaps are used in wiring this base for 16 V AC supply.

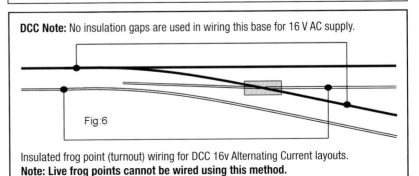

Fig:6

Insulated frog point (turnout) wiring for DCC 16v Alternating Current layouts.
Note: Live frog points cannot be wired using this method.

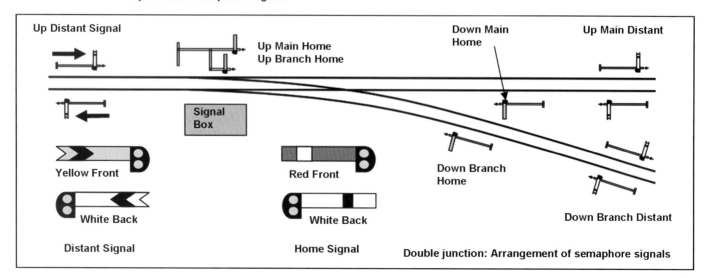

Double junction: Arrangement of semaphore signals

Above: This shows a diagrammatic layout of the signals at a typical double junction on a main line that has a branch line spur.

SIGNALS IN USE

Home and distant semaphore signalling was introduced on sections of track that had long distances between signals, as a safety measure. (Trains were travelling faster.) The method used was a single movable arm fitted onto a post.

The 'Home' signal arm was painted red (Command signal) and the 'Distant' signal arm was painted yellow, and indicated the position of the next command signal. (Yellow signal reading meaning the next signal is red or clear to proceed). This method allowed the train to travel at a greater speed between signals whilst providing a greater distance for the train to stop if need be. To reduce the cost of signalling, second hand material was used; hence we have solid wood, fabricated metal, old rails, tubing etc used for posts. Finally oil lamps were very reliable and extremely inexpensive to run!

SIGNALS

When there was just a single track and one train signals were non existent, but the moment other trains were added to the track some method of controlling the train's movements became necessary. The first signals were very basic involving hand gestures and fist fights, to decide who had the right of way.

To overcome this problem some of the first signals involved a stick, the possessor of the stick having the right of way. Another method used was a ball and a pole, when the ball was raised it meant give way and when lowered proceed. The same applied to a board that was rotated 90 degrees; when it was turned face on, it could be seen and when it was on edge, it almost disappeared from view. This worked fine on small sections of track, but as the amount of track available expanded and joined other sections of track this method of controlling the movement of the trains become impractical.

Semaphore signalling had been used by the military for a long time to relay messages over long distances and the principle was very simple. The transmitter consisted of a person waving two flags (or bats) held with arms outstretched and depending upon the position of the arms, the letter it represented. This then evolved into a building with two poles, and on each pole was attached a single board that represented the out-stretched flag. The position of the boards representing a letter was read by an observer at the other end of the sight line. This basic principle was applied to the railways, whereby the outstretched arm represents 'Stop' or to give it its correct term 'Section in advance blocked – Stop' and when the arm drops 'Go' or to provide the correct definition 'Section in advance clear'.

Unfortunately a technical problem became apparent with the arm dropping. The problem was that the 'Go' was incorrectly indicated by a signal with a broken cable, which caused an accident. Therefore to remedy this problem it was decided that if the signal arm was pulled upwards by the cable, and if the cable snapped, the signal would fall to the

'Stop' position. (This we must assume was one of the first forms of automated fail-safe installed on the railway associated with signalling.) The 'arm down' still remained, but redesigned and counter weighted so that the signal had to be pulled to the down position, and if the cable broke or malfunctioned, would automatically show the stop position.

Unfortunately several hundred tons of train cannot stop very quickly, and because trains were encouraged to travel faster, and by the time a driver was able to see a 'stop sign' and the train stopped, the train could well be a long way past the signal! To overcome this problem two signals were introduced, the 'Home' and 'Distant' each at times attached to a single post or in pairs: The top one is the present signal, the lower arm the next signal's setting. Therefore the driver knew to slow down because the next signal could well be a command to stop. To define the outline of the signals 'the present signal' had a square end, normally painted red with a white stripe. (White on reverse with a black stripe) The distant signal was painted yellow and has a fish tail cut out at the end and marked with a black chevron. (White with a black chevron on the back) so that by looking at the signal's shape, the crew of the train knew what type of signal that had come into view.

Night Signals: So that the signal could be seen at night, the arm of the signal had a spectacle plate attached containing coloured glass. Two types were used, the home (red signal) that indicated the compulsory sign, the 'stop' position contained red glass the 'go' position blue glass, because oil lamps were used. (The oil lamp burnt with a yellow flame therefore blue plus yellow showed as green.) The second advisory signal (Yellow) was fitted with a red glass (Next signal stop) and a yellow glass (Next compulsory signal clear) to their corresponding positions.

This formed the basics of signalling, but since nothing was standardised variations of this basic theme of semaphore signalling can be found, including specials such as used as a calling on arm, used to permit a loco to pass the 'stop' signal for a

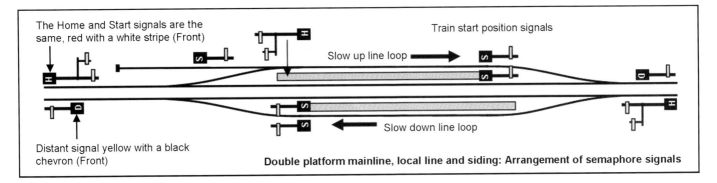

The Home and Start signals are the same, red with a white stripe (Front)

Train start position signals

Slow up line loop →

← Slow down line loop

Distant signal yellow with a black chevron (Front)

Double platform mainline, local line and siding: Arrangement of semaphore signals

short distance for marshalling purposes. Repeater signals, ground signals etc, and coloured light signals can also be found.

Coloured Light Signals: Semaphore Signals cannot be seen in the darkness; therefore in long tunnels signals fitted with arms were useless. To overcome this problem the arm was dispensed with and only the spectacle plate remained. With the advent of reliable 'electric' bulbs the oil lamp was dispensed with, and the design changed to become a single lamp house, with each lamp showing a particular colour. The very basic is the two light arrangement which shows stop (Red) or go, (Green) followed by the three light arrangement. (From top: green, yellow, and red) and the four light arrangement. (From top: yellow, green, yellow, and red.) This four-aspect coloured light arrangement provided yet further information for the driver, allowing him to judge his speed because the signals have now become standard in their interpretation. I.e. Green: Section in advance clear. Double Yellow: Next signal is yellow. Single yellow: next signal is red. Red: Section in advance blocked (therefore stop). There is one last signal, the one found at the end of the platform, the starter signal. This indicates to the driver when he can be ready to start his journey, and when given the all clear by the guard or station staff, by a whistle and green flag he can start the train on its journey.

Positioning Of Signals: Signals are used to indicate one of the following situations:
1: That the line up to the next signal ahead is clear/blocked and it is safe/unsafe to proceed.
2: The driver has the authority to proceed with care and caution.
3: That the path the train is to follow has the points (turnouts) correctly set.
4: The setting of the next signal. (Distant)

Signals Can Be Placed:
1: At the start of a section of track.
2: At the approach of an obstacle i.e. a set of points, where tracks diverge and cross, a road level crossing etc.
3: At the approach to a platform (Distant)
4: At the end of the platform at the start position of the train. (Home)

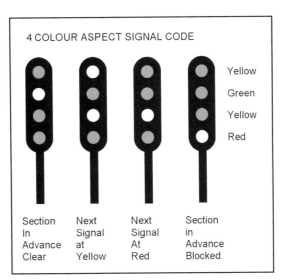

4 COLOUR ASPECT SIGNAL CODE

Yellow
Green
Yellow
Red

| Section In Advance Clear | Next Signal at Yellow | Next Signal At Red | Section in Advance Blocked |

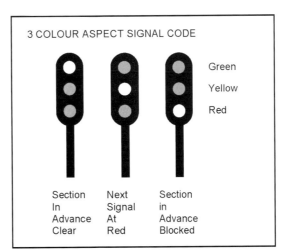

3 COLOUR ASPECT SIGNAL CODE

Green
Yellow
Red

| Section In Advance Clear | Next Signal At Red | Section in Advance Blocked |

Top row:
Both signals set at 'Stop' or to give its correct term: the way ahead is blocked.
Middle row:
The home signal indicates the way ahead is clear. The lower Distant signal indicates the next home signal is 'Stop'.
Lower row:
Both signals indicate the next sections of track are clear, and it is safe to proceed.
The signals are designed that if a cable breaks, or any other malfunction occurs, the signal automatically goes to the 'Stop' position. This is known as the fail-safe position.
Left: Disk signal near Traffic lights.
(Kent 2007)

The illustrations right show the baseboards joined together using flexible cable fitted with a plug on each end. These plugs fit into a corresponding plug fixed to each base. The track on each base is split into electrical isolated sections, with each section controlled by a double pole on-off-on switch, (Fig:2) so that adjoining sections can be switched on or off as required.

Two controllers can be used and wired (Fig:3) using a series of double pole on-off-on switches.

Because switches always seem to get damaged when mounted on the side of the base (when the base is moved) the switches could be mounted on the baseboard top, or wired back to a control panel.

JOINING BASEBOARDS

The track's major function is to steer the rolling stock along a predetermined path. To do this effectively it must be properly laid on a smooth surface and the worst situation is transferring rolling stock from one base to another, because a major join in the track is encountered. To work efficiently the rails must align within fractions of an inch of each other, so the rolling stock can pass over the join without derailment.

If a layout is built solely for your own use and does not have to align with other people's layouts, it also has straight track at the join; the task is simpler. This is because the join is relatively easy, i.e. the two baseboards can be aligned and bolted together, complete with locating pegs.

The track is then laid over the join and fixed into position. On both edges of the baseboards' joints, brass screws are fixed into the base, on the outside edge of each of the rails, and then soldered to the rails so they are firmly fixed into position. (Alternatively, printed circuit board can be used. The centre part of the copper coating is filed away, and the rails are then soldered to this.) Either way, the rails are then cut through with a razor saw (Fig:1) along the join line to separate each baseboard. The bolts are dismantled, allowing the two bases to be parted. On re-assembly the locating pegs align the bases into the correct position, and the bolts secure the baseboards together.

Greater difficulties arise when the track runs diagonally to the join, and increase further still when it has to align with someone else's layout, or when building a layout that is interchangeable with itself. It is now virtually impossible to use the above method of fixing the track to obtain the critical track alignment, and therefore it becomes necessary to devise some means of adjusting the track. This needs to be built-in at an early stage of the layout's construction if it is to be successful. (See Chapter 2 page 29 track adjusters.) The track adjusters should permit slight sideways movement to both tracks, *not* individual rails, so as to re-align the baseboards' track joints.

The track join itself, although diagonal, should be cut square, so that both wheels on an axle encounter the join at the same time, otherwise derailments occur due to uneven wheel bounce.

Wiring a Series of Bases: By treating each base as a separate item, the wiring becomes easier to understand. Each base will present its own problems i.e. The base 01 with all its sidings appears complex, but it is similar to a house, whereby you switch on or off individual hall way and room lights as you go. Therefore the house wiring breaks down into a lot of individual sections. We do the same with the layout's wiring.

The main lines are treated as separate parts and controlled by their own controllers, power being fed from one base to another base. (In Fig 3 the sidings are controlled from a slave controller.) The controller for base 01 is a master, controlling all movements within the sidings and the main line. Within the sidings each set of points has a set of isolating switches, so that individual track control is obtained. As previously explained (Page 155) the points (turnouts) are electrically isolated so that to continue across the point and along the track behind it requires a switch to be thrown to complete the electrical circuit. This happens in each case. Alternatively, a point motor that has a built in switch (Page 160) can be used. This type of point automatically switches on the power to the track it is set to and makes wiring considerably easier, but in some cases is less flexible in use.

Wiring Bases 01, 02 And 03: These are treated in the same way as the single oval layout, only this time they have to be linked together using plug-in leads. By connecting the leads in various combinations, different controlling methods can be used. One of the simplest ways to arrange this is through what is called 'zone control'.

Since the interchangeable bases are constructed as individual electrically insulated sections, and each section having to be plugged into the next, it is a very easy procedure to treat each base as a 'zone'. The plug-in leads which connect each of the bases is replaced by leads fitted with slave controller and switches, the power to which is fed directly from the master controller.

By setting the master controller on full power and then using a slave controller, control is transferred to the slave controller. Alternatively separate transformer controllers of the 'Gaugemaster' ® type with power input control can be used for smoother 'zone' change over, set on simulated load, as this reduces the change-over 'power step' difference on handing over from controller to another controller. The slight difference in setting between the units is taken care of by simulated coasting or gradual build-up of power, unlike other units which immediately show this difference.

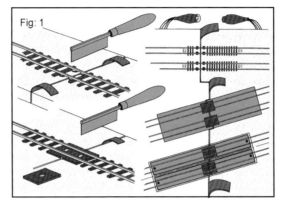

Fig: 1

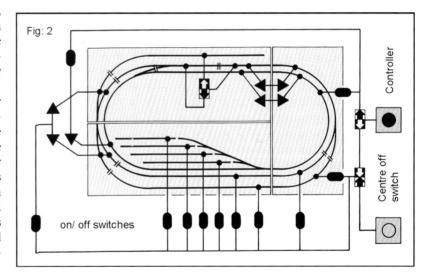

Fig: 2

on/ off switches

Controller

Centre off switch

Left: The baseboard join using the copper printed circuit board method. Properly done this provides years of trouble free running. This also applies to all the other joins in the track, so make all track joins as smooth as possible. Also, solder all fishplate rail connections when the track is being used to supply power.

Left: By inserting card between the bases when track laying, it makes cutting the track joins easier and loses the saw cut thickness, so the tracks butt tighter together.

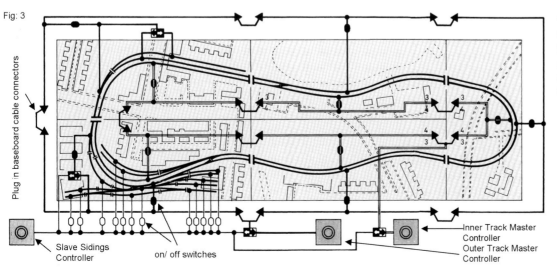

Fig: 3

Plug in baseboard cable connectors

Slave Sidings Controller

on/ off switches

Inner Track Master Controller

Outer Track Master Controller

To control and provide even voltage around the track, the power is fed to the centre of each base from a switched, plugged-together wiring loom.

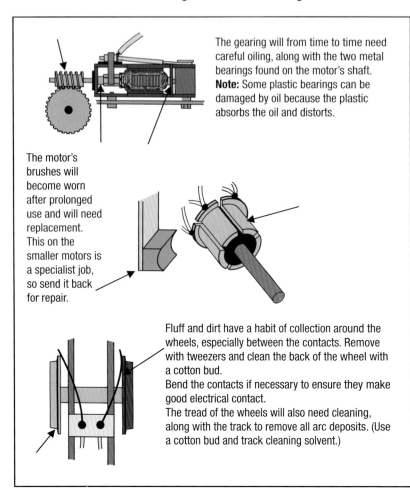

The gearing will from time to time need careful oiling, along with the two metal bearings found on the motor's shaft. **Note:** Some plastic bearings can be damaged by oil because the plastic absorbs the oil and distorts.

The motor's brushes will become worn after prolonged use and will need replacement. This on the smaller motors is a specialist job, so send it back for repair.

Fluff and dirt have a habit of collection around the wheels, especially between the contacts. Remove with tweezers and clean the back of the wheel with a cotton bud.
Bend the contacts if necessary to ensure they make good electrical contact.
The tread of the wheels will also need cleaning, along with the track to remove all arc deposits. (Use a cotton bud and track cleaning solvent.)

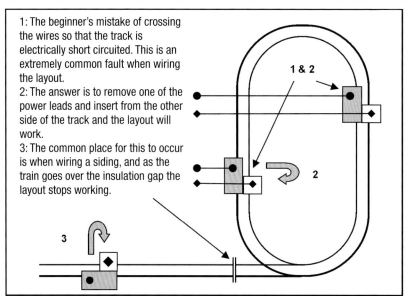

1: The beginner's mistake of crossing the wires so that the track is electrically short circuited. This is an extremely common fault when wiring the layout.
2: The answer is to remove one of the power leads and insert from the other side of the track and the layout will work.
3: The common place for this to occur is when wiring a siding, and as the train goes over the insulation gap the layout stops working.

The Multi-meter supplied by Radio Spares® has a buzzer setting which is extremely useful for speedily finding short circuits; because you don't have to keep looking at the dial you just listen for the bleep.

It can also be used to take DC and AC current readings as well as resistance readings, useful for checking out the armatures of electric motors, polarity of diodes etc.

FAULT FINDING

You have to retain your sense of humour when you are fault finding because it is normally the easy answers that catch you out time and time again. When the layout is in full working order and suddenly stops, what is the cause? The symptoms generally fall into different categories i.e. sudden loss of electrical power and is it a track fault or is it because somebody tripped over the power cable, and pulled the plug out? Or has the engine ceased to work? The first thing to do is make a quick visual check to ensure the power is still on and then check the track to see if a metal object (pliers or other tools) has been placed across the rails. (If that is what happened remove the object and wait a few minutes for the auto cut-out to reset.) If this was not the problem remove all rolling stock from the track. This splits the search for finding the fault into two areas.

The Engine: If a locomotive stops working, first make a visual check of the model to see if anything has fallen off. If no problem can be found place it on a section of track known to be working. One of two things will happen when power is applied. Either the overload will cut out and switch off the power or the engine moves. If the engine does not move keep a visual check on the engine for a thin column of blue smoke which will indicate that something very serious is occurring. If nothing happens place a known working engine on the same track. If nothing happens with both of them take a reading across the track with a multi-meter just to confirm power is being supplied to the rails. If the model works place it onto the track that has a problem. If it works then it is the other engine, if it doesn't then it is electrical supply on the layout.

Test Track Readings: Place the engine on the track and then take a resistance reading using the meter's own power source to establish whether an open or short circuit has occurred on the model. If it is an open circuit dismantle the loco and inspect for a broken connection, paying special attention to the pick-up wipers which rub onto the wheels because these do tend to wear out or pick up fluff, and making them ineffective (see illustration). Do this both visually and by taking a resistance reading by placing probes in appropriate places. An easy check is to replace the locomotive on to the track, position the probes on each rail and take a reading. If no resistance is found then place one probe on the rail and the second on each of the motor's brushes in turn. This should produce two direct readings from the four taken. If an open circuit to one is indicated repair as necessary, if more than two check the insulation for a short circuit.

If there is still a problem and both rail to brush circuits are good, replace the probes on to the rails and rotate the motor's armature by hand whilst taking a reading. If an intermittent reading is found the problem lies within the brushes, the commutator or a winding of the motor's armature. If both the brushes and commutator are clean and in good condition and only one section of the armature does not work a coil is broken or burnt out. This is a replacement job as the rewinding of a single coil is extremely difficult.

Unfortunately, dismantling an electric motor disturbs its magnetic field so that on re-assembly it is never the same unless re-magnetized. This loss can be ignored for general purpose work but will show itself if the motor is required to work hard, as it simply will not work as well as it used to. In general terms it is usually quicker and cheaper to replace the entire motor in the event of a coil burning out.

If all the coils are good clean out the motor's commutator gaps, its surface and replace the brushes if necessary. New brushes, like a new engine, need running in until they take up the commutator's shape, as before they do this they are working inefficiently.

The Track: If it is the track that has the problem switch off the power supply and set all switches to the off position. This is when the centre off switches come into their own because each section will now be isolated and readings can be made for a short circuit or if the power is supplied. If the track, with all the rolling stock removed and switches set at off, still shorts out, check each section between the controller and switches. If this does not reveal the fault, switch on one section at a time, checking for power using the multi-meter set to voltage in both forward and reverse modes. If all is well then switch on adjoining sections in pairs. The illustration on the right shows a typical number of problems, associated with points (turnouts) the circuit works in one direction but when a point is changed a short circuit occurs.

Basically there is little to go wrong with a straight length of track, but points generate a whole series of problems. This is when it is worth investing in a simple volt meter, that shows volts and has a battery powered resistance dial, for trouble shooting.

For example using probes; use the multi-meter set on resistance so the meter supplies its own power and check the insulated joins to each of the sections of rail. Both rails should provide a zero reading, if there is a reading then the insulation gap has been bridged and is no longer functioning. Clean the gap until a zero reading is obtained. Remove probes, switch the power back on and recheck with the meter set on volts. If it still does not work continue by repeating this procedure until the fault is clear. The turnouts are particularly good at finding bits to short circuit them so these should be checked both visually and electrically very carefully.

One of the biggest mistakes is to clean the track with wire wool, because this deposits tiny pieces of wire all around the track, which attach themselves to the train's electric motors' magnets and short circuit everything.

The unit/engine stops on the point.

Clean the contacts attached to the rails or carefully bend the contacts until they make electrical contact. (Don't paint them!)

Both the live frog and insulated points suffer with the problem of contacts failing to work. The symptom is the power unit/engine stops on the point and works when pushed to the next powered section of track.

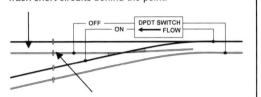

Track short circuits behind the point.

Having reset all other points inline place all switches to off and remove all rolling stock, clean/re-cut the insulation gap behind the point.

The live frog point is prone to short circuiting the following section of track when the isolating gap between the rails becomes bridged. The classic reason is that the gap was cut when the rails were cold, and the rails have expanded during warm weather.

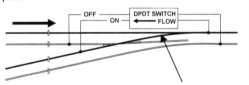

Carriages come off the track as they go over the point.

This is normally the classic: Was the point set in the right direction for travel of the train!

We all do this one; whilst having the engine at the far end, whilst pushing/shunting the carriages or trucks etc, they all come off at the points, simply reset the points for the correct direction of travel.

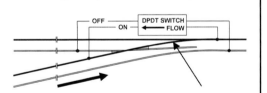

The unit/engine stops as it comes to the point.

This is normally another classic. The point is set in the right direction for the train to travel but it stopped; did the next section of track have the power switched on?

We all do this one; all sections of track need to be powered for the train to travel, so if a train suddenly stops first check the power switch is on! It is only when the power switch is on you will need to look elsewhere.

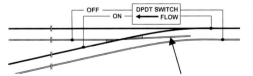

The engine/unit stops as it goes over the point, but other engines work without problems.

From time to time this problem occurs with just one particular engine as it passes over a live frog point. What can happen is the wheels touch the back of the open switch blade and this electrically short circuits the point.

This problem is a real pain to resolve, because the engine can work without problems elsewhere, it is only one point that causes trouble. The answer can be to replace the point with a larger radius one, and re-lay the track. Alternatively it could be a loose switch blade and the gaps narrowed.

SOLDERING WIRES

Learning how to solder is one of the most important tasks to master. Poor soldering will doom a layout to a constant stream of electrical failures.

The secret of successful electrical soldering is to use a hot iron, clean the job well and apply the solder to the job and not the iron.

The purchase of a good pair of wire strippers is a must, as these remove the casing to expose the wire without damage. This is very important since reducing the number of wires affects the electrical carrying capacity of the cable. A single small strand of wire in many cases can be a fire risk, because it alone cannot carry the amperage required and it will get hot.

THE CONTROL PANEL'S USE

The choice of the control panel's appearance is very much up to the individual, as so many factors govern its design. For example, will the layout be used at home most of the time? Will the layout be exhibited? At present the self-contained oval fits into my estate car, minus the control panel. The choice is: Should I make the panel permanently fixed in place, and hire a van for the move when it is exhibited or do I bolt it onto the baseboard so that it is removable, involving lots and lots of plugs to join all the wiring together.

The self-contained layout with a built in control panel suffers from none of the problems of plugs not working and the control panel is built to suit the baseboard. If the points (turnouts) are to be changed manually, a control panel is not even needed since the track isolating section switches can be built into the layout's baseboard and wired back to the controller.

This provides a choice: should the control panel be a separate unit or built in? The fundamental point governing this is how the points (turnouts) are to operate. If they are mechanically linked the logical choice for reliability is to build them into the baseboard and avoid all the problems of disconnecting and reconnecting linkages each time the layout is moved. If the turnouts are electrically-operated the connection problem is much simpler, as a suitable plug-in system can be built. This then allows all of the switch gear to be installed on the control panel and connected via the plugs to the layout, keeping the landscape clear of switches.

Controllers are another personal choice. I prefer one that allows the rolling stock to slow down naturally, rather than skidding to a standstill when the power is turned off. Gaugemaster produce a range of controllers which permit simulated control over the locomotive, i.e. When full power is applied the engine does not depart like a rocket, but slowly builds up speed to reach its maximum and vice versa, the operator applying the braking as necessary to stop the momentum of the train.

The simulator can also be switched off to allow fine shunting manoeuvres. This gives the operator another problem, however, which is observing these delicate movements closely. To overcome this a hand-held infrared controller can be used, which enables the operator to move around the layout without the need for cables attaching it to the control panel. Another problem with small slow manoeuvres is electrical contact, as the rails become dirty with time and use, and this prevents continuous electrical flow to the locomotive's motor which in turn causes intermittent stopping and starting, so that in the end it will not restart until pushed by hand to a fresh piece of track. The answer is to keep the track clean, by using a special track cleaning rubber (produced by Peco).

Appearance And Design: The use of plastics for the facia of the control panel makes their construction easier, as plastic can be drilled and cut with hand tools, and LEDs can be glued in position using PVA glue (removable in case of failure). Plastic can also be masked and sprayed complete with the layout diagram so that it looks smart and impressive. The use of miniature switches also helps considerably to reduce the panel's size. Alternatively the turn-out motors can be operated by an electric pencil, (Page 161) and the track and signalling diagrams can also be made to light up. Always tag the cables for ease of identification.

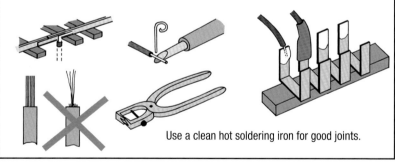

Use a clean hot soldering iron for good joints.

The same problem arises when using single-strand bell wire, the resistance of which absorbs the electrical energy; so that over a long length it shows a voltage drop sufficiently to be noticeable. To avoid this problem use multi-strand electrical cable. Maplin Electrical® is an ideal source.

Track plan marked out on facia panel using the mask and spray method.

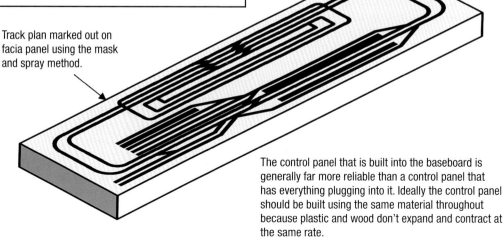

The control panel that is built into the baseboard is generally far more reliable than a control panel that has everything plugging into it. Ideally the control panel should be built using the same material throughout because plastic and wood don't expand and contract at the same rate.

Semaphore signals are visually far more exciting than coloured lights, but coloured light signalling is easier to make work. The reason for this is that point motors are available with built in switch gear, and as the motor changes the points, it also changes the coloured light signal. The outcome is automatic signalling, unlike semaphore signals which require either a separate cable or a relay to physically move the signal arm. (See page 161)

The problem is compounded with 'N' scale, because of actual size, and therefore coloured light signals are far more reliable and robust than working semaphore signals at this small scale.

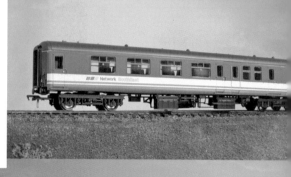

9. ROLLING STOCK

Modifying rolling stock is an enjoyable part of model making and at a exhibition I came across these inexpensive brightly coloured 4 wheeled coaches and my thought was 'they will make good line side old or disused coaches'.

The first stage was to dismantle the coach, cut off what was not required and apply a coat of primer.

The bodywork was then painted using household water based emulsion paint that had been thinned, so that the primer could still be seen underneath.

The gold trim was applied by using a rubber that was thinly coated with coloured emulsion paint. *(Press rubber over the raised surface of the coach; which will transfer the paint to the body.)*

Finally, the coach was given a 'dirty' emulsion wash and allowed to dry.

Below: The rather old looking coaches at the town end of the Wishton Halt layout.

Dismantle 4 wheel carriage, including wheels.

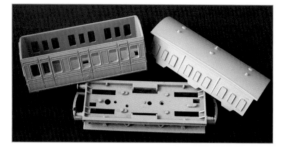

Prime using car spray with thin coats of paint.

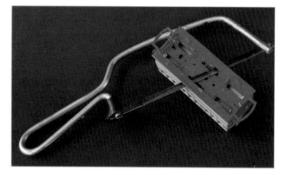

If required remove axle boxes etc, with a small saw, file and clean as required.

Above: Using a small rubber, coated in a thin layer of paint press over the raised surfaces to produce a lining effect and allow to dry.

Left: Finally to produce a weathered effect use thinned emulsion paint 'dirty wash' over the entire coach. (Use a tin foil tray to contain the paint.)

READY-TO-RUN ROLLING STOCK

One of the great things about ready-to-run rolling stock is the selection available from both the main manufacturing concerns and the professional model makers who offer kit building services, who extend the range of available rolling stock further still. A good example of one of these companies is TMS Models (www.tmsmodels.biz) situated in the UK, which offers a very large choice in the way different kits are built. This starts with the 4 mm range and progresses through to the larger '0' super detailed models.

This type of specialised service allows the individual (provided the kit is available) to obtain a rare item of rolling stock finished in a unusual livery, all of which is hand-painted and lined, for one's collection. Collecting locomotives which are displayed in show cases is also part of railway modelling, as the model, instead of being shown on a shelf, can be displayed in a small diorama, so that it looks at home in a setting. This caters for the person who enjoys landscaping rather than building rolling stock, but wants an unusual prototype immaculately finished. This type of service is impractical for the mass-market manufacturer.

Research Into Available Rolling Stock: The easiest way to gather information on rolling stock is to visit your local dealer, or to go up on the web and visit various sites, and obtain a series of catalogues on various manufacturers' products. The reason for exploring several dealers is because there is a tendency for a particular shop or site to specialise in a small number of manufacturers' products. Because the range is so vast, it is impossible to stock everything.

By consulting the catalogues at a very early stage whilst designing the layout, a number of things can be taken into consideration, such as the availability of rolling stock, the types and the countries of origin. Are cars, people and buildings available to suit the type of rolling stock and are there any other accessories that are made to add interest to the layout?

Peco, for example, produce a comprehensive range of track work in several gauges to suit the different scales. They also back up this range with turnout motors and switchgear, line side accessories such as tunnel portals, stations, huts and buildings. They also produce kits and ready-to-run rolling stock, including both standard and narrow gauge prototypes, all of which can be used to add character to the layout. To further back this up and to help the modeller Peco also produce booklets which cover track plans, both large and small, using both Setrack® and Flexible track, and most important of all they provide information sheets printed to modelling size on their Streamline turnouts and crossings to aid the planning of a layout.

Just as the range of different rolling stock available is enormous, so is the range of scales, giving the modeller a very wide choice. The most popular scales are HO/00, probably due to the fact that they established themselves so many years ago. Also very popular is N gauge, the possible reason for this being its small size which allows more countryside to be included on the layout, so that it looks more realistic, and permits a smaller physical size of layout, which is convenient for storage. All the remaining gauges vary in their popularity from country to country.

The terms scale and gauge can lead to misunderstandings as the same gauge can be used for various scales. The gauge of the track means the distance that the running rails of the track are spaced apart. The term scale is the ratio of the model size to the full size prototype. For example, if the model is 76 times smaller than the real prototype the scale is expressed as 1:76. This is modelled at 4 mm to a foot, which is not quite correct but a close equivalent. This error is so small that it is ignored and is a factor common to all the scale modelling size ratios. (See page 12 for further details.)

Narrow gauge modelling is one of the specialist areas of modelling because most of the rolling stock has to be made by the modeller. The beauty of narrow gauge modelling is in the fact the scale of the model is larger i.e. it is almost like running '00' scale rolling stock on 'N' scale track. See below for size comparison.

Narrow gauge scales run on standard track sizes, but have tighter curves!

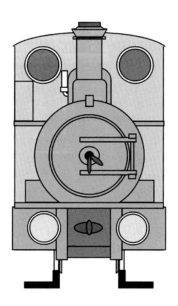

SM-32 Gauge 32 mm Scale 16 mm

0-16.5 Gauge 16.5 mm Scale 7 mm

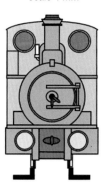

00-9 Gauge 9 mm Scale 4 mm

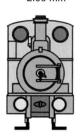

N-6.5 Gauge 6.5 mm Scale 2.06 mm

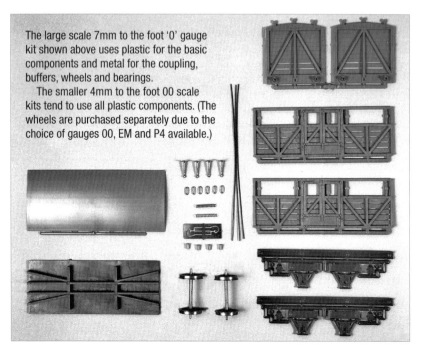

The large scale 7mm to the foot 'O' gauge kit shown above uses plastic for the basic components and metal for the coupling, buffers, wheels and bearings.

The smaller 4mm to the foot 00 scale kits tend to use all plastic components. (The wheels are purchased separately due to the choice of gauges 00, EM and P4 available.)

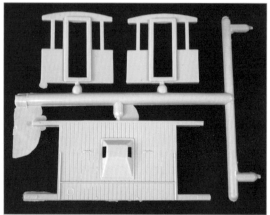

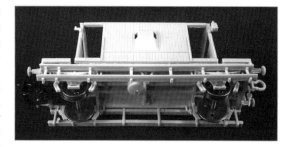

PLASTIC KITS

The plastic kits available tend to be trucks and wagons, rather than coaches and locomotives. The possible reason is the cost of tooling, which would be very expensive compared with the cost of acid etched components and white metal castings.

The weight of the model is also important, because if the locomotive is not very heavy the wheels will spin, due to lack of adhesion. The weight provides grip.

Opposite above: Use a jig to make square cuts when altering plastic kits.

Several manufacturers of rolling stock produce plastic kits, providing a wide choice of subjects for the modeller. Dapol® for example still produce plastic kits that were available over 45 years ago under the names of Rosebud® and Airfix® etc.

Other companies such as Plastruct and Evergreen produce a wide range of plastic strip and embossed plastic sheeting. Slater's® are probably best known for its plastic sheet, sold under the name of Plastikard®. (10, 15, 20, 30, 40, 60 & 80 thou thick, black, white & clear sheets) Perspex® Oraglass® produce considerably thicker plastic sheeting that has a very different working characteristic and is much nicer to use. Unfortunately it does need power tools to work with the thicker material efficiently.

The companies mentioned have been established a number of years and during this time most of these companies have developed a wide range of accessories and services which include chemical milling. Most people know this as acid etching and is a useful service to know how to use, as your skills develop and your modelling becomes more adventurous.

The photo sequence on the right shows the basic construction assembly of a Dapol® CO38 Brake Van. The kit contains the bits needed except glue. The kit's construction starts with the chassis and you remove the components from off of the sprue as you go with a sharp knife and fix in place using a liquid cement, applied with a paint brush.

The kit's instructions are very basic but easy to follow and is ideal for the beginner to make as their first model. Painting is straight forward and how to do this is covered in another chapter. The kit could be finished as a line-side disused piece of rolling stock, without its wheels!

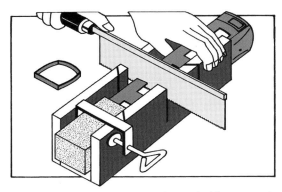

Since plastic is a very easily workable material, it lends itself to adaptation, which is useful as a number of commercially produced ready-to-run models are scale-wise too short. This is especially true of coaches. By cutting two coaches at a suitable point they can be joined to form a corrected length of coach. The jig shown can be made from wood; the saw fitting into the gap so that its blade is guided to produce a good clean straight cut.

Plastic can be laminated in layers to form thicker pieces by using liquid cement or solvent, and then shaped, being either carved with a sharp knife or filed. Double-sided sticky tape can be used to temporarily fix small pieces, which would be difficult to hold, on to a larger piece of plastic, so as to form a handle.

For gluing plastic components together, Slater's® market a solvent called 'Met-Pak'. (In the trade we use a solvent called dichloromethane.) Being a solvent it does not have a gap filling property so joins must be a good fit. Because poor joins will cause problems, therefore all kits should be carefully inspected as assembly takes place, to make sure that the components fit snugly. Cyanoacrylate and other glues of this type do not join plastic together very well, so therefore they should be avoided.

Filling gaps when components do not fit very well is always a problem. Car body filler is a good general-purpose material but it does have its limitations. Unfortunately some makes set very hard, making it difficult to sand flat or remove in difficult places. I have found through practice that epoxy putty can be superior as this can be modelled to shape whilst it is still soft, can be smoothed with water and requires no further work. For finer gaps I have found that filler called 'Brummer'® Stopper (as used in woodworking) is ideal. Since this filler is water based, it can be cleaned off with a damp rag, unlike other fillers that require filing or sanding, producing the risks of damaging the component's surface. Dents, unfortunately, will require keying by scraping and drilling so that the filler can grip the plastic. Alternatively, a mixture of liquid glue which has had scrap plastic dissolved in it can be used, built up in a series of layers. This method works very well when the component has no fine detail. All plastics will require priming with a paint that is specially formulated to key to plastic. Having primed the plastic finish with any non-cellulose based paint because this type of paint will destroy the plastic's surface.

Commercially available ready to run plastic rolling stock or kits are a prime source of model updating, whereby the model is cut to pieces and reassembled slightly differently to represent an earlier or later version of the existing model.

Page 174 of this book shows a basic bit of kit bashing, whereby an inexpensive carriage was converted into a useful piece of rolling stock.

Buildings can also be 'bashed' whereby they are not assembled as the manufacturer intended (see page 132).

Below: The 'Bachmann' Market Hampton range of buildings are ideal for accompanying rolling stock for skillful adaptation and repainting to meet the layout's needs.

The model shown right is a fine example of the GWR 1028 County of Warwick. The model was made by Ron Cadman, who in 1986 professionally produced these models.

SCALE SPEED

To look realistic rolling stock needs to travel at a scale speed. Every thing can be scaled apart from time which always remains a constant.

The speeds shown can be converted to scale speed by dividing the distance by scale size i.e. 5280 feet is one mile.

Modelled at 2mm per foot (N scale) equals 10560 mm; divide by 60 minutes equals 176 mm per minute. Convert to inches equals 6.90 per minute and multiply by miles per hour, i.e. 50 mph equals 28.75 feet travelled per minute.

Note: Because of fractions the feet figures have been rounded up to even numbers.

METAL KITS AND MASTERS

The method of manufacturing white metal components has been developed to a fine art over the years. The masters for these are produced in metal by hand. This is necessary because the most common method of making the rubber moulds requires the use of heat and pressure.

Two uncured rubber discs are used, the master being embedded into these to form the mould's shape by being squashed between them. To cure the moulding rubber so that it retains its shape, heat is applied whilst the material is under pressure. When this process is finished the moulds are separated and the master is removed. Next the moulds are placed in a centrifugal casting machine. The void created by the master is filled with molten white metal, which is removed from the mould when it has cooled.

Since this procedure is a simple one, skilful modellers can make their own masters and have them cast. This service and others is offered by a number of companies which advertise regularly in modelling magazines and specialise in white metal casting and chemical milling procedures.

Making Masters: The technique for producing the master is to shape the components from brass and solder additional pieces in place; hollow components being cast in two pieces due to the difficulty of making a suitable core plug (examine a kit closely). The components have to be produced fractionally larger than required, due to shrinkage of the hot metal in the mould. Since this is a constant the easiest way of allowing for it is to photographically enlarge the drawing by approximately two per cent and work to the new slightly enlarged photocopy. The percentage by which the drawing will need to be enlarged will depend upon the specialist company producing the casting, because various casting metals have slightly different shrinkage rates. The method of mould production also influences this, as a cold cured rubber mould expands with heat, thus almost neutralising the shrinkage rate of the metal.

Cold cure rubber is an expensive material, so it is not used by all the casting companies. This means that in the end the modeller will have to do some research to establish from the company what shrinkage rate should be allowed for. The master can then be made proportionally larger as necessary and any other points can be discussed at the same time.

The advantage from the modeller's point of view of cold cure rubber is that masters can be made from suitable plastics, but as with all masters, the final result can only be as good as the planning, the fitting of the components and the standard of workmanship involved.

The commercially available metal kits are produced using two methods, either by casting or by chemical milling (known as etching). The latter technique is used to produce the fine brass components and again is a method that the advanced modeller can use, after producing their own artwork for the components required.

Chemical Milling (Etching): For this an accurate drawing is required, produced at least twice size so that it can be photographically reduced. This enhances the artwork of the components and helps to minimise the size of any drafting errors.

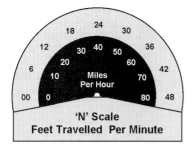

'N' Scale
Feet Travelled Per Minute

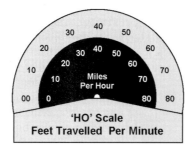

'HO' Scale
Feet Travelled Per Minute

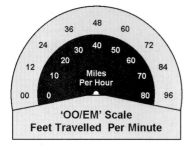

'OO/EM' Scale
Feet Travelled Per Minute

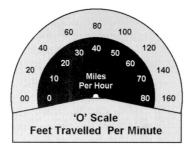

'O' Scale
Feet Travelled Per Minute

Left: A finished LNWR inspection coach used by F. W. Webb. The model was built and painted by Ron Cadman from a 'Premier kit'.

The locomotive is the Cornwall, which was used exclusively with this coach for many years.

The engine and carriage has been placed onto a small landscaped base, so that it forms a small diorama for viewing.

The drawing can be produced on art-board (identical back and front etching) or on drafting film (etching on each side different). The advantage of using film rather than tracing paper is that it is unaffected by humidity and stays the same size. By using special inks and rubbers, the drawing can be altered without destroying the surface of the film unlike tracing paper that damages easily. Another advantage of using film rather than art-board is that a provisional drawing in pencil can be produced first, and the components then moved around to make maximum use of the area which will constitute the fret: The term given to the etching on its surround.

Lost Wax Casting: Another method commercially available is the lost wax process. This is used to make the round brass components of a kit when strength is required on small pieces, or for those kits made entirely from brass. This time the master can be made from any suitable modelling material, because a cold cure rubber mould is made from the master first, this then being used to produce a wax copy casting. The wax copy is embedded into a solid block by immersing it in a special fine cream-like mixture of plaster. The wax copy can either be dipped in the plaster or the plaster can be poured over it. Note that a wax 'sprue' must be left between the wax casting in the centre of the plaster and the open air. Once the plaster has set, the wax copy will be solidly encased apart from the tip of the 'sprue'. The plaster is then gently heated to both dry the mould and melt the wax, which is poured out through the hole that contained the 'sprue'. The shape of the wax casting is thus left in the block. Using a centrifugal casting machine, molten brass is then injected into the plaster mould. Once it is cool the plaster is broken away to reveal the brass casting. This is a very specialised procedure, and is expensive!

The production of a model from a metal kit is very time consuming but is extremely rewarding.

The kit extras will include the electric motor, the wheels, couplings etc. And also specialist paint.

The brass will need to be thoroughly cleaned before painting as any wax or oils, acid stains from fingers etc will affect the way the paint sticks to the surface of the metal. A good scrubbing in hot soapy water with some pumice powder and an old tooth brush is thoroughly recommended!

Left: Brass kits are produced using chemical milling. The fret is etched from both sides and by only etching from one side some limited depth can be added. i.e. wood panelling lines etc.

The bulkier items such as axle boxes, springs, hoses etc, are produced in white metal.

This kit shown was produced by 'Micro Rail' and is of a R C Horsebox.

The original was built at St Rollox from July 1907 to 1908.

Like all these brass kits the wheels are purchased separately, i.e. 00, EM or EEM etc, because the track gauge is different.

Above: The GWR 5700 engine built at 7mm to the foot (O gauge) built from a 'Vulcan Kit'® made by Ron Cadman and came complete with wheels and electric motor.

Below: Using a sheet of glass carefully align the chassis so that the axles are square, the chassis does not rock and the wheels run smoothly.

ADVICE FOR THE BEGINNER

If you are building your first metal kit, start with the tender's bodywork after assembling the chassis. Make sure it aligns with the locomotive's running plate height by temporarily assembling the tender using Blu-Tack®, sticky tape and elastic bands to hold it together, so that the entire assembly sequence is understood. Fortunately a tender can have a separate under-frame which eases adjustment of the riding height. When you are thoroughly familiar with the way and in which order the components go together, assemble the tender using glue or solder. Just tack the joints to begin with,

so that as assembly continues adjustments can be made. When satisfied fillet the corners and across the joins with glue or solder on the inside. Ideally master the art of soldering, purchase low melt solder, and obtain a good temperature controlled soldering iron!

Each kit will require its own special construction methods and since there are so many kits of different prototypes, the variations in assembly techniques are endless, although the basic techniques of soldering and gluing remain the same.

Other principles also apply to all kits. Always dry-assemble components and check the fit of the running components for clearance, as it is easier to make adjustments when the kit's components are in separate pieces. The kits all have explicit instructions and as your skills and confidence increase, more complex kits can be built. As always start with a simple kit that needs the minimum amount of work, because it is far more satisfying to complete a kit than be defeated by it.

Having finished the assembly of the kit, filled in any holes and dents and made good the joints, thoroughly cleaned the entire model in lukewarm soapy water, scrubbed the stubborn dirty bits clean with pumice powder and an old toothbrush, and then rinse everything well, the final bit is to dry the model in a warm dust-free place so that it is ready for painting.

Note: For the beginner there is a soldering exercise on page 186/187. This shows how to make an end stop (buffer) and has been designed to use leftover pieces of track and low melt solder. I strongly recommend that this test piece is successfully completed before attempting to solder any metal kit together.

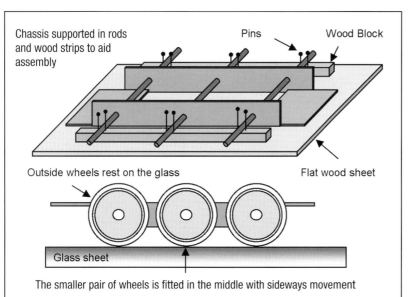

Chassis supported in rods and wood strips to aid assembly

Pins

Wood Block

Outside wheels rest on the glass

Flat wood sheet

Glass sheet

The smaller pair of wheels is fitted in the middle with sideways movement

Chassis Assembly, White Metal Or Brass: Assembly of the kit always starts with the chassis, so that wheel clearances, axle alignment and the riding height can be checked. The axle alignment is done using push fit, long straight metal rods through the axle bearings, the distances between them being measured and aligned for squareness. The axles and wheels are now fitted as per the manufacturer's instructions and checked so that they are smooth and free running, complete with spacing washers and crank pins. A point to remember when fitting wheels on locomotives with more than four driving wheels is that the fractionally smaller ones fit in the middle. This is to prevent the chassis rocking up and down on the middle two sets of wheels (easily checked on a sheet of glass) and to restrict sideways movement on the 'outside', as per the following example: front set no sideways play, middle set sideways movement; rear set no play (0-6-0 wheel configuration).

This no-play situation also applies to the axle on which the gearing is situated. The middle wheels' side play will be governed by the minimum radius used, so this will need to be checked on the track; at the same time look for places where the wheels may foul on the bodywork or any part of the driving mechanism. When satisfied, and after the body has been checked for its fit with the motor temporarily in place, dismantle as necessary and paint the chassis, before reassembling to continue.

Fitting the motor comes next. The alignment of the gears must be carefully checked and shimmed with thin brass sheet until just the finest of play is felt in the gearing. When satisfied that the motor's output shaft, gearing and wheels run freely, by rotating the armature by hand, lubricate the gears and axle bushes. Finally apply a fifteen-second burst of half power, reducing this until it is zero, whilst carefully listening for a continuous and even tone, to denote that there is not a mechanical tight spot. (Repeat in the opposite direction.) When satisfied that all is well, run in the assembly for three (half speed) five-minute sessions in each direction, whilst constantly checking that the motor is not over-heating. Make any adjustments as necessary. This very careful alignment and running in should produce a sweet-running chassis, which will be a sound basis for the rest of the model. Assemble the rest of the model and carefully paint to suit.

Below: The GWR 850 kit laid out showing the basic components. The wheels, the gears and the electric motor are purchased separately because it allows choice of drive.

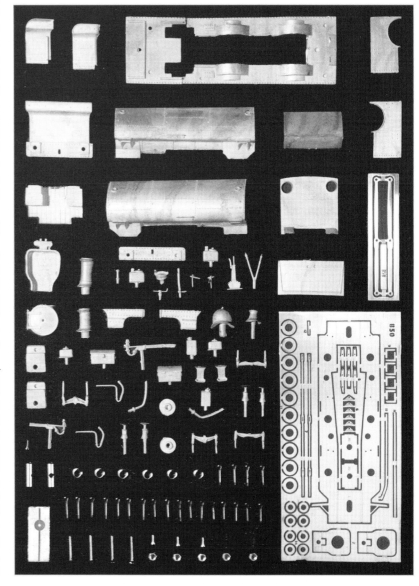

Above: This shows the LMS 4-6-0 Highland Light Infantry locomotive awaiting its turn of duty. (Modelled at '00 scale by Ron Cadman).

This is an extremely nice model, which needs a good degree of model making skills to make and paint. Note: The beginner is strongly recommended to start with a simpler project.

FIXING METAL COMPONENTS TOGETHER

The components can be joined together in various ways, but by far the best method is soft soldering. On white metal kits the use of special low-melt solders and fluxes is strongly recommended, followed by epoxy two-part glue and super glue (cyanoacrylate). The advantage of soldering is that the model does not fall apart with age, but is a procedure that many modellers still avoid, probably due to fear of melting the white metal components. This is easily overcome by using a variable low heat soldering iron, operated on twelve volts from the controller's transformer. The ideal soldering iron is the Oryx, twelve-volt, five-watt model. Note; 240-volt soldering irons are not recommended for white metal, as their working temperatures are far too hot, exceeding the melting temperature of the metal used to produce the kit's components. (This is not a problem with brass and a 240-volt mains soldering iron can be used.) The low-melt solders start from around the boiling point of water upwards (100 degrees centigrade), and are available in various grades of melting points. Note: Under EU Law low melt solders have restricted use. The technique is to start with the high melt grades and work down to the low melt grades, as this allows a solder join to be made without melting a join that is nearby. (This also applies to brass kits.) A second way around this problem is to use wet cotton wool draped over the adjacent joins to keep them cool (wet cotton buds are also useful).

The soldering iron's bit will have to be tinned and cleaned regularly, and at times reshaped to suit the particular job in hand. A building board will also be found useful as the components can be pinned into position, or held square by using wooden blocks taped into position with double-sided sticky tape. For brass kits I prefer to use a 'Microflame' gas torch, as by tinning the components and fluxing, heat is applied very quickly to a localised area, which minimises heat travel. On completing assembly of all the components, thoroughly wash everything to remove all traces of flux. File and scrape off excess solder.

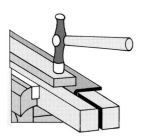

Most metal kits will require some form of light metalworking facilities. The vice should have the minimum of a 2 inch jaw width and a reasonable opening and depth. Cover the serrated jaw teeth with hardwood blocks, held in place with double sided sticky tape. Finally smooth and polish the head of the hammer to avoid bruising the metal and don't use it again for hammering in place any nails!

Use the fret table and a jeweller's piercing saw (Page 44) for cutting thin pieces of brass, supported on 2mm plywood. (Cut through both.) The fret table is difficult to find ready made, (Hobbies Store) so it is quicker to make your own from 9mm plywood and fixed to the table with a small 'G' clamp.

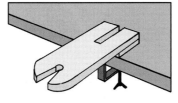

Cleaning: Before soldering or gluing, all of the kit's components will have to be cleaned in batches as packed, to remove the manufacturer's machining or release compounds. My favourite method is to use a kitchen pan cleaner, i.e. Vim (pumice powder) and an old toothbrush or wire wool and some liquid detergent. Work in an old bowl, cleaning the pieces until they shine, then rinse them in a sieve under running water, keeping the plug in the sink at all times just in case a piece escapes. (Count the pieces before and after washing.) The components are then dried using paper kitchen towel and stored in self-seal plastic bags.

Assembly of the components can now start, each piece being individually checked for fitting, and reshaped as necessary until you are satisfied. The components are then washed a second time to remove any oils deposited by the fingers; stubborn dirt is removed by scraping or sanding, so that the join area is absolutely clean prior to soldering or gluing. This is very important as white metal oxidises very quickly and dirt will affect the way solder flows when heated or the strength of the bond when glue is used.

Restoration: One of the good ways of developing modelling skills is to restore an old metal bodied engine, which by its very nature can only be improved upon. The photograph shown top right is a typical example of a model that has seen better days. The electric motor is missing, the body has been dropped and the wheels are bent out of alignment. Therefore there is not much to lose!

Start by making a decision: will the restored model be a working or a static model? If static then apart from a clean up, the existing wheels can be used. If it is to be a working model then the chassis will need to be rebuilt or a working donor found. (Salvaged from a plastic body loco.) Alternatively a brand new brass chassis could be built complete with new wheels, gearing and motor. I would advise that the first restored model (as shown above) is kept as a static model!

Painting: The first paint on bare metal is always a priming coat preferably of the two-part self-etch type. This provides a good key on the bare metal's surface, on top of which all the finished colours are applied. This first self-etch coat will have to be left for at least 24 hours to dry before you apply the first coat of colour. Having done this, the first rubbing-down can commence. Start by using 1,000 or 1,200 grade wet and dry sanding paper, gently smoothing off any bits that feel like tiny pieces of grit in the paint's surface but taking care not to go through the paint's surface. Dust off and apply the second coat, then again carefully and lightly sand down, repeating until an even, smooth coat is obtained. The thickness of each coat should be kept as thin as possible, to avoid too great a paint build-up, which would obscure detail. See Chapter 6, Painting and Weathering.

Above: Clean off the old paint with a conventional paint stripper and soak off with lots of running water and remove stubborn bits of paint with an old tooth brush. Fill dents with car-body filler and sand. Finally clean with wire wool until all traces of dirt are removed. Prime using a bare metal primer for full size car bodies.

Above: This old metal bodied GWR engine would make an ideal restoration project, because if the painting you attempted failed to look satisfactory, the paint can be stripped off and another attempt can be made; until you are satisfied with the final result. Note: Don't be surprised if it takes a number of attempts!

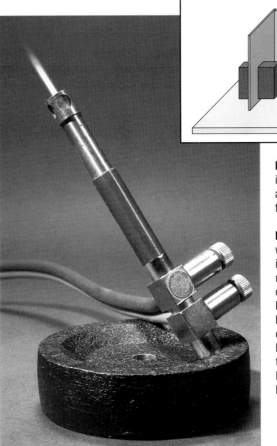

Left: The Micro Flame torch is a very useful tool for applying extremely hot heat to a small area.

Note: When soldering with a torch secure items in place with blocks of metal. (Wood burns and contaminates the join area.) Ideally purchase some fire bricks from a good DIY centre to make a soldering hearth, which will contain the heat for silver soldering. Don't try to silver solder brass shim sheet, it melts!

There are numerous preserved railways scattered around the country and each one preserving history normally associated with the area.

The above picture depicts a busy scene associated with the arrival of a train with passengers alighting prior to passengers boarding the train.

In this case the curve of the platform adding interest to the photograph. From the modeller's point of view it is impossible to retain a scale clearance between the platform and the rolling stock, therefore the clearance will governed by the rolling stock used.

PRESERVED RAILWAYS

One of the best ways to become familiar with railway procedures is to visit one of the many preserved railway lines that are scattered around the country. These are run by people who undertake this voluntary work for fun and are deeply committed enthusiasts, who have between them a great knowledge of the railway. What is nice is the fact that many are keen to share their knowledge, and will find time to explain to you the basic principles and terms used for most railway memorabilia.

The steam era was not noted for its clean environment, because all clothes quickly become soot stained, therefore even today it is advisable to wear clothes that are older and of a darker colouring when making such a visit!

To the beginner it may seem very daunting at the start, but bear in mind that there are hundreds of other people who have had exactly the same problem and have gone ahead with railway modelling, and they not know how or where to start.

When you make your visit to the preserved railway centre, check on the limitations of taking photographs, because some centres are totally unreasonable with their limitations, whilst others are so relaxed that you go back again and again. What you will need to photograph are the basic things that you expect to model, i.e. the track and the ballast, the platform, buildings and signals. The position of the start signal, its type e.g. is it a semaphore upper or lower quadrant signal or is it a coloured lights signal etc.

Model Clubs: The books and magazines available may contain a tremendous amount of information, but this on average is aimed at the reader who already has some model making experience. (Although to be fair regular articles written for the beginner are published). For the complete beginner who really does need to gain the basic knowledge, modelling clubs also play a crucial role, because they provide the chance to meet various people, who are at different stages of learning and experience. Because of their combined knowledge, they will be able to help solve many of the beginner's fundamental early problems and this should help prevent repeating many common mistakes.

The first stage in locating a club is to attend one of the exhibitions, details of which are generally well published in magazines and local newspapers. Having done this of course, one can wander around the exhibition and have a chat with the various exhibitors who are running their layouts. Knowing modellers as I do, I have found that the vast majority will be only too willing to help the newcomer to the hobby. At the same time an exhibition will provide a chance to look at the various scales, so that an assessment can be made on the size that will be required for a layout. You can also visit the manufacturers' and retailers' stands, and obtain their catalogues, etc. Finally, at the end of the day an overall gathering of information has been accomplished and hopefully some new friends have been made.

Hobbyists: Railway modelling is a hobby that interests people in all walks of life, but it is surprising just how few people will not discuss this; for fear of ridicule. Many years ago I was loading my car with prototypes of dolls, and amongst great giggles a group of young mums that I knew accused me of playing with my dollies. I then produced the engineering drawings, the prototype doll heads and the complicated mechanism required to make the eyes work. Suddenly a change in attitude became apparent; it was a fascinating job to do for a living. But I was still teased for many years afterwards!

The attitude of many people towards model making has changed and the hobby has gained a great deal of respect, probably partly due to *Star Wars* and other science fiction films which use a considerable number of models to produce the special effects. TV and films are great consumers

4ft 9in is a nominal distance because this distance varies with the curve of the track, the tighter the curve the greater the gap.

4 foot 9 inches

3ft 6in from the top of the track to the platform surface.

of mode sets, since in many cases the reality does not exist and creating the illusion that it does exist becomes a job for the model maker. This skill has gained recognition over the years had led to several full time model making courses at the Higher National and Degree level of education. Model making is also a supportive subject to many other subjects, architecture being a prime example, the model being easier and quicker to understand than a handful of drawings, or a computer animation.

My advice to the beginner is start in a small way, begin with simple kits, both for buildings and rolling stock, experiment with a less expensive kit. *(A goods van is a useful starting point as if it does not work properly; you can always remove its wheels and use it as a makeshift line side hut.)* Make a second one and try to avoid the mistakes made on the first one. If that one does not work you have two makeshift huts and can have a third go! The same applies to bits left over – since they are scrap in the first place, nothing is lost if the construction tried does not work, but you will have learned what not to do! I am yet to meet a model maker, who has not made a disaster that has ended up being thrown away. Don't be put off, skill and knowledge take time to learn and years of work are needed to produce an exhibition winner!

Professional Modelmaking: The approach to professional model making is very different to making models for a hobby. This is because the cost determines the amount of time spent. For the hobbyist the time costs nothing, so that the amount of detail shown is unrestricted. Therefore it is well worth a visit to the Model Engineering Exhibition in London because even the professionals stop to admire the workmanship.

Below: Coupling the vacuum hoses etc. before departure.

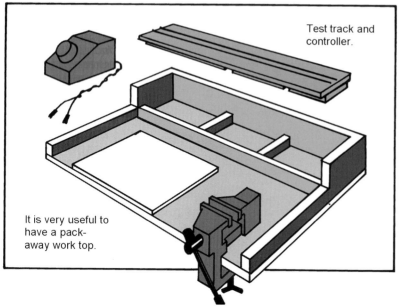

Test track and controller.

It is very useful to have a pack-away work top.

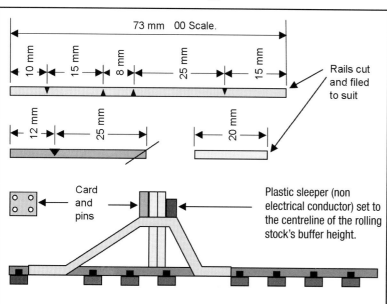

73 mm　00 Scale.

10 mm
15 mm
8 mm
25 mm
15 mm

Rails cut and filed to suit

12 mm
25 mm

20 mm

Card and pins

Plastic sleeper (non electrical conductor) set to the centreline of the rolling stock's buffer height.

Above: The buffer is constructed using spare rail. This is one of those projects you do because you want to, since it is easier to purchase them ready made. The only advantage is the fact that the buffer does not come off the end of the rail when the train hits it!

The larger scale buffers are quite nice to make, because they can be made using a metal cutting saw, a three sided file and a good soldering iron.

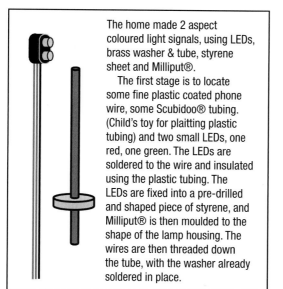

The home made 2 aspect coloured light signals, using LEDs, brass washer & tube, styrene sheet and Milliput®.

The first stage is to locate some fine plastic coated phone wire, some Scubidoo® tubing. (Child's toy for plaitting plastic tubing) and two small LEDs, one red, one green. The LEDs are soldered to the wire and insulated using the plastic tubing. The LEDs are fixed into a pre-drilled and shaped piece of styrene, and Milliput® is then moulded to the shape of the lamp housing. The wires are then threaded down the tube, with the washer already soldered in place.

BUFFER (END STOP) CONSTRUCTION

This is a nice little project and the drawing contains the sizes of each of the components. The project starts by cutting four equal lengths of rail. Mark out and notch as detailed using a Swiss 3 sided file. Use the first one as a master by cramping in a vice along-side the other rails, filing them one at a time to match the master rail. Do the same with the second shorter length of notched rail and bevel it to suit the track. Then cut four more lengths of rail and a length of wood or use a plastic sleeper (do not use metal or it will short circuit the track), and finally cut out and drill the two end plates. This supplies us with all the components needed.

Thoroughly clean all the metal rails and pin in position on a piece of wood as shown. Bend one of the four notched rails and lay it in place on top. When you are satisfied with the alignment solder together by pre-fluxing the join, then apply heat from the iron to the rail. Apply solder to the rail (not the iron), using as little solder as possible – this saves a lot of cleaning up! Keep applying heat from the iron so as to allow the solder to run properly and form a good sound join. Repeat this on the other joins and when they are cool remove the rail and turn it over, clean and re-pin in position. Now lay the second notched and bent rail in position, align carefully and solder in place. Repeat the sequence for the second side to make a pair.

Slide the longest lengths of rail back into position on the sleepers, taking care not to miss one. Do this until they touch the rail soldered to the track. Do exactly the same on the short length of rail behind the buffer. Finally fit a short length of sleeper between the bent rails, by cutting away the web on the chairs. Square the track and uprights by pinning the wooden strip into position using the plastic plates. The track and buffer can now be pinned down in place as required on the baseboard, joining additional track via insulated fishplates, and carefully wiring back to the isolator switch on the buffer side of the track. Paint the track to represent weathering and add ballast, emergency sand, stop lights, etc, for effect. Repeat procedure as required.

Other Projects: Soldering is a far more efficient way of joining metals together, but not all metals solder. For example, aluminium and other similar metals do not solder. Stainless steel will solder but needs a special solder and flux. White metal will solder, but needs a special low melt solder and soldering iron. Low melt solders start at around water's boiling temperature, and silver solder is the hottest of all the solders, at almost 'red hot' heat.

Hints and tips on soldering: Always use a medium fifty watt iron for track work and for safety's sake use a cradle and point the hot tip of the iron away from you. Clean and re-tin the iron regularly and wipe off excess solder with a damp rag. Clean metal and plenty of heat is the secret of successful soldering.

Wood or plastic, do not use metal rail or it will short circuit the track.

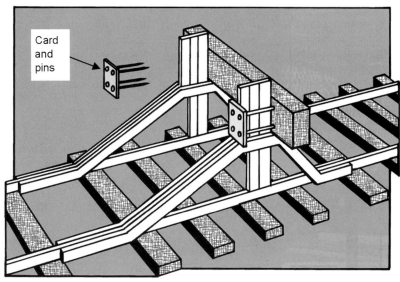

Card and pins

Above: The finished buffer ready to be installed on the layout. The middle 4 sleepers will need the chairs cut away, by carefully using a sharp knife so as to fit onto the track, because the new rails soldered to the track prevent the chairs from sliding down the rails.

Above: Use a large hot soldering iron that has a clean tip, and apply the heat to the rail, and apply the solder to the rail, not the iron because it will burn the flux off on the iron and not clean the surface to be soldered. Apply the heat until the solder runs.

Above: This is a dirty soldering iron tip which will need to be cleaned. Do not dip the tip into the flux, because it erodes the plating of the tip and causes the above problem.

Right: When the tip is cleaned by wiping on a damp rag or sponge, wait a few seconds for the tip to regain its heat, and then tin with solder, and wipe the excess off with a damp rag.

Left: The clean tip should look bright and shiny. This bright tip should be maintained clean throughout all soldering operations so as to produce a swift heat transfer from the iron to the component being soldered. The work should also be clean and free of grease and dirt, Baker's Fluid is extremely corrosive, therefore wash off thoroughly.

Warning *Baker's Fluid is poisonous and should be kept out of the reach of children. It is also corrosive, so avoid breathing the contaminated steam when soldering, and keep away from tools and skin. If they get splashed, wash off with lots of soap and water and dry thoroughly. If your eyes get splashed, seek medical attention immediately.*

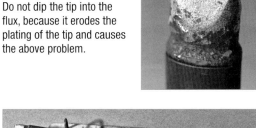

Above: When not in use the iron should be placed in a cradle, to prevent the iron rolling around on the work bench which could result in serious burns.

Right: If all else fails you can always purchase a plastic end stop (buffer) and install this at the end of the line, ballast the track, paint and weather to suit and try not to crash into it with any rolling stock!

10. ADVANCED LAYOUT MODELLING

The multilevel layout is designated as having 'North' at the town end of the layout. (See pages 200 & 201.)

Therefore in the view shown right, we are looking 'South' and down the hill to the bridge. The change in road level from the town (+90ft) to under the bridge (+30ft) is 60 feet.

USING SCALE MEASUREMENTS

I can almost feel the metric thinkers amongst you, saying to yourselves: What's all this measurement in feet – we use metric now, all that feet and inch stuff was made redundant years ago.

Well the bad news is that British Model Railways are measured as 2mm, (actual 2.0625mm) to the foot, and 4 mm to the foot etc.

This is despite the introduction of metric measurement in the U.K. So I have used the old Imperial measurement of feet and inches, because it can be used to describe heights on any scale of layout, and of course being of the older generation I can relate to this type of measurement.

INTRODUCTION

Since 1983, when the first draft pages of this book were written, the traction power of model locos has greatly improved. This is because the modern electric motors are far more powerful. In the early years most very small 'N gauge' electric motors were of a 3-pole design, and then they changed to 5 pole. (In the meantime, 00 & HO models have reaped the benefits of 7 & 9 pole electric motors, fitted with flywheels!)

The modern model train, fitted with a powerful electric motor can pull a considerable number of carriages: But in the end the governing factor is wheel slip. This is the grip between the wheel and the rail, and if this is exceeded the 'engine' will remain static, with its drive wheels going around, i.e. when the incline of the track is too steep, for the engine to pull 100 wagons up the slope!

On a flat layout most 'engines' will pull between 60 and 100 goods wagons, but start to climb up a gradient and this number starts to drop, the steeper the hill, the fewer the wagons. In practical terms this means that if we are going to hide the fiddle yard, or store rolling stock underneath the layout's main track level, we have to be careful not to have a very steep ramp. For example the type that is used in multi storey car parks, to get us from one level to the next.

The New Multi Level Layout : By using this book as a reference by referring to the earlier chapters, we can compare the new multi level layout with the simple oval layout: shown on page 46. The basic shape of the old layout has remained, only this time instead of looping the track back on itself at the same level; it goes underneath and down to a lower level. The advantage of this is; that we now have twice the amount of track, without the layout becoming twice the size. This is because now we have a double layered layout.

Note: The design of the new layout, can be simplified by joining the two ends of track that go down the ramps together. This will then form an oval shaped track, that can be built on one level. The disadvantage of doing this is that you will considerably restrict the running potential of the layout, and will be similar to the old oval layout.

Research: With the benefit of hindsight, I had a look at what the critics had to say when this book was first published, for constructive comments. From these remarks two statements are very true. (1.) No matter what type of layout you decide to make, you will still need to construct a baseboard. (2.) The layout should have a good working potential, and easily operated.

I also researched to find out what the average modeller wanted from a layout and needed to know. So I went to club meetings, exhibitions, etc. and prepared a list of priorities. (1) To show how to build a small compact layout on a single baseboard that dismantles for servicing. (2) For convenient transportation to exhibitions, the size of the layout must be small enough to fit into the back of the average estate car. (3) That at least 2 people can operate the layout simultaneously. (4) That each person can control at least 2 trains. (5) The layout must have a continuous loop – for hands free operation! (6) Finally, some parts of the layout should be automatically controlled!

With these 6 requirements in mind, a lot of thought went into the design of the new layout. The existing small oval layout shown in the book, has limited working potential, but all the methods of construction were shown, and from the drawings it would be easy to change the design so that it became a multi level layout.

The Oval Layouts: Comparisons: The new oval design, as described in this chapter, will show you how to make a multi layered layout that has far more running possibilities than the basic oval layout shown on page 46.

Note: At times it probably will help to re-read the baseboard construction methods, starting with chapter 3: Constructing the layout, (page 42) and compare the methods shown.

I now refer you to page 46: this shows the plan of the oval layout, whilst the illustrations on page 47 show the basic levels. Have a look at these and you will find that the ground contour levels are higher (+75ft) and lower (+25ft) than the track's unchanging level of +50ft.

Unfortunately slopes on the track do cause problems, i.e. because if you construct a siding or station, that is built on a slope, the carriages, wagons, etc., will always need to have the 'engine' coupled in place to prevent them rolling down hill, and causing chaos to the lowest part of the layout.

This problem accrues, with baseboard 5, (Lower plan; with the fields and station; page 55.) The track starts on the left at +50ft, rises in the middle to +55ft as it goes over the road, and then drops down to +50ft on the right hand side. This is only an 11 mm rise, but the carriages will roll down hill on their own.

If you look at all of the other bases, the track level remains at +50ft, and the ground rises or falls below the track's height.

I now refer you to page 48 plan of base 01: The level of the ground of this completely flat base is +50ft and is typical of many beginners' layout. The first stages of making the layout look more interesting are plans 02 & 03 and this is because the ground's contour levels rise above the track level to +75ft. This will allow us to build a road bridge across the tracks, rather than at the same level as the track. (As per the level crossing, base 01.)

It is much the same story for plans 4, 5, 6 & 7; with each base becoming more difficult to make; because of the huge variation in the contour levels above (the top of cliff is +230ft, base 7) and below the track level. (The water level is at +20 ft at its lowest point, on base 6.)

Whilst the multi-level base looks complex to make, a better understanding will be achieved by making a cardboard model first, at say 3 inches to the foot. (¼ inch equals 1 inch therefore quarter full size) and solving any construction difficulties encountered.

Do you know that we still build houses with 4 brick courses to the foot; (13 to the metre.) Our brick sizes have not changed; only the method of measurement has. (See Surveying pages; 102, 103.)

NOTE: Some readers may find it difficult to obtain rulers at 1:76, (00.) 1:87, (HO.) and at 1:160 (N.) scale: But it is very easy to make your own 2, 3, or 4 mm to the foot scale rules. (See page 14/15 on scale sizes.)

Having provided you with a good reason to copy the scale rules in the front part of this book, we can now use them to measure the heights on this more complex layout!

The layouts shown in the book use ground levels that reflect material thicknesses, i.e. 12mm MDF equals 6ft at 2mm to the foot (N) and 12mm at 4mm to the foot would measure 3ft (00). 50mm soft wood batten measures 25ft at 'N' scale and 12.5ft at '00' scale, etc.

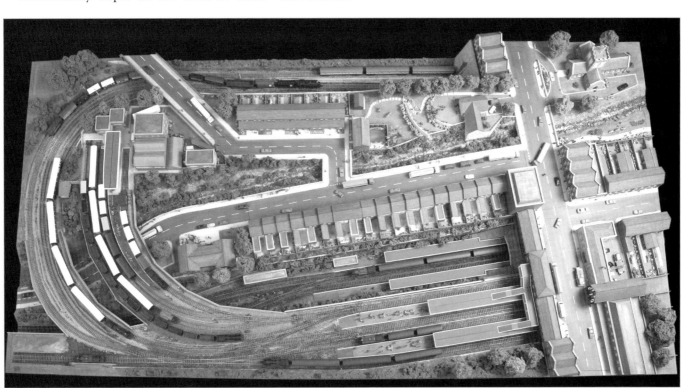

Right: The front view (West) of the layout showing the access holes to the lower level. The removable hatches on the top allow access to central lower track areas.

Below: The same layout during its construction. The materials used are a mixture of MDF, softwood batten and car body filler. The paving is cardboard and the paint used is standard household matt emulsion. To help reduce noise the track is laid on cork, which is painted ballast colour before laying the track.

Opposite: The top photo shows the platforms and the signals at the end of the platform. The track within the station and in the sidings is built on a flat area, so as to prevent rolling stock without an engine rolling down hill! The slope starts on the track at the bridge that goes over the road and then drops below the road bridge before continuing into the tunnel. The track in the tunnel continues to descend until it reaches the storage level. The height from the upper to the lower level is 60 scale feet. The gradient from the upper level to the lower level is 4% and is the maximum recommended slope for model engines to pull a series of coaches.

The maximum number of coaches or wagons that an engine can pull is governed by wheel friction. I.e. some rolling stock has less friction than others, and will roll down the slope of the track on their own; others with high friction will not. I recommend that you replace the wheels on high friction stock.

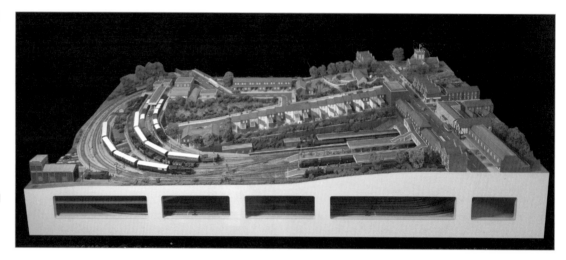

GRADIENTS

The overall size of the new 'N Scale' layout has also changed; from 4ft x 3ft (1220mm x 910mm) to 5ft 9in x 3ft (1750mm x 910mm) an increase in length of 1ft 9in, (531mm) so as to allow for the rise and fall of the track's level. The gradient on the track should always be kept to the minimum. It is recommended not to exceed a 4% rise. This is a rise of 4in, for every 100in of track length (4mm in 100mm = 4% gradient). The new layout has a length of 112.5in; (2850mm) for our sloping track, and this calculates out to be the maximum difference of 4.5in (114mm) at 4%, between the two levels.

In real life, the track is kept as flat as possible by following the ground's contours; so as to stay within the 2% (2mm in 100mm) main line gradient. But in Britain the Hopton incline is almost 7% (1 in 14) on the Cromford and High Peak line. Once the gradient exceeds 7% it becomes normal to use a central third rail, fitted with a rack, and the engine is fitted with a corresponding pinion (gear wheel).

The equivalent layout built at 00/HO would measure 11ft 6in x 6ft, and would provide 216in of sloping track. This then calculates out as 9in (228mm) between the two levels. I now refer you to page 35; and by using selective compression, the multi levelled layout can be built 00/HO scale to have a baseboard size of 4ft 6in x 9ft and would provide 6in (150mm.) gap between the two levels.

The gap between the two baseboards' levels is critical: too narrow and you cannot get your arm inside, so as to reach things; too wide and the gradient between the baseboards becomes unnecessarily steep, so it is a compromise. Therefore to solve the majority of the access problems, we can use a series of removable hatches on the model.

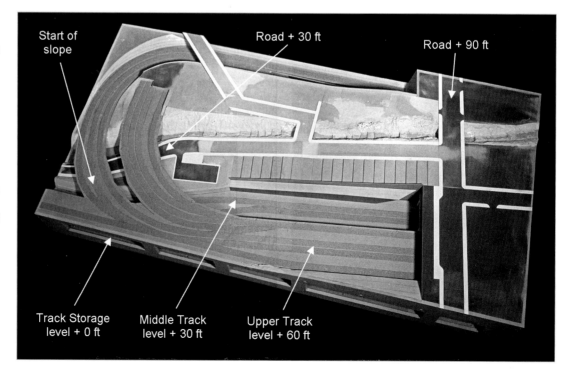

Start of slope

Road + 30 ft

Road + 90 ft

Track Storage level + 0 ft

Middle Track level + 30 ft

Upper Track level + 60 ft

This will then allow us easy access to reach into the layout to retrieve de-railed rolling stock etc., at the lower levels. But to make life easier, it is also useful to have access from all the 4 sides, and these holes need to be large enough, so you can see what you are doing, whilst reaching for the bits!

Purchase Precut Materials: The construction starts with cutting out two pieces of 6mm ply or MDF, the same size. The easiest way is to have them cut for you, at the same time as you purchase the timber. Have these cut at 2ft 11in x 5ft 8in (890mm x 730mm) which will allow for the 4 sides, each measuring 12mm thick, to be added to the outside of each edge. The measurements of the outside 12mm thick MDF pieces are slightly different; you need two at 5ft 9in x 7in wide (914mm x 180mm) and two at 2ft 11in x 7in wide (730mm x 180mm). You will also need about 10ft of 1-inch-square (25mm square) and 20ft of 2in x 1in (50 x 25mm) smooth-finish softwood batten, and at least 100 of 1in (25mm) mild steel cadmium-plated no.8 counter sunk wood screws, of the cross-head type; plus a 500ml bottle of PVA woodworker's glue!

The off cuts can be cut into strips of 4.5in (114mm) wide, and will be used to form the honey comb type of construction used on the base.

Baseboard Construction: The baseboard's construction starts by assembling the lower track level, by using one of the 890 x 730 mm x 6 mm thick boards and edging it with the 2" x 1" smooth finish batten. (Note: Be careful fixing the edging batten to the lower level. to make sure the edges are in line, and are square. Trim the battened edges with a hand plane if necessary. Do not cross batten at this stage.) The lower baseboard then forms a good drawing board for marking out at full model size the track, the roads, and the buildings positions etc., on a sheet of tracing paper. Work from the upper levels, starting with the position of the points, outside of the station.

The best way is to assemble all of the points and track for this area. Start by positioning the toe of the long point 20in (510mm) from the end edge of the board, and inset it by 1in (25mm) measuring to the nearest rail, from the edge of the board. (Note: Ignore the 12mm edge thickness, this is added later when the outside edge is fixed in place.) The long point, you will find, sets the angle of the straight length of track that goes into the station. From this key position, carefully work outwards in all directions, adding short pieces of track as necessary, so as to ascertain the remaining point positions.

The choice of insulated frog points produced by Peco® will make the wiring of this layout simpler. This is because live frog points back feed (see page 155) and therefore the track will need to be broken into a large number of electrically insulated sections; each wired to a separate switch.

Above: This is a view of the storage loop level and shows the wiring to the point motors that operate the upper track level. Note how the formers have been angled to provide maximum access for hands!

Far right: This shows the basic honeycomb formers (walls) and the track levels. (The edges of the base are not shown.) The first stage is to mark out the position of the upper track and to cut the walls to height. Do not cut out the lower level 'holes' at this stage, until the top level is finished, otherwise you can find yourself with a lot of 'loose bits'. The idea is to retain as much as you can of each former in one piece! You will probably find that there will be a slight difference between the illustration shown and your arrangement of the formers. Don't worry, as long as it works.

Having drawn out all of the track work and marked in the positions of the stations; for the upper level, begin to mark out the position of the middle level of track, on a separate sheet of tracing paper using your first drawing as a guide. (Note 1: At one place you will find that to obtain clearance for the train to pass under the point, (Turnout) the 'Point Motor' will need to be moved and operated via a push rod fitted in a tube, and another will need to be countersunk.

Having finished drawing out both the upper level and the middle level, now draw the lower level on tracing paper, using the other levels as a guide. When all the drawings are finished, remove them and place the lowest level drawing at the bottom; so that they read– lowest level, middle level and upper track level and finally the top road level.

Study these drawings for mistakes, and when satisfied remove the middle level and upper level and 'only' mark out on the appropriate pieces of MDF that will form the honey comb. To mark out the lower 'holes for the track', place the upper level drawing on top of the lower level and mark out the upper track levels. Finally mark out the middle track level. The formers (walls) should now begin to look like those shown in the illustration bottom right. Place in their correct places on the previously battened lower level baseboard.

Having finished battening all four edges of the lower base, cover the lower base and the lower level drawing with polythene sheet and wrap around the edges and secure in place from the inside. (The reason for doing this is that we will be building a lot of layers on top and we do not want to stick the top layers to the bottom layer.) Now fix the sides (not cut to height as yet) temporarily in place using

wood screws and start the assembly of the basic honeycomb. (see page 194) Having cut out the cross members, and having temporarily secured them in place, cut the spacers to length that fit between. Fix all the components in place using masking tape, or screws – just for the time being! Because the construction of the honeycomb is a something similar to a jigsaw, you are constantly trying to get bits to fit, so there is a lot of removal and putting things back involved.

Having assembled the basic honeycomb, marked out everything and satisfied yourself, cut out and lay the upper track level in place. Mark its position on the formers and number the formers! Then only mark out the upper level track height, do not cut anything until everything is marked out and you are satisfied that no mistakes have been made.

By referring to the drawing underneath the polythene sheet mark out the lower level clearance heights, and transfer the information to the honey comb cross members. When you are satisfied that every thing is correct- cut out only the top track level part of the formers to suit and replace in position. Now replace the upper track level in position, and adjust the honeycomb cut outs as necessary to make it fit. Don't glue anything together yet, no matter how many times the formers fall over! Repeat with the middle level, by cutting out the track and the bases for hatches 3 & 6 which sit at the same level. (+30ft) Now you can see how the upper level works it is time to cut out the lower level openings, so remove the formers one at a time and cut out the lower openings. Replace each piece as they are cut, and renumber if necessary. The numbering of the formers is very necessary to avoid the confusion associated with all the pieces looking similar.

Left: This view shows the track that can be seen and the track that descends to the lower storage level which is hidden from view by hatches 4 & 6, and a wall (see pages 61, 124 and 127).

Don't glue anything together yet, until the storage level and the basic hatches are made. The next stage is preparing the hatches, which might mean modifying the formers to suit!

Storage Level Construction: It is now time to dismantle the honeycomb, start by removing the edges and build the lower level ramp; which explains why it is important to number all the formers.

Having marked out the lower level; cut out the curve that forms the ramp from a separate piece of MDF, using a jig saw fitted with the correct blade. Take your time to get a good clean cut that runs along the line. Then carefully cut the lower baseboard, in the same arc as the ramp to form a tongue, about 300mm long. Trim the end square and insert a piece of scrap MDF cut to the same radius, underneath the tongue and fix in place using glue and small wood screws. Then fix the ramp to the scrap piece making sure that the joint is level and the curve is inline and not kinked. The blocks that form the ramp supports are now inserted under the ramp and a piece of straight material is joined onto the curve using screws. Don't glue this bit yet! Repeat with the second ramp, then reassemble the honeycomb (don't glue anything yet!) and fit the upper track level. Now the lower ramps can be trimmed to length to suit the upper track level.

Reassemble: The lower level should now be built to the stage shown in the photograph (top left page 194) minus the track, but with the walls around the ramp. Do not make these walls too high, or they will hinder retrieving derailed rolling stock. Having achieved this cover with polythene sheet; cutting it away around the ramps and tape the sheet down with masking tape as required. Fit the outside edges in place and assemble the honeycomb, adjust as necessary to fit and provide clearance for the rolling stock along the ramp area. Fit the upper track level in place, adjust as required

and then insert the middle track level. Insert the public house baseboard, and the terraced houses' base into position, which will lock the lower level base in place. Place the two upper level hatches in position: Now you are ready to start the construction of the last two hatches.

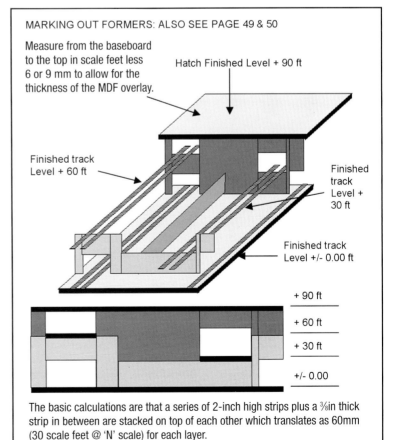

MARKING OUT FORMERS: ALSO SEE PAGE 49 & 50

Measure from the baseboard to the top in scale feet less 6 or 9 mm to allow for the thickness of the MDF overlay.

Hatch Finished Level + 90 ft

Finished track Level + 60 ft

Finished track Level + 30 ft

Finished track Level +/- 0.00 ft

+ 90 ft
+ 60 ft
+ 30 ft
+/- 0.00

The basic calculations are that a series of 2-inch high strips plus a ⅜in thick strip in between are stacked on top of each other which translates as 60mm (30 scale feet @ 'N' scale) for each layer.

Photo 1: This shows the basic lower level baseboard that has been constructed as per the instructions found on page 49, baseboard 01, but without the cross battens. (Don't fit these until the point motors are fitted in place.) The track is marked out (all levels) and the ramps constructed by cutting through the board and bending to the desired angle for a short distance. This is followed by a separate piece of board cut to the required shape, suitably supported so as to finish the ramp. At the end of the ramp construct a firm reinforced support level for both this ramp and the ramp fitted to the upper level. Don't fit the cork or track yet!

The next stage is to build the honeycomb that fits over the lower level, using corner blocks and a screw together method. Do not glue at this stage because parts of the honeycomb will be assembled, dismantled cut and altered, and reassembled several times before you get this right!

Start by cutting the width uprights first, (four all at the same height +61ft as the upper track level) and one at +90ft, slightly longer (angled).

Mark out the track positions and clearances required for the lower tracks. (As per page 49 and illustration page 191.)

Repeat as necessary until all are marked out. When satisfied, cut them out using a power operated jig saw (Page 44) or a hand operated fret saw fitted with a wood cutting blade, as per health and safety requirements.

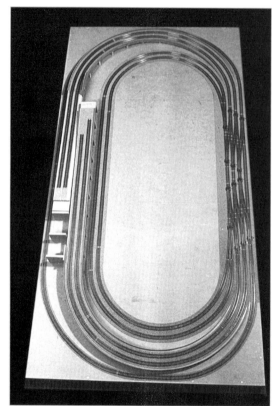

Photo 1: The lower level storage loop complete with half ramp to upper level.

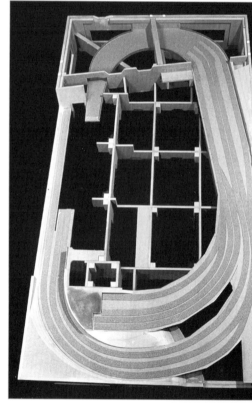

Photo 2: The upper level complete with half ramp to lower level.

PROGRESS

The photograph 4 shows how the upper part of the baseboard should look, after a lot more work and it is all glued together. The baseboard has all the hatches in place and the cork underlay fixed in place ready for the track. Note; by strategically placing the paving along the joins, most of the gaps between the hatches are covered. The paving is made from thick cardboard, cut to shape and fixed in place with PVA woodworker's glue.

The photograph 5 shows the underside of the honeycomb, note how the stream is attached to the underside of the upper track level. Also note the cut outs in the honeycomb for the cables.

The photograph 3, shows how the two bases should look when placed on top of each other and with the sides trimmed to height. The bottom corner has been filled in and so has the embankment adjacent to the station. Also note how other little pieces of reinforcement have been added to support the hatches.

The most useful tool that I used for shaping the contours of the hatches is the Powerfile® and the most useful filler is the Easysand® make of car body filler; which is in two parts and when mixed sets in a matter of minutes. The secret of using car body filler is to mix small quantities at a time, and to constantly clean the mixing board and spatula, as the filler starts to harden. By wearing a pair of rubber gloves, the filler as it hardens can be rubbed between the palms of the hands, causing the filler

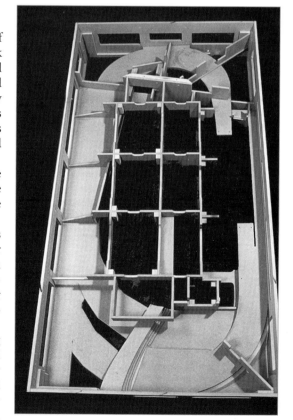

Photo 5: The underside of the upper level showing the honeycomb construction that holds the levels in place. Note the use of blocks to strengthen the joins, which are glued and screwed in place.

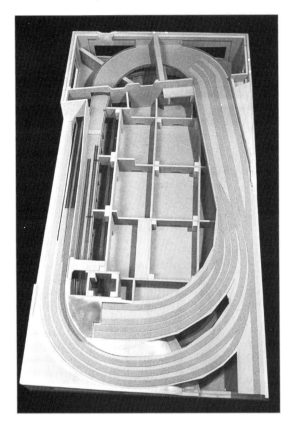

Photo 3: The upper level fitted onto the lower level, with the ramps now joined.

Photo 4: The upper, the middle, the lower levels and all the hatches.

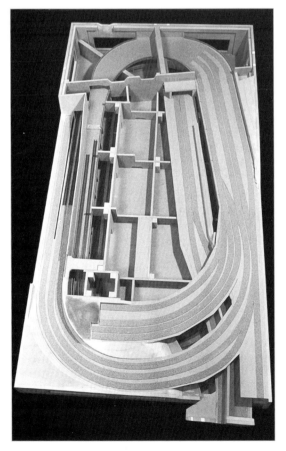

Photo 6: The middle level slides out from under the railway bridge, after the removal of all the hatches.

to crumble; this makes small rocks, that can be sanded. The best of these 'rocks' we will use later on to fill the bottom of the stream that is a feature of the hilly landscape.

The Track Levels: The storage track level's datum is +/- 0.00 ft, therefore we can use this to calculate all the other levels. For example the middle track finished level is +32ft (64mm at 'N' scale or 128mm at '00' scale) whilst the upper station track level is 61ft and the road at the highest point is 90 ft above the storage tracks' level.

The middle level (+32ft) is removable and is trapped in place by the other hatches. The reason for having the middle level removable is for servicing, because if anything goes wrong this level will need to be removed to get at the lower track etc. Therefore cut out the board that forms the base for the middle level and hatches 3 & 6 at the same time and place into position on top of the honeycomb, check that everything fits and adjust the honeycomb to suit. Now I think you can see why all these components that make up the honeycomb structure are not glued together at this stage; because of all the alterations needed to make other things fit. The hatches are no exception and you will find that you will make further alterations to the honeycomb to make everything fit!

Note: The honeycomb is built with a series of arches; these are for the cable runs associated with all the different power supplies necessary to operate the layout.

Photo 2: Shows the honeycomb and upper track level as viewed from the top. Whilst this looks complex it is in fact a series of strips of wood cut to predetermined heights, with holes in and which support other pieces of wood, that form the hatches and track etc.

The edges should be screwed into place from the outside, to enable easy removal during construction, and only finally trimmed to shape after everything, including the hatches are made. The very last stage is to cut the access holes in the sides.

Photo 3: Shows the upper level fitted onto the lower level, whilst making sure that the ramps align with each other with the minimum of gap.

Photo 4: Shows the hatches in place and the cardboard paving. It is at this stage that the cork underlay for the track can be laid, followed by laying the track, complete with point motors. Also at this stage the wiring should be installed because holes for wiring will need to be drilled and cables run on both the top and the underside of track levels etc.

Photo 5: Shows a view of the underside of the honeycomb. Note how little remains of the cross members and other supports, and that arches have been cut to allow for cable runs on the lower level.

Photo 6: Shows the middle level partially removed, which does not have any cables fitted underneath its baseboard (track level) because these would prevent the base from being removed for servicing.

Right: This shows the shape of the middle level base, that is partly withdrawn from the main baseboard. To remove the middle level base all hatches are removed to allow access for 'fingers' and to be able to manipulate the base under the bridge.

The clearance under the bridge fixes the maximum height of the components on the base, and therefore the staircase from the platform is removable as a separate item.

Below: Note the arrangement of the surface mounted point motors and wiring because the underside of the base must be kept flat.

Bottom: The base being refitted into position after the station signs, people etc, have been added.

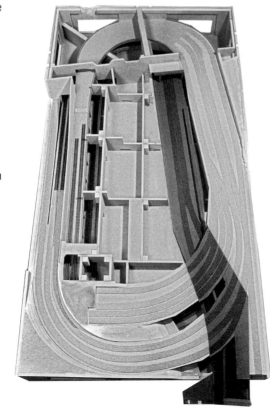

THE MIDDLE LEVEL TRACK

This is best described as a mini layout, because it is totally self-contained on its own baseboard. The track work is very simple and contains 3 sets of points and 5 short lengths of straight track, with each end of the straight fitted with a diode. This diode is inserted so that it bridges a cut made in the track, to control the stopping of the train at a predetermined position. This is a key part of the automatic running of the lower level.

To make the track look as if it is electrified, it has a third rail, which has been super glued in place. The points are operated via push rods that run through a short piece of tubing, because the point motors need to be surface mounted. The same applies to the wiring, because the underside of the base needs to be completely flat, so that it can be removed at any time for servicing. (See bottom photograph.)

The ballast and landscape texture is used to cover the wiring and tubing, so groove the base as necessary to countersink some of the wiring. (See middle photograph.) The platform, canopy and walls are also attached to the base, but not the staircase or bridge– these are kept separate and loosely drop into position. Make this base and hatch 3 (Terraced Houses) and hatch 6 (Pub) so that they are removable; before finally gluing the honeycomb together! *(Temporarily fix the honeycomb together using screws and wooden blocks, so that it can be easily dismantled and altered.)*

Hatches: The layout has six individual hatches that are described in the order of construction. The first hatch has the Station and the Tudor building, plus other shops etc., constructed from a flat board that has been cut to shape. The second hatch has the church, a stream and a bridge, and therefore the flat board will need to be cut away to accommodate the lower water level. The third hatch is the one with the houses going down hill. The datum level

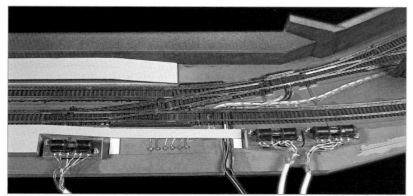

for this hatch is the underside of the middle track level baseboard support; from which it is built back up to street level.

This hatch has to be completely removable, so that it is possible to remove the middle level station and track in one piece for servicing. Hatch four: has the bungalow and sloping garden. This hatch also has the stream that joins hatch two at one end and hatch five at the other end. Hatch five contains the goods yard's industrial buildings, complete with road bridge, housing, etc,. Hatch six: this has the pub and car park, that goes under the railway bridge and is built up from a series of layers – again from the same level as hatch three. This hatch also has to be removable, because it locks the middle level station baseboard in place. The construction for hatches 1, 2, 3, 4, 5 & 6 are similar; whilst the middle track level is like a mini layout on its own baseboard.

Hatches Construction: The hatches are constructed using MDF, cut to shape. The thickness of 9mm, pre-sets the contour levels at 4.5ft, (at N scale) so that the first drop in level for the stream's surface on hatch two automatically becomes 4.5ft lower than the existing street level – when we place a second piece of MDF underneath. If we cut an area of the –4.5ft level of the stream away, and insert a third board underneath. we can further reduce the stream's surface level down to –9ft from the street level at this point.

The method described is called bread and butter construction, and is used for construction of model boat hulls etc. The principle is to cut the segments to shape, glue the bits together and then to smooth to shape, both inside and out. The advantage is that most of the unwanted material has been previously cut away, so that it makes the job easier. On hatch five, we take full advantage of this method, to form the terraces.

Hatch One: This is the easiest hatch to make and requires a single piece of 9mm MDF cut to shape, fitted with the buildings. (Photograph top right.) The methods used for constructing the buildings that are made from Perspex are shown on page 108, and the methods used for making and casting the stone textured walls is shown on pages 117 & 118.

Hatch Two: This is similar to hatch 1; and again uses 9mm thick MDF but because it has a stream it will require the base to be cut away to lower the water level. Cut along the outline of the stream using a jig saw, and shape the embankment with a 'Powerfile' (dade by Black & Decker) then insert a new piece of 9mm MDF under the base. Cut away just before the bridge; trim to shape and fix in place with PVA glue. Cut a second piece of MDF and insert to produce the lower level of water under the bridge. When the glue is dry carve to shape with the 'Powerfile' including underneath. To bring the scene to life landscape as per chapter 4 by adding small bushes people and cars.

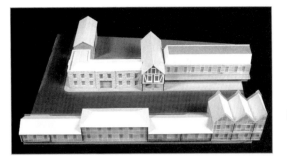

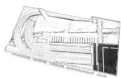

Station Hatch 1

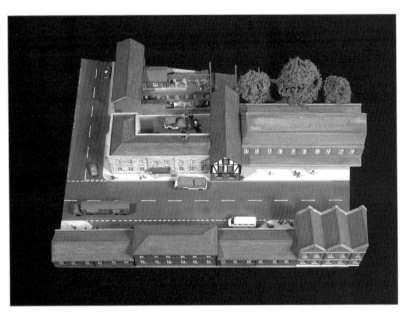

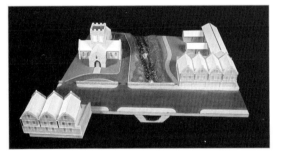

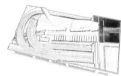

Church Hatch 2

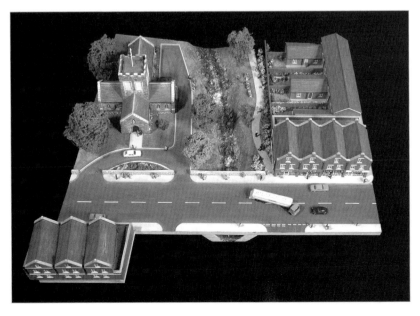

Terraced Houses Hatch 3

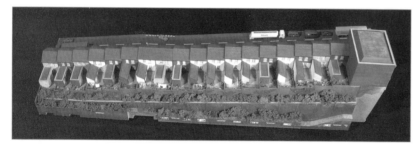

The Retirement Home Hatch 4

Hatch Three: Terraced Houses: The base for this should have been previously prepared because it is used to lock the middle level track in place. If not; place the middle track level in position and mark out the size of base for hatch 3 (Terraced Houses) and also cut and fit the pub base for hatch 6. (Note: mark this out to the centre of the paving on the stream side for both these hatches, so that the paving can be used to cover the join.) Mark both these bases out on 9mm thick MDF, and cut out to shape. Mark and cut out three profiles that follow the ground's contour levels; these start at the top of the hill, (finished levels +90ft) where the road joins in the middle (+49ft) and the bottom of the hill (+42ft). (Lower track level datum +/-0.0ft.) Deduct 18mm to allow for the thickness of the road, and for the board previously cut out. Mark and cut out the road, making it half the width of the paving wider on the stream side, and the full width of the paving on the housing side. Fix the profiles in place and insert scrap material as necessary, to form the ends.

Note: It is very important to keep all the profiles upright or the hatches will be difficult to remove. Fix the road in place. Cut from 6 mm MDF, the strips that form the ground for the houses and fix in place. Mark and cut out and then temporarily fix in place the wall and the embankment; using double sided tape. Place in position on the baseboard's framework.

Hatch Four: The Retirement Home: Start the construction of hatch four, after finishing the levels of hatch 3; because we will use the road's contour line to form the hatch's profile. (See the lower two photographs left.) Start by marking out a plan on a sheet of paper and by using carbon paper; transfer the information onto a series of 9 mm pieces of MDF. Build this up to thickness using the bread and butter method of construction, to form a series of laminations, each slightly different in size. Cut and trim as necessary so that it will fit into position.

Place this in position on its support on the main framework and cut out the contours above this level, cutting away the stream and to provide overhead clearance for the trains on the concealed track as necessary. Mark and cut out the bits that fit underneath. When satisfied, carefully glue the pieces together, using PVA; starting with the lower components.

Note: make sure that you retain the straight edge, that aligns with hatch 3 and cover the edge of hatch 3 with masking tape to prevent hatch 3 & 4 being glued together.

When the glue has dried and everything is firmly joined together, carefully carve to shape using a 'Power File' (made by Black & Decker) fitted with a very coarse grit. The basic hatch is now ready to model the walls of the stream with car body filler, (Note: Use Easysand® and not the type that sets rock hard. See chapter 4 on Rocks and Cliffs page 64.) The buildings and walls etc, are added later.

Hatch Five: Goods Depot: The construction of this base (photograph top right.) is similar to hatch 4, except that the bridge that goes over the track is a separate piece added on top; to provide extra clearance for the trains. The bridge over the stream is part of the main hatch. The contours of the stream are built below this level using the lamination method, and carved to shape using the 'Powerfile'.

The embankment of this hatch continues under the bridge, as a separate piece and is attached to the main base. (See photo page 194, bottom right, showing the underside of the base, which also shows the laminations of the embankment.) It is probably easier to build the hatches 4 & 5 and the embankment that goes under the stream together, so that they align height wise.

Hatch Six: Public House: The base for this hatch (photographs bottom right) should already be made, so all it will need is an extra thickness of 9mm MDF fitted under the bridge to form a mound to give some contours to the base and provide extra support for the pieces of wooden dowel that form part of the bridg's structure. These dowels should be slightly shorter than the bridge height to provide clearance during removal of the hatch from under the bridge.

The Honeycomb Glue And Fix: Having built the hatches, and satisfied that they all fit, carefully mark out the sides, the access holes etc, and remove each side one at a time. Cut each side to shape and fix back in place, repeat on the other three sides. Carefully remove each hatch as required and glue the honeycomb together, one piece at a time! Finish gluing the honeycomb and strengthen joins with scrap softwood batten as necessary. Part the top base from the lower base and flood all joins with glue.

Buildings: The methods used for construction are covered within Chapter 5, only unlike the other bases shown in the book, all the buildings on this layout are scratch built.

Landscaping: The technique I used for the stream and the embankment was the crumpled kitchen foil and car body filler method. I worked with small areas at a time and overlapped each join. Note: You will find that as the filler sets, it reaches a point when the tin foil can be removed, but if you leave it too late it is permanently fixed in position. Don't worry if this happens, just paint over the tin foil.

The next stage is to prepare a runny Polyfilla® mixture of ground coloured emulsion paint, and PVA. This is spread with a paint brush down the centre of the stream. Whilst usable add small stones etc. to form rocks and boulders etc, stipple the surface with a paint brush to make it look like running water, wet as necessary to smooth out: Note: Make sure that you obtain the finish you want because adding PVA to Polyfilla® makes it set like concrete. Therefore it is impossible to sand once it has set!

Goods Depot Hatch 5

Public House Hatch 6

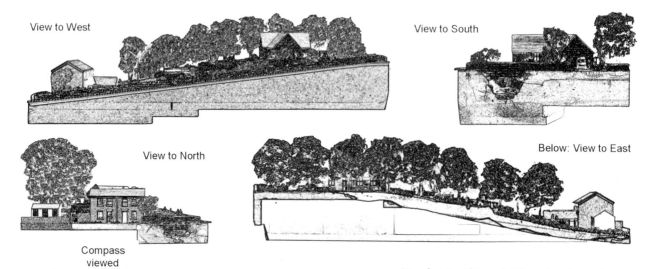

View to West

View to South

View to North

Below: View to East

Compass
viewed
underneath

W

N ← → S

E

Use the methods shown and alter the design to suit your own design of layout. On a lightweight base which remains in one piece (no removable sections) 6mm plywood and battens can be used to make the support for the polystyrene. In this case the hatches will get a fair amount of handling during their working life therefore they need to be made from a robust material. The paint used is standard household matt emulsion.

Hatch 4 & 5 (Bases): These hatches 4 & 5 are good examples of how the bread and butter system of construction can be used to produce bases with various levels. The fact that these are small bases (hatches) is unimportant, because what is important is the method used. Chapter 4, pages 67, 68 and 70 show in detail the method used for the 'bread and butter' construction, using expanded styrene, pulp board etc. On this page we show it in practical use, whereby the outline of the base is first cut out and additional layers are added as necessary. The layers are added on a trial-and-error basis, whereby if it looks good it stays there, if not it gets altered. (Note: This is where double sided sticky tape becomes very useful – for temporarily fixing the layers together.) This is on the grounds we know what we want to achieve, but we are not working from detailed drawings, and we don't know what the outcome of a decision we make will have on the next problem, and if it was a bad decision it will need to come to pieces. For example I have chosen these two bases (hatches) because they join together.

Hatches in place over the track to hide the track to the lower level, which is also hidden from view by an easily removable wall.

View to South

View to East

Below: View to West

View to North

W
N — S
E

Compass
viewed
underneath

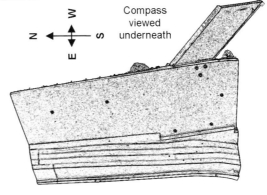

Choice of Material: Because I have a good well-equipped workshop, I choose materials that suit me. Other people are not so fortunate and therefore their choice of material will reflect on what they can use. The material I chose for these bases is MDF, which needs to be cut with an electrically powered saw (jig saw). The contours can be carved with a chisel, but an electrically powered chisel and power file makes life easier. If pulp board or expanded polystyrene is used it can be cut with a knife, but it is extremely fragile.

The next material is modelling foam, which is similar to expanded polystyrene, but far denser and therefore stronger. This can be cut with a sharp knife and pad saw (hacksaw blade with a handle) and fixed together with a special contact adhesive. (PVA woodworker's glue is air drying and will not harden trapped between plastic sheets.) Carving and sanding is a straightforward process, because the material is soft and easy to carve. PVA will adhere to its surface and water bound paints will not attack the surface. This material is the best alternative to MDF for the bases.

Above: The view from the South shows the end of the block of houses, the section through the stream and some trees.

The view to the East shows the back of the row of houses, and at the right hand end the road bridge. This is a separate layer, which has been tapered down from its thickest part to meet the main base level.

The view to the West shows the gully to the stream and the smoothed outside edge to the base.

The view from the North shows the end of the depot block of buildings, the section through the stream and some trees.

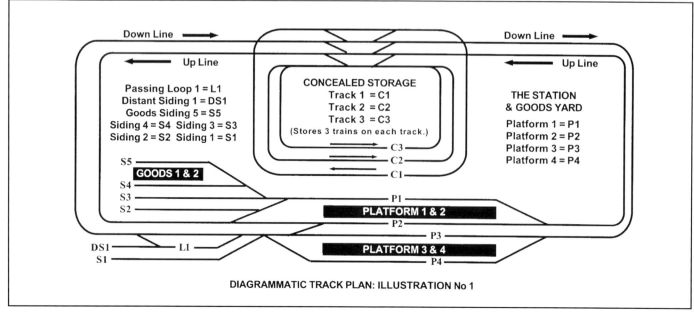

DIAGRAMMATIC TRACK PLAN: ILLUSTRATION No 1

11. TIMETABLES

WISHTON STATION

Running Procedures & Timetables: The multi-level layout depicts a very busy main line interchange station that also links up with a local line. Therefore to efficiently manage the daily routine of this station, a fully up to date and well informed train timetable is required.

This station has a busy day, because not all of the trains that arrive are through running, and for some this station is their final destination. Finally, to meet the varying demands for trains during the day, some trains are stored in the station's sidings, until they are due for departure.

At the scheduled time; the train is moved from one of the sidings, to its departure position, so that the passengers may embark, before the train sets off on the start of its journey.

From our point of view, a busy situation will allow a very wide range of running procedures to be carried out, and is an ideal subject to model. But for the layout to work in a convincing way, we need to store extra trains in a hidden siding (Fiddle Yard) so that the same trains are not continuously run.

The problem with most fiddle yards is that they are dead ends and this means that the train must be reversed out. In addition to this it normally requires the awkward job of uncoupling the steam engine – the introduction of a second steam engine so that it is facing the correct way, as the train comes out of the yard etc., etc.

Note: This is not a visual problem with the drive from 'any end' modern train, but mechanically it places the drive unit at the back; so that it pushes the carriages around the track, causing derailments. It is always preferred that the drive unit pulls the carriages, because the model is far more stable.

To overcome the problem on the station layout, I have used a hidden circular fiddle yard. The advantage of this is; that the circle can be split up into segments and each segment can store several complete trains. The real bonus is that the engine (Drive Unit) can remain at the front, because it is not necessary for the train to reverse out. The only disadvantage of the circular fiddle yard is that the trains require to be shuffled around, so as to release them in a different order to which they arrived.

If we unravel the plan of the track and illustrate it in a diagrammatic way, it is far easier to understand. This will then help us to use a small amount of track to its full advantage.

Because we will be operating a model, we can dispense with some of the rules and regulations, regarding full size practice. For example, a busy main line would not permit any shunting operations to be carried out on it, because of the dangers involved.

If we look at diagram number 1, you can see that certain positions on the track have been given codes, i.e., Platforms P1, P2, P3 & P4, Sidings S1, S2 S3 & S4 etc, and the trains have been given numbers. It is important to memorise the positions on the track, so that you know which points on the track need to be changed, so that the train can be moved from one place to another safely! Although the number of trains installed on the track may not always be the same.

The following pages show a series of diagrammatic illustrations representing the multi-level layout track plan.

The levels have not been split into upper or lower levels, but combined so that the path of a train can easily be followed. I.e. the train in platform 2 departs along the up line goes around the loop and back to platform 2. In reality the train departed from platform 2, and went down the slope, through the lower level, and climbed back up to the higher level and finally arrived at the station platform 2. The train need not stop, it could pass through, and could repeat this several times, before being diverted into the hidden siding, and another departs back onto the up line and arrives at platform 1.

Finally our diverted train reappears from the hidden siding and arrives at platform 2 and stops whilst the train in platform 1 departs to the hidden siding, etc.

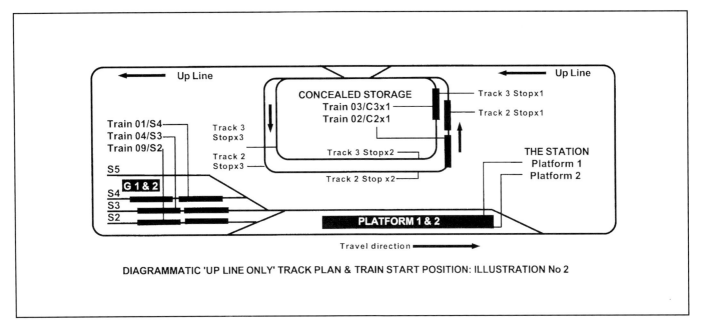

DIAGRAMMATIC 'UP LINE ONLY' TRACK PLAN & TRAIN START POSITION: ILLUSTRATION No 2

Running Procedures: The Up Line:
Moves 1 & 2
From Train 01/S4 To Train 01/P1 &
From Train 01/P1 To Train 01/C2 x2.

If we look at our first diagram, and find train '01', we can see that it is waiting in the 'S4' siding, and it is ready to be moved into the station at platform 1. After a brief stop, the train departs and passes by the entrance to the Concealed Storage Loop, before it comes back into the station on the platform 2 line. We could stop the train, or let it continue through the station without stopping. We choose not to stop, and for a second time it passes the entrance to the Concealed Storage Loop; the station on the platform 2 side; without stopping. Finally, we divert the train into the Concealed Storage Loop. We then have a choice to make: do we stop the '01' train behind train '02' or train '03'? Say that we stop it behind train '02' on track 2 so that it ends its journey. We now have another choice to make: do we move the passenger train '02' or do we move the goods train '03'?

Note: Because the **C**oncealed **S**torage **L**oop is constantly referred to, we will use the initials **CSL**.

Moves 3 & 4:
From Train 03/C3 x1 To Train 03/P1 &
From Train 03/P1 To Train 03/S4

We choose to move the goods train '03' from the CSL, and travel along the main line. Prior to the station, it turns off and goes into the station at platform 1. It could continue through the station and go back into the CSL, or it could stop and be reversed into one of the station sidings. We choose to reverse the train '03' into the S4 siding.

In effect what we have achieved with the first two moves is: (1.) To move the first train out of the siding, (leaving a parking space in the S4 siding) and park the train in the CSL, and (2.) Removed one train from the CSL and park the train in the S4 siding, adjacent to the goods yard platform, via the main station platform 1.

Move 5:
From Train 02/C2 x1 To Train 02/P1

We now have the choice as to which train to pick from train '01' or '02' in the CSL, and we choose to move train '02' on track 2. This train also turns off the main line, as it arrives at the station, and stops at platform 1.

The criticism of the earlier simpler oval layout was that it was restricted in its use. This is something I agree with, because its first function was to show how to model a contoured base.

To overcome this criticism the multi level layout was designed, using the basis of the original simple oval, and placing it on top of a storage yard, rather than extending the base sideways so that the layout became twice the size.

The requirement was 'It had to fit into the back of an estate car' when the layout needed to be moved, etc.

Left: The up-line platforms 1 & 2 are on the right and without trains. From 'S3' a goods train is arriving into platform 1, which won't stop. The clear tracks next to the goods train lead to sidings 4 & 5. In siding 2 the back of a wagon can be seen.

Platforms 3 & 4 are on the left and have trains waiting to depart. (The points for Train 3 are set.)

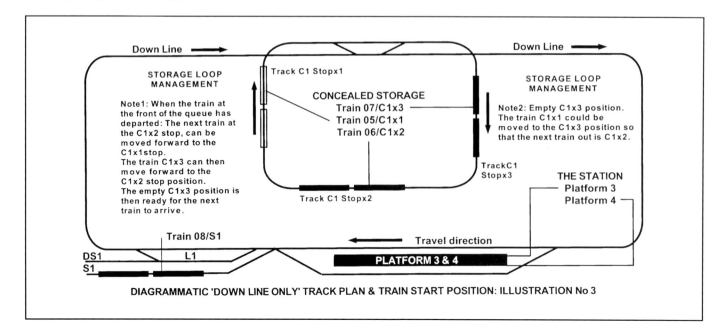

DIAGRAMMATIC 'DOWN LINE ONLY' TRACK PLAN & TRAIN START POSITION: ILLUSTRATION No 3

Because it is not easy to see the track needs to be split into electrical sections, so that a train arrives on a dead section of track and stops.

This regrettably increases the wiring to the track, but it does save underground collisions! (Fishing out 30 trucks that have derailed is very time consuming, especially when it was not your fault: This time.)

Like all track, the rails will need regular cleaning to remove accumulated 'Arc Deposits' caused by the minute sparks that are generated whilst the electricity is picked up from the track through the trains' wheels.

There is no answer to this, you just have to thoroughly clean the track using a track cleaning rubber or a soft cloth and plenty of rubbing.

Do not use wire wool, because the tiny fragments that break off from the pad will either electrically 'short out' the track or get picked up by the engines' magnet field, and cause irreversible damage to the motors.

Move 6:
From Train 01/C2 x2 To Train 01/C2 x1
The train '01' on track 2, now departs from the CSL, and goes through the station on the platform 2 side without stopping, and goes back into the storage loop, stopping at position C2 x1 on track 2.

What we have achieved with this is; to move the train '01' forward a space; from C2 x2 to C2 x1 on track 2. But by taking it all the way around the track, we have our fast non-stop train passing through the station on the platform 2 side, whilst the train on platform 1 waits.

Move 7:
From Train 02/P1 To Train 02/C2 x2
The train '02' on platform 1, now departs, past the CSL, and then passes through the station on the platform 2 side; without stopping. The train's journey finally stopping in the CSL behind train '01'.

Move 8
From Train 03/S2 To Train 03/C3 x1
The goods train '03' is then moved from the siding, through the station on the platform 1 side, without stopping and into the CSL. It then stops on track 3 in the 3x1 place, so that it is back in its start position.

Moves 9 & 10:
From Train 01/C2 x1 To Train 01/P1 &
From Train 01/P1 To Train 01/S4
We then move the train '01' on track 2, from the CSL and stop it in the station at platform 1. It is then reversed into the 'S4' siding so that it is back at its start position. We could now repeat the above sequence, but as yet the train '04' has not had its turn!

Moves 11 & 12:
From Train 04/S3 To Train 04/P1 &
From Train 04/P1 To Train 04/P2
Train '04' moves from the siding 'S3' and into platform 1 and stops. The train then departs from platform 1, and moves past the CSL and stops at platform 2.

Move 13:
From Train 09/S2 To Train 09/P1
The train '09' moves from the siding 'S2' and stops at platform 1.

Move 14:
From Train 04/P2 To Train 04/C3 x2
The train '04' departs from platform 2 and moves past the CSL, not stopping at platform 2, and into the CSL. This time stopping at C3x2 on track 3, behind the goods train.

Move 15:
From Train 03/3x1 To Train 03/3x3
The goods train '03' on track 3x1 is moved from the CSL, and passes through the station, on the platform 2 side, without stopping. It then enters the CSL and stops behind train '04' on track 3, in the 3x3 position.

Moves 16 & 17:
From Train 09/P1 To Train 09/P1 &
From Train 09/P1 To Train 09/S2
The train '09' departs from platform 1, passes the CSL, and goes through the station on the platform 1 side, without stopping. It passes the CSL a second time and then stops at platform 1. Finally it is reversed into the 'S2' siding.

Moves 18 & 19:
From Train 04/C3 x2 To Train 04/P1 &
From Train 04/P1 To Train 04/S1
The train '04' departs from the CSL, and stops at platform 1. Finally, is reversed in its designated start position of 'S3' in the siding.

Move 20:
From Train 03/C3 x3 To Train 03/C3 x1
The train '03' on track 3 at x3 is moved out of the CSL and travels through the station without stopping, and back into the CSL, stopping on track 3, at position C3x1, the starting position.

Move 21:
From Train 02/C2 x2 To Train 02/C2 x1
The train 02/C2 x2 moves forward one position

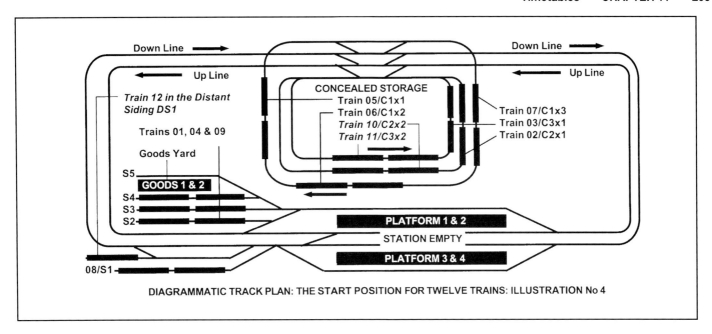

DIAGRAMMATIC TRACK PLAN: THE START POSITION FOR TWELVE TRAINS: ILLUSTRATION No 4

to C2 x1 position, by going all the way around the track.

Running Procedures: The Down Line:
Move 1:
From Train 05/C1 x1 To Train 05/P4
The first Train '05' on the track 1, parked in the Concealed Storage Loop, starts its journey and stops in the station at platform 4.
Move 2:
From Train 06/C1 x2 To Train 06/L1
The Down Line Goods train '06' on track 1 in the CSL starts its journey and passes through the station on platform 3 side and stops on the passing loop 'L1' just outside of the station.
Move 3:
From Train 07/C1 x3 To Train 07/C1 x1
The last train '07' on the track 1, at the 1x3 position, in the CSL, starts its journey, and passes through

the station on the platform 3 side; without stopping, and returns to the CSL, stopping at C1 x1.
Move 4:
From Train 06/L1 To Train 06/P3
The train '06' that has been waiting in the passing loop, now departs and goes past the CSL and arrives at the station at platform 3, and stops.
Move 5:
From Train 05/P4 to Train 05/C1 x2
The train '05' on platform 4 now departs and stops in the CSL, behind train '07' on track 1.
Move 6:
From Train 08/S1 To Train 08/P4
The train '08' reverses from the siding and into the station, stopping at platform 4.
Move 7:
From Train 06/P3 To Train 06/C1 x3
The train '06' departs from platform 3, and goes into the CSL, stopping behind train '05' on track 1.

Easy access to the storage loop is vital so the minimum gap between levels needs to be at least 13 cm (5 inches) so that there is sufficient clearance for a hand to grab at anything that has derailed, or to clean the track etc.

Unfortunately this gap was not always possible, so a lot of hatches are used to provide the required access.

Left: The 'Wishton Arms' has siding 2 nearest the camera and can store 13 trucks. Siding 3 can store 4 coaches and engine. Siding 4 has a platform and can store 7 mixed rolling stock and 1 engine.

Siding 5 also has a platform and can store 9 trucks and 1 engine. Because the track is flat in the sidings the rolling stock can be detached from the engine without the danger of them running away.

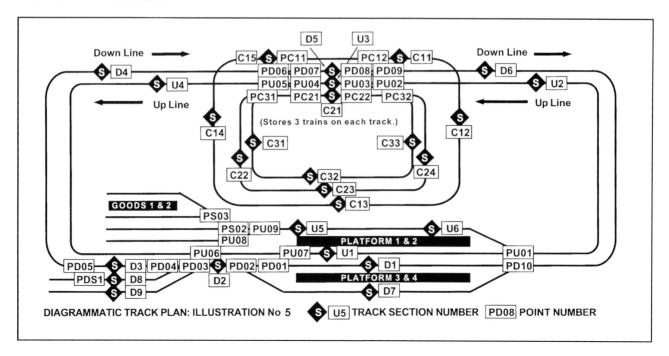

DIAGRAMMATIC TRACK PLAN: ILLUSTRATION No 5   ◆ U5 TRACK SECTION NUMBER   PD08 POINT NUMBER

Note: The sequence of events described within this chapter can be changed to suit each individual's requirements since it is only a guide to how a layout could be run.

The multi level layout has the advantage of being split into two 'Controller Zones', the first is the up line, the second is the down line, (excluding the middle level) so that each zone can run a totally different timetable, without interfering with the running of the other zone.

But, rolling stock can be handed from one zone to the other. For example a goods train can be moved from S5 to Platform 2 via platform 1 (Up line) and have the engine uncoupled.

The engine sitting in DS1 could move to platform 2 and couple-up to the trucks and wagons in the station, so that the fresh engine faces the new direction of travel. The train then departs via the points onto the down line, as it starts its journey. Repeat as required!

Move 8:
From Train 07/C1 x1 To Train 07/P3
The Train '07' moves from the CSL, passing through the station without stopping on the platform 3 side, passes the CSL again and back into the station. This time it stops at platform 3.

Moves 9 & 10:
From Train 08/P4 To Train 08/P4 &
From Train 08/P4 To Train 08/S1
The train '08' departs from platform 4, goes past the CSL and re-arrives at the station, on platform 4 and stops. Finally, it is then moved forward into the 'S1' siding, so that it is back in its start position.

Moves 11 & 12:
From Train 05/C1 x2 To Train 05/P4 &
From Train 05/P4 To Train 05/L1
The train '05' moves from the CSL and stops in the station at platform 4, it then departs and stops in the passing loop, just outside the station.

Move 13:
From Train 06/C1 x3 to Train 06/P4
The train '06' moves from the CSL and goes around the track, via P4 without stopping, and then returns to the station and stops at Platform 4.

Move 14:
From Train 05/L1 To Train 05/C1 x1
The train '05' departs from the passing loop, and stops at its original start position, in the CSL; track 1, position x1.

Move 15:
From Train 06/P4 to Train 06/C1 x2
The train '06' departs from platform 4 and stops at its original start position, in the CSL; track 1, position x2.

Moves 16, 17, 18, 19, 20 & 21:
From Train 07/P3 to 07/P3 (Repeat 4 times.)
From Train 07/P3 To Train C1 x3
The train '07' in the station departs from platform 3 past the CSL and stops at platform 3, It repeats

this 4 more times, before departing from Platform 3, to go back to its original start position in the CSL; track 1, position x3.

The sequence is now ready to be repeated.

Real-Time: Timetable: If a single person was to run all of the nine trains using the 42 procedures described above, at two minute intervals, it will take 84 minutes from start to finish. But because the tracks are independent of each other, and two people can operate the layout simultaneously, therefore, between them the time taken is only 42 minutes to make all of the moves. (21 moves each x 2 minutes per move = 42 minutes.)

The Running Schedule: The art of compiling a running schedule is to remember two basic rules. (1.) This is to have an empty space available; at the train's destination. (2.) To have a clear track; between the place of departure and the destination. In our case we have three places, i.e. the Siding, the Station and the CSL, and it is like driving down the road, and stopping at each set of traffic lights; because they are at red. When the lights change, you can move off again. Plan each move as a start and stop procedure, that goes from 'A' to 'B' i.e., siding 1, to platform 4. Provide each move with a number, i.e., 1, 2, 3 etc. Finally allot each move a length of time, with a time gap in between each move. Remember, you nearly always have to wait for a train; because you have just missed one, or the next train has not arrived!

The layout can be run with fewer trains, i.e. the minimum of 4, and these can be started from the sidings. Say train '01' in siding S1 moves to the station and stops, then departs into the CSL, so as to hide it. You can do much the same with the other trains; bringing them out on an 'as and when basis' so that you make up your own running order. Visually it always looks good to have at least one train on the layout, stopped in a station or siding, otherwise the layout will look deserted. Finally; it is also nice to have two trains continuously running, and just sitting back and watching!

Middle Level: The middle level is set up to run two trains automatically and uses two separate power inputs (see page 162) to provide a greater visual appeal. A third train is on standby and with the flick of a switch, this train can run. The illustration 1 shows all trains parked in the sidings, one of which can be seen, the other two are hidden from view. The sequence starts with train 1 moving into the station, at platform 1 and stopping. If we leave the setting as it is the automatic control will make the train go backwards and forwards at around 1 minute intervals. We could now start train 2 and send the train into platform 2. Again, If we leave the setting as it is the automatic control will make the train go backwards and forwards at around 1 minute intervals. We could return train 2 into the hidden siding, change the points and train 3 can be set to run automatically back and forth, between station 2 and the hidden siding. In effect it would look like a commuter terminus, with trains coming and going at intervals. Finally, by setting things on the manual setting train 3 could be moved to platform 1, and train 2 moved to hidden siding 3, etc and the trains repositioned etc. The automatic setting restored, and the rolling stock arrives and departs from a different location.

I hope that this new edition will provide much thought, provoke a discussion and an understanding that most of the information can be adapted to suit other layouts. This middle level mini layout was designed to show how a small self contained automatic layout can be made that occupies the minimum of space, whilst the final chapter contains sufficient information so that you can take some photographs of your layout, to show your friends.

All the best, John Wylie, July 2008

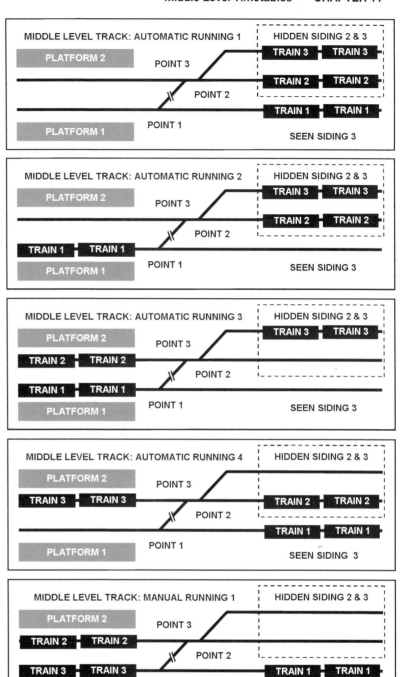

Left: The middle level back and forth part of the layout which is awaiting the arrival of third rail rolling stock.

Unfortunately, no commercial manufacturer to date produces track or ready to run 3rd rail rolling stock. This is a pity considering the large area of south east England that runs this type of stock.

The model portrays pre-electrification!

12. PHOTOGRAPHY

Photography is changing so rapidly with the advent of digital video and stills cameras, whose electronic images can be quickly downloaded onto a computer. The outcome is that conventional photography has now declined to the point that film based cameras may not exist within the next few years.

Nevertheless the same rules apply to digital and video cameras, as it does to conventional photography. First you have to understand how to capture the image, before it can be turned into a good photograph.

I bet many of us do not still have our first layout, but there is a good chance that a photo of the layout survives. Therefore document what you make for posterity, i.e. look at the photographs of what granddad used to make . . .

Top: The Nikon D50 Digital Single Lens Reflex camera that uses interchangeable lenses.

Right: The Canon compact IXUS 70, digital camera is ideal for gathering information photographs.

It takes time to learn how to take a good photograph; because there is far more to it than just pressing the button. This statement is based on the fact that I have been teaching photography for a long time and the fact that most photographs can be greatly improved, with a bit of thought.

Ever asked yourself why some photographs are better than others? The general answer from new students is: they all looked good through the view-finder when I took them!

What was not taken into consideration was how the camera interpreted the scene. For example, you are photographing the model with the room lights on and everything looks very nice. Then the camera uses its flash, and burns out the foreground, and the background is left in total darkness: Therefore the resulting picture is very different to the way the scene was originally viewed.

From the professional model maker's point of view, to be able to use a camera is a necessary skill because it is a very quick way to record visual information. Most simple digital cameras these days will produce a reasonable photograph, but a basic digital camera may not meet our needs. This is because most of our research will require a wide selection of different types of photographs, i.e. close-up and distance photographs.

Digital Photography: The digital camera is now well and truly established as a photographic media. Its main advantage is it does not require film, chemistry or a darkroom and the fact that a photograph can be taken, downloaded onto a computer and printed in a few minutes! The disadvantage is capture size; your camera will need to have at least a 4mb chip, and an optical zoom macro lens.

One of the things that people fail to understand is the fact that it does not matter if it is video, digital or film based, a camera is a camera, and much the

same rules apply. Therefore, the camera is just another tool that is useful to know how to use.

Research: Ideally, all research photographs should be taken to include all four sides of the subject, plus a large number of photographs that show every small detail – taken from every angle! Because it is very important to obtain a good set of photographs on the first visit and thus avoiding going back umpteen times to take some more.

The Camera: It is extremely easy to use the camera to record information, but to use the camera for model photography requires the total understanding of all the camera's functions. It is only by having total control over the camera that you can expect to produce a good photograph.

Film Camera Types: The range finder camera has a viewing window alongside the lens, and is not suitable for model photography. The single lens reflex camera views the scene through the lens, and because it has interchangeable lenses, a macro lens can be fitted; it is the ideal camera for model photography.

Digital Camera Types: These are best measured in pixel size, 1 megapixel, 2 megapixels etc. through to 12 megapixels plus. This figure relates to the number of pixels (light recording sensors) found on a micro chip. The greater the number of pixels, the greater the amount of information that can be gathered about the image projected onto it. For the average person a compact camera with aperture priority and manual settings, and the minimum of a 4 megapixels image sensor, will produce a good A4 print (10 x 8in) and excellent smaller sizes; this will meet most people's needs.

Format: This is a term that describes the film camera's size: The 35mm cameras are classified as small format; the 6 x 6cm, and 6 x 9cm are classified as medium format. The 5 x 4 inch and the 10 x 8 inch are large format cameras. For our use the 35mm format camera is more than adequate.

f 2

f 22

To use a camera as a tool you will need to understand its six basic functions.

The most difficult function to understand is the depth of field, and this is the key to good, sharp model photographs.

The key factor is to use the smallest aperture setting available i.e. f22 at all times (Note some cameras have f16 or f8 as the smallest aperture.) and use a sturdy tripod to hold the camera steady during the long exposures.

The top picture has been taken using an aperture of f2. Because this aperture setting has a poor depth of field, most of the photograph is out of focus.

The lower photograph has been taken using an aperture setting of f22.

Notice how sharp this picture appears to be compared with the first photograph. The focus was not changed, only the aperture setting.

The f22 aperture setting will need a longer exposure time than f2, i.e. from f2 @ 1/2000 second, to f22 @ 1/30 second exposure time. (Consult the owner's manual or use the camera's aperture priority setting.)

The choice of lens focal length also plays an important role, because a 250mm telephoto lens has a poor depth of field at f22 compared with a 28 mm wide angle lens set at f22.

Therefore it is recommended that you use a wide angle lens, rather than a standard, (50mm) or telephoto lens for all model photography.

Finally, for model photography it is also recommended that a tripod is used to avoid camera shake and do not use the camera's built in flash.

The Film: The film is made up of a clear backing that is coated with a thin layer of light sensitive emulsion. (This is a compound that reacts to light, so that it retains an image.) To stabilise the image, it will need to be processed in a series of chemicals. After the emulsion has been processed, the emulsion will no longer react to the light.

Film Speed: Natural light changes considerably, so the manufacturers produce different types of film. Therefore, to standardise how the film's sensitivity to light is measured, the film is rated as having an ASA/ISO number. The popular films are 25, 50, 100, 200 and 400. The ISO 25 is the slowest film, and the 50 ISO film is twice as sensitive to light than our first film, whilst the 100 film is four times as sensitive as a 25 ISO film. The 200 ISO film is eight times more sensitive to light than the 25 film, whilst the 400 ISO film is 16 times more sensitive than the 25 ISO film. The 100 ISO film is the recommended film to use in bright sunlight, and the 400 ISO for a dull and overcast day, evenings, etc. If this is not set automatically by the camera, you must set the film's ISO yourself, as found in the camera's hand book.

Digital Cameras: The ISO setting on a digital camera mimics the film's sensitivity to light, measured as ISO 100, 200, 400, 800, and mimics film etc, whereby as each number doubles, the camera's electronic sensor becomes twice as sensitive to light. DIN is another standard way of measuring the camera's film/sensor sensitivity to light, which is still found on some cameras and films. It is recommended that the lowest ISO setting is used, because the higher settings reduce picture quality due to electronic noise (looks like snow flakes).

Exposure: The film/sensor will need to be very carefully exposed to the light, because the emulsion/sensor reacts almost instantly. By restricting the amount of light that reaches the film's/sensor's surface, we can control how the image is formed.

In practical terms this means that excessive or inadequate amounts of light will produce a poor image. Therefore we have to get the amount of light just right. By good fortune most cameras have an automatic setting, which will do all the exposure calculations for us, and get it right most of the time: Note I say most of the time and not always!

The aperture of the lens controls the amount of light that enters the camera and onto the film's surface.

The calculation formula for the size of the aperture is governed by the lens diameter and the focal length, e.g. a 100mm diameter lens that focuses at infinity at 100 mm is classified as an F1 lens. (Focal length divided by diameter = F1.) Therefore a 50mm diameter lens that focuses at infinity at 100mm is classified as a F2 lens. (Focal length divided by diameter = F2.)

Using the same calculations, a mechanical method can be used to restrict a measured amount of light that will pass through the lens, i.e. The lens size is 50mm x 100mm focal length, but the aperture size is 25mm, therefore this will be described as an F2 lens set at F4. (Focal length divided by the aperture diameter = F4.) The same formula is used for the following aperture settings, F5.6, F8, F11, F16, F22 etc.

The aperture size affects the depth of field, the area in front of the lens that is in sharp focus. It also affects the shutter speed; the larger the aperture, the faster the shutter speed and vice versa.

The nearest focus of the standard lens is normally too far away to take close-up pictures; the alternative to extension tubes is close-up lenses that fit over the front of the camera's lens.

The secret is to take your time when taking photographs.

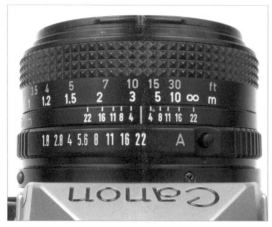

Above: The aperture of the lens is set at f22, and is the best setting for model photography on all cameras.

Below: The 35mm film camera needs an extension tube between the camera's body and the lens for close-up photography.

Film Quality: Different brands of film i.e. Fuji, Konica etc, provide good colour saturation under a wide range of lighting conditions. The slower ASA films generally provide a higher quality of colour saturation, whilst the faster films record subtle variations of hue and tone in low lighting conditions.

The sharpness of the print will also depend on the film speed; slower films have a smaller grain size, so that they appear to be sharper than a faster film.

The daylight colour negative and positive films are balanced to be exposed under natural daylight or electronic flash conditions. This is between 5200k and 5800k, of the light colour temperature range. If you wish to expose daylight film under artificial lighting conditions (3200k) a suitable filter (80B) must be fitted over the camera's lens, or light source. With black and white film, the light source does not matter.

Digital Image Quality: Different brands of cameras vary in their rendering of colours; Fuji, Nikon, Canon and Pentax cameras provide good colour saturation under a wide range of lighting conditions. They also render a good black, important if the shadow area is not to look muddy. The sharpness of the image will also depend on the pixel count, the greater the number, the better the image quality. The lens also plays an important role in picture sharpness.

The daylight and artificial colour settings of the camera can be automatically set, as can the quality of the daylight, e.g. sunny, cloudy, dull etc.

The ideal digital camera for use will have auto and manual settings, so that a choice can be made for tricky lighting situations.

Exposure Fault (Automatic Cameras): If we look at the photographs (Page 211) of the viaduct, we can see that the top picture shows a lot of detail, whilst the lower one does not. this is because in the first picture the sun was behind the camera and the light meter correctly read the situation. In the second picture the sun was in front of the camera, and the light meter misread the situation. If you have a simple camera, with no override controls, it is best to avoid this problem, by photographing the scene when the sun is in a different position. (At another time of the day.) The ideal position of the sun is at 45 degrees to the subject; from behind the camera. Hazy sunlight reduces the contrast range, and is the ideal lighting for taking photographs.

If you have an advanced automatic camera, the method used is to take a light reading from the shadows and to lock the camera's exposure control – or to set the camera on manual, with the exposure set for the shadow area, and then to take the picture.

In effect what you will be doing is to expose the film for the shadow side of the viaduct, and not for the sky. When you expose for the sky and the sun, the result will be under exposed shadow areas. This is why the viaduct is silhouetted against the sky, in the second photograph.

The Camera's Controls: The camera has six easily explained functions, but some of these are interlocked with each other. This means that it is necessary to learn and to fully understand each of the six camera controls, before it is possible to obtain the maximum use of the camera as a tool.

1. The Camera's Body (film). This is a light tight box that contains a complex mechanism for moving the film forward; so that the next frame of unexposed film is ready. The body may also contain the camera's shutter.

2. The Shutter. The shutter controls the amount of light entering the camera's body, by opening for a predetermined amount of time. The amount of time that the shutter can open, can be measured in hours, or it could be measured in fractions of a second.

3. The Lens. This is a series of magnifying glasses that have been specially shaped, so as to focus the rays of light in a very precise way: by changing the distance between the lens and the film's surface the lens can be focused.

3a. Lenses Choice (35mm Film Camera). The wide angle lens provides a broad view of the scene and makes things look further away. The telephoto lens will magnify a small portion of the view, so that it looks nearer. The standard lens views the scene at the same angle as the human eye's cone of vision.

The ideal lens for both outdoor use and model photography is the 28/200 mm variable focal length lens, with a macro facility; this is because of its all round performance. Note: The macro facility is used for focusing on a subject that is very near to the camera. Extension tubes do exactly the same.

3b. Lenses: Wide (35mm Camera). The lenses 17mm, 20mm, 24mm, 28mm and 35mm, in focal length; are classified as wide angle lenses.

3c. Lenses: Standard (35mm Camera). The lenses 50mm and 55mm are classified as the standard lens.

3d. Lenses: Telephoto (35mm Camera). The lenses with the longer focal length of 70mm, 100mm, 200mm and upwards are classified as telephoto lenses.

Note: digital cameras quote different focal lengths on different sensor sizes, therefore manufacturers refer to 35mm equivalent focal lengths.

4. The Aperture (F Number). This controls the amount of light that passes through the lens, by opening or closing. When the aperture is fully open, (i.e. F4) it will allow the maximum amount of light to pass through the lens. When it is fully closed, (i.e. F22) it will minimise the amount of light that can pass through the lens.

5. The Available Light Meter. This is a device for measuring the amount of continuous light that is available. Flash light is not continuous; it is a short burst of light.

5a. The Flash Meter. This is a device for measuring a short burst of light and therefore it will not measure continuous light. Some makes of automatic cameras have this meter/sensor built into the camera's body, whilst with other makes this is built into the flash gun.

6. ISO Setting (same on digital cameras). This is either set manually, or automatically depending upon the make of the camera. Film cameras: On a fully automatic film camera, as you insert the film, the ISO bar code printed on the cassette, pre-sets the camera to match the film type.

Image Capturing Method. In addition to the above six items, which relate to the camera only; we also need to understand the limitations of the image capturing method used.

Pixels and Dots Per Inch. Digital cameras like film grain size is measured in the number of grains/ pixels per inch, the greater the number the more difficult they are to see. I.e. we can see 50 or 100 grains/dots per inch, but we cannot see 300 plus, per inch. Therefore if our digital camera can capture an image in excess of 300 'Pixels Per Inch' (PPI) and we print the image greater than 300 Dots Per Inch (DPI) the digital image will be better than that captured on film.

The photographs show the difference between high contrast and low contrast lighting.

The top photograph shows what happens when additional lighting is added to the scene, which makes a considerable difference to the appearance of the subject

The high contrast photograph (Lower Photo.) contains little or no detail in the shadows. This is because only one light source was used, and the exposure made for the highlight. Therefore the contrast range was beyond the film's/sensor's working capabilities.

Depth of Field Control: The camera's lens is fitted with a method of controlling the light that passes through it, called the aperture. In the early days it was a series of metal discs, each disc was drilled with a single hole and each disc had a different hole size. These were called stops. In the modern lens; the aperture is an adjustable iris, which changes its size by opening or closing.

Because it is important that we know what size the iris has been set to; it is indicated by numbers, e.g. 4, 5.6, 8, 11, 16, 22. The numbers for reference purposes, are prefixed with the letter 'f' i.e., f8, to indicate that they are aperture numbers, to avoid confusion with shutter speed numbers. The 'f' number also has a direct relationship with the depth of field – the part of the picture that is in focus, i.e. f4 has very limited depth of field, whilst f22, provides the maximum. Therefore, all the pictures we take need to be at the smallest aperture setting of f22. (film cameras) f16, f8 etc the small aperture on digital cameras.

Small Aperture and Long Exposures: Unfortunately the small aperture reduces the amount of light, that enters into the camera's body. To compensate for this, extra time – for the light to reach the film's/sensor's surface must be allowed for.

In practical terms it means that the higher the 'f' number, the slower the shutter speed. (Note: all the following aperture/shutter combinations are for the same exposure settings.) i.e. Starting with the largest aperture size and a fastest shutter speed: Aperture set at: f4 @ 1/1000 second shutter speed. Set at: f5.6 @ 1/500 second. Set at: f8 @ 1/250 second. Set at: f11 @ 1/125 second. Set at: f16 @ 1/60 second. Set at: (smallest aperture setting) f22 @ 1/30 second (slow) shutter speed.

It is very similar to filling a cup up with water; turn the tap on very slowly and the cup takes its time in filling, turn the tap on full and the cup fills almost instantly – get it wrong and the water makes a real mess! The same applies to the exposure, get it wrong and the picture is spoilt.

The Tripod: Having established that the best aperture to use for model photography is f22, and the big disadvantage is the long exposure time: Use a sturdy tripod to solve the problem. Also by using a tripod it will prevent the camera moving back and forth, side to side etc., as you try to focus on the subject- as it does when hand held. The extra advantage of using a tripod is that you can now study the scene through the camera's viewfinder, and look very carefully at what it contains; so as to compose the picture to its best advantage. You can also let your friends have a look, and add their comments, before you press the shutter.

Lighting: Most cameras have a built in average available light meter, but it will not measure the contrast between the brightest area and the darkest area of the scene, unless you know how take a reading properly. For example: bright sunny cloudless days tend to produce soot and white wash photographs; that have the highlights burnt out, and contain very dark shadows. The ideal day for photography is a slightly hazy day, which diffuses the light, and reduces the contrast.

What is interesting about these two photographs is the way the people cease to blend in with the background. The viewpoint has also been lowered and moved very slightly.

The camera has been carefully positioned, so that the uprights remained vertical and the eye level remained horizontal. This opens up the debate as to which is the best photograph, which I leave you to decide.

STUDIO LIGHTING

The secret of lighting is to make the scene look natural, atmospheric, moody, dramatic etc. To achieve this it requires a great deal of skill and understanding of how to light the subject to meet the camera's needs and not the eye. It does not matter whether the lighting source is natural, electronic flash or tungsten, the skill needed remains very much the same.

The sensor of a digital/film camera has a limited working exposure latitude therefore the lighting must be set within these tolerances. The single light source whilst being dramatic is generally beyond the sensor's latitude, so a second light source is necessary. This secondary light could well be in the form of reflected light.

The photograph shows the main light (left) arranged at 45 degrees, and 45 degrees above the subject. This will provide the 'aperture setting'. This is the key light, from which the second light is balanced. The second light (right) is the diffused shadow fill in light source, set 45 degrees right and 45 degrees above the subject. This light is adjusted by using distance to be 1, 2, or 3 stops below the key light, and will depend upon the lighting effect required.

On a larger setup/layout more powerful lights are used. The art of lighting is in balancing the light to create a natural looking light, with a sparkle and does not look flat.

Do not diffuse all the lighting sources otherwise the lighting will become totally flat. The key light can be changed from a pin point to a broad source by using a silver reflector. Do not use the white surface; because it will soften the light.

Experiment with the key light and fill in light ratios by changing the value of the fill light and also try additional background lights and change the ratios by increasing them above and below the value of the key light. This will lighten or darken the background. Keep a set of notes, you will soon learn!

The photograph of the train emerging at speed on page 60 was a trick of the camera. The method used was a long shutter speed and the model pulled slowly along using black cotton! Because the cotton moved it did not 'show'.

The same method must be used with artificial lighting, a directional light must be balanced with a diffused light, which is used to fill in the shadows. (The heat resistant diffuser over the right hand light.)

Exposure Latitude: The problem is that negative film/digital sensors have a limited exposure latitude. For example: Over exposure a factor of three, and under exposure by minus five times; a contrast range of eight. (3 over, 5 under, 1 normal = 9 stops.) Unfortunately, bright sunny lighting can have a contrast range of 15, which is beyond the film's latitude/sensor, so it needs additional lighting to help reduce the contrast.

Lighting Set-Up: The best way to photograph a model is outdoors, and to use a large sheet of white expanded polystyrene, to reflect the light back into the shadows. This will also work indoors with artificial light, but a better way is to use a second light, and a sheet of heat restraint translucent film. Tracing paper could catch alight if placed near the lamp. The method is to set the main lighting that represents the sun, at about 45 degrees to the left of the subject; viewed from behind the camera. Move the light up and down to obtain the best effect. Finally; take a light reading through the camera. Set the aperture to f22 and say the shutter speed reads 1/30 of a second. (Note: Because each camera is different, you will have to consult your own camera's instruction manual on how to set the camera on manual use.) Now turn off the light that represents the sun, and switch on the diffused fill in light. (A sheet of translucent film will diffuse the light.) This should be placed at 45 degrees, on the right hand side of the subject. Move the light up and down to gain the best effect. Take a light reading, with the aperture still set at f22, and move the light back and forwards until the shutter speed reads 1/15 of a second. This represents minus 1 stop exposure, move the light away from the model, until the shutter speed reads 1/8 second; this represents 2 stops under exposure. (Ideal for colour.) If you move the light further back, you can obtain minus 3 stops. (Ideal for black & white films.) **(Important: reset the camera's shutter speed back to 1/30 of a second, before taking the photograph or the exposure will be wrong.)** The effect obtained with both lights on is to expose the film within the films/sensors working latitude. The net result should be detail within both the highlight areas and the shadow areas of the photograph. Finally, because the photograph's composition has been carefully considered, it should look interesting, as well as being in sharp focus. Note: A sky background always looks better than a room full of flowered wall paper. Further details available in books from the Public Library.

The lighting used to photograph a layout does not need to be complex, because two 150 watt x 240v garden lights will provide sufficient lighting for video and digital cameras. If you use a conventional camera and colour film fit an 80A (Daylight film conversion to Tungsten lighting) filter over the lens. For black and white films no correction filter is required.

For digital cameras reset the white balance for tungsten lighting and switch off the camera's built in electronic flash (not needed).

The tungsten lighting can be exchanged for off camera electronic flash guns, set on manual, because they will confuse each other when set on auto.

GLOSSARY

Abutment: Structure used for support on each side of an arch or bridge.

Adhesive Weight: Weight of the locomotive borne by the driving wheels, used as friction grip.

Alternating Current: (Single phase AC) Cycle of household electrical current, pulsing between full power and zero, hence the live side and neutral. Three phase incorporates the other half and doubles the supply.

Ampere or amp: Unit used to measure electrical strength.

Aqueduct: Bridge carrying water.

Armature: Series of wire-wound bobbins (each one classified as a pole) fixed to the shaft of an electric motor and, when switched on, forming a rotating electromagnetic. See Commutator.

Articulation: Pivoting driving wheels on separate frames complete with their own steam cylinders or electrical power units to help the locomotive to negotiate tight bends more easily.

Articulated: See above

ATC: (Automatic Train Control) System designed to assist the driver and help prevent misreading of signals ranging from simple cab warnings to full automatic control.

Automatic coupler: One that locates itself and locks into position; can be uncoupled with the use of a ramp or electromechanical device.

Ballast: Chippings spread underneath the track, and is used for bedding, levelling and distribution of the weight of the passing rolling stock.

Banking: See Super-elevation; Also see 'Cant' and Camber.

Banking: Assisting the single locomotive with one or more additional engines to assist a train up a steep gradient. The additional engines can be attached at the back or the front of the train.

Baseboard: Structure on which the model railway is built.

Bay Platform: A short platform built on one side of a through platform generally used for terminating local or branch line trains.

Bellows: (American Term) The flexible corridor connection between passenger coaches.

Bench-mark: Spot height shown on a map and marked at the actual location (usually on a wall etc).

Big Boy: The popular name given to the largest Union Pacific 4-8-8-4 steam locomotive.

Block Train: One made up of identical wagons and vans.

Bo-Bo: Diesel or electric locomotive with two driving axles (i.e. four driving wheels) on each of the two bogies.

Body Shell: Basic structure of a model without the fittings.

Bogie: Swivelling assembly carrying wheels mounted below a locomotive or coach.

Boiler: The part of the steam engine in which water is heated.

Bolster: Principal weight-carrying cross-member of a bogie on which the pivot is fixed.

Bow: Wire strip bent with the aid of string, used to draw curves.

Box car: American term for a van or covered freight wagon.

Brake van: Sometimes known as the guard's van; Used in trains without inter-linked brakes to supply braking power at the rear.

Branch Line: Secondary line departing from a main line.

Buffers (also end stop): Used to stop rolling-stock at the end of sidings etc.

Buffers: Sprung shock-absorbing fittings, fixed at each end of all rolling stock.

Bunker: Coal container built into the rear of a tank locomotive.

Cab: Driver and fireman's compartment of a locomotive usually sheltered with a roof.

Caboose Car: American term for the rail crew's compartment, often at the rear of the train and used as an office for the conductor. Sometimes used as a living quarters by rail crew on long-haul travel.

Camber: Normally applied to roads, whereby the outside edge of the bend is higher than the inside of the bend in the road. The straight road is also cambered whereby the middle is higher than the outside edge, so that rainwater can drain.

Canned Motor: Electric motor enclosed in a tin casing.

Cant: The amount that the outer rail is raised above the inner rail on a curve.

Car: American term for carriage or wagon.

Catch-points: Set of points facing away from the direction of travel used to catch rolling stock running away backwards, as on a gradient.

Catenary: Arrangement of suspended wires for overhead current collection.

Centre-swing: Amount the centre of the vehicle overhangs the track on the inside of a bend.

Chairs: Iron castings bolted or spiked to the sleepers and used to secure the rails.

Chipboard: Board made from wood chippings bonded together with resin.

Clear Signal: Signal displaying green, indicating the section of track is clear of obstructions and it is safe to proceed.

Clearway: Clearance gap between running tracks.

Clerestory Roof: One with a central vertical extension, the sides of which are glazed.

Co-Co: Diesel or electric locomotive with three driving axles (i.e. six driving wheels) on each of the two bogies.

Collector: Electrical contact rubbing on the live rail or wire.

Commutator: Segmented electrical contact ring fixed on to the shaft of an electric motor, used to pass the electricity from the two brushes into the winding of the armature, the number of segments of the commutator corresponding to the number of poles. (As it rotates along with the armature on the shaft of the motor, it switches on or off the windings, controlling the effect of the rotating electro-magnets against the static magnets.) This produces the driving force of the motor.

Compound Curve: One formed from a series of radii.

Contour: Line joining places of equal elevation, used to indicate changing levels on a flat sheet such as a map or plan.

Converter: Transformer or other unit for converting AC current to DC or vice versa.

Coupling: Device used for connecting items of rolling stock.

Crossing: Tracks that cross each other at the same level.

Cross-tie: Longer than standard sleeper used beneath points etc.

Current: Rate of flow of electricity.

Curve: Track that is no longer straight and falls into various categories. These categories restrict rolling stock use. i.e. a tight curve can be used by small engines and wagons only to prevent derailment.

Curve: Simple, Single and Compound. (Ideally between each curve install a length of straight longer than the longest carriage used on the layout to prevent buffer locking.)

Cut-Out Circuit Breaker: Automatic device which operates to open the circuit in the event of an electrical overload.

Cutting: Excavation through high ground to maintain railway/road level.

Dead End: A length of track that ends at the buffers (End Stop).

Dead-man's Handle: A safety device fitted in the cab that automatically brings the train to a stop should the driver become incapacitated whilst at the engine's controls and on the move.

Decal: (transfer) Printed logo or lettering, removable from its backing, used instead of hand painting.

Diagram: A diagrammatic display of the track showing key information that displays the settings of the signals and points (turnouts) which is normally found in the signal or control box.

Diesel: A compression ignition internal combustion engine that theoretically ignites the fuel solely by compression. In reality to reduce the compression ratio a glow plug is used to ignite the fuel. This reduces the knocking sound associated with the diesel engine.

Direct Current: Continuously flowing single direction electrical current.

Distant Signal: Signal showing approaching trains the condition of stop signal ahead.

Double-Heading: The use of two locomotives to power one train. See also banking engines for gradients.

Double-Slip Point: Crossover also incorporating sets of points in both directions.

Down Line: That travelling away from the company offices (usually London).

Drawbar: Device for connecting the locomotive to the tender.

Drop Sided Wagon: A wagon or carriage in which the door or sides drop downwards to facilitate loading. Cattle and horse boxes tend to have drop sided doors.

Dual Gauge: Track laid as three rail in which one is used as the common rail so that two different types of train can share the same track, e.g. Broad gauge and standard gauge or standard gauge and narrow gauge rolling stock.

Dumb Bell: A single straight length of track that has a return loop at each end, which is complex to wire. The beginner is advised to use dual track along the straight, so that it becomes a squashed oval.

Earth: A designated power escape route to dissipate electricity safely. All mains equipment should be earthed for personal safety unless double insulated to EU standards.

Electric Pencil: Conductive rod used to make a short electrical contact; its prime use is for changing points.

Embankment: Built-up ground to carry a railway/road over low ground; can also be found along river banks to contain the water's flow.

End Stop: See Buffers.

End-Swing: Amount the end of the vehicle overhangs the track on the outside of a bend.

End-to-End: A simple shelf layout that stops at each end. i.e. a branch line layout with a terminal and a fiddle yard.

Engine: Alternative name for a diesel power unit or steam locomotive.

Fiddle Yard: Concealed area of a layout used to manually assemble the trains.

Firebox: The part of the steam engine in which the fire is lit to warm the water in the boiler.

Fishplate: Plate used to join lengths of rail together (should not be relied upon for electrical connection).

Flange: Part of a wheel's rim which engages the rail's inside edge, used to keep rolling stock on the track. The complete profile is known as the tyre.

Flash: Unwanted material on injection moulded components (caused by incorrect fitting of the dies).

Footplate: Platform on the locomotive for the driver and fireman.

Freight Yard: American term for a goods depot.

Frog: Break in the rails of points allowing wheels to pass through where they cross.

Gauge: Actual width, centre to centre, between rails. This is a set of standard measurements that governs the width.

Goods: The British term for freight.

Goods Yard: The British term for a freight yard or depot.

Governor: Device used to self regulate a train's speed irrespective of incline or descent.

Gradient: Slope or incline usually expressed as a ratio, e.g. 1:150.

Gravity Shunting: See also Hump Yard

Grouping: The name given to the amalgamation of the major railway companies in Britain (Excluding Northern Ireland) to form what became the LMS, LNER, GWR and SR railways many years ago.

Guards Van: The last piece of rolling stock attached to a train.

Half-Wave Rectification: Electronic method of controlling the current, providing a very precise control of full power.

Halt: Stopping place for local services without normal station facilities.

Headshunt: Length of track allowing the locomotive to disengage from the rest of the rolling stock (as at a terminal platform) or track on to which a train can draw before setting back into a goods yard.

Home signal: Stop signal at the entrance to the next block' of signals controlled by a signal box.

Hopper Wagon: Vehicle that discharges its load through the floor.

Horn-Hook: Efficient out of scale coupling.

Horsebox: Specialist covered wagon or van for transporting horses.

Horsepower: A measurement of a known unit of power, i.e. 0.7457 kilowatt is classified as being one horsepower.

Hot Box: The term given to an over heated axle box, normally indicating that the bearing has not been lubricated.

Hump Yard: Marshalling yard with an artificial hill down which wagons roll into the selected sidings; Also known as gravity shunting.

Inspection Car: Normally a self-propelled covered specialist equipped vehicle that is used by engineers to inspect the track, using various electronic and mechanical methods.

Interchange: Normally a point that a series of train routes meet and passengers can transfer conveniently from one route to another.

Island Platform: One with tracks on both sides.

Island site: Layout with access from all sides.

Jumper Cables: Wiring fitted with plugs and used to connect portable baseboards.

Leading Wheels: Wheels fitted in front of the driving wheels on a locomotive.

Level Crossing: General term for a road, path or railway crossing the track on the level, controlled by gates, lights and bars or signals.

Light Engine: Locomotive travelling without rolling stock.

Limit of shunt: Indication board on a main line beyond which any rolling stock may not pass during shunting operations.

Livery: Colour scheme used by railway companies.

Loading Gauge: Hanging framework used to check the height of a load before it leaves a siding.

Local Line: Routes normally allocated to slow frequently stopping passenger trains that are short in distance, possibly single line track operation and come to a dead end.

Loop: Up and down lines linked together via a half circle, allowing the turning of rolling stock in a train length without uncoupling.

Loose Coupling: The joining of goods wagons and vans using three link chains. Anybody who lived near a goods yard knew when the wagons were being shunted around, because the noise of the buffers clattering against each other down the entire length of the train, each time the wagons moved.

Mail Train: Express intercity train fitted with letter collecting and delivery at speed devices and sorting on route.

Main Line: The route used by the majority of fast intercity rail traffic.

Marshalling Yard: The area where rolling stock is sorted out into train lengths for different destinations.

Micro-chip: Minute electronic integrated circuit designed to do a particular task; used in Digital Command Control units.

Motive Power Depot: Engine shed used for servicing and preparing locomotives for running.

Motor Bogie: Powered bogie fitted with driving wheels.

Motorman: Driver of a diesel or electric engine.

Multiple Aspect Signals: Those using electric lamps to give a series of aspects, red, amber and green.

Multiple Track: Track with running lines in addition to the up and down line.

Multiple Unit: Two or more power units or locomotives controlled by one driver.

Narrow Gauge: Any railway track of less than the standard gauge.

Pannier Tank: Locomotive carrying water tanks fitted on the sides of the boiler.

Pantograph: Current-collecting sprung frame used for collection of electricity from overhead wires.

Passing Loop: A single length of track that splits into two tracks and then back into one track; so that trains can pass each other.

Permanent Way: The term for fixed in position track bed and track.

Pick-up: Electric current wiper contact fitted to rolling stock. Could be a pantograph for overhead pick-up or located by the wheels as used by the 3rd rail Southern Region trains.

Pick-up Freight: A train that picks up and drops off goods at pre-selected places on a regular or as required basis. This could involve loaded or empty wagons and vans.

Piggy Back: Drive on road vehicles carried on railway flat cars. Used in America to avoid driving long distances.

Pilot Engine: Locomotive used for marshalling empty rolling stock at a terminal station or an additional engine coupled at the front, providing assistance to help pull a heavy load up a steep incline.

Platelayer: Track maintenance engineer.

Platelayers Hut: The small line side shed used to store equipment in, brew tea and shelter from the rain etc. This could also be a disused railway carriage, with the wheels removed.

Points: Track work allowing change from one track to another.

Pullman Car: The more expensive way for passengers to travel because of the comfort and service it provides.

PVA: A water-based glue favoured by woodworkers.

Railcar: Self propelled single or double carriage passenger transport vehicle.

Reception Road: Track used for the arrival of trains at a goods yard.

Release crossover: Set of points towards the buffer end of a headshunt to allow a locomotive to depart leaving other rolling stock at the platform.

Reverse Curve: Curve followed by one in the opposite direction.

Reverse loop: Length of track turning back on itself, used to turn a train in the opposite direction. It must be used with a reversing switch and electrically segmented track.

Right of Way: Normally operated on single line track, whereby a stick, key or letter is given to the driver of a train giving him the sole authority to proceed. All others must stop and allow him to pass.

Rolling Resistance: Drag caused by the friction of the axle bearings, wheels etc and opposing the pulling effort.

Rolling Stock: General term for all vehicles that travel on the tracks.

Roundhouse: Engine shed arranged in a part or full circle with a turntable in the centre.

Saddle Tank: Engine fitted with a water tank shaped to fit over the boiler.

Scale: Relationship of any dimension in direct proportion to that of full size, i.e. 1 in on a model representing 1 ft on the full size item would be one-twelfth scale.

Scissor Crossing: Parallel tracks fitted with points and a diamond crossing allowing trains to change over from any direction.

Semaphore Signal. Older bar-type indicator, with a painted arm and lamp-lit coloured spectacles.

Shunting Neck: Similar to head-shunt, a single track which then divides up into sidings.

Shuttle: Train that runs back and forth normally over a short distance on a regular basis.

Side Tanks: Water containers fitted on either side of the boiler.

Sidings: Lengths of track used for shunting, storage etc. away from the main line.

Siding: A line that departs from the main line and used to store or sort on a temporary basis rolling stock. The siding could have several sections of track, a platform and a resident engine.

Signal: Warning indicator fitted alongside the track, used to control the movement of rolling stock.

Signal Aspect: Coloured lights mounted on a post that indicate the condition of the track in front. I.e. clear or occupied.

Signal Box: Building from which signals and points are operated, having control over specific area of track.

Signal Semaphore: A method of using a moveable arm mounted on a post, which indicates by its position the condition of the track in front, i.e. clear or occupied, and at night by displaying a single coloured light.

Single Slip: Crossover incorporating points in one direction only.

Six-Foot Way: Clearway between tracks.

Sleeper: Concrete or wood cross-member used to support the track.

Solebars: Main front and back cross-members at each end of the wagon frame.

Starter Signal: One permitting a train to proceed into the next signalling block section ahead.

Station Throat: Complex of track-work outside a large station.

Strapping: Metal strip reinforcement on rolling stock bodywork. Stretcher locomotive's or bogie frame's cross-member.

Stud Contact: Metal, round headed spike fitted on the sleeper between the tracks, used for electrical contact on older types of electric model trains.

Super-Elevation: Laying the outside rail higher than the inside rail on a tight curve, enabling the rolling stock to travel around it at a higher speed.

Tank Engine: Locomotive which carries its own water and coal supply on one chassis.

Tender: Wheeled vehicle carrying coal and water supply, attached directly behind the engine.

Trailer Coach: Un-powered carriage fitted to a railcar or railbus.

Trammel: (beam compass) Used for drawing large-radius curves.

Transfers: See Decals

Transformer: Unit for converting mains electricity into safe low voltage suitable for model railway use.

Tread: Slightly coned face of a locomotive's wheel which is in contact with the track.

Truss Rod: Bracing used diagonally in the underframe to make it more rigid.

Turnout: See Points

Turntable: Rotating device for turning stock or aligning it with other tracks that radiate from it, e.g. in a roundhouse.

Underframe: Load-carrying structural framework which supports the body of a carriage or wagon.

Underlay: Material used beneath the track on a layout to help reduce noise.

Underpass: A road or pedestrian tunnel going under the track or road etc.

Up Line: That travelling towards the company offices (usually London).

Valve Gear: Mechanism which opens and closes the steam ports of the cylinders of a steam locomotive.

Van: A roofed wagon or truck used for carrying goods.

Viaduct: The name given to describe a brick or stone built series of arches that supports the track above low lying ground between two places of higher ground in hilly countryside.

Voltage: Electromotive force measured in volts (equivalent of pressure).

Wagon: Normally an open topped truck used for the conveyance of goods.

Wheel Arrangement: (4-6-2, 2-6-0, 0-6-0 etc) Formula representing the number of wheels in front of the driving wheels, the number of driving wheels and the number of wheels behind the driving wheels (on the engine only).

Worm Drive: The name given to a type of gearing used to turn the drive through 90 degrees and reduce the electric motor's shaft speed by a ratio of around 30 to 1 This increases the power to the drive wheels.

Zero One: Early Hornby system of using two-wire digital control for the entire layout.

ACKNOWLEDGEMENTS

THANKS
I would first like to thank my wife Jean for all the typing, for the contribution she made towards the book and for putting up with the layouts around the house for a considerable number of years.

I would also like to thank the following manufacturers for all their help and support: Wills Finecast, Ratio, Gauge Master, Form Craft, West Coast Kits, Vulcan, Premier, Seep and Hornby.

With special thanks to Graham Farish and Bachmann UK for their enormous support during the production of the new edition.

PHOTOGRAPHY
Craig Semplis, page 32
Brian Monaghan, pages 58, 59, 121.
Your Model Railways, pages 121.
West Coast Kits Ltd, pages 182.
Margaret Dickson, page 184.
Ron Cadman of Vulcan and Premier Kits Ltd, pages 178, 179, 180, 181.

All other photographs, John Wylie.
INK LINE ARTWORK BY:
Andrew Timmins and Christion Still:
Pages 13, 14, 17, 20, 21, 24, 26, 28, 29, 39, 64, 68, 75, 76, 77, 79, 80, 81, 82, 83, 92, 103, 107, 109, 118, 120, 127, 170,186.
Paul Wylie:
Pages 61, 79, 100, 101, 102, 141, 142, 146, 182, 186.
Colour artwork page 72: Andrew Timmins.

All other ink artwork, scanning and toning: John Wylie.

ORIGINAL PENCIL & COMPUTER GENERATED ARTWORK BY:
John Wylie

MODELMAKERS
Medway College of Art and Design, Fort Pitt, Rochester, Kent. (3 Year Higher Diploma Industrial Model Making). Special thanks to Amanda Bristow, Graham French.
Team Members: Tim Adcock, Damian Barrell, Mark Dawson, Simon Fox, Andrew Freeman, Alison Hardy, Paul Higgins, Richard Majillius, Ian Poisden-Watts, Paul Persigetti, Raoul Reesinck, Stella Winter, Stuart Woods.

Additional help: Paul Wylie, Jean Wylie. All new models made by John & Jean Wylie.

Note: You can see a sample of the model making methods shown in this book on display in Rochester and Upnor Castles (Kent). Rochester Castle is open all year but Upnor is only open during the summer months (April–September).

INDEX

Photographs front and back page: The 'N' scale bases 01 and 02 built at 2mm to the foot, which formed part of a much larger layout when all the bases were joined together.

The layout appeared on television and was also on exhibition for over 8 years in Merley House (Now closed) as part of a public exhibition.